Praise for this book

'At last a book that digs deeply into what it means in practice for humanitarian and development agencies to adopt a political philosophy of rights as they respond to people suffering from poverty, war and disaster. The case studies are clear and revealing. The advantages and the risks of a rights-based approach are openly discussed.' *Dr Hugo Slim, Chief Scholar, Centre for Humanitarian Dialogue, Geneva*

'This is a timely and important contribution to the rights and development literature. The moral appeal of what have become known as "rights-based approaches" is irrefutable on a superficial gloss, accompanied in recent years by a burgeoning volume of policy statements, programming guidelines and scholarly analyses. But the virtuousness of the rhetoric masks a great many hard questions as to how such putatively transformational approaches can be applied in practice, and more fundamentally still, how far these approaches must themselves be examined for consistency with the ideals they purport to embody, and how far they can go in attacking the complex and varied "root causes" of poverty and injustice in any given situation. While shunning pretences at easy answers, this book frames these dilemmas coherently and articulately, based on practitioners' own experiences, against an engaging account of the philosophical underpinnings and history of human rights and rights-based approaches. The result is a critical and nuanced analysis that will appeal to practitioners, academics and policy-makers alike.' *Mac Darrow, Coordinator, Human Rights Strengthening (HURIST) programme, UN Office of the High Commissioner for Human Rights, Geneva*

About this book

Human rights now occupy a central position in the discourse surrounding international development. Recognition of the fundamental links between the denial of rights and the persistence of poverty has propelled rights-based approaches into the policy and practice of many development NGOs, UN bodies and aid agencies. The development practitioners authoring the present volume have had concrete experience in trying to apply a rights-based approach in their work. Their aim here is to contribute to a greater common understanding of the approach. Top-down attempts to formulate coherent rights-based policy have, the editors argue, largely failed to convince sceptics that they go beyond mere repackaging of existing best development practice. Instead what is needed is a bottom-up approach based on the insights provided by practical experience.

This volume also seeks to identify what difference a rights-based approach makes in practice. The concrete experiences reported here help answer the questions: How does a rights-based approach alter the practical work of development? What is the 'value added' of a rights-based approach? What possibly new difficulties arise?

Addressing the range of development areas influenced by this approach, the volume spans development, humanitarian relief and conflict resolution. It also examines contemporary challenges to its implementation, including the politicization of aid and the 'war on terror', neo-liberal economic policies, and the clashes between universal human rights standards and specific cultural norms.

Reinventing Development? is a valuable pulling together of the field experience and reflection on the many issues raised by the new rights-based approach to development. It concludes that there is the potential not only for human rights to reinvent development, but for development to reinvent human rights.

PAUL GREADY AND JONATHAN
ENSOR | editors

Reinventing development?

Translating rights-based approaches
from theory into practice

Zed Books

LONDON | NEW YORK

Reinventing development? Translating rights-based approaches from theory into practice was first published by Zed Books Ltd, 7 Cynthia Street, London N1 9JF, UK and Room 400, 175 Fifth Avenue, New York, NY 10010, USA in 2005

www.zedbooks.co.uk

The Swiss Agency for Development and Cooperation generously provided financial support for the realisation and publishing of this title and in order to make it available in developing countries.

Cover designed by Andrew Corbett
Set in Arnhem and Futura Bold by Ewan Smith, London
Printed and bound in Malta by Gutenberg Press

Distributed in the USA exclusively by Palgrave Macmillan, a division of St Martin's Press, LLC, 175 Fifth Avenue, New York, NY 10010.

A catalogue record for this book is available from the British Library.
US CIP data are available from the Library of Congress.

ISBN 1 84277 648 7 hb
ISBN 1 84277 649 5 pb

Contents

Introduction

PAUL GREADY AND JONATHAN ENSOR

In recent years human rights have assumed a central position in the discourse surrounding international development. A recognition of the fundamental links between rights denial, impoverishment, vulnerability and conflict has led to the incorporation of rights-based approaches into the funding strategies, policy formulations and practice of a diverse range of actors, including United Nations agencies (UNDP, UNICEF), major donors (the UK's Department for International Development [DFID], the Swedish International Development Cooperation Agency [SIDA]), international NGOs (ActionAid, CARE, Oxfam) and local grassroots NGOs and social movements. While there is a growing literature on policy formations and the politics and principles of rights-based approaches, it is clear (i) that there is a great diversity in understandings of what constitutes a rights-based approach, and (ii) the next major step for this approach requires assessments of opportunities, advantages and challenges in the realm of practice.

This volume seeks to address these issues. Its first aim is to contribute to a small but growing body of studies that attempt to identify what difference a rights-based approach makes in practice. What is the 'value added' by a rights-based approach? How does a rights-based approach alter development work and programming? What, possibly new, difficulties and tensions arise? Secondly, the collection aims to make a contribution to a greater common understanding of a rights-based approach. Top-down attempts to formulate policy coherence in relation to rights-based approaches have made some progress towards identifying common themes, but have largely failed to convince sceptics that they go beyond repackaging existing best development practice. While acknowledging the diversity of rights-based approaches and practice, and seeking to explore its implications, this collection aims to build a greater common understanding of its core components, from the bottom up, based on insights provided by practitioners.

In Parts I and II of the book the experiences of practitioners are detailed in case studies of rights-based approaches in practice. Authors in this section are from the NGO and inter-governmental organization (IGO) communities from across the spectrum of development, humanitarianism and conflict resolution. Part III contains three longer chapters exploring contemporary challenges facing the implementation of rights-based approaches: the implications of rights for development in an era of neoliberalism and 'good-governance', the relationship between rights and culture, and aid politicization and the 'war against terror'. This Introduction sets out a theoretical, historical and political context for the chapters that follow. It provides a (re)conceptualization of human rights that speaks to the international political and economic changes associated with globalization that have accompanied and contributed to the rise of rights-based approaches. Following on from this foundation, it outlines the history, recent emergence and policy content of the relationships between human rights and development. The Introduction ends by detailing some of the major critiques of the rights-based approach, drawing out a series of thematically organized questions. These questions are returned to in a Conclusion that uses the practice-based contributions to both provide some provisional answers and to continue what will undoubtedly be an ongoing conversation.

The first human rights revolution

The modern era of human rights began during the Enlightenment with the US Declaration of Independence (1776) and the French Declaration of the Rights of Man and the Citizen (1789). Two concepts of enduring significance to human rights jostle for influence within these documents: natural law/rights and the social contract.

The declarations had a common foundation in natural law and rights. In natural law/rights, foundations and justifications are located in God and religion, nature (the 'state of nature', given or inspired by nature), in the nature of 'man', and/or through a shared capacity for reason. Rights are potentially universal in all these guises – individuals, for example, can be seen as having rights simply by virtue of their common humanity and shared characteristics – in the 'state of nature' outside and before the formation of any social grouping, political arrangements or legal dispensation. But rights are also simply a matter of faith. Not surprisingly, such a theory of rights, once secularized and stripped of religious justification, has come under sustained criticism from philosophers, political theorists and lawyers.

Macdonald writes: 'It seems a strange law which is unwritten, has never been enacted, and may be unobserved without penalty, and peculiar rights which are possessed antecedently to all specific claims within an organized society' (1984: 22). A host of challenging questions have threatened to sweep natural rights aside: which rights are natural? Who decides? How

2

can disagreements over these issues and changing views over time and across cultures be adjudicated? What are the implications of the chasm between ideal and reality? But, as we shall see, this conception of rights has enduring and cross-cultural significance because it speaks to the idealism and activist agenda of human rights. To claim that we are all free and equal, that we have original rights, is, arguably, a moral fiction, but it can be a very empowering fiction and has had profound political impact.

The social contract moves beyond rights as an article of faith to provide them with a socio/political-contractual grounding (Rachels 1993). Hobbes, who, alongside Rousseau, is most closely identified with social contract theory, famously believed that life in the 'state of nature', without rules or accepted enforcement mechanisms, would be a state of constant war. To escape this condition, the individual joins in voluntary association with others to form rules to govern social relations and to establish an agency – the state – with the power to enforce the rules. Certain rights are sacrificed in exchange for an agency to enforce and protect those rights that remain. In short, we exchange unconditional freedom in return for the advantages of social living, as a balance is sought between our rights and the rights of others, and between rights and responsibilities. Under such a set of rules a society can develop in which everybody is better off and in which we can afford to become moral agents. The social contract is therefore rational, and the rationale for rights is located in relationships, reciprocity and mutual benefit rather than in religious, or increasingly secular, belief.

The idea of the social contract, which entrenched the notion that there is no divine or absolute right to rule but, on the contrary, a right to government by consent, was truly revolutionary: '[The US and French Revolutions] are revolutions in the sense that they sought a radical transformation of the accepted principles of social organization, rather than a mere seizure of power within the existing order' (Evans 2001: 17). The relationship between the individual and the state was transformed. By challenging an organic, hierarchical vision of society, feudalism, the aristocracy, the church, monarchy and colonialism, the traditional relationship between the rights of rulers and the duties of subjects was inverted. Specifically, this meant that the relationships between the state and the individual, state legitimacy and consent to be ruled, were founded on respect for human rights. Both the US and French declarations contain rights that formed the basis on which the individual consented to be ruled, and rights thereby constituted the justification for rebellion in the event of their violation. The rights revolution was, therefore, both conceptual and, in time, political.

Natural rights and the social contract remain significant in contemporary human rights discourse and practice. Natural rights are philosophically

3

contested, but undeniably real. They are real in the sense that history is littered with examples, from the suffragettes and the anti-slavery movement to opposition to apartheid and the communist regimes of the former Eastern Europe, of occasions when individuals and groups have acted on a powerful moral sense of injustice, believing that they are neither mere pawns nor property. They do so not because states or laws encourage and protect such protests – in fact, more often than not they hinder and oppress – but instead they mobilize support through a shared belief that something is unequivocally wrong in a higher court of morality. The natural law approach to legal interpretation insists on a necessary link between law and morality, where moral principles are sought if necessary beyond the confines of the text and legislative intent. A bold interpretive strategy argues that an amoral law is not law. It is useful for our purposes to examine the recurring use of this conception of rights, and its seminal role in struggles over their conception, construction and implementation.

Confirmation of this understanding of rights comes from the contributions to this volume, for example, when participants in a study of the impact of a human rights training course developed by the Danish International Development Agency (DANIDA) and the International Law Institute, Uganda (ILI-U), state that the rights-based approach 'helped me recognize that one is born with these rights and they are not given' and 'I came to realize that rights are free and are for all' (Okille, DANIDA/ILI-U).[1] Rights are not, and cannot only be, seen 'in postinstitutional terms as instruments', but must also be understood as 'a prior ethical entitlement' (Sen 1999: 229).

The social contract, similarly, resonates through contemporary societies, politics and international relations. Various social and political arrangements – from discussions about the challenges of reforging official aid relationships through partnership along the continuum from conditionality to 'contractuality' (Maxwell and Riddell 1998), to Poverty Reduction Strategy Papers (PRSPs), described as a new form of social contract with donors (World Bank 2003: 13), to corporate codes of conduct – are discussed in these terms. Criticisms of the social contract theory also retain their relevance today: what do the powerful, the rich and those with superior knowledge gain from such rules? Given power imbalances, is there any guarantee that the rules will be fair? How can the social contract be extended beyond the state, or the international community of states, as its basic unit(s)? Why would an agent comply with a rule if there is no effective sanction? But the social contract, here seen in a new guise as operating within and across states but not yet at the level of a global contract, remains a means through which power imbalances and inequities can be challenged by allocating rights and responsibilities to all parties, in the interests of all parties, backed up with monitoring mechanisms and sanctions. Although there are significant critiques and other important theories of relevance to human rights – consequentialism/utilitarianism, positivism, Marxism, constructivism, postmodernism – the argument made here is that rights continue to evolve at the interface of natural rights idealism/activism and social contract pragmatism/enforcement, and indeed must involve an ongoing interaction between the two to remain vibrant and responsive to change. Examples of contractualism from the case study chapters are discussed in the following section. If the Enlightenment heralded the first human rights revolution, conceptually and ultimately politically, the current era of globalization contains and demands a second revolutionary break with the past.

The second human rights revolution

The second human rights revolution is ongoing, inextricably implicated in the era of globalization. The post-Second World War era – the establishment of the UN, drafting of the Universal Declaration of Human Rights (1948), and subsequent proliferation of human rights treaty and non-treaty bodies – is better understood both conceptually and politically in evolutionary rather than revolutionary terms, notably in relation to natural law/rights and the social contract (Marks 1998; Morsink 1984; Shestack 1998). Contemporary globalization, while retaining an important role for these two core concepts, constitutes and demands a more radical break with the past. It resituates the nation-state, both in terms of its dominance as a political actor and in terms of its relationships. In short, government has become governance, with significant implications for a human rights regime based on the relationship between the state and the individual. While some argue that the state is declining in importance, with the global market marginalizing it to a merely administrative and facilitative role, many aspects of globalization remain driven by state-based policy decisions. However, the state is unquestionably now only one site of power alongside other power-brokers such as IGOs, multinational corporations (MNCs) and NGOs.

Equally importantly, relationships between NGOs and other actors, including states, are increasingly characterized less in adversarial and competitive terms, and more in terms of complementarity and partnership. The reasons for this move towards cooperation include an initial post-Cold War opening up of international politics and strategic decisions on all sides, in both the human rights and development fields, about the need for greater effectiveness, dialogue and utilization of complementary capacities. More specifically, there was an increased use of NGOs as service

5

deliverers and subcontractors in the provision of development aid and humanitarian relief, and an incremental, more constructive, but also increasingly contested use of human rights discourse beyond its conventional range. Such developments have complex implications for NGOs in terms of funding relationships, independence, accountability, power relations and their ability to combine both advocacy and partnership. The second human rights revolution can thus be characterized as inextricably linked to the shift from government to governance, from 'anti-statism' to 'collaborative activism' (Falk 2004), and to the diffusion of human rights into new areas, in the search for, and struggle over, a new rights regime. The rise of rights-based approaches to development is part of this revolution.

More concretely, how are these changes manifesting themselves? The chapters in this collection repeatedly illustrate the ways in which new actors are being framed as rights holders and more particularly as duty bearers. Jonsson notes: 'There is a need to extend the claim–duty relationships to include all relevant subjects and objects at sub-national, community, and household levels.' International actors are also often added to the mix. The system of claim–duty relationships is called the 'pattern of rights', with each understood as roles individuals/actors may perform, rather than immutable labels. Individuals/actors often occupy both roles simultaneously in relation to other individuals/actors at different levels of society. Building on this conceptualization, pattern or role analysis – the identification of key claim–duty relationships for specific rights – can become an important component of programming (Jonsson, UNICEF). Within such an expanded human rights terrain, NGOs, IGOs and others seek to build the capacities of rights holders to claim rights and of duty bearers to meet their responsibilities (also Brouwer et al., Oxfam; Jones, CARE Rwanda; Theis and O'Kane, Save the Children). In short, the vertical pole of rights (state–individual) is complemented by a consideration of horizontal relationships (Jarman, Institute for Conflict Research; in the Northern Ireland context about which Jarman writes this includes paramilitaries and communities in conflict).

Relationships between the relevant actors are redrawn in a variety of ways. The stress is on alliances, coordination, complementarity, or on balancing such partnerships with advocacy, lobbying and critique, from local to global levels. Contributors talk of the dual role of civil society, advocacy and service delivery (Mander, consultant; Okille, DANIDA/ILI-U); of developing networks between community organizations to influence local and national policy (Antunes and Romano, ActionAid Brazil; Akerkar, ActionAid India; Theis and O'Kane, Save the Children); of blending a 'violations' and a 'promotional' approach (Jones, CARE Rwanda), or a prescriptive human rights approach with the facilitative conflict management approach (Galant and Parlevliet, Centre for Conflict Resolution); while Oxfam assert: 'Working ... from the local level upwards, building the awareness and capacity to promote human rights, and joining forces and linking different actors and different levels are strategies that – when done well – give expression to Oxfam's quest for global equity' (Brouwer at al., Oxfam). These reformulated relationships, and their implications for human rights, constitute the building-blocks of the new contractualism.

The Sphere Project, for example, can be categorized as a new form of social contract, and it engages with all aspects of the second human rights revolution (a range of different actors, reformulated relationships, and an expanded, creative, contested use of rights). The Sphere Project, initiated in 1997, consists of the Humanitarian Charter, a declaration of principle(s), and Minimum Standards in Disaster Response, largely by sector, e.g. health services.[2]

It is an attempt to establish system-wide quality and performance standards. Human rights pervade this project in various ways (Darcy 2004). Crucially, the service standards are framed as entitlements, indicating a willingness on the part of those who subscribe to Sphere to be accountable for their performance measured against the standards. The Minimum Standards are an attempt to define the minimum content of a 'right to life with dignity'. In doing so, Sphere draws on international human rights law, international humanitarian law and refugee law as the basis for more specific, sector-based formulations, for example in health services, of minimum requirements for humanitarian assistance. Thus, Sphere is an extrapolation and development of rights. It also includes what are, in effect, new rights, notably the 'right to assistance', seen as implicit in the right to dignity. Those affected by conflict and disaster become rights bearers rather than objects of charity and benevolence.

Drawing an analogy between Sphere and commercial and public sector 'performance' charters in which customer rights are articulated in the form of minimum service standards, Darcy identifies a further way in which Sphere is 'rights-based':

> [Public service] charters were based on an actual or presumed contract between the service provider and the 'customer', and provided a basis for holding public sector bodies to account for their performance in a way that was becoming familiar in the commercial and professional sectors. In the broadest sense, this could be seen as an articulation of the social contract between state and citizen. More specifically, such charters usually referred (explicitly or implicitly) to more general rights principles ... By

7

reference to such principles, the individual citizen becomes a legitimate claimant with regard to public services, and the service charters provide a vehicle for defining the substance of the claim. Unlike a true contract, these were unilateral declarations of intent, but were based on an assumed relationship that could be seen as analogous to that between humanitarian agencies and their 'beneficiaries'. (Darcy 2004: 116)

Darcy notes the lack of consumer choice or political sanction in this particular context, although the humanitarian ombudsman concept (again drawing on a public service model), now the Humanitarian Accountability Partnership, represents an attempt to fill the accountability gap.[3] However, mechanisms for ensuring accountability and enforcement remain underdeveloped.

Finally, rights have importantly informed the stress on responsibilities. NGO accountability is situated within a wider framework of legal and political responsibility. Darcy identifies diverse actors – the UN, the International Committee of the Red Cross (ICRC), the International Monetary Fund (IMF) and World Bank, military and commercial actors – under the heading 'the globalising of responsibility' (2004: 120). Both the nature and degree of responsibility, or duty, varies, but that there is debate and evolution in this area is beyond question. Within a hierarchy of responsibility, Darcy, echoing Sphere itself, cautions against exaggerating the role, power and responsibilities of humanitarian agencies, noting their dependence on political actors and parties to conflict and that outcomes are contingent on factors beyond agency control. Darcy argues that states retain primary responsibility, and that the political contract between governments and people remains crucial and should not be undermined.[4] While largely an NGO initiative, Sphere has gained widespread support from other parts of the humanitarian system (the UN, ICRC, bilateral and multilateral donors). Over and above such support, Sphere can be used as a platform or advocacy tool to appeal to responsible political actors and lobby responsible parties, a basis for negotiations over access, resources and relief provision, and as a standard of assessment for all actors and for the humanitarian system as a whole.[5]

Sphere is one of numerous, related strands within an emergent human rights regime, many of which are informed by the rights-based approach. What does this mean for our understanding of what rights are and how their use can be, and is being, justified? One of the arguments of this volume is that locating rights at the intersection of natural rights and contractualism places rights, and the securing of rights, firmly within the realm of moral, social and political processes. Law, ideally, frames the everyday and provides a last resort in terms of enforcement. However, if we had to go to court for everything to which we felt entitled we would have time for little else. Most rights are violated and secured in everyday life and relationships, in social and political processes. Furthermore, the interaction between the everyday and the extraordinary, and the private and the public, and the way the one folds into the other, is often overlooked in mainstream human rights discourse and practice.

These understandings of human rights guard against what can be called the legal reflex within human rights discourse, the automatic and unthinking resort to the law in the belief that it is the most effective and perhaps the only form of protection and remedy. The legal reflex can be counterproductive because the law is oppressive (part of the problem rather than part of the solution), because it is inaccessible, or because no effective legal system or remedy exists. Jonsson (UNICEF), in this volume, argues that human rights standards and principles are not precise enough to concretely inform development programming, while Galant and Parlevliet (Centre for Conflict Resolution) concur that a narrow, legalistic interpretation of rights provides little guidance for operationalizing how rights can be integrated meaningfully into conflict management processes. Okille (DANIDA/ILI-U) notes as a recommendation that as the judicial and social/political environment is inhospitable to the legal approach (the context is Uganda), human rights training should emphasize the search for alternative, 'home-grown' ways of ensuring accountability that can work within local contexts, while Akerkar (ActionAid India) notes how vast sections of the Indian population continue to be discriminated against not only because of unfair laws, but also due to the failure to implement progressive laws.

A narrow, legal approach is also unhelpful because establishing legal recognition can become an end in itself – as alluded to above, the real life of even progressive laws can easily become implicated in preserving the status quo as rights become institutionalized – and because the ambiguity of legal recognition can include a reduction in creativity with regard to activism. Formal recognition of a right is not enough (Tomas, UNDP). In the field of development, the legal reflex can sometimes be seen in relation to children's rights and the right to health, where reference to the Convention on the Rights of the Child and the International Covenant of Economic, Social and Cultural Rights (ICESCR, specifically Article 12 and General Comment 14), can serve to preclude combination strategies, that may include but go beyond the law, and the non-legal innovations detailed in this volume. Again it should be noted that these arguments do not seek to deny the importance of the law, but they do seek to establish the equal importance of political and social processes in securing human rights.

9

Contributors to this collection speak directly to a broader understanding of human rights. For them, justice is a social process, utilizing informal and formal mechanisms, and not purely legal (Jonsson, UNICEF; also Okille, DANIDA/ILI-U above); rights-based approaches act in the social, political and economic spheres as well as the legal (Akerkar, ActionAid India); how people relate to the law and its institutions is critical, not just the content of the law itself (Tomas, UNDP); human rights are more than just a legal code as, more fundamentally, they represent an ethical framework for human relations, applicable to all (Jones, CARE Rwanda); and rights-based approaches target laws and regulations, but also beliefs and public opinion (Brouwer et al., Oxfam). Mander (consultant) points out that rights approaches 'may derive strength and legitimacy [from sources such as] socially acknowledged ethical principles of equity and justice, or from the organization and struggles of poor people's organizations'.

More conceptually, the equal importance, indeed interdependence, of processes and outcomes is a common refrain. Galant and Parlevliet (Centre for Conflict Resolution) write 'the quality, legitimacy and sustainability of the outcome depends on the process used to achieve it', while for Jonsson (UNICEF) human rights standards define benchmarks for desirable outcomes (the minimum acceptable level of an outcome) and human rights principles should inform the process designed to achieve the outcome (the minimum level of conduct, values, e.g. participation). Good process can itself be understood as the achievement of a human rights outcome (Jones, CARE Rwanda). The most useful and comprehensive conceptualization of human rights as the everyday is provided by Galant and Parlevliet (Centre for Conflict Resolution) in their discussion of 'dimensions of rights' – rights as rules, rights as structures/institutions, rights as relationships (like Jarman, highlighting the vertical and horizontal axes of rights), and rights as processes. As the application of this schema in the case study of Pieter Mambo High School illustrates, it provides a framework for analysis and intervention.

The study by Okille (DANIDA/ILI-U) on the impact of human rights training in Uganda generates useful insights into the ways in which participants from various walks of life applied the knowledge gained of human rights in their everyday lives. Shifts were reported in mind-sets and attitudes, values and belief systems. Aside from using rights in new ways in the workplace (government ministries, local government, schools, NGOs and community organizations), impacting on staff and inter-personal relations, programming, policy and legal formulation, and more, rights also influenced family life, personal development and confidence, and political awareness.

Two final points on the human rights of the everyday, as essentially social and political processes, can be drawn from the analysis above. First, culture and local specificity are integral to this agenda as indigenous justice mechanisms may be more real than formal legal structures (Tomas, UNDP), and culture is among the factors influencing local authority and power structures (Ensor, consultant). Moreover, the local dynamics that underpin discrimination and power may be observable by or understandable only to those within communities, highlighting the need to ensure that problem analysis also comes from within affected communities (Akerkar, ActionAid India). Whereas fundamental human rights and justice can be construed as absolute concepts and non-negotiable, the application, interpretation and realization of rights and justice are negotiable within the context of specific political, historical and cultural conditions (Ensor, consultant; Galant and Parlevliet, Centre for Conflict Resolution; Jarman, Institute for Conflict Research; Jonsson, UNICEF; Okille, DANIDA/ILI-U; Theis and O'Kane, Save the Children; Tomas, UNDP). The second point is that a conceptualization of rights as implicated in social and political processes is intrinsically 'generative', with rights continually under construction within social and political struggles (Antunes and Romano, ActionAid Brazil; Brouwer et al., Oxfam; Ensor, consultant; Jonsson, UNICEF; Mander, consultant).

Among the range of conceptual and theoretical formulations that speak to this emphasis – one avenue alluded to but not explored in detail here, for example, is legal pluralism – is the distinction between choice and interest theories of rights (Edmundson 2004; Ensor, consultant). Choice theory argues that a right exists when a right holder is able to exercise control over his/her claim on another's duty. In essence, a right requires a right holder and that right holder has the power to enforce or waive the duty relating to the right. This is most persuasively a legal theory of rights. Interest theory grounds rights in the interests of the rights holder, identifying interests as the justification and foundation of rights. In this volume, Ensor argues that an alternative 'mode' of rights-based practice is revealed through focusing on the interests that rights represent rather than on the legal formalization of those interests. Complementing the legal mode, an attention to interests implies constructive engagement with cultural norms, draws attention to the processes of individual and communal change, and suggests that the struggle for justice is at times best served through rights defined locally first and globally second. By grounding rights in individual interests – that is to say, well-being – the political, social and moral necessity for legal rights is also revealed, and their aspirational aspect, emphasizing what *should* happen over what *can* happen, is explicitly stated. This latter point is particularly pertinent as it underpins the social change function of rights. As Edmundson points out, interest theory 'exhibits a kind of generative power that many find attractive, but others find disturbing' (2004: 122).

In a related argument, stressing the need for greater flexibility in the relationship between rights and duties, Sen utilizes Kant's distinction between 'perfect obligation' ('a specific duty of a particular agent for the realization of that right') and the broader notion of 'imperfect obligation' ('[t]he claims are addressed generally to anyone who can help, even though no particular person or agency may be charged to bring about the fulfilment of the rights involved') (1999: 230). This Introduction emphasizes the interest theory of rights and the notion of imperfect obligations, not to the complete exclusion of their twin concepts, but in the belief that these understandings of rights are both neglected and speak to the challenges and dynamism of the second human rights revolution. The Sphere Project, for example, can be located within both of these conceptualizations of rights.

Given the backdrop that globalization provides to the new human rights regime, the idea that there are rights in search of duties, rights holders in search of duty bearers, is not only relevant, but necessary. Otherwise, rights will be too legal, too state-centric, too static and conservative to assist in the pursuit of social justice. Both a natural rights and social contract influence are evident in this reformulated social, political and legal agenda, as the former go in search of the latter. While an expansion in our understanding of duties and duty bearers is necessary, it needs to be informed by an acknowledgement, such as that in the Sphere Project, that the responsibilities of different actors will inevitably vary. Here the distinction between the duty to respect (a negative obligation of avoidance, not to interfere in the enjoyment of, or violate, a right), to protect (measures to protect people from rights violations committed by others/third parties), and to fulfil (the adoption of appropriate measures to aid and assist), and the need for the performance of multiple kinds of duties to secure the complete fulfilment of a right, provide a useful set of conceptual tools (Shue 1996).

In sum, the case study chapters in this book illustrate that the rights-based approach is being driven by and through diverse sets of actors, forging new sets of governance relationships, often using social contracts in the form of 'unilateral declarations of intent' and innovative reworkings of the rights–duties binary, and reinventing and contesting human rights in everyday life. Agencies seek to set up circuits or contracts of rights and responsibilities, to link real rights to equally real duties in reciprocal relationships of recognition, legitimacy and accountability, in their work and spheres of operation. These contracts, like Sphere, are not legal contracts, but exist within social and political processes. Accountability is potentially profoundly, and positively, reworked and redirected downwards by new contractualism. But, within the broader context of partnership and collaboration with more powerful actors such as states/donors, making accountability real also represents its major shortcoming and future challenge. Mander (consultant) hopes for more active states that can intervene on behalf of the poor, taking back a layer of accountability currently ceded to the market. National and international law, citizenship and building local civil society capacity to hold national governments to account, and the evolving legal position on non-state actors, constitute part of the picture. But they are not sufficient to deliver broad-based accountability.

In redrawn vertical and horizontal relationships, a wide range of individuals and actors are reconceptualized as accountable for their actions. Notably, advocates of a rights-based approach also attempt to alter relationships with the recipients of their goods and services, constructing such recipients as rights bearers and their own agencies as duty bearers (CARE, Oxfam, UNICEF: this is less true of governmental donors such as DFID who remain reluctant to see themselves in this light). Some of the specific examples detailed in this volume – such as CARE Rwanda's participatory, interactive monitoring tool designed to provide a forum for orphans and vulnerable children to critique and direct CARE's work (Jones, CARE Rwanda) and the code of conduct developed by Somali civil society, including standards to which civil society aspires to adhere and a monitoring mechanism (Brouwer et al., Oxfam International) – raise questions, beyond declarations of intent and socio-political process, of whether those with less power in the arrangements have access to real sanction and redress. The Afghanistan government reconfiguring its relationship with donors by stressing pledges made and donor responsibility is an interesting attempt to enforce a rights-based accountability, but ultimately faces similar challenges (O'Brien, CARE Afghanistan). As Cornwall and Nyamu-Musembi note, rights-based approaches will mean little if they do not transform power relations among development actors themselves (2004: 1,432). Tomas (UNDP) is forthright on this point, noting that while the potential for improving the accountability of state actors and power holders is one of the key contributions of rights in development, the lack of monitoring and accountability within, between and over NGOs and donor agencies is the critical obstacle to its successful implementation.

A final development within the second human rights revolution relates to the much-proclaimed interdependence and indivisibility of human rights, mainly with reference to civil-political rights and social-economic rights. In mainstream human rights discourse this has become a mantra, epitomized by the Vienna Declaration and Programme for Action of the 1993 UN World Conference on Human Rights, which proclaims: 'All human rights are universal, indivisible and interdependent and interrelated.' From the mainstream human rights community the claim remains rhetorical, more a statement of intent and a recognition of the need to be more relevant to new, particularly Southern, audiences and constituencies, than it is reality. The literature that most effectively both conceptualizes human rights indivisibility and interdependence, and seeks to validate the argument with concrete examples, comes from within development. Two seminal examples are the work of Sen (1999: 160–88) and de Waal (1997) on famine. As the following sections of the Introduction indicate, through the history and conceptual evolution of the relationship between human rights and development, these interactions were largely hidden. However, interdependence and indivisibility were to be of defining importance in the emergence and content of rights-based practice.

The rights-based approach to development is at the heart of the transformations that characterize the second human rights revolution, spanning the various actors involved, reworking the relationships identified, and irrevocably changing the ways in which rights are understood and used. Whether these transformations will deliver a political revolution in Evans's sense – a radical transformation of the accepted principles of social organization, or even a mere seizure of power within the existing order – remains to be seen. Conceptual changes, as with the earlier revolutionary era, inevitably precede a protracted set of political struggles. Despite still drawing on versions of natural rights and the social contract, what is not in doubt in the developments already underway and documented in this volume is the current reality of significant conceptual and political change. Not only are human rights possibly reinventing development, but development has the potential to reinvent human rights.

The evolution of the relationship between human rights and development

The history of development is one of ongoing change, influenced to varying degrees and at different times by diverse pressures: dominant political ideologies; particular regional circumstances; trends in academic and non-governmental discourse; and the continuing failure to generate lasting solutions to poverty and human insecurity, to name but a few. While the changes in development practice inevitably form a continuous process, a review of the last fifty years reveals a series of trends that can be broadly associated with each of the last five decades of the twentieth century. However, as will be demonstrated, the second human rights revolution constitutes a decisive moment in the relationship between human rights and development.

14

The modern era of development emerged as overseas aid in the 1950s, in an environment dominated by independence movements and the gradual ending of the colonial period. Aid was provided by European states to their dependants, soon to be demanded as a duty by former colonies, and large capital injections were provided in the belief that modernization projects would have a catalytic effect on emergent economies. Aid was considered to be a transitory arrangement which would induce 'take-off' and was accordingly defined by an economic agenda: growth was sought and large-scale infrastructure projects were the mechanism for its achievement (Tomaševski 1993: 30–1). Ethical issues, such as welfare and rights, were, if considered at all, assumed to follow as a consequence. However, while the macro-economic effect of aid, measured in terms of indicators such as Gross National Product, was occasionally positive, it became clear during the1960s that even where growth was achieved it often failed to improve conditions for the poorest sections of society. The realization that aid would not have the immediate effect that had been hoped for forced donor countries to reassess their role, leading to the institutionalization of hitherto diverse aid delivery mechanisms and the birth of a longer-term goal known as 'development'. The unanticipated failure of aid resulted in a period of transition during the 1960s in which the delivery and purpose of assistance was questioned by recipients and donors alike. Much that is familiar today in development emerged during this period: demands for fairer trade and aid policies, which would become the proposals for a New International Economic Order (NIEO), resulted from the first UN Conference on Trade and Development (UNCTAD, a forum that lives on) (Looney 2001: 1,128); aid flows stagnated or reduced; political and commercial 'conditionalities' emerged (Tomaševski 1993: 31); and direct approaches for improving welfare were sought to replace unsuccessful growth-based mechanisms. This latter point drew out development as a multidisciplinary endeavour for the first time, resulting in a redefinition that was to characterize development practice during the 1970s.

The upheavals of the 1960s brought about a new vision of development, characterized by anti-poverty initiatives and welfare and gender strategies, and as a 'broad-based, people-oriented or endogenous process, as a critique of modernisation and as a break with past development theory' (Elliot 2002: 46). This redefinition became known as the basic needs approach. Stung by the failure of earlier macro-economic strategies, economists championed 'redistribution with growth' in an attempt to pass on the benefits of financial surplus, but a failure to reduce poverty sharpened the focus on basic needs. The new approach proposed three themes: to increase income for the poor through labour-intensive production; to promote public services;

and to encourage participation. However, participation remained narrowly defined (Mohan and Holland 2001: 182), while in most countries, only an increase in pro-poor public services materialized (Jonsson 2003: 2), with programmes designed to meet basic needs such as health, education and farming receiving donor agency funding. Despite the promises of the new agenda, the targeting of aid towards poor or excluded groups during this period proved to be a transitory phenomenon. The debt crisis at the start of the next decade, fed in part by private lending to Southern governments seeking to free themselves from the ties of increasing aid conditionality, prompted a swift retreat from human-focused development. The introduction of structural adjustment policies in the 1980s reflected a contraction of donor thinking, once again focused on narrow financial goals, with recipient states being required to enter into supposedly palliative financial administration in order to qualify for aid. Four decades of development had, therefore, been sufficient for aid policy to turn full circle, from the failure of economic growth strategies, to poverty alleviation and back to growth.

This characterization of development history offers a simple schematic of the dominant themes that arose following the moral and political collapse of the colonial system. However, while discourse, and investment, undoubtedly followed the trends outlined above, challenges to the ideologies and mechanisms employed in aid and development remained a constant feature. It is in this sense that rights can be seen as having had a continuous relationship to development throughout its history, even if the link emerged as a defining feature only after five decades of remaining largely hidden.

The 1948 Universal Declaration of Human Rights (UDHR) both coincides with the emergence of the modern development era and represents one of the strongest statements of rights as the mechanism for human realization. The UDHR not only redefined the relationship between the individual and global political order (Sano 2000: 737), but did so by declaring the individual to have both civil and political freedoms and the right to cultural, economic and social welfare. While the relationship between the different rights became disputed political territory, due in no small part to the polarization of global ideologies in the post-Second World War period, the unified presence of all rights in the UDHR is clear and relates to the goals of personal and social well-being that are synonymous with the modern development agenda. However, the separation into civil and political rights on the one hand, and cultural, economic and social rights on the other was reified by the approval of the UN General Assembly of two related, yet indisputably distinct human rights covenants two decades later in 1966 (the International Covenant on Civil and Political Rights [ICCPR] and the

16

International Covenant on Economic, Social and Cultural Rights [ICESCR]). As mentioned above, it was to take until the 1993 Vienna Declaration to secure rhetorical reconfirmation of the indivisibility that was clear in the text of the UDHR.

Outside the partisan power struggles of international politics, the inter-relationship between the rights identified in the UDHR and their centrality to development continued to be recognized. In 1959 at the New Delhi Congress of the International Commission of Jurists (ICJ), the indivisibility of rights was affirmed within an expanded understanding of the 'Rule of Law', a view reinforced in subsequent meetings of the Congress and through the urging of lawyers to maintain and enforce cultural, economic and social rights (MacDermot 1981: 25). Moreover, the ICJ traces its relationship with development back to this time and, in 1978, made its understanding of the relationship between development and rights clear: 'development should not be conceived of or understood simply in terms of economic growth, nor as an increase in per capita income, but should necessarily include those qualitative elements which human rights constitute and which provide an essential dimension' (ibid., p. 27).

Mohan and Holland observe that in the negotiation of the human rights covenants 'the priority [for newly independent African countries] was development' in which 'abstract debates about rights had little relevance to this cohort of modernisers who used centralised mechanisms to push through grandiose development plans' (2001: 180). This role, or rather absence, of human rights in development did not go unnoticed. As Tomaševski points out: 'the review and appraisal of the first UN Development Decade [the 1960s] encompassed in its critique of development the disregard of human rights' (1993: 12). The purpose of this criticism was limited to raising human rights awareness in development, seeking to ensure respect for human rights rather than extending to protection or fulfilment. The 1969 Declaration on Social Progress and Development, however, was significantly more forthright. Article 2 of the Declaration begins: 'Social progress and development shall be founded on respect for dignity and value of the human person and shall ensure the promotion of human rights and social justice.' The idea that development should 'ensure the promotion of human rights' is a radical statement at the end of a decade that struggled to shake off the economic imperative in development discourse and practice.

While the dominant paradigm of the 1970s shifted to anti-poverty strategies and basic needs, human rights remained a theme among those critical of or seeking to expand the concept of development. Participation came to be an accepted aspect of programming during this period. Although predominantly focused on using local knowledge in development projects rather than popular political participation (Mohan and Holland 2001: 182), not all shared this narrow conceptualization. In 1976 the Director General of the International Labour Organization (ILO) observed that 'a basic needs oriented policy implies participation of people in making the decisions which affect them ... For example, education and good health will facilitate participation, and participation will in turn strengthen the claim for the material basic needs' (ILO 1976: 321). Basic needs, when taken in this broader sense, served to raise awareness of the fulfilment of human rights as fundamental, 'not as ends in themselves but also to contribute to the attainment of other goals' (ibid.). However, it is characteristic of an idea whose time had yet to arrive that the ILO's 1976 World Employment Conference resolution ultimately failed to include reference to the role of human rights.

Important developments did arise during the 1970s in which human rights gained a prominent profile, including the coming into force of the two international human rights covenants and the instrumental role of the Carter administration in exposing international politics to human rights. However, it was the third meeting of UNCTAD in 1972 that brought rights squarely into the development discourse through the claiming of the right to development by the governments of the South. Although it would be 1986 before the Declaration on the Right to Development would be adopted by the UN General Assembly, the idea gained significant momentum within the UN in the intervening years. In 1977 the Commission on Human Rights prompted the Secretary General to undertake a study into the international aspects of the right, and two years later the Commission affirmed the existence of the right to development (Alston 1981: 101). As part of his report, the Secretary General attempted to outline a definition of development. The content of this definition is worth reproducing here, if only due to its strikingly rights-based quality, and the Secretary General's opinion that it is representative of a 'general consensus' on the meaning of development in 1979:

> the central purpose of development is the realization of the potentialities of the human person in harmony with the community; the human person is the subject not the object of development; both material and non-material needs must be satisfied; respect for human rights is fundamental; the opportunity for full participation must be accorded; the principles of equality and non-discrimination must be respected; and a degree of individual and collective self-reliance must be achieved. (ibid., p. 102)

From this background it becomes less surprising to find that alongside the rise of fundamentalist market economics, the momentum behind ideas that embraced both development and rights continued through the 1980s. The central and perhaps best-known advocate to emerge in this period was Amartya Sen. Sen has now become famous for challenging the technocratic approach to managed, welfarist economic development and introducing the notions of freedom, agency, capabilities and entitlement. Undoubtedly, his early 1980s challenges to conventional development wisdom and ultimate redefinition of the overall goal of development – development as freedom – has played a central role in the emergence and acceptance of the interrelationship between human rights and development. The link to rights is made strongly through the 'entitlement' concept, which captures those things that a person is in control of, or has command over, in life. Entitlements are acquired by virtue of the attainment of rights. Sen postulated that complex interdependencies link matters of life and death, such as starvation and famine, with rights, through the entitlements concept: mass starvation occurs through a lack of entitlements in a population (or more probably a particular, disenfranchised section of a population) rather than as a result of shortages in food production (Sen 1981). Moreover, through capabilities, Sen is concerned with the ability of individuals to choose and achieve different and important aspects of life (or 'functionings' in the Sen lexicon), encompassing physical needs (such as nourishment) through to more complex social elements of well-being such as participation and self-worth (Sen 1999: 74–6). In this latter sense, Sen's approach echoes the broader understanding of basic needs argued for by the ILO Director General some years previously, while more generally it is possible to see Sen's contribution as a coherent and, importantly, an economist's contribution to the ongoing rights-based discourse.

While the significance of Sen's work is beyond challenge, it remains important to see his contribution in the broader historical context: by situating Sen's ideas within a continuum of thought relating rights and development it is possible to see the eventual emergence of rights-based approaches as the product of an evolution in thinking rather than the result of a revolution instigated by the work of one individual. This context is also important for understanding how the emergence of rights-based approaches constitutes a significant break with previous development strategies. By providing a body of documents that identify rights as a challenge to mainstream development, the history of rights-based thinking offers a perspective that presents the recent emergence of rights-based approaches as the achievement of a contested goal rather than a simple 'repackaging' of the status quo (Uvin 2002: 2). The turn of the decade at the end of the 1970s provides several examples: the rights-based understanding of development

19

outlined by the UN Secretary General in 1979; Sen's seminal contribution; and the outcome of the ICJ's 1981 conference entitled 'Development, Human Rights and the Rule of Law'. Convened in the same year as Sen's work on famine was published, the conference brought the ICJ's understanding of the relationship between rights and development to a head. In a conclusion that is underpinned by the need for the indivisibility of rights, global action and revised social contracts – the pillars of the second human rights revolution – and that resonates with many of the chapters in this book, the ICJ synthesized three decades of discourse:

> the satisfaction of basic needs would be permanently achievable only with structural changes at all levels, local national and international, that would enable those concerned to identify their own needs, mobilise their own resources and shape their own future in their own terms. Development should, therefore, be seen as a global concept including with equal emphasis civil and political rights and economic, social and cultural rights. (ICJ 1981: 224)

The emergence of rights-based approaches

The 1980s are now well known for the adjustment policies that formed the reaction to the debt crisis and the demands of the New International Economic Order (NIEO). However, the foregoing offers a view of how understandings of the role of rights in development were sufficiently broadly held, in institutions such as the ILO and the ICJ, in sections of the UN, and by individuals such as Sen, that they were sustained through the reversals of the 1980s. A critical backlash against structural adjustment emerged towards the end of the decade, embodied in concepts such as 'Adjustment with a Human Face', launched by UNICEF in 1987 (Cornia and Jolly 1987) and the World Bank's rhetorical engagement with poverty alleviation (Einhorn 2001: 26). UNICEF's influential challenge to adjustment advocated empowerment policies and people-centred development, and was scathing of the marginalization that had taken place under economic stabilization programmes (Jonsson 2003: 2). More broadly, Molyneux and Lazar identify a 'conceptual shift' across a range of large international NGOs towards the end of the 1980s, in which NGOs moved from being 'needs-based and service-driven to a more *strategic* approach, in which rights issues were increasingly incorporated into their work' (Molyneux and Lazar 2003: 6, emphasis in original). Thus, after several decades on the sidelines of development discourse, the failure of the neo-liberal reaction provided an environment receptive to an alternative development paradigm, allowing the human rights approach to emerge.

Recognition of the shortcomings of structural adjustment coincided with a profound shift in the global political context brought about by the ending of the Cold War. From a rights perspective, the most striking evidence of this change was the content of the Vienna Declaration. Released from the ideological stalemate of superpower politics, the Declaration was a work of compromise between North and South rather than East and West, in which the indivisibility of rights was conceded by the North in return for an acceptance of universality by the South. The broadening of the accepted definition of rights that took place at UN conferences throughout the 1990s (Hamm 2001: 1007) was aided by the increased participation of NGO representatives at international fora, including in influential agenda-setting processes (Molyneux and Lazar 2003: 23). Indeed, Molyneux and Lazar argue that NGOs operated decisively in the transformation of development priorities. With many NGOs having adopted the language of rights, the centrality of their role is demonstrated by the range of levels across which they operated in the 1990s: along with participating in the flurry of 'end of millennium' UN conferences, NGOs were influencing and being influenced by donors' demands for a broad-based, social justification for project funding, while also communicating and reacting to the concerns of their Southern partner organizations (ibid., p. 24). In societies that were transforming themselves from authoritarian regimes, civil and political rights were assumed, and used to demand cultural, economic and social justice. Social movements understood Katarina Tomaševski 's observation that 'impoverishment and disempowerment are two sides of the same coin' and therefore 'economic and political governance ... became the target of popular protests' (1993: 5). Thus indivisibility finally started to be realized across a range of actors, not only from above in the rhetoric of governments, but crucially also in the emergence of 'development from below' (Sano 2000: 739). In terms of the emergence of rights in development, this transition towards a common recognition of all human rights proved crucial: as those who had articulated a vision of rights-based development had identified for more than three decades, indivisibility of rights forms the key element in the approach. Thus, with the ending of the Cold War and a consequent opening up of international politics, the threads of failing neo-liberalism, resurgent indivisibility, social movement activism and long-standing intellectual support combined to form a bond tying rights to development.

The contributors to this volume reinforce this view of rights indivisibility as a core component of rights-based approaches (see, for example, Brouwer et al. on Oxfam's five 'aims' and the importance of freedom of information, expression and assembly in sustaining short-term subsistence gains, and

Antunes and Romano [ActionAid Brazil], defining a struggle for the right to food in terms of a fight for citizenship). They provide a wide-ranging argument for a holistic interpretation of the indivisibility and interdependence of human rights, including not only civil-political and economic-social rights but also process and outcomes; multiple levels from the local to the global, top-down and bottom-up approaches, and a Northern NGOs focus on home government policies as well as the international arena (Brouwer et al., Oxfam; Jones, CARE Rwanda; Jonsson, UNICEF); public and private actors/spheres (the everyday); and new as well as existing rights extending to include both individuals and collectives (Antunes and Romano, ActionAid Brazil; Ensor, consultant). The case study chapters demonstrate the indivisibility of human rights in practice, and as a fundamental component of good development practice. Through concrete examples, such practice can genuinely inform a theoretical understanding of indivisibility that is coherent and grounded in reality.

Undoubtedly, a broader range of factors than those outlined above combined to forge a new consensus around rights at the start of the 1990s. Perhaps most significantly, the search for a normative discourse with which to address an increasingly globalized world with multiple and diverse nodes of power, along with a pre-existing international framework of rights standards and mechanisms contributed as underlying, rather than proximate, causes for the emergence of rights (Hamm 2001: 1007; Mohan and Holland 2001: 180). It is also an oversimplification to suggest that rights arrived into a world that was remade at the end of the 1980s; structural adjustment has since been rebranded and found a new home in some Poverty Reduction Strategy conditionalities, rather than having been displaced entirely; the broader neo-liberal paradigm lives on through economic globalization (Hamm 2001: 1007); and the gradual dismantling of Cold War institutions and ideologies has been neither rapid nor complete (demonstrated, for example, by the USA's ongoing refusal to ratify the ICESCR). However, without the positive synergies between component parts of the second human rights revolution, realized to a large extent through the many faces of indivisibility, it would have remained unlikely that an idea as potentially challenging as rights would have taken root as a developmental concept at all.

Despite theoretical and rhetorical convergence, the content of rights-based development differs with regional and thematic focus and with the degree of institutional commitment to and particular understanding of the relationship between rights and development. This diversity is apparent from the contributions in this volume, but core commonalities can also be identified. Maxine Molyneux and Sian Lazar, in examining the role of rights in development projects in Latin America, identify a number of key elements common to rights-based practice in the region. In particular, they highlight building 'micro–macro linkages' to transform personal values and interpersonal relationships as a crucial step in actualizing the content of otherwise abstract legislation. Similarly, they describe the process of 'changing mentalities' in which those who express their needs move from a focus on charity and favours to being claimants with rights (Molyneux and Lazar 2003: 9). These themes are also common to the rights-based practice detailed in this volume and are significant in taking up the challenge that rights represent. Rather than seeking only technical or quantifiable outcomes, an engagement with rights stimulates a political transformation in which the ideas that rights represent in a particular context are drawn out and emphasized in ways that are relevant to everyday life, in socio-political as well as legal processes. Such transformations can challenge established, often hierarchical structures within society and are therefore not uncontested. Moser and Norton bring this aspect into sharp focus by demonstrating how rights may be used as an entry point to challenge power relationships. Used in this way, rights offer both a tool for analysis of who owes a duty to whom and a mechanism for framing the legitimate claims that are identified (Moser and Norton 2001: 16).

Molyneux and Lazar's study develops the transformational aspect of rights by highlighting their use as a mechanism for 'strategic action' that encourages active participation and at best will 'empower the poor to analyse their own personal situation, attribute responsibility and work out the means to improve it'. Further, by assisting the poor to 'find their own voice' and thus define their own development objectives, the projects in the study are found to be both more effective and more likely to be sustainable (Molyneux and Lazar 2003: 10). Taking up the importance of voice, Urban Jonsson, a major contributor to UNICEF's human rights approach and the author of a chapter in this volume, sees communication as being of central importance to rights-based practice, with rights realization 'triggered by the process of communication; that is by an interaction between claim holders and duty bearers that admits the former into the decision making process'. Communication of this sort is characterized as an empowering, two-way, interactive process that enables claim holders to identify desired changes, and is contrasted with 'behaviour change strategies' that are designed to persuade marginalized people to adopt desired practices (Jonsson 2003: 27; also see Jonsson's contribution to this volume).

At the level of policy, the Office of the High Commissioner for Human Rights (UNHCHR) in the Asia-Pacific region instituted a study in 2002 of the emerging features of rights-based approaches to development (Nguyen

23

2002). Drawing on the documentation of eighteen UN agencies, development cooperation agencies and NGOs, the study identified four 'levels' of integration of rights into the development process.[6] The policies surveyed reveal different understandings of the causal relationship between development and human rights at each level of integration, described under the headings: successful development leads to respect for human rights; respect for human rights contributes to sustainable development; realization of human rights as a goal of development; and realization of all human rights as the ultimate goal of development. The range of attitudes described by the four categories demonstrates that within the field of development the role that is afforded to rights remains extremely variable. In the first category, rights are seen as an outcome of development and therefore only incidentally related to intervention programming. Illustrative of this understanding is the World Bank, which takes the view that 'the advancement of an interconnected set of human rights is impossible *without development*' (ibid., p. 3, emphasis in World Bank original). However, the latter three categories all see rights as an increasingly integral part of the development process, with the final policy group in fact inverting the relationship and defining development itself as the achievement of human rights.

The analysis provided by the UNHCHR study demonstrates that an institution's understanding of the relationship between rights and its function (in this case, development) is fundamental in determining the role that rights play. For some organizations, rights are mentioned only to locate their work with respect to what is perceived to be the latest terminology or trend. Others, however, identify rights as instrumental to or even as the definition of their function and purpose, and set their policy goals accordingly. Those organizations that fall into Nguyen's final category, in which development is defined as the achievement of rights, include Oxfam and DFID, whose overarching rights-based principles are summarized as: 'accountability, equity, non-discrimination and participation. Situations are analysed through a human rights analysis framework, which ... poses questions about power relations within society: political, economic, social and cultural' (ibid., p. 6–7).

A review of the policy documents of NGOs such as ActionAid and CARE reveals that this integrated role of rights in development practice is representative of many interpretations (ActionAid 1999; CARE 2002), including those found in a study examining Danish rights-based aid policy: '[the policies studied reveal a focus on protection of individuals and groups against power exertion ... a focus on non-discrimination, equal opportunity and participation ... a focus on enabling support that allows individuals and groups to lead a life in dignity, free of poverty, with access to certain minimum standards of living, health, water, and education' (Sano 2000: 751).

These examples point to an interpretation of the rights-based approach in which the central components of development work, such as participation and empowerment, are reclaimed and repoliticized from neo-liberal instrumentalism and mainstream appropriations by powerful institutions such as the World Bank. Participation, for example, is not a needs-based consultation for specific projects but becomes a more inclusive and democratic process of popular involvement in decision-making over decisions that affect people's lives, based on rights and responsibilities (Cornwall and Nyamu-Musembi 2004). Moreover, these interpretations point to an approach that constitutes a challenge to power. Some of the infrastructure of this challenge has been outlined already. Expanding the range of those considered rights holders and duty bearers, in relationships in which the latter individuals/actors are reframed as accountable, is not a neutral act. Many contributors to this collection suggest that rights-based approaches address the root, structural causes of poverty and conflict. Poverty is understood as a symptom of deep-rooted inequalities and unequal power relationships, in short as a state of powerlessness and rightlessness (Akerkar, ActionAid India; Brouwer et al., Oxfam; Mander, consultant); and human rights abuses are conceived as symptoms and structural causes of conflict (Galant and Parlevliet, Centre for Conflict Resolution). If rights violations underpin poverty and conflict, the relevant relationships and situations need to be transformed by questioning power and resource imbalances. Interventions focus on the poorest, the marginalized, on discrimination and inequalities, and seek to mobilize, empower and more. Rights-based approaches problematize policy trade-offs that are harmful to the poorest, and both help to protect people from the unjust exercise of power and can be used to challenge power (Jonsson, UNICEF).

The experiences relayed by Antunes and Romano (ActionAid Brazil) specifically focus on reclaiming power for the poor and marginalized from social systems that perpetuate inequality. Populist, elite politicians who provide services but prevent the formation of people's organizations and drug gang bosses who provide public services across their territory in exchange for loyalty, are identified as the power holders that have trapped populations in poverty and dependency. The struggle for sustainable food and nutrition for the poor is therefore met by developing the agency of and providing support to community groups and social movements, who in turn offer an overt challenge to the dominant political authority. Notably, a key contribution of the international NGO in this work is the provision

25

of accurate information, for example on the extent of malnutrition or the numbers of people migrating due to poverty, highlighting the relationship between knowledge and power (see also Akerkar's description of ActionAid in India).

O'Brien (CARE, Afghanistan), while acknowledging that aid has always been political, makes the useful distinction between capital 'P' 'Political' and lower case 'p' 'political'. The former is partisan, promotes particular political actors and non-consensual values, whereas the latter asserts that aid should be informed by certain core, higher, consensual or universal political values and takes sides to the extent that it is pro-poor. O'Brien's argument is that the core political values of humanitarianism (neutrality, impartiality, humanity) have been found wanting in complex politicized scenarios such as the 'war against terror', and need to be supplanted by the values or principles of human rights. All such values are 'political' because they inform processes through which resources and power are allocated and used. O'Brien explores how a rights-based approach has enabled humanitarians to provide a principled response to aid 'Politicization' in Afghanistan, addressing specifically the core dilemmas of the militarization of humanitarian action and funding. O'Brien argues that the rights-based approach can give NGOs the ability to define and affirm their own values when faced with competing political demands.

The challenging of power can take a wide variety of forms at a concrete level. Recipients of a human rights training course in Uganda spoke of a new confidence that would help them to raise human rights concerns and challenge violations, from demanding a list of tender awards from the district administration to seeking justice. Again, knowledge is a form of power:

> [w]henever a policeman senses that you have some knowledge of your rights they will treat you with more respect and will not intimidate or harass you. For instance, whenever I ask a policeman, 'Please, officer, can I know your number', he senses that he might get in trouble later if he is up to anything funny, and usually will not pursue a request for a bribe. (Okille, DANIDA/ILI-U)

Similarly, Akerkar (ActionAid India) reports that, for several of those involved in projects set up following the communal violence in Gujarat, the engagement with rights was a 'transforming experience', giving them the confidence to challenge authority and fight for justice.

Jones (CARE Rwanda) states that the rights-based approach reorientates NGOs from purely technical solutions to socio-political action. So, for example, CARE's programme in Gikongoro province, heavily focused on HIV/Aids, complements technical interventions such as strengthening the health system and access to voluntary counselling, testing and anti-retroviral therapy, by attempting to emphasize the deeper societal issues of ignorance about HIV/AIDS, stigma, discrimination and exclusion. Jones also raises the issue of resistance to the rights-based approach, both within CARE Rwanda itself as well as society and the broader body politic. In a polarized and fragile society, recovering from genocide and with little by way of a culture of public debate and participation, there is a political sensitivity to anything perceived to be divisive and limited space for the critical engagement and challenges to the status quo that rights-based approaches require. Okille (DANIDA/ILI-U) and O'Brien (CARE Afghanistan) concur that assertions of rights can be seen as a threat or irritant by those in power. This insight is nuanced by noting that a lack of understanding of the processes of change can be a central problem; Tomas (UNDP) asks how rights-based actors can manage change in both the realization of previously repressed rights and in the location of decision-making power in such a way as to minimize or mitigate the challenge to vested interests.

Various issues are raised by this discussion of rights and power. Perhaps the most important is again Evans's point: does a rights-based approach attempt to transform radically, or simply modify, the prevailing neo-liberal economic order? This, in truth, is not clear from the contributions to this book. While rights-based approaches can be top-down and appropriated from above, they can also take their place in a long history – spanning anti-colonial and anti-apartheid struggles, campaigns for the Right to Development and the New International Economic Order (NIEO), and the ongoing activities of social, anti-globalization and anti-war movements – of attempts to use, construct and appropriate rights from below to challenge power holders. However, while the rights-based approach identifies structural concerns, can it transform them? The challenges to power often appear local and fragmentary (within particular projects or NGO programmes) rather than systemic, with structural factors often beyond the control of the relevant actors. Jones (CARE Rwanda) states that '[t]he ultimate aim of RBA has to be systemic change, independent of external support, that achieves lasting gains in human rights and poverty reduction', while for Antunes and Romano (ActionAid Brazil) '[t]he biggest problem in the fight for existing or new rights is how to consolidate ... practices and obligations, in order to not depend on politically favourable governments'. How structural change might be achieved requires much greater clarification, both conceptually and practically. A further issue requiring more research is how NGOs combine a strategy of challenging power with relationships characterized by partnership, collaboration and varying degrees of financial dependency. Finally, and as a related point, it should be noted that the application of a rights-based approach, and reframing relationships in terms of rights holders and duty bearers, does not inevitably result in resistance or conflict. As the chapters by Jarman (Institute for Conflict Research) and Galant and Parlevliet (Centre for Conflict Resolution) show, the successful acceptance and internalization of rights and responsibilities, both one's own and those of others, by a range of actors, can defuse rather than ignite conflict.

The history of the relationship between rights and development highlights the role played by the broader political context in defining the emergence, function and impact of rights. The emergence of the rights-based approach during the 1990s rather than the 1980s, for example, had more to do with the international political reconfigurations that took place during each period than with changes in appreciation of the need for rights. What, then, is to be the role of rights in the new millennium? Undoubtedly, the post-9/11 context has yielded setbacks through a flexing of muscles by economic and military power holders against rights. New challenges to indivisibility have emerged as focus is drawn away from economic and social and towards civil and political rights, both through new attacks on liberty (internment including at Guantanamo Bay and in the UK; abuse including at Abu Ghraib; and crackdowns throughout the world under the guise of the 'war against terror') and through attacks 'for' liberty (Afghanistan, Iraq). However, the experiences described in this volume repeatedly highlight how rights assume greater relevance when attacked or when they are systematically denied to populations and, moreover, the framework for action provided by rights becomes even more necessary and relevant in places such as Afghanistan and Iraq where the space for intervening is narrowed by the 'war on terror' (O'Brien, CARE Afghanistan). Just as the history of rights is characterized by advances and setbacks, the contest over ownership of rights, and their very meaning, is now continuing in new political contexts. Current and past challenges to the role of human rights in development will no doubt be matched by new variants in the future as local and global political environments evolve; the task for rights-based practice is not only to respond to the changing environment but also to play a part in shaping it.

Critiques of rights-based approaches

This section by and large summarizes the arguments of key authors who have critiqued rights-based approaches. It is structured thematically and each section ends with a set of questions raised by the critiques. The questions should be seen as challenges to which subsequent chapters and the Conclusion need to rise. The Conclusion to the volume returns to the questions posed in the Introduction, and attempts to provide some provisional answers drawing not on academic or policy literatures, but on the practice-based contributions in this book. Three critiques are addressed in some detail: overreach, politicization and false hope.

Overreach Accusations of NGO overreach have been levelled at facets of work ranging from moral and political ambition to operational skills and capacity.

For humanitarianism, Rieff (2002) argues that overreach has its origins in frustration at dealing in failure, with a limited, isolated role addressing short-term needs rather than long-term, systemic, root causes. Haunted by the mantra that there are 'no humanitarian solutions to humanitarian problems', Rieff argues that humanitarianism invested in the idea of itself as a force for social transformation, a force to build new societies. Overthrowing the Taliban, for example, appeared to be a much better way of meeting the humanitarian needs of the Afghan people than trying to work with an essentially obstructionist regime. This has led humanitarians to look beyond relief to human rights, but also to intersections with development, peace-building, conflict resolution, democracy and good governance. Rieff condemns 'holistic' humanitarianism as 'anything and everything' (2002: 272); 'a serious, wonderful, and limited idea has become a catchall for the thwarted aspirations of our age' (p. 335).[7] Chandler, citing Nicholas Leader's (1998) classification, makes a similar argument about humanitarianism's 'deepening' (solidarity and advocacy for victims in conflict situations in terms of protection, security and human rights) and 'broadening' (from humanitarian relief to longer-term development) (Chandler 2002: 26–40). Crucially, for Chandler, this overreach is more interventionist in scale and duration, requiring NGOs to seek the support of states and international institutions. These developments looked as if they might ally humanitarian objectives to the power and resources to ensure success.

Overreach required an emphasis on complementarity and coordination, which Rieff submits to trenchant critique. These processes have operated across principles, policies and actors. Rieff argues that not all competing claims – '[t]ruth and justice, peace and justice ... human rights and humanitarianism' (2000: 283) – can be reconciled. For one, rights often conflict with each other. The question of whether principles clash spans the fields of human rights, humanitarianism, development and conflict resolution, for example in relation to the relief–development continuum, the convergence of human rights and development/humanitarian discourses, and peace versus justice. In Duffield's view, the complementarity of development

29

and humanitarianism, founded in rights, is claimed by the development community in order to secure its own future in the face of an almost continuous history of failure. If humanitarian action suffers or is sacrificed as a consequence, it 'would appear to be a price worth paying to maintain the concealment and responsibility of the development profession' (2001: 93). Duffield is similarly forthright in denouncing a regime that embraces conflict resolution and post-war reconstruction: 'one could well argue [that] donor governments are expecting a child to do the job of an adult' (p. 88). However, for advocates of a rights-based approach, the binding glue in these proposed complementarities is human rights, seen as the clearest bearer of shared values, and as a means of addressing abuse of power, inequality, the root causes of problems and providing sustainable solutions. Human rights can appear particularly prone to being appropriated as a source of legitimacy for failed discourses and an answer to everyone's problems. There are also questions about whether NGOs have the capacity to undertake the necessary analysis and interventions.

The frequently claimed tension between peace and justice can be depicted in the following terms: 'conflict managers' stress a swift end to war, which may require compromise and amnesties, while the 'democratizers' emphasize human rights, prosecutions for perpetrators, democratic institutions and the rule of law (Baker 1996). These approaches are shot through with differing emphases on processes and outcomes, pragmatism and principles, short-term and long-term objectives, immediate needs and structural causes, that lend themselves to claims of incompatibility on the one hand, but also complementarity and the need for coordination on the other (see Galant and Parlevliet, Centre for Conflict Resolution). The call for greater coordination has been directed at all levels, from international interventions to local, community programmes. Putnam (2002), for example, argues that international human rights organizations need to show greater tactical and political flexibility, particularly in the early stages of peace implementation, balancing the 'enforcement approach' to human rights protection with an emphasis on providing education/training and building domestic institutions, such as the police force and judiciary, on which the former approach depends. Her assertion is that human rights are best served by coordination, integrating human rights into peace implementation missions and collaborating with post-settlement governments. At a national and community level, contributors to a recent issue of *Human Rights Dialogue* (2002) indicate that in conflicts such as those in Northern Ireland and Sri Lanka, which are characterized by inter-group tensions, splits within and between human rights and conflict resolution approaches can mirror splits in society. In such contexts these political and politicized appropriations may in part be overcome by greater coordination. But, as Rieff reminds us, the price of such coordination can be high.

If humanitarian actors have embraced greater coordination, within and beyond the humanitarian system, the result has, for Rieff, been confusion, a blurring of lines between, say, NGOs, states and militaries. NGO–state links are not new – American humanitarianism has a long tradition of cooperation with government and was deeply implicated in US Cold War foreign policy – but they have expanded and deepened dramatically in the post-Cold War era, in large measure due to a dependency on state funding, with NGOs often becoming, in effect, subcontractors. These interrelated issues – funding; the subcontracting of previously state functions in welfare, service provision, development and humanitarian relief; resulting implications for independence and accountability – affect NGOs across all the issue areas addressed by this book.

What Rieff calls 'state humanitarianism' crowds out autonomous humanitarian space, in part because one way in which its power is exercised is by subordinating humanitarianism to other agendas. Most provocatively, humanitarian objectives have been used as a rationalization for war. Other examples, such as the role of the UNHCR as 'lead agency' and gatekeeper for the humanitarian effort in Bosnia, powerful in relation to the NGOs yet powerless in comparison with the major states, similarly brought home some of the stark realities of coordination infused with unequal power relations. Rieff prefers the more modest aims of an independent humanitarianism – of Médecins Sans Frontières (MSF) and French humanitarianism more generally[8] – over the prevailing ethos of linkages, coordination and mainstreaming. Thus, for him, the implication of stressing complementarity and coordination is a third C: cooption: 'Historically, no social movement has ever succeeded for very long in retaining sole custody of the ideas it has championed or the values it has tried to stand for. Cooptation has been the historic destiny of most if not all large moral ideas' (Rieff 2002: 288).

The encounter with state power and institutionalization is fundamentally transforming. Mohan and Holland make a similar point with regard to human rights and development: 'The emergence of RBD [rights-based development] discourse ... has created an operational space for an absorption of the rights agenda within the neo-liberal policy frameworks' (2001: 182), and 'the neo-liberal establishment has successfully repositioned itself with respect to the rights-based agenda by championing accountability, transparency and the role of citizen participation in demanding their rights' (p. 183).

The theme of overreach speaks directly to the challenges that characterize the second human rights revolution: complex relationships between diverse actors; complementarity, coordination and cooption in new regimes of governance; the challenge of whether to work with or against governments (see Rieff 2002: 291); and struggles over the appropriate role for and meaning of human rights, including the search for appropriate duty bearers and rights indivisibility. Under the umbrella of 'overreach', this volume will seek to address the following questions:

- Is there evidence for the claimed complementarity between human rights and other agendas such as development, humanitarianism and conflict resolution in the search for more holistic, longer-term solutions?
- Is it possible to say in what circumstances coordination, notably with states, leads to negative results (incoherent organizational mandates, blurred divisions of labour, cooption) or positive outcomes (increased influence and effectiveness, maintenance of space for independent action and effectiveness)?
- Do NGOs and IGOs have the capacity to operationalize rights-based interventions (especially when it involves working outside traditional areas of knowledge and competence, significant retraining, the capacity to do necessary research and political analysis, and so on)?

Politicization One of the most frequently articulated challenges to the growing influence of human rights is that it politicizes NGO work that is often more traditionally thought of in the guise of various combinations of independence, impartiality, neutrality and so on.

The politicization of humanitarianism for relief agencies, for example, is a result of the wider role humanitarianism has come to play in global politics. The humanitarianization of world problems represents a form of depoliticization and political disengagement by states. Hence the bleak view that in countries of little strategic interest, humanitarian assistance became the paradigm for North–South relations in the post-Cold War era (ibid., p. 87, citing a UN official in eastern Congo). As Bosnia and Rwanda exemplified, where states, the media, and to some extent NGOs, characterize political problems as humanitarian, humanitarian relief can become a substitute for real political action, and an alibi for state inaction and a lack of political will. States could simultaneously appear to do something while substantively doing nothing. Humanitarianism, so the critique goes, became an impediment to genuine understanding and appropriate action. And humanitarian agencies found themselves mired in their powerlessness, dependencies and complicity (here the allegations range from complicity in ethnic cleansing and helping to stop Bosnians leaving for the West in the former Yugoslavia, to assisting the Rwandan *genocidaire* to regroup in the refugee camps of eastern Zaire/Congo). 'It is now commonplace to read of humanitarian aid prolonging wars, feeding killers, legitimising corrupt regimes, creating war economies and perpetuating genocidal policies' (Chandler 2002: 43). The primary sickness afflicted the major power-brokers (states and, to a lesser degree, the UN), but a secondary ailment affected the humanitarian NGOs (Rieff 2002: 123–93).

The irony is that at the same time as states and inter-governmental actors have sought at least rhetorically to depoliticize their activities – although the post 9/11 era of accentuated aid politicization has stripped some of this mask away – shrouding foreign policy in a mantle of humanitarianism and human rights, NGOs have embraced human rights as politics. Aid has been identified by NGOs across the development–humanitarian spectrum as inherently political. And the embrace of human rights was an acknowledgement of this fact, a means of contesting the depoliticization of foreign policy *and* 'Politicization' of aid and of driving the rubrics of expanded-/over-reach, confronting power and longer-term sustainability in complex, compromising political contexts and emergencies. Set against this trend and cutting across the categories of humanitarianism, development and conflict resolution, some practitioners remain wary of human rights politics to the degree that it is perceived to judge and marginalize constituencies they feel need to be engaged with in the humane and pragmatic pursuit of basic needs and peace. The depoliticization/politicization nexus is thus a nuanced one, dividing NGOs and other actors internally and from one another.

The engagement with politics and human rights means many things: advocacy and the lobbying of governments to live up to their responsibilities; forms of political analysis and calculation; a framing of development, humanitarian and conflict resolution work in terms of rights and responsibilities; a preparedness to withhold aid and assistance, and even withdraw from particular situations, if it is calculated that they will prolong conflict and undermine human rights; and more.

There are a range of critiques of the various forms in which politicization and human rights have begun to influence international politics. Duffield differs from many in condemning what he sees as an illusion of political engagement, despite the frequent reference to politics from within the NGO community. For him, 'the new humanitarianism fails to make a radical break with the technicist and (despite the adoption of the term political) apolitical nature of development discourse' (2001: 92). The failure of humanitarian actors to be political in the sense of being 'capable of

33

altering outcomes' is at the heart of Duffield's critique (p. 96). A genuine political engagement would address the complex reality that surrounds humanitarian disasters and design programmes accordingly. The politics of the new humanitarians, however, is merely 'politics as policy', amounting to an admitting of and transparency in the compromises that humanitarian actors are forced to make in the course of their work – that is, their policy decisions – rather than the design of overtly political programmes that aim to impact on the prevailing socio-political environment. This represents, in effect, a call for more politics (overreach, ambition), not less.

Another set of critiques questions the subordination of sovereignty and democracy to human rights, development and humanitarian interventions. Chandler denounces what he sees as an era characterized less by the demise of state sovereignty in the service of individual human rights than by the end of sovereign equality between states – a radical construction that lay at the heart of the UN and the international legal system it created – in which powerful states have come to be seen to have a moral right, unilaterally or collectively, to uphold human rights even if their actions are legally questionable. On the one hand sovereignty is increasingly porous for weak states, while on the other hand for strong states it is increasingly free from international legal constraints. When state sovereignty is seen simply as a cover for human rights abuse and, as a result, sovereignty is trumped by human rights, this, Chandler argues, is the unpalatable outcome (2002: 120–56). He asserts, further, that a human rights-driven world of external interventions (such as aid conditionality and UN protectorates), discredited UN consensus politics, new hierarchical international relations governed by power, and policy and political arenas colonized by lawyers and NGOs, constitute an attack on popular democracy and democratic accountability, and a 'retreat from political equality', at both the domestic and international levels (pp. 192–219).

Many critics concur that turning aid on and off on the basis of how it might contribute to the protection and promotion of human rights undermines sovereignty, and deepens interventions, through new forms of conditionality. Chandler identifies as a key differentiating attribute of rights-based humanitarianism 'the end of the strict separation between strategic ends-based state assistance, which was often highly selective and conditional on certain economic and political policy choices, and needs-based NGO humanitarian activism, which was based on unconditional need' (2002: 26–7). This blurs the difference between 'Politics' and 'politics'. Such conditionality can subordinate people's needs to the imperatives of human rights, holding people hostage to the good behaviour of states. It undermines the humanitarian principles of universalism, neutrality and

34

impartiality, and clearly increases the political nature of development and humanitarian assistance. Some are appalled at the ethics of such calculations and conditionality in the interests of wider interests, or the long term – by the instrumentalization of aid – and, indeed, of the couching of strategic and policy choices in ethical rather than more honestly political terms:

> The politicization of humanitarian aid has led to even greater leverage over non-Western societies as NGOs and international institutions increasingly assume the right to make judgements about what is right and just, about whose capacities are built and which local groups are favoured. Where humanitarian aid started out as an expression of empathy with common humanity it has been transformed through the discourse of 'human rights and human wrongs' into a lever for strategic aims drawn up and acted upon by external agencies. (ibid., p. 47)

A further set of political critiques question the nexus between the twin universalisms of neo-liberalism and human rights, asking whether it sidelines non-market alternatives to development while privileging individual rights at the expense of structural change: 'At the root of RBD is a liberal belief that development is a matter of personal choice and effort, but that this is tempered by the prevailing social and political conditions,' state Mohan and Holland (2001: 183), followed later by this judgement: 'we do not believe that the rights-based development agenda, as currently constructed, will challenge the structures which create underdevelopment' (p. 195).

Critics also argue that the politicization of aid set in motion a susceptibility to the ultimate logic of taking sides and pursuing strategic, political ends under a moral banner, humanitarian war: 'no version of the intermingling of humanitarianism and human rights makes sense except in the context of a world order in which humanitarian military intervention, or at least its credible threat, is one standard response (it need not, however, be frequent) to a so-called humanitarian crisis' (Rieff 2002: 320). The central issue, linking back to concerns about cooption, can be stated simply: can, or should, war be used to secure human rights or humanitarian ends?

The argument that linking humanitarianism to human rights has militarized humanitarianism is made by Rieff and Chandler. From having been 'used' by states in the interests of doing too little in Bosnia and Rwanda, arguably humanitarianism opened itself up to be 'used' to do too much in Kosovo, Afghanistan and Iraq. Concepts such as humanitarianism and human rights have such wide appeal, in part, because they sugar-coat the unpalatable (an argument that could also be applied to increased aid conditionalities): 'It was as if war had become impossible for a modern Western country to wage without describing it to some extent in humanitarian terms' (ibid., p. 240). Unsurprisingly, this set of linkages and outcomes, this redefinition and depoliticization of war and claiming of a higher moral agenda, has proved highly controversial. In Rieff's view 'a humanitarianism that supports the idea of war carried out in its name is unworthy of that name' (p. 258), while Chandler states even more provocatively: 'Through human rights discourse, humanitarian action has become transformed from relying on empathy with suffering victims, in support of emergency aid, to mobilising misanthropy to legitimise the politics of international condemnation, sanctions and bombings' (Chandler 2002: 51). Rieff is not anti-war, per se, but disputes the humanitarian pretext and cover, arguing that the use of a moral argument seeks to put war beyond debate. Again, the reality of power relations in such collaborations means interventions will be more military and less humanitarian. NATO in Kosovo, for example, was a belligerent in the conflict, but sought to control both military and humanitarian agendas.

As a result of militarization and forceful interventions, particularly in the post-9/11 era, humanitarianism and human rights have become bound up in the 'war against terror', and agendas and accusations of empire. In Ignatieff's nation-building as 'empire lite' – the new imperial project of 'consolidating zones of stability in areas of vital national interest' – he argues that there are some problems (state failure/collapse) for which there are only forceful, imperial solutions. Some nations cannot heal their own wounds, imperialism has become a precondition of democratic self-government (Ignatieff 2003: 24, 125). Chandler argues that the pursuit of human rights and 'international justice', with the framework of international law either overridden or selectively applied, institutionalizes global political inequalities and heralds a return to the power politics, interventions and motives of an earlier imperial age (Chandler 2002: 120–56). While such dynamics arguably have a long history – Rieff also traces to European colonialism the long association between charity (initially missionaries, faith-based), intervention/invasion and empire, between the alleviation of suffering and the agendas of power (Rieff 2002: 57–89) – these are none the less challenging associations.

It is important to stress that the militarization of humanitarianism does not solely mean war. It can involve, for example, military protection, by actors as diverse as NATO and armed militias, for the distribution of relief; negotiations over access; and interactions in the context of UN peacekeeping or the policing of peace agreements. One price of this increased protection for humanitarian agencies is, perversely, increased insecurity through association. In this volume, O'Brien (CARE Afghanistan) provides an interesting discussion of the civil–military dilemma, in the form of the mingling of military and humanitarian/ reconstruction agendas in the Provincial Reconstruction Teams (PRTs) in Afghanistan. It is also important to tease out the role of NGOs in bringing about militarization, and especially war in humanitarianism's name. Rieff and Chandler paint a picture of general NGO support for and acquiescence to militarized humanitarianism. There are important distinctions to be made between particular agencies (human rights and humanitarian) and conflicts, and on the continuum between directly calling for or supporting, overtly or tacitly, armed intervention, creating the climate for or seeming to invite such acts of aggression (Rieff's argument that a transformed humanitarianism 'readily lent *itself* to this official interpretation ... [i]t had all but begged for the chance to be used as a moral warrant for warfare' [2002: 20, emphasis in original]), and taking no position on or opposing intervention. There is also the issue of the use of human rights reporting to justify military interventions and questions about NGO responsibility and accountability that this raises.

A more nuanced analysis of this issue is provided in an International Council on Human Rights Policy report entitled *Human Rights Crises: NGO Responses to Military Interventions* (2002). This report engages with many of the challenges detailed above, including the strong disagreements and lively debate within NGOs and the NGO community. It also recognizes that calls for action take many forms, e.g. prevention; the need to engage with international *and* national NGOs as well as perspectives in countries where intervention has occurred and those in which it has not; and the difficulties of developing a coherent, unified position on the issue.

A lack of genuine political engagement by states with solving global problems, preferring the extremes of neglect, neo-liberalism and war, provides the backdrop to the politicization of NGO work in development, humanitarian and conflict scenarios, and the introduction of human rights to direct this process. This backdrop has generated contested new governance and rights regimes. Hence, a second series of questions:

- In what ways do human rights politicize NGO work, and is such work too political or not political enough?
- As a dimension of both overreach and politicization, are human rights a new form of imperialism, used to provide an increasingly intrusive attack on sovereignty, democracy and political debate/processes?
- Does the rights-based approach seek a radical transformation of the prevailing economic and political order, a mere seizure of power within the existing order, to provide alternatives (to neo-liberalism, empire), or is it hopelessly compromised by complicity and cooption?
- To what extent is 'force' – in forms ranging from aid conditionality to

37

war – a characteristic of the rights-based approach? Is this use of 'force' legitimate?

False hope A final challenge is the charge that human rights constitute an 'offer of false hope' (Rieff 2002: 12). Like many critics of human rights, Rieff takes an exclusively legalistic view of rights. The 'judicialization of the world' (p. 10) view of human rights is not the vision of human rights that informs this book. Rieff's assumptions lead him to argue that basic rights require a legally administered cosmopolitan society, thereby confining their achievements and immediate potential to the West, and an international community, the existence of which he repeatedly denies. He slams the human rights norms culture as a utopianism adrift from reality.

> [T]o me it remains not just an open question, but a question that desperately needs to be asked, what [an improvement in human rights norms] has actually accomplished for people in need of justice, or aid, or mercy, or bread, and whether it has actually kept a single jackboot out of a single human face ... every state paid lip service to the new norms, but when those who had the power to kill thought it was time to start killing, these laws and conventions saved not a single life. (ibid., pp. 15, 71–2)

Affirming this point, Chandler, under the heading of 'rhetoric without responsibility', argues that the success of human rights resides in its capacity to provide 'legitimacy without accountability' (2002: 69). In the international arena this potentially applies to all relevant actors – states, militaries, international institutions, NGOs – raising critical questions about who is accountable to whom, the challenge of selectivity, and the gap between rhetoric and reality. Chandler champions what he sees as real political rights secured within the state, formal democracy, and by the empowered, equal, self-governing subject/citizen, contrasting them unfavourably to the diminished, disempowered subject/victim of universal human rights, dependent on external assistance/intervention and liberal elites, offered rights without adequate means/agents of implementation, enforcement and accountability (pp. 89–119).

While this world-view smacks of a bygone age, and of a rather naïve faith in states and democracy, it also articulates a very different vision of human rights from that contained in this volume. Chandler sees human rights as a legal and moral/ethical discourse that constitutes an attack on the traditional sphere of politics and the agency of the human subject. Rights are predominantly a top-down stick with which to beat non-Western governments and a means of ethically sanctioning elitist, external interventions and regulation. There is little sense here of non-legal manifestations of rights, Southern people and organizations claiming their own rights, or of agencies using rights in collaborative and constructive relationships with power holders. Even within a top-down paradigm, Cornwall and Nyamy-Musembi's comments about the uneven and contradictory nature of the colonial project are pertinent: 'The paradox of the ways instrumentalist intervention was actively transformed by people into something that they could make use of in securing freedoms has considerable contemporary resonance' (2004: 1,421).

More persuasively, Uvin (2002) looks at the implications of incorporating human rights into the development enterprise for relations of power and inequalities, internally and externally. In short, do human rights really change anything, and if so, what? Uvin, in a manner reminiscent of Nguyen (2002), takes us through three levels of integration. At one end of the continuum is 'rhetorical, feel-good change' (p. 1), 'little more than thinly disguised repackaging of old wine in new bottles' (p. 2), which alters terminology, but rather than challenging traditional development discourse simply elevates it to a higher moral ground. A re-description of development as, always or in a new guise, promoting human rights, in reality rationalizes the status quo. Duffield concurs with this view: '[r]ather than actually changing what aid agencies do, the rights based approach appears linked to the need to reinvent a new identity periodically in an increasingly competitive and sceptical world' (2001: 223). At the second level, human rights objectives are added to the goals and criteria for agencies, allowing for new programmes with specific human rights aims, e.g. the World Bank focus on good governance. This level can also constitute a form of appropriation, as in the case of good governance which is used to blame Southern governments for their own underdevelopment.

The third and most radical level redefines the mandate of development, in part at least, in human rights terms, with a potential for bringing about a fundamental rethinking of the development paradigm. The two approaches become linked agents of social change. Uvin cites Sen's *Development as Freedom* (1999) favourably, as the bible of this new paradigm, but critiques Sen for providing 'no politically grounded analysis of what stands in the way' of what is an approach with a considerable history (Uvin 2002: 8). Secondly, he argues that Sen does not go beyond 'broad paradigmatic insight' (ibid.), meaning that agencies which convert 'remain committed to little more than improved discourse' (ibid.). And so we are back to levels i and ii, characterized by the search for the high moral ground, competition for donor funds, blaming others, visions and conceptual formulations, 'but zero practical guidelines or obligations ... adopting [Sen's thinking] costs nothing' (ibid.).

Ultimately, Duffield advocates greater engagement with rights. Building on his call for a real political engagement, he decries a version of rights-based work that focuses only on economic and social rights and avoids the more complex problems found in the 'sensitive' civil and political sphere (2001: 223). This restricted application of rights is in effect business as usual for the NGO community: '*it is the aid agency reforming its concept of human rights to bring it into line with the work that it already does*' (p. 222, emphasis in original). While agencies may work with the aim of social transformation, it is argued that unless political and legal issues are addressed directly through demands for civil and political rights, that aim will not only fail to be met, the dominant social structures will be reinforced (pp. 248, 250). Thus, the rights-based approach in its current form 'holds out little hope' of impacting on the pervasive violence of abusive regimes (p. 224). Duffield ultimately presents another version of the call for rights to be understood as indivisible and interdependent.

Mohan and Holland argue that 'the balance sheet in favour of rights-based development, as it is currently conceived, is relatively empty' (2001: 193), while a recent IDS Policy Briefing states: 'The full implications of putting a rights-based approach into practice remain to be tested' (IDS 2003: 1). The challenge, and one engaged with directly by this book and the questions below, is whether there can be, and indeed has been, movement along Uvin's continuum; whether ideals, discourse and policy formulations can be and are being translated into effective political strategy, real obligations, and concrete social and political change.

- Is the adoption of rights-based approaches more than rhetoric and re-packaging? If so, what are the obligations and value added?
- If social contracts are creating new circuits of rights and responsibilities, and reinterpreting rights indivisibility, how are these rights being made real?
- Is the balance sheet in favour of rights-based development still relatively empty?
- From the practical experience of applying rights-based approaches so far, what lessons can be learnt and what challenges remain?

Notes

The authors would like to express their sincere thanks to Olivia Ball for her invaluable comments and editing assistance with this volume, and to the Swiss Agency for Development and Cooperation for their financial assistance towards the writing and dissemination of the book.

1 Contributors to this edited collection are cited in the Introduction in this manner (name, organizational affiliation). The latter refers to affiliations

at the time of writing, or to the organizational experiences written about.

2 See the Sphere Project: Humanitarian Charter and Minimum Standards in Disaster Response at <www.sphereproject.org> (Geneva 2004).

3 See Humanitarian Accountability Partnership International <www.hapinternational.org/en> (Geneva 2004).

4 It can also be argued, however, that macro social contracts such as Sphere will remain largely unenforced and unenforceable unless and until they are politicized. Rights ideally need to be secured through normative/legal and political/economic processes with failure exacting a price on both counts. The need for political contracts is particularly urgent when, as across the humanitarian system, the normative/legal framework is weak/uneven. This rationale can apply to all relevant actors within this system, including NGOs (Gready 2004).

5 There is healthy disagreement about the coherence, appropriateness and effectiveness of Sphere – see for example a recent special issue of *Disasters*, 2004, 28 (2) – and there are a range of other, related initiatives in the humanitarian field. It should also be noted that some of those who have signed up to Sphere have embraced its technical standards and sidelined its rights-based dimension. The main point being made here is that initiatives like this provide vital fora for debate and the working through of issues at the heart of the second human rights revolution.

6 The development organizations surveyed are: UNDP, UNICEF, UNIFEM, WHO, World Bank, UNAIDS, AusAid, CIDA, DANIDA, DFID, European Commission, JICA, NORAD, SIDA, CARE, CRS, Oxfam GB, Save the Children Sweden.

7 Rieff (2002: 91–120) argues that humanitarianism became a 'saving idea', the 'reigning utopia', in the Western imagination as the twentieth century drew to a close. Its rise coincided with the rise of neo-liberalism and the decline of communism, development and liberation politics/Third Worldism. Humanitarianism was at once an anti-political bolt-hole for the Left and more generally provided a form of sentimental engagement for the socially concerned, enabling people to feeling better while leaving the status quo intact. Exemplifying this context were humanitarianism's fixation with market share and media coverage. This contradicts the idea of humanitarianism as a force for significant change.

8 Critics of human rights-based humanitarianism do not agree in their classification of MSF. In contrast to Rieff, Chandler describes MSF as 'the leading advocate of the new human rights-based humanitarianism' (2002: 43).

References

ActionAid (1999) *Fighting Poverty Together: ActionAid's Strategy 1999–2003* (London: ActionAid).

Alston, P. (1981) 'Development and the Rule of Law: Prevention Versus Cure as a Human Rights Strategy', in ICJ (ed.) *Development, Human Rights and the Rule of Law* (Oxford: Pergamon Press).

Baker, P. (1996) 'Conflict Resolution Versus Democratic Governance: Divergent Paths to Peace?' in C. Crocker, F. Hampson with P. Aall (eds),

Managing Global Chaos: Sources of and Responses to International Conflict (Washington, DC: United States Institute of Peace).

CARE (2002) *Defining Characteristics of a Rights-based Approach, Promoting Rights and Responsibilities* (Atlanta, GA: CARE).

Chandler, D. (2002) *From Kosovo to Kabul: Human Rights and International Intervention* (London: Pluto Press).

Cornia, G. and R. Jolly (1987) *Adjustment with a Human Face* (Oxford: Oxford University Press).

Cornwall, A. and C. Nyamu-Musembi (2004) 'Putting the "Rights-based Approach" to Development into Perspective', *Third World Quarterly*, 25 (8): 1,415–37.

Darcy, J. (2004) 'Locating Responsibility: The Sphere Humanitarian Charter and Its Rationale', *Disasters*, 28 (2): 112–23.

de Waal, A. (1997) *Famine Crimes: Politics and the Disaster Relief Industry in Africa* (African Rights and the International African Institute in association with James Currey [Oxford] and Indiana University Press [Bloomington, OH]).

Duffield, M. (2001) *Global Governance and the New Wars: The Merging of Development and Security* (London: Zed Books).

Edmundson, W. (2004) 'The Nature of Rights: "Choice" Theory and "Interest" Theory', in W. Edmundson (ed.), *An Introduction to Rights* (Cambridge: Cambridge University Press).

Einhorn, J. (2001) 'The World Bank's Mission Creep', Foreign Affairs, 80 (5): 22–35.

Elliot, J. (2002) 'Development as Improving Human Welfare and Human Rights', in V. Desai and R. Potter (eds), *The Companion to Development Studies* (London: Arnold).

Evans, T. (2001) *The Politics of Human Rights: A Global Perspective* (London: Pluto Press).

Falk, R. (2004) 'Human Rights and Global Civil Society: On the Law of Unintended Effects', in P. Gready (ed.), *Fighting for Human Rights* (London: Routledge).

Gready, P. (2004) 'Introduction', P. Gready (ed.) *Fighting for Human Rights* (London: Routledge).

Hamm, B. (2001) 'A Human Rights Approach to Development', *Human Rights Quarterly*, 23 (4): 1,005–31.

Human Rights Dialogue (2002) Integrating Human Rights and Peace Work, Series 2, no. 7.

IDS (Institute of Development Studies) (2003) 'The Rise of Rights: Rights-based Approaches to International Development', IDS Policy Briefing, issue 17, May.

Ignatieff, M. (2003) *Empire Lite: Nation-Building in Bosnia, Kosovo and Afghanistan* (London: Vintage).

ILO (International Labour Organization) (1976) 'Employment, Growth and

Basic Needs: A One World Problem', Director General's Report to the World Employment Conference, ILO.

International Commission of Jurists (1981) 'Summary of Discussions and Conclusions', in ICJ (ed.), *Development, Human Rights and the Rule of Law* (Oxford: Pergamon Press).

International Council on Human Rights Policy (2002) *Human Rights Crises: NGO Responses to Military Interventions*, International Council on Human Rights Policy, Versoix <www.ichrp.org>

Jonsson, U. (2003) *Human Rights Approach to Development Programming*, (Kenya: UNICEF).

Leader, N. (1998) 'Proliferating Principles; Or How to Sup with the Devil without Getting Eaten', *Disasters*, 22 (4): 288–308.

Looney, R. (2001) 'New International Economic Order', in R. J. Barry Jones (ed.), *Routledge Encyclopaedia of International Political Economy*, Vol. 2 (London: Routledge).

MacDermot, N. (1981) 'Opening of the Plenary Discussion', in ICJ (ed.), *Development, Human Rights and the Rule of Law* (Oxford: Pergamon Press).

Macdonald, M. (1984) 'Natural Rights', in J. Waldron (ed.), *Theories of Rights* (Oxford: Oxford University Press).

Marks, S. (1998) 'From the "Single Confused Page" to the "Decalogue for Six Billion Persons": The Roots of the Universal Declaration of Human Rights in the French Revolution', *Human Rights Quarterly*, 20 (3): 459–514.

Maxwell, S. and R. Riddell (1998) 'Conditionality or Contract: Perspectives on Partnership for Development', *Journal of International Development*, 10: 257–68.

Mohan, G. and J. Holland (2001) 'Human Rights and Development in Africa: Moral Intrusion or Empowering Opportunity?' *Review of African Political Economy*, 28 (88): 177–96.

Molyneux, M. and S. Lazar (2003) *Doing the Rights Thing* (London: ITGD Publishing).

Morsink, J. (1984) 'The Philosophy of the Universal Declaration', *Human Rights Quarterly*, 6 (3): 309–34.

Moser, C. and A. Norton (2001) *To Claim Our Rights: Livelihood Security, Human Rights and Sustainable Development* (London: Overseas Development Institute).

Nguyen, F. (2002) *Emerging Features of a Rights-Based Development Policy of UN, Development Cooperation and NGO Agencies*, Discussion Paper, OHCHR Asia-Pacific Human Rights Roundtable, no. 1 (October).

Putnam, T. (2002) 'Human Rights and Sustainable Peace', in S. Stedman, D. Rothchild and E. Cousens (eds), *Ending Civil Wars: The Implementation of Peace Agreements* (Boulder, CO: Lynne Rienner).

Rachels, J. (1993) 'The Idea of a Social Contract', in J. Rachels, *The Elements of Moral Philosophy*, 2nd edn (New York: McGraw-Hill).

Rieff, D. (2002) *A Bed for the Night: Humanitarianism in Crisis* (London: Vintage).

Sano, H.-O. (2000) 'Development and Human Rights: The Necessary, but Partial, Integration of Human Rights and Development', *Human Rights Quarterly*, 22 (3): 734–52.

Sen, A. (1981) *Poverty and Famines: An Essay on Entitlement and Deprivation* (Oxford: Clarendon).

— (1999) *Development as Freedom* (Oxford: Oxford University Press).

Shestack, J. (1998) 'The Philosophic Foundations of Human Rights', *Human Rights Quarterly*, 20 (2): 201–34.

Shue, H. (1996) *Basic Rights: Subsistence, Affluence and US Foreign Policy*, 2nd edn (Princeton, NJ: Princeton University Press).

Tomaŝevski, K. (1993) *Development Aid and Human Rights* (London: Pinter).

Uvin, P. (2002) 'On High Moral Ground: The Incorporation of Human Rights by the Development Enterprise', *Praxis: The Fletcher Journal of Development Studies*, 17: 1–11. <http://fletcher.tufts.edu/praxis/xvii/Uvin.pdf>

World Bank (2003) *Toward Country-led Development: A Multi-Partner Evaluation of the Comprehensive Development Framework*, Synthesis Report (Washington, DC: World Bank).

ONE | **Case studies: Africa**

1 | A human rights-based approach to programming

URBAN JONSSON

Up until the early 1990s there was very limited contact and exchange between people working with human development and people working with human rights. The development people focused on effective and goal-oriented transfers of resources and increased social well-being. The aim was to meet people's basic needs in a sustainable and sustained manner. They worked primarily in the area of social and economic development. People working with human rights, on the other hand, worked on strengthening international human rights norms and institutions and protecting recognized human rights. Most of them focused on civil and political rights and targeted governments (Nelson and Dorsay 2003). Two trends in the 1990s contributed to a gradual convergence of the two approaches (Sano 2000): (i) developing countries increasingly demanded international assistance as an entitlement. Development assistance was increasingly seen as a right rather than an instrument of solidarity. And (ii) developed countries increasingly demanded good governance and the democratization of developing countries as a condition for assistance.

The Vienna Declaration states that, 'development exists within a human rights framework ... Development should rightly be seen as an integral part of human rights.'[1] In other words, human development is a necessary but not sufficient condition for human rights realization. The Social Development Summit in Copenhagen states that human rights are an 'integral element of the development agenda'.[2] The rule of law, access to justice and so on are necessary conditions for human development. In other words, the realization of human rights is a necessary but not sufficient condition for human development.

A similar convergence took place between human rights groups and human development groups. This was very much the result of human rights NGOs becoming increasingly interested in social, economic and cultural rights (for example, Amnesty International and Human Rights Watch). At the same time the development NGOs became more interested in the links between development and the protection of civil and political rights. The cooperation between the two types of NGOs has increased tremendously during the last decade. Many of them are now struggling to operationalize a human rights-based approach to programming or a human development approach to human rights. On a larger scale some of the new social movements (e.g. the women's movement, the green movement and the indigenous peoples' movement) combine human development and human rights (Stammers 1999).

In spite of the fact that human rights constitute the very foundation of the United Nations, through the UN Charter and Universal Declaration of Human Rights, the organization did not take a lead in promoting human rights during the first forty years of its existence. The major reason for this was the very different positions held by member states during the Cold War. Immediately after the end of the Cold War a dramatic change took place, to a large extent because of the commitment and work of UN Secretary General Kofi Annan. In 1997 he launched a programme of UN reform with a clear emphasis on human rights. In a statement to the Commission on Human Rights two years later he explained: 'As the Secretary-General of the United Nations I have made human rights a priority in every programme the United Nations launches and in every mission we embark on. I have done so because the promotion and defense of human rights is at the heart of every aspect of our work and every article of our Charter.'[3]

In September 2000 the largest-ever number of heads of state and government gathered at a summit in New York, which ended successfully with the adoption of the Millennium Declaration,[4] a powerful document outlining the crucial aspects of a desirable future world. Unfortunately, most organizations have reduced the Millennium Declaration to the two (out of thirty) paragraphs identifying a set of Millennium Development Goals (MDGs). This is very problematic, because the MDGs must be seen in the broader context of the Declaration. And the broader context includes the fundamental role of human rights. The respect for all internationally recognized human rights and fundamental freedoms, including the right to development, forms the normative basis for the Declaration.

A human rights-based approach to programming (HRBAP)

A definition of human rights Development requires the satisfaction of at least two conditions: the achievement of a desirable outcome and the establishment of an adequate process to achieve and sustain that outcome. Most of the health, education and nutrition goals in the Millennium Declaration, for example, represent specific, desirable outcomes. Effective human development demands a high-quality process to achieve such outcomes. Participation, local ownership, empowerment and sustainability are essential characteristics of a high-quality process. In an HRBAP the required process qualities are set by human rights principles.

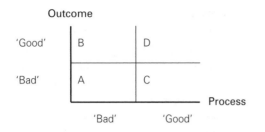

FIGURE 1.1 Outcome and process

Level of outcome and quality of process define a two-dimensional space for social action, as illustrated in Figure 1.1. Most development starts at A, and the ideal, final stage is D. Unfortunately, many development programmes move into one of the two areas represented by B or C. The former represents a good outcome at the expense of, for example, sustainability (an aspect of a good process), and is as ineffective as C, a good process without a significant outcome. Some Unicef-supported immunization programmes in the 1990s had rapidly moved into B but proved unsustainable, while some NGO-supported community-oriented programmes had moved into C but proved impossible to move to scale (Jonsson 1997a).

While monitoring of the achievement of human development outcomes has improved considerably during the past ten years, far less progress has been achieved in monitoring the quality of processes – largely because good process has seldom been defined.

Human rights standards define benchmarks for desirable outcomes, while human rights principles represent conditions for the process. There is some confusion about the difference between standards and principles. Basically, a human rights standard defines the minimum acceptable level of an outcome or results, while a human rights principle specifies the criteria for an acceptable process to achieve an outcome (minimum level of conduct, values). A list of the most important human rights principles has been proposed by UNDP (2003a) as shown below:

- universality and indivisibility
- equality and non-discrimination
- participation and inclusion
- accountability and rule of law

A human rights approach requires equal attention to outcome and process. This has been particularly emphasized in the discussion on the right to development (Sengupta 2003).

An easy way to define human rights would be to say that human rights

A human rights-based approach

are those entitlements codified in human rights covenants and conventions. Such a definition, however, is too dogmatic and not very useful for an HRBAP. It would also miss the point that human rights are human constructs, which means that new rights will be constructed, gradually codified in conventions and accepted by ratification.

The relationship between rights holders and duty bearers also constitutes a core component of a human rights approach, but most scholars in the area of international human rights law recognize obligations only on the part of the state. There is a need to extend the claim–duty relationships to include all relevant subjects and objects at subnational, community and household levels. It is interesting to note that the Preambles of both the International Covenant on Civil and Political Rights (ICCPR) and the International Covenant on Economic, Social and Cultural Rights (ICESCR) support such an interpretation, stating: 'Realising that the individual, having duties to other individuals and to the community to which he belongs, is under a responsibility to strive for the promotion and observance of the rights recognized in the present Covenant.' Similarly, Article 29 of the Universal Declaration on Human Rights states that human rights are not limited to the relations between citizens and the state (ICHRP 1999).

Claim holders and duty bearers are not labels applied to specific individuals, but roles that individuals may perform. It is important to recognize that most individuals enter into the roles of both claim holder and duty bearer at the same time, but in relation to actors at different levels of society. It is equally important to realize that an individual very often cannot meet his/her duties, because he/she has some of his/her own rights violated. Parents, for example, have a duty to provide food for their children, but may fail to do so due to lack of a job or cultivable land. In such cases parents cannot be held accountable for not providing food for their children.

This system of claim–duty relationships is called the pattern of rights. This pattern must be understood in an HRBAP.

Towards a common understanding Many UN agencies have made serious efforts to operationalize an HRBAP. UNDP and Unicef have been in the forefront. A UN informal working group has been active during the last few years on this issue. Meetings were arranged in Princeton in 2002 (UNDP 2001) and in Stamford in 2003 (UNDP 2003b). At the Stamford meeting an agreement was reached by most participating agencies on a Common Understanding of a HRBAP, which contains the following three principles:

1 All programmes of development cooperation, policies and technical assistance should further the realization of human rights as laid down in the Universal Declaration of Human Rights and other human rights instruments.

2 Human rights standards contained in, and principles derived from, the Universal Declaration of Human Rights and other international human rights instruments guide all development cooperation and programming in all sectors and in all phases of the programming process.

3 Development cooperation contributes to the development of capacities of duty bearers to meet their obligations and/or of right holders to claim their rights.

Based on these three principles the meeting agreed on the following unique and specific characteristics for a programme adopting HRBAP:

1 Assessment and analysis in order to identify the human rights claims of rights holders and the corresponding human rights obligations of duty bearers as well as the immediate, underlying and structural causes of the non-realization of rights.

2 Programmes assess the capacity of rights holders to claim their rights and of duty bearers to fulfil their obligations. They then develop strategies to build these capacities.

3 Programmes monitor and evaluate both outcomes and processes guided by human rights standards and principles.

4 Programming is informed by the recommendations of international human rights bodies and mechanisms.

During the development of HRBAP (both in theory and practice) it became increasingly clear that the number of good programming practices from years of learning become obligatory rather than optional in HRBAP.[5] It is important, however, to recognize that the application of good programming practices does not by itself constitute an HRBAP. They are necessary, but not sufficient, conditions.

Implications of the common understanding for programming Internal reviews and country case studies of the adoption and use of a human rights-based approach to programming in Unicef country programmes of cooperation has clearly shown that there have been a wide variety of interpretations of the meaning of HRBAP. The situation almost reflects the philosophy of anarchy that 'anything goes'. Many country offices refer to one or several of the following in reporting on the adoption of HRBAP: (i) the Convention on the Rights of the Child (CRC) and the Convention on the Elimination of all Forms of Discrimination Against Women (CEDAW) are explicitly recognized as the foundation for the Unicef Country Programme of Cooperation; (ii) goals and objectives are formulated in human rights language; (iii) human rights principles are explicitly referred to as guiding planning and implementation; (iv) support is given to the development of human rights institutions; and (v) offices engage in advocacy for and information gathering about human rights. None of these, however, would qualify for HRBAP according to the criteria proposed by the Stamford meeting.

Similarly, in other agencies there is a plethora of concepts that are very seldom explained, including 'human rights approach to development', 'rights-based approach to development', 'programming in a human rights perspective', 'CRC/CEDAW programming' and 'programming through a human rights lens'. This confusion is to a large extent a result of different understandings of the relationships between human rights and (human) development. There is, therefore, a need to be clearer about criteria that must be met in order to qualify for an HRBAP. The Common Understanding provides such criteria in its three principles.

The first criterion in the Common Understanding requires that all programmes should contribute to the realization of human rights. This is a necessary, but not sufficient, condition. Most Unicef-supported programmes and projects in the past have contributed to the realization of children's and women's rights by achieving desirable and human rights relevant outcomes. Currently, many Unicef-supported programmes and projects define the objectives in human rights language, while the actual programming is done as usual.

The second criterion, that human rights standards and principles should guide all programming in all sectors and all phases of the programming process, is very often adopted in rather vague forms. The ambiguity of the term 'guide' has resulted in a number of different interpretations, as mentioned earlier. The simple fact is that programming cannot just be guided by standards and principles, because these are not precise enough to inform concretely the operations of programming. But programming can be assisted by recognizing that human rights standards determine the outcomes while human rights principles define the conditions of the process. The third criterion specifies the objectives of 'guiding'. It states that programming should contribute to the development of the capacity of claim holders to claim their rights and of duty bearers to meet their duties.

In conclusion, each of the three conditions is necessary, but not sufficient in isolation. Sufficiency requires that all three conditions are met at the same time.

A method for applying HRBAP

Based on the first two principles of HRBAP detailed above, a method has been developed on how to apply an HRBAP in practice. This method has been adopted by Unicef and is being applied in a large number of Country Programmes of Cooperation. The method consists of five consecutive steps logically linked and with some new tools to manage information.

Step 1: Causality analysis The first step is to identify the immediate, underlying and basic causes of the problem. Without a reasonable consensus on causality, there is not likely to be consensus on solutions. Identification and analysis of the causes of a problem is facilitated by the use of an explicit conceptual framework (Jonsson 1997b). In this causality analysis the problems identified are understood to reflect human rights violations (disease, malnutrition, lack of basic education, exploitation, discrimination). This is an example of a situation in which human development analysis assists and adds value to human rights analysis. The causality analysis will result in *a list of rights that are either being violated or are at risk of being violated*, together with the major causes of these violations and the key actors involved.

Step 2: Pattern analysis Pattern analysis aims to identify key claim–duty relationships in a particular societal context. First, key actors – those who are likely to enter the roles of claim holders and duty bearers in relation to a specific right – should be identified. This will be based on the causality analysis. As already mentioned, the same individual or group of individuals often may enter the roles of both claim holder and duty bearer. A teacher may have a duty to parents to provide good teaching, but may at the same time have a claim against the government to receive a salary. Teachers, however, do not just have duties to parents. They may also have valid claims on parents, for example, that parents bring girls to school. This is illustrated in Table 1.1, which includes examples of claim–duty relationships in relation to the right to basic education. Most often the key claim–duty relationships cluster around the diagonal of the matrix, i.e. the parents/teachers, teachers/district and district/national government relationships, reflecting a bottom-up chain of claims at the lower level, create claims at higher levels. In reverse, a top-down chain reflects the fact that higher-level duties create duties at lower levels.

Step 3: Capacity gap analysis After the key claim–duty relationships for a specific right have been identified, the next step is to analyse why the right is not realized. A basic assumption underlying the approach proposed here

TABLE 1.1 Pattern analysis of the right to basic education

Claim holders	Children	Parents	Teachers	District	National government
Duty bearers					
Parents	Allow girls to go to school		Allow time for homework	Assist in construction of classrooms	
Teachers	Provide good-quality teaching	Establish parent–teachers associations		Participate in training workshops	Follow established curricula
District	Stop all recruitment of child labourers	Provide material for classroom construction	Retrain teachers		Use funds correctly
National government	Legislate free and compulsory basic education	Policy on exemption from school fees for poor parents	Ensure adequate salaries for teachers	Allocate adequate funds for education	

TABLE 1.2 Capacity gaps of teachers to meet their duties to parents

Responsibility	Do not feel that parent–teacher associations (PTAs) are of any importance; teachers know what is best for the school
Authority	Establishment of a PTA requires approval from the district authorities
Resources	Lack of funds to make PTA meetings attractive for participants
Decision-making capability	Do not feel that the views of parents are useful for the management of the school
Communication	Do not speak the local language well

is that rights are not realized because claim holders lack the capacity to claim the right and/or duty bearers lack the capacity to meet their duties. The analysis of capacity gaps is called capacity analysis.

Capacity is defined in a broader sense, including the following five components:

- Responsibility/motivation/commitment/leadership: referring to the acknowledgement by an individual that he/she *should* do something about a specific problem. It means acceptance and internalization of a duty, and is often justified in legal or moral terms.
- Authority: this refers to the legitimacy of an action, when an individual or group feels or knows that they *may* take action, that it is permissible to take action. Laws, formal and informal norms and rules, tradition and culture largely determine what is or is not permissible. The structure of authority in a society reflects its power relations.
- Access and control of resources: if an individual accepts that he/she *should* do something and *may* do it, it may still be impossible to act because the person lacks resources. Capacity must therefore also mean that the person is in a position to act, or *can* act. The resources available to individuals, households, organizations and society as a whole may generally be classified into the following three types: (i) human resources, (ii) economic resources and (iii) organizational resources.
- Communication capability: the ability to communicate and to access information and communication systems is crucial for individuals and groups of individuals in their efforts to claim their rights or meet their duties. Communication is also important in connecting various key actors in the social fabric into functional networks able to address critical development issues.

- Capability for rational decision-making and learning: rational decision-making requires evidence-based assessment and a logical analysis of the causes of a problem. Actions should be based on decisions informed by the analysis. After action has been taken, a reassessment of the result and impact will lead to improved analysis and better action in the next round. Such interactive learning-by-doing relies heavily on the ability to communicate (Jonsson 1993).

Each dual claim–duty relationship generates five lists of capacity gaps. An example is illustrated in Table 1.2.

Step 4: Identification of candidate actions These are not the finally selected actions, just candidates for them. To summarize the method so far, causality analysis results in the identification of a set of rights that are being violated or at risk of being violated. Role/pattern analysis identifies key claim holder–duty bearer relationships for each specific right. Capacity analysis defines the capacity gaps of claim holders to claim their rights and of duty bearers to meet their duties. A programmatic response aimed at the realization of rights must contribute to narrowing or closing these capacity gaps.

Candidate actions are those actions likely to contribute to reducing or closing the capacity gaps of claim holders and duty bearers. Such actions should aim to increase responsibility, authority, resources and the decision-making and communication capabilities of claim holders and duty bearers. An example of candidate actions to close the capacity gaps of teachers to be able to meet their duties to parents is illustrated in Table 1.3. A similar process is required to show the candidate action for closing the capacity gaps of teachers to claim their own rights.

TABLE 1.3 Candidate actions to close the capacity gaps of teachers to meet their duties to parents

Responsibility	Launch a campaign among teachers about the importance of PTAs
Authority	Convince the district authorities that teachers may decide on PTAs
Resources	Use community funds for providing tea at every PTA meeting
Decision-making capability	Arrange meetings between teachers, parents and children to discuss the management of the school
Communication	Provide training of teachers in the local language

Step 5: Programme design The priority actions or activities selected should be aggregated into projects and programmes. This is the reverse of most current programming practices, which disaggregate programmes into projects, and projects into activities. Activities can be clustered, or aggregated, according to the level of society in which claim holders and duty bearers operate. At each level some activities will aim at developing the capacities of individuals as claim holders, while others will aim at developing the capacities of individuals as duty bearers. Some activities will do both, sometimes even in relation to more than one right. For example, the development of teachers' communication skills will strengthen teachers both to meet their duties to children and to claim their rights in relation to the Ministry of Education.

The selection of priority activities and the division of labour among UN agencies should take place within the UN Development Assistance Framework (UNDAF) of a given country and the ongoing preparation of Poverty Reduction Strategy Papers (PRSPs). A clear division of labour for supporting the government should be agreed upon, including UN agencies, bilateral agencies and NGOs.

Practical experiences with the adoption of HRBAP

In January 1996, the Unicef Executive Board adopted a first-ever Mission Statement in which the human rights of children and women, as enshrined in the CRC and CEDAW, were recognized as the foundation of Unicef's cooperation. In April 1998 Unicef issued an Executive Directive to all field-offices, Guidelines for Human Rights-based Programming Approach, in order to reorient country-level programming towards HRBAP (Unicef 1998). The principles contained in the May 2003 Common Understanding had been promoted in Unicef Eastern and Southern Africa region since 1998.[6] It was therefore possible to evaluate some of the Unicef Country Programmes of Cooperation by 2003. The experience from Mozambique and Uganda will be briefly discussed, followed by some findings in a recent global review of the adoption of HRBAP by Unicef in the field.

Mozambique An external evaluation of the Mozambique programme (2002–04) was undertaken in 2004 to 'identify lessons learned about both successes and constraints in the process of applying HRBAP' in the implementation of the cross-cutting HIV/AIDS programme (Häusermann 2004).

The evaluation found that the preparation of the programme had met all four unique characteristics defined in the Common Understanding. The adoption of an HRBAP had significantly changed the design and strategies in the Country Programme. A strategic focus was given to capacity development, particularly of communities. The design of the programme was influenced by the strong participation of children and young people. In a survey, about 60 per cent of rights holders were satisfied with their involvement in the causality analysis, although many of them admitted that they lacked basic knowledge about human rights. Most rights holders also thought that they had developed their capacity to claim their rights. There was a strong agreement that HRBAP had developed capacities at all levels of society to respect, protect and fulfil rights.

The adoption of HRBAP had meant that most good programming principles had been adopted, including the recognition of poor people as key actors in their own development, a focus on empowerment, local ownership, reducing inequalities and more clear accountabilities. Insufficient attention, however, had been paid to gender analysis and the economic and socio-cultural causes of HIV infection.

A common complaint among duty bearers was that they wanted to know more about their own rights in order to be able to claim these rights and as a result be more able to meet their duties as duty bearers. This reflects a serious problem in the programme, where rights holders and duty bearers are labels attached to certain people, rather than roles that most people may perform. An interesting finding was that most participants agreed that Unicef project staff should be accountable to rights holders. This is, indeed, a significant change from past practice.

In conclusion, the Mozambique programme successfully adopted HRBAP, but much more training is required, together with better monitoring of the process.

Uganda The adoption of HRBAP in the Uganda Country Programme of Cooperation (2001–05) was reviewed as a part of the mid-term review in 2002 (Unicef 2003). Similarly to Mozambique, the adoption of HRBAP required significant changes in programme content and practice.

The use of HRBAP had increased the ability to address exclusion and disparities. For example, 80 per cent immunization coverage, praised just a few years ago, was no longer acceptable. The 20 per cent excluded must be reached. Children and young people participated much more than before at both strategic and operational levels. Adults started to recognize their roles as duty bearers and appreciated the contributions of young people to the programme. Throughout the implementation a deliberate effort had been made to address both outcome and process. The Early Childhood Development (ECD) project had been most successful in finding the right balance.[7]

HRBAP led to a district-focused approach, aiming at the development of the capacities of duty bearers, the development of partnerships and strengthening communities to address issues that affected them. The programme had been successful in the few areas selected for implementation, but it had been difficult to expand the programme due to resource constraints (both economic and human resources).

Similar to the case of Mozambique, it was found that most duty bearers were not aware of their own rights and did not have sufficient capacity to claim their rights. Again, a more complete pattern analysis would have avoided this problem.

Local government District Implementation teams play a crucial role in rural development in Uganda. A major challenge for successful implementation is the fact that the strength of the team depends on a few individuals. Poor delegation and weak supervision by district heads of departments are additional challenges that must be overcome in order to expand the adoption of HRBAP to larger areas of the country.

Global review In 2004 an organization-wide review was made to find out the experiences with the adoption of HRBAP in Unicef (Raphael 2004). It was found that about 20 per cent had used HRBAP to guide programme implementation and that about the same percentage of staff had understood the approach. The adoption of HRBAP, however, is very uneven among the regions, with countries in the Latin American and Eastern and Southern African regions representing more than 70 per cent of those countries that had adopted HRBAP.

The review concluded that much more training is required, both of Unicef staff and partners. A special effort should be made to engage UN Country Teams to promote HRBAP in the preparation of the Common Country Assessment (CCA)/UNDAF and PRSPs. There is also a need for more clear guidance from headquarters.

Conclusions

There is an emerging consensus that HRBAP has significant advantages compared to basic needs and human development approaches to programming. The most important are summarized below:

1. Increased accountability as a result of explicitly defined claim–duty relationships. These are different from entitlements which do not identify any specific duty bearer. A duty is also different from a promise or an interest.
2. HRBAP makes most good programming practice obligatory, and not

just optional. Human rights-based programmes are therefore effective even when measured by traditional development criteria.

3. HRBAP offers better protection of people who are poor by ruling out trade-offs that are harmful to them. The most common trade-offs promoted in development work are: (i) the needs trade-off: relatively high levels of poverty should be accepted in order to maximize investment and future economic growth; (ii) the equality trade-off: initially economic growth will create inequalities that should be accepted; and (iii) the liberty trade-off: civil and political rights must be temporarily suspended in order to allow for economic growth (Donnelly 1989: 164–5). HRBAP, therefore, pays more attention to exclusion, discrimination, disparities and injustice, and emphasizes basic causes.

4. HRBAP focuses on legal and institutional reform, and promotes the rule of law. When applying HRBAP, access to justice means the people's ability to seek and obtain remedy for grievances, through formal and informal justice mechanisms, and in conformity with basic human rights principles and standards. Currently, access to justice is most of the time limited to people's ability to use public and private justice services. In HRBAP, justice is seen as a social process, not just a legal one.

5. A human rights approach better protects people from power exertion and can be used to challenge power. HRBAP stimulates social movements and mobilizes civil society.

6. In a human rights approach to development, development assistance can no longer be based on charity or solidarity only; it will be a result of national and international obligations (including obligations on Unicef).

The United Nations has an obligation to respect, protect, facilitate and fulfil human rights in all development and humanitarian work. There is therefore a need for an operational HRBAP. UN agencies have moved fast in the process of agreeing on criteria for an HRBAP, manifested in the Stamford Inter-agency Consultation's Recommendation Towards a Common Understanding. There is, however, a significant gap between agreements at the UN agency headquarters level and the reality at the country level. Very few agencies, and in very few countries, have mainstreamed human rights in their work. Therefore, training of UN Country Teams should be a top priority for all agencies.

The current UN reform promotes stronger cooperation among UN agencies. HRBAP is new to all UN agencies and could therefore become an effective catalyst in the efforts to move towards a real UN team approach, including joint programming. Finally, the current strong focus on the achievement of the MDGs must be balanced with a greater attention to the overall implementation of the Millennium Declaration, which provides the context in which the MDGs should be addressed.

Notes

1 Vienna Declaration and Programme of Action (para. 25–26), United Nations World Conference on Human Rights, 1992.

2 The Copenhagen Declaration and Programme of Action, United Nations World Summit for Social Development, 1993.

3 Secretary General to the Commission on Human Rights:, 'I Have Made Human Rights a Priority in Every United Nations Programme', 7 April 1999.

4 General Assembly Resolution 55/2, United Nations Millennium Declaration, 18 September 2000; General Assembly Resolution 55/162, Follow-up to the Outcome of the Millennium Summit, 18 September 2000.

5 At the Stamford meeting the following good programming practices were identified:

- people are recognized as key actors in their own development, rather than as passive recipients of commodities and services
- participation is both a means and a goal
- strategies are empowering, not disempowering
- both outcomes and processes are monitored and evaluated
- analysis includes all stakeholders
- programmes focus on marginalized, disadvantaged and excluded groups
- the development process is locally owned
- programmes aim to reduce poverty
- top-down *and* bottom-up approaches are used in synergy
- situation analysis is used to identify immediate, underlying and basic causes of development problems
- measurable goals and targets are important in programming
- strategic partnerships are developed and sustained

6 During 1998–2000 a number of draft proposals and guidelines on a Human Rights Approach to Programming/Community Capacity Development were prepared by the Unicef Regional Office for Eastern and Southern Africa (ESARO).

7 The ECD project in Uganda is a community-based project implemented in three districts so far. The project was planned through a community dialogue and is multidisciplinary in addressing all the important causes of inadequate ECD for children below five years of age. Positive results have been achieved, increasing child survival and improving care and protection of the children at the critical early age. Plans are underway to expand the project to other districts.

References

Donnelly, J. (1989) *Universal Human Rights in Theory and Practice* (Ithaca, NY: Cornell University Press).

Häusermann, J. (2004) *Mid-Term Evaluation of the Application to the HRBAP in the HIV/AIDS Priority of the Mozambique Country Programme of Cooperation, Government of Mozambique and UNICEF, 2002–2006, Final Report*, September (New York: Unicef).

ICHRP (International Council on Human Rights Policy) (1999) *Taking Duties Seriously: Individual Duties in International Human Rights Law – A Commentary* (Sydney: ICHRP).

— (1997a) *Success Factors in Community-based Nutrition-oriented Programmes and Projects in Malnutrition in South Asia*, Unicef Regional Office in South Asia (ROSA), Publication no. 5 (Kathmandu: ROSA).

— (1997b) 'An Approach to Assess and Analyze the Health and Nutrition Situation of Children in the Perspective of the Convention on the Rights of the Child', *International Journal of Children's Rights*, 5: 367–81.

Jonsson, U. (1993) *Nutrition and the United Nations Convention on the Rights of the Child*, Innocenti Occasional Papers, CRS 5, November (Florence: CRS).

Nelson, P. and E. Dorsay (2003) 'At the Nexus of Human Rights and Development: New Methods and Strategies of Global NGOs', *World Development*, 31: 2,013–26.

Raphael, A. (2004) *HRBAP Progress Review 2003. Implementation of Human Rights Approach to Programming in Unicef Country Offices (1998–2003)* (New York: Unicef).

Sano, H. (2000) 'Development and Human Rights: The Necessary, but Partial Integration of Human Rights and Human Development', *Human Rights Quarterly*, 22 (3): 734–52.

Sengupta, A. (2003) 'The Human Right to Development', paper presented at the Nobel Symposium, Oslo, 13–15 October.

Stammers, N. (1999) 'Social Movements and the Social Construction of Human Rights', *Human Rights Quarterly*, 21 (4): 980–1,008.

UNDP (2001) 'Recommendations of Inter-Agency Workshop on Implementing a Human Rights Approach in the Context of the UN Reform', 24–26 January (Princeton, NJ: UNDP).

— (2003a) *Poverty Reduction and Human Rights*, March (New York: UNDP).

— (2003b) 'Report from the Second Inter-Agency Workshop on Implementing a Human Rights-based Approach in the Context of UN Reform', 5–7 May (Stamford, CA: UNDP).

Unicef (1998) Guidelines for Human Rights-based Programming Approach, Executive Directive CF/EXD/1998–04, 21 April.

— (2003) *Mid-term Review Report of the Uganda Country Programme* (Kampala: Unicef).

2 | The experiences of Oxfam International and its affiliates in rights-based programming and campaigning

MARJOLEIN BROUWER, HEATHER GRADY,
VALERIE TRAORE AND DEREJE WORDOFA

Oxfam International (OI) was created in 1995 as a confederation of twelve independent non-government organizations dedicated to fighting poverty and injustice around the world. The affiliates share a global strategic plan and pursue joint efforts in campaigning and programming (both development and humanitarian), aiming to achieve greater impact through their collective efforts.[1] They support more than 3,000 counterparts in approximately 100 countries, committing their moral, human and financial resources to work with partners and allies as part of a global movement to promote economic and social justice.

Oxfam[2] starts from the premise that poverty is a state of powerlessness in which people are denied their human rights and the ability to control crucial aspects of their lives. In the experience of Oxfam's partners, poverty is a symptom of deeply rooted inequities and unequal power relationships, institutionalized through policies and practices at the levels of state, society and household. Moreover, although some forms of unequal power relationships are rooted in age-old injustices, new forms are being generated by economic globalization and by imbalances in negotiating power between rich and poor countries.

Faced with this changing context, and recognizing that its traditional ways of thinking and working were becoming less effective, Oxfam took the formal decision in late 2000 to adopt a rights-based approach (RBA) to the alleviation of poverty and the ending of exclusion and social injustice.[3] For Oxfam and many other agencies, embracing an RBA was a response to the limited success of previous approaches, which aimed to respond to basic needs or promote sustainable livelihoods, by giving greater emphasis to the impact of power inequalities in the development process. Decades of entrenched and chronic poverty around the world, compounded by conflict and insecurity, had left huge numbers of people unable to achieve the basic requirements for human development and a life of dignity. Their situation was exacerbated by increasing inequalities within and between societies, and the appropriation by elite groups of the resources required for development.

For a development and humanitarian agency such as Oxfam, the underlying purpose of a rights-based approach is to identify ways of transforming the self-perpetuating vicious cycle of poverty, disempowerment and conflict[4] into a virtuous cycle in which all people, as rights holders, can demand accountability from duty bearers, and where duty bearers have both the willingness and capacity to fulfil, protect and promote people's human rights. Oxfam implements universal standards in a practical and action-oriented way,[5] using a rights-based planning framework to challenge states and others to be accountable to their citizens and to promote non-discrimination and equality in order to redistribute resources and opportunities within and between societies. Oxfam's ability to reach global institutions such as the World Bank, IMF, the World Trade Organization (WTO) and multinational corporations enables it to promote links between local communities and global decision-makers in the struggle to achieve human rights. Furthermore, a rights-based approach enables Oxfam to target the two main factors seen to prevent the realization of human development and human rights: lack of political will, and insufficient capacities to claim and fulfil rights.

In addition, rejecting the notion that people living in poverty can meet their basic needs only as passive recipients of charity, Oxfam works with people around the world who are the active subjects of their own development, in their efforts to realize their rights.[6] This of course compels Oxfam and other rights-based agencies to 'raise the bar' on their own accountability, because civil society organizations (CSOs) themselves may unwittingly perpetuate outmoded notions of charity, overlook discrimination and exclusion, and even reinforce existing imbalances of power.

Rights, aims and 'strategic change objectives'

For Oxfam, a key aspect of its rights-based approach is support for the fulfilment and protection of all human rights, including economic, social and cultural rights, civil and political rights, and rights in international humanitarian law. Just as human rights principles enshrine the indivisibility of rights, so Oxfam felt it important to incorporate this spectrum of human rights in the five 'aims' contained in the planning framework that was formalized in 2000. Thus, Oxfam programmes are designed to work with others to ensure that all people have the following entitlements:

- the right to a sustainable livelihood
- the right to basic services (in particular education, healthcare and water)
- the right to life and security

- the right to be heard (an aim which includes the promotion of civil and political rights, institutional accountability and global citizenship)
- the right to an identity (an aim including the promotion of gender equality and social and cultural diversity).

The general human rights documents that underpin this approach are the Charter of the United Nations and the Universal Declaration of Human Rights of 1948, which laid the framework for the promotion of the dignity and worth of all human beings, as well as conditions for justice, respect and social progress.[7] In addition, many treaties, conventions and declarations reflect the five rights-based aims of Oxfam. Under each of the five aims, Oxfam targets the achievement of specific 'strategic change objectives' (SCOs), identifying them jointly at the international and regional levels.[8] These SCOs explicitly state the rights to be exercised, supported by Oxfam programmes over an agreed time-frame. To achieve them, Oxfam delineates desired 'policy and practice changes' associated with each of the SCOs. In its recently developed 'toolbox' (Wilson-Grau 2003), Novib Oxfam Netherlands has begun to assess, together with partner organizations, which of their outcomes could contribute to achieving the policy and practice changes, and ultimately the SCOs and aims that Oxfam has identified.

Table 2.1 gives examples, aim by aim, of rights-based changes in policy and practice, both in the domain of laws and regulations and in 'beliefs' or public opinion (Wilson-Grau 2004: 3).

Oxfam has attracted some criticism for generating its own list of rights, which was viewed by some as a repackaging of the standard international framework. In its defence, Oxfam would claim to have pioneered a way to use international norms and standards to reinforce its existing programmes and campaigns, and to have implemented a rights-based approach in an innovative and organic way (because the new formulation was built on what already made sense to staff and partner organizations around the world). Others have appreciated Oxfam's genuine efforts to embed its 'own rights' within the existing international instruments (see for example Marks 2003).

While arguably the Oxfams have not gone far enough in helping all staff to understand human rights instruments and principles, the use of practical rights-based aims was an important move towards giving programmes an intrinsic focus on rights which both recognizes international norms and standards and translates them to related national constitutions and legislation. It is at the national and sub-national levels that Oxfam – and indeed many other international NGOs – can best support CSOs and the public at large to hold relevant duty bearers accountable for fulfilling, protecting and respecting human rights.

TABLE 2.1 Examples of rights-based changes in policies and practices

Oxfam's five aims	Governmental and corporate laws and regulations and their adherence		Religious, cultural and social beliefs and their observance	
	Changes in policy	Changes in practice	Changes in policy	Changes in practice
To a sustainable livelihood	Parliament passes a law mandating an agrarian reform	Ministry of Agriculture distributes land titles to landless peasants	Agro-industry recognizes the economic potential of farming without the intensive use of chemical fertilizers and pesticides	Commercial farmers adopt large-scale organic farming practices
To basic social services	Ministries of Health and Commerce rule that the importation and production of generic anti-viral medicines will be permitted	Pharmaceutical companies initiate local manufacture and sale of low-cost anti-virals	Roman Catholic archbishop modifies religious doctrine to permit the use of condoms	Religious faithful regularly use condoms to block the transmission of the AIDS virus
To life and security	Interior Ministry issues a decree prohibiting the public from carrying concealed weapons	Civilian population stop the carrying of concealed weapons in public	Families reject their belief that nothing can be done in the face of perennial flooding	Communities implement flood-preparedness plans
To be heard – social and political citizenship	Referendum and constitutional amendment requiring local government to consult citizens on budget planning and implementation	Citizens participate in the municipal budgeting process	Citizens' groups become convinced that government corruption must be combated	Civil society organizations act as watchdog on municipal officials
To an identity – gender and diversity	Managers' Association adapts corporate guideline prohibiting ethnic discrimination.	Members of minority groups file increasing numbers of formal charges for corporate harassment	Community elders declare every woman's right to be free of domination by men	Parents support girl students in denouncing sexual abuse by their male teachers

Raising awareness of rights at home and around the world

Most of the Oxfams devote significant efforts in their home countries to raising public awareness of the relationships between poverty and the denial of rights, for example through 'global citizenship' programmes.[9] Much of the campaigning work of Oxfams to Make Trade Fair, to Control Arms, and to Make Poverty History[10] is designed to spur their home-country citizens to hold their own governments accountable for economic, political and social policies that will reduce disparities between rich and poor, and curtail the self-interest of richer nations. Implicit in this is Oxfam's belief that all of the world's people bear responsibility for securing not just their own rights, but also the rights of others. Building an active citizenry and strengthening the relationship between citizens and the state is essential to this process,[11] as is working through collective, participatory action. Other key messages are the need to ensure that social justice is accorded at least equal priority with economic growth, and insistence on the fact that the prosperity of some must not be allowed to perpetuate the poverty of others. In all of this, alliance building, good partnership and working effectively with others in coalitions are crucial for the legitimacy of the process and to ensure good outcomes.

Different Oxfams – a range of approaches

Different Oxfams may accord different emphases or priorities to the five rights-related aims, depending upon their national context and other factors, such as history and experience. Yet the principles that underlie the campaign for the realization of rights – equality, non-discrimination, participation and accountability – are at the heart of all of Oxfam's programmes and strategies.[12] The next section provides examples of how Oxfam puts a rights-based approach into practice. A number of Oxfams have programmes in each of the countries concerned, but each case study is written from the perspective of one affiliate.

Responding to the impact of globalization on Sahelian cotton farmers
Creating more space for the representatives of Southern NGOs in international fora, in order to link local activists and global decision-makers more effectively, is one of the strategies pursued in the Oxfam International Campaign to Make Trade Fair. Often a long-term process of building capacity and trust precedes such linking. The case of Sahelian cotton farmers, who together with Oxfam International succeeded in voicing their views effectively at the WTO meeting in Cancún in 2003, is a good illustration of this process.

Hundreds of village-based farmers' associations were founded in the 1980s and 1990s in the Sahelian countries of West Africa. A number of Oxfams supported poverty-alleviation programmes, in addition to investing in work to build the organizational capacities of village associations through intermediary NGOs. The next step was to move from developing organizations to supporting lobbying and advocacy by and on behalf of people living in poverty. Realizing that local solutions are not always enough, the village-based organizations started creating regional organizations that were in a better position to influence policies. The NGOs adjusted their capacity-building programmes and adopted an approach of 'linking and learning' between village associations in various parts of the Sahel to support this process. As a result, farmers, cattle owners and fishermen and women in several areas formed national federations and regional unions.

Globalization has negative effects on weak economies and ultimately on rural households. The Sahelian farmers' organizations recognized globalization as a new challenge. The millions of farmers in the Sahel who produce cotton for export are directly affected by subsidies paid to domestic cotton farmers by the governments of the USA and other countries. The income of African producers dropped as the price of cotton fell on the world market. They responded by setting up ROPPA, a regional farmers' organization, in 2000.

At the WTO ministerial conference in Cancún in 2003, ROPPA successfully called attention to the plight of Sahelian cotton farmers. Oxfam contributed to research on the issues, provided advice to governments and farmers' representatives, and sponsored a media tour in the northern hemisphere for representatives of the groups affected. But such efforts on the global stage bring neither immediate nor permanent positive impacts, and CSOs must remain vigilant in the struggle for justice. Fortunately, following a subsequent complaint by Brazil in a similar case, a WTO dispute-settlement panel found that US cotton subsidies are contrary to WTO rules.[13] This decision was a major step forward in the fight against the dumping of subsidized products on world markets, and Oxfam is confident that the decision will strengthen the initiative taken by West African governments to end the European and American subsidies.

This case shows how an RBA requires consistent capacity building within the Oxfams and with partner organizations. Apart from the need for increased investment in education in citizenship and human rights,[14] there is an enormous need to continue to strengthen the capacity of people who want to claim their rights. Changes in policy and practice can be achieved only if the people whose rights are violated are able to express their views about what should be changed. As one staff member of Oxfam observes: 'We recognize that lone social actors rarely can achieve policy and practice changes. Work is required on a significant scale in alliances with social actors working at all levels. We consider that in any country, it is local citizens, organized as civil-society actors, who know best what policy and practice changes are achievable and how to achieve them' (Wilson-Grau 2004: 3). In this context, the Oxfams play an important role by helping to influence the policies and practices of multilateral institutions and multinational corporations, in addition to funding local development actors working towards policy and practice changes of their choice.

The right to sustainable livelihoods: the Ethiopia coffee crisis One of Oxfam's aims is to support poor people to claim their right to sustainable livelihoods, but it goes further than typical development programmes that aim to increase income and productivity. Oxfam's work in support of this aim includes support for food and income security, natural-resource management and promotion of labour rights for those in waged employment. Within the context of social justice and the realization of human rights, promoting sustainable livelihoods is not concerned merely with access to resources, but also with increasing the capacity to secure one's livelihood. This takes into account the reality of poor communities: a livelihood that has sustainable human development as its outcome depends on other human rights, such as the right to be heard (addressing 'voice poverty'). Oxfam's rights-based approach also takes into account the imperative need to hold duty holders accountable for their responsibilities to marginalized communities.

Since the beginning of the coffee crisis in Ethiopia, Oxfam has supported Ethiopian coffee producers to overcome the disastrous blow to their country's economy and their livelihoods. Sixty per cent of Ethiopia's national earnings comes from coffee, so when world coffee prices fell to an unprecedented level a few years ago, the national economy, the coffee industry and coffee producers had to absorb the shock. Coupled with the international coffee crisis were Ethiopia's problematic domestic trade rules, which denied farmers and cooperatives access to international buyers, leaving farmers dependent on unfair prices and exploitation by exporters. In addition, coffee farmers were unaware of international coffee prices and of their role in the coffee market.

Oxfam played a key role in three ways: first, in developing relationships with all stakeholders, including producers, government officials and corporations; second, in strengthening the voice of producers through providing information, building capacity and promoting networking; and third, bringing all stakeholders around the same table to find appropriate solutions to the crisis.

Given the fact that national policies were largely to blame for the producers' failure to recover from the damage done to their livelihoods, a large element of Oxfam's strategy was to hold the government of Ethiopia accountable for protecting producers from further marginalization. Lobbying of the government by Oxfam partners and staff eventually led to an official agreement to lift the restrictions on farmers and cooperatives, allowing them to sell coffee directly to international buyers. Although sceptics doubted the likely effectiveness of the government's decision, and the capacity of the cooperatives to take advantage of it, the reform represented a huge step towards reform of the coffee industry in Ethiopia.

What followed was active and extensive work to develop the trading capacity of the coffee cooperatives and ensure the highest quality of coffee, to match global quality standards for speciality coffee. Oxfam organized a national conference to address concerns about the deteriorating quality of Ethiopian coffee.

The achievements of one Oxfam partner, the Oromia Cooperative Union, speak for themselves. In 2001, one container of coffee was exported. In the next year, with the addition of volunteer staff, the cooperative sold ten containers. In 2003, sixty containers of coffee were sold on the international market. By May 2004, the Oromia Union had sold all of its 120 containers.

The changes in Ethiopia's coffee industry go beyond the increased sales to a full government endorsement of policies more favourable to farmers and cooperatives. Since 2001, when the campaign for reform began, the following results have been achieved:

- Coffee farmers who could not sell directly to international markets now have direct access to international buyers, with no intermediary, thus increasing their profits.
- Coffee farmers and cooperatives are now exempt from paying tax.
- National banks have begun giving farmers and cooperatives credits and loans which used to be restricted to exporters.
- Taxes on travel from coffee-producing regions to other regions have been lifted.

Cooperatives have stabilized the coffee market, and the removal of restrictions has eliminated the middlemen. In addition, the steady restoration of the coffee-based economy has meant that not only coffee farmers, but the chain of other industries and people that depend on coffee exports, are heading for financial stability.

Promoting sustainable livelihoods in Malawi and Zambia through advocacy on institutional accountability The following case study demonstrates work aligned between country, regional and global levels that pursues two of Oxfam's aims: the right to a sustainable livelihood and the right to be heard. This is a joint programme, managed by Oxfam GB with the support of several Oxfam affiliates.

In August 2002, Oxfam International produced a briefing paper entitled 'Death on the Doorstep of the Summit' for the World Summit on Sustainable Development in Johannesburg. The paper sought to link the food crisis in Southern Africa to the agricultural liberalization policies imposed on Zambia and Malawi at the behest of the World Bank and IMF. It demonstrated that by requiring these countries rapidly to dismantle state support for agriculture, the Bank and the Fund had gravely compromised the food security of poor women and men in the region, making them even more vulnerable to destitution.

The paper was accompanied by significant media work in Zambia, including a televised interview with the Minister of Agriculture, in which he questioned the policies of the World Bank and the IMF. This footage was compiled in collaboration with Oxfam staff and partners in Zambia, and was used both at the Johannesburg summit and in Zambia itself. In Malawi, further country-specific research was conducted, which contributed to the creation of a broad campaign involving civil society, media and parliamentarians. The campaign succeeded in getting assurances from donors and government ministers that they would not privatize the state marketing board ADMARC, given that it had a clear social role to play as the source of cheap agricultural inputs and farm produce for poor people in rural areas.

The immediate outcome of this work was to highlight the link between agricultural liberalization and increased food insecurity in the region, and the role of the World Bank and IMF in promoting liberalization policies. The campaign's longer-term impact on poor people has been twofold, in terms of livelihood and in terms of increased accountability. In Malawi and Zambia it contributed to a reversal of donors' policy on agriculture. In Zambia, the government has reintroduced a certain level of subsidy on maize, with the tacit support of the IMF. In Malawi, the World Bank recognized that ADMARC has a key social role to play in keeping open unprofitable markets in distant rural areas, which on pure economic criteria were losing the government support that was key to the survival of poor communities. In both countries there has been or will be a direct effect on the lives of poor women and men, as evidence developed by the World Bank itself shows that per capita consumption by poor families in rural areas with access to the state ADMARC markets is as much as 20 per cent higher than the average.

In terms of the right to be heard, in Malawi poor rural women and men actively engaged in a series of radio debates, broadcast nationally from villages in Mulanje where Oxfam works. The debates focused on the role of ADMARC in supporting the livelihoods of the poor. In Malawi and Zambia, Oxfam's campaign and policy work stimulated national debates about agricultural policy, engaging civil society and parliamentarians, and increasing public discussion of poverty-related issues. There has also been a shift in donor policy on this issue in Zambia and Malawi, although it is still necessary to maintain pressure on the policy-makers.

Other rights-related topics were opened up; for example, women became involved in radio debates about gender equity; discussions included gender-related aspects of food security, for example the frequently ignored situation of female-headed households. And civil society partners active in both countries became more actively engaged in advocacy and strengthened their advocacy capacity. This experience of campaigning and lobbying helped to build a broad alliance for change, and the base for a long-term movement of civil society actors around this issue.

As is the case with other policy work, the gains made could easily be reversed; for this reason CSOs must continue to monitor privatization conditions on World Bank loans in Malawi, for example. Nevertheless, this case study illustrates the effectiveness of joined-up programming by the Oxfams for advocacy at national, regional and global levels. This instance was prompted by a reaction to a region-wide crisis, but it has clear national and global implications.

Capacity building in a stateless society: Somalia Oxfam believes that promoting responsible citizenship, through supporting the work of local autonomous partner organizations, is a crucial step towards improving the capacity of people to claim their rights and towards seeking the accountability of those in power.

Somalia is a war-torn country that has not had a functioning government for twelve years. Its social fabric has been all but destroyed. Warlords have ruled through fear and the silencing of people. In response to their worsening plight, some courageous individuals began implementing development projects. A number of Oxfams work in Somalia and this case study is based on an experience of Novib Oxfam Netherlands who began to support these initiatives in 1995. What began as development work has slowly expanded into an engagement in public debates and advocacy for peace and human rights. In 2002, Novib Oxfam Netherlands was invited by the European Commission to launch a project called 'Strengthening Somali Civil Society'. At the start, Somali researchers mapped civil society throughout the country (identifying NGOs, religious leaders, elders, community-based organizations, the media, professional organizations, and artists) and studied donors' policies to understand why they were not investing in Somalia and Somaliland. This led to the Civil Society Symposium in the city of Hargeisa in February 2003, where 400 representatives of civil society came together to review the findings. They impressed upon the attendant donors the need to invest in education, but also to start thinking in terms of partnerships with local organizations.

Meanwhile, a Code of Conduct was developed by Somali civil society, prescribing standards to which civil society aspires to adhere. Somali networks have subscribed to the Code and set up a monitoring mechanism. Furthermore, ten human rights organizations were trained in investigation, documentation, monitoring and advocacy, with the aim of systematically documenting abuses of human rights and addressing violations that are not visible to the international community. Cases were presented to the UN Human Rights Commission in Geneva, and the support of Amnesty International was obtained to protect defenders of human rights. Finally, a newsletter and a website were developed to promote the work of Somali groups. Somalis can now communicate with fellow Somalis, both within the country and in the diaspora. The work and the debates have made it possible for civil society actors to contribute to reconciliation. Two campaigns in particular, Civil Society in Action and the Hadrawi Peace March, have raised hopes that people can regain power over their own lives.

Oxfams – the advantages of difference

Each of the Oxfam affiliates is working on the commitments made in the strategic plan of 2000, including the incorporation of a rights-based approach. Yet differences remain, not surprisingly in view of the fact that the confederation was formally established less than ten years ago. For Oxfam International, narrowing some differences, and accepting others, is an ongoing process, informed by a lively debate among partners, allies, and critics in other institutions. While consistency is important, the differences provide comparative analysis of effectiveness and impact among peers, and give sufficient 'room for manoeuvre' for innovation.

Two examples illustrate the breadth of this 'room for manoeuvre'. One concerns the efforts of Oxfam GB to build capacity on both sides of the human rights equation. While much of Oxfam GB's support for civil society is similar to that of other Oxfam affiliates, it is distinctive in that it explicitly seeks to improve the capacity of duty bearers to respond to the demands of citizens and civil society organizations. This is due primarily to its history of operational programmes, whereby Oxfam GB teams in country programmes work in direct collaboration with government, as well as with civil society. While this area of work is clearly important (Tomás 2003: 11–16), Oxfam is mindful that where governments are not genuinely interested in justice and promoting rights, a commitment to capacity building must not provide a façade to deflect criticism and action.

By contrast, Novib Oxfam Netherlands has consistently worked to strengthen the capacity of autonomous partner organizations and NGOs in particular, both at an internal/micro level (organizational development) and at an external/macro level (institutional development). Over time, this institutional development has deepened into alliance-building, lobbying and advocacy, and building citizenship, which is well illustrated in the Somali case study presented above. In a recent policy paper (Novib 2004), this standing policy has been reaffirmed: a strong civil society is crucial in order to create a system of checks and balances between the agency, the government and the private sector.

A common language and a coordinated approach

As this chapter has demonstrated, a variety of methods to promote the fulfilment of human rights has emerged from the adoption of a rights-based approach across the Oxfams and in different national contexts. Although the emphasis and *modus operandi* of particular Oxfams may differ, common to all are the shifts that occurred when they redefined their work according to five rights-based aims and related strategic change objectives, and when programme and campaigning work focused on well-defined targets for holding institutions accountable for their policies and practices. Despite some differences in their ways of working, the Oxfams have demonstrated how a rights-based approach can be implemented in programmes and campaigns to transform a spiral of poverty and human rights abuses into a virtuous circle, in which rights holders benefit, and duty bearers fulfil human rights. This can take place at regional, national and international levels, or indeed – and most powerfully – at multiple levels combined.

The examples presented here illustrate efforts by one or more Oxfams to develop their rights-based approach further. One way is to assess the outcomes of partner organizations' work against rights-based aims and strategic change objectives. Another is to improve the awareness and capacity of duty bearers, either the state or multinational corporations, to meet their obligations to respect human rights. A third is to strengthen the voice of local actors through capacity building and multi-level advocacy and media work. A fourth is to ensure that the full continuum of rights is addressed, whether by Oxfam or others.

While the implementation of a rights-based approach in terms of institutional accountability has become a significant feature across the work of the Oxfams, there has been less discussion and collaboration on an equally important component of the RBA: that of incorporating human rights principles throughout Oxfam's practice. These principles are of course enshrined in Oxfam's stated intent; but ensuring that they are consistently put into practice, not merely enshrined in institutional rhetoric, is a continuing challenge.

The extent to which Oxfam staff practise these principles in their day-to-day work depends on a whole host of factors, including levels of awareness, capacity and willingness to uphold the standards through programme and campaign cycles. It also depends on how well staff and their counterparts are supported to uphold these standards in the face of other organizational demands.[15] Arguably, Oxfam struggles with translating theory and good intent into good practice no more or less than the typical international NGO. But because of its increasingly high profile, it is particularly important for Oxfam to be mindful of its responsibilities when it describes itself as an agency with a rights-based approach at its core. A focus on global-level campaigning must not lead Oxfam to overlook the real situation of local communities, and Oxfam must meaningfully evaluate whether global successes are being translated into improvements for the world's most marginalized people. Rights such as the freedom of information, expression and assembly must be exercised everywhere, or short-term gains will be lost. Indeed, the requirements of broad-based campaigning and the increasing demands on CSOs for sophisticated planning and reporting mechanisms are in some ways competing with this imperative for attention and resources. Nevertheless, it is evident that mainstreaming the principles of human rights will be an increasing aspect of Oxfam discussions, both internally and externally with counterparts and other stakeholders, in the coming years.

Oxfam faces other challenges in implementing a rights-based approach. Many people are not aware of their rights, so awareness-raising will be a lengthy process. Some governments are not committed to protecting and promoting rights; even in cases where they express commitment, they may lack the necessary resources. And at times, Oxfam refrains from pressuring governments about specific violations, for fear of risking legitimacy or of creating future risks to staff and programmes.

Despite these challenges, the universal language of rights has helped the Oxfam affiliates and their partners to speak a common language, and to express in authoritative and internationally accepted terminology the essential elements for achieving human development and global justice. The unequal power relations that constrain human development can be confronted more forcefully when international principles and instruments of human rights can be brought to bear on national legislation, and in turn citizens can draw on both levels to demand their rights. Rights-based development programmes and campaigns are an important complement to the longer-established activities of organizations dedicated to the protection of human rights. Working on these issues from the local level upwards, building the awareness and capacity to promote human rights, and joining forces and linking different actors and different levels are strategies that, when done well, give expression to Oxfam's quest for global equity.

Notes

1 For more information, see Oxfam International (2000); available at <www.oxfam.org/eng/about_strat.htm> Hereinafter, references to programme or campaigns encompass both development and humanitarian goals and activities.

2 In this chapter, 'Oxfam' is used when it is applicable to the twelve affiliates of Oxfam International, rather than any specific affiliate.

3 When adopting the OI Strategic Plan 'Towards Global Equity' (2000), the RBA was one feature of the OI profile, the other three being 'humanitarian response and development action'; 'action, advocacy and learning'; and 'working with autonomous, local partners'.

4 For more on this vicious circle, see Williams (1995).

5 For an excellent overview of how an analysis of rights holders versus duty bearers is intrinsically linked to the action-oriented character of rights, and human rights in particular, see the contribution of Bas de Gaay Fortman in Boerefijn et al. (2001: 49).

6 Through claiming respect for and protection and fulfilment of rights. The legitimacy of development actors to contribute to fulfilling rights is described in an analysis of Henry Shue's work on the trinity of obligations (Brouwer 2001: 18).

7 The Millennium Declaration, adopted by the UN General Assembly in 2000, which has generated the Millennium Development Goals as specific targets for 2015, can be seen as a reaffirmation of the UN Charter.

8 The twelve Oxfams have organized their work globally into twelve 'regions' that form units for coordination and joint action.

9 For example, Oxfam GB's Global Citizenship programme has had a significant impact on the development of global citizenship studies within the UK National Curriculum.

10 Make Poverty History represents a shift in Oxfam's Education Now campaign towards a broader alliance and the goal of persuading governments and donors to achieve the Millennium Development Goals.

11 For more on this relational character of rights, see Lund-Madsen 2001: 3–4.

12 Interestingly, these are classified as elements of 'the human rights approach', 'the responsibilities approach' and, to a lesser extent, 'the human rights education approach' (Marks 2003: 5–6, 16–22 and 23–6).

13 The WTO panel found that $3.2 billion in US cotton subsidies and $1.6 billion in exports credits (for cotton and other commodities) contravene WTO rules. This represents almost all cotton subsidies and close to 50 per cent of all export credits used by the USA in 2002.

14 This emerged as a key priority during consultations conducted among the staff by Oxfam America and Novib Oxfam Netherlands on implementing an RBA. A comparison of the outcomes of those consultations may be obtained from the OI secretariat (Brouwer 2003).

15 For example, by taking advantage of opportunities for policy dialogue that do not permit thorough consultation with affected communities.

References

Biekart, K. (2003) *Dutch Co-financing Agencies and Civil Society Building (Synthesis Study)* (The Hague: Steering Committee for the Evaluation of the Dutch Co-Financing Programme).

Boerefijn, I., M. Brouwer and R. Fakhreddine (eds) (2001) *Linking and Learning in the Field of Economic, Social and Cultural Rights*, SIM Special no. 27 (Utrecht: Netherlands Institute of Human Rights [SIM]).

Brouwer, M. (2001) 'Making ESCR Meaningful to People', paper submitted to the conference of the Netherlands Institute of Human Rights (SIM), Following Up the Good Work, 28–29 September.

— (2003) *Comparison of RBA Consultations, Oxfam America and Novib Oxfam Netherlands* (Washington/The Hague: OI).

Lund-Madsen, H. (2001) *Assessing the Impact of Human Rights Work: Key Elements for a Methodology*, May (The Hague: Novib Oxfam Netherlands).

Marks, S. P. (2003) *The Human Rights Framework for Development: Seven Approaches* (Boston, MA: François-Xavier Bagnoud Center for Health and Human Rights, Harvard School of Public Health).

Novib (2004) *Novib in Action: Civil Society Building, Vision, Policy and Practice* (The Hague: Novib Oxfam Netherlands).

Oxfam International (2000) *Towards Global Equity: Strategic Plan 2001–2004* (Oxford: Oxfam International).

— (2002) *Death on the Doorstep of the Summit: Oxfam Briefing Paper 29*, August (Oxford: Oxfam International).

Shue, H. (1996) *Basic Rights: Subsistence, Affluence and US Foreign Policy*, 2nd edn (Princeton, NJ: Princeton University Press).

Tomás, A. (2003) *A Human Rights Approach to Development: Primer for Development Practitioners* (Kathmandu: UNDP).

Varga Mas, O. de la (2003) 'Oxfam International and the Rights Based Approach' *Ontrac*, 23 (7) (Oxford: INTRAC).

Williams, S. (1995) *Basic Rights: Understanding the Concept and Practice of Basic Rights in Oxfam's Programme: A Resource for Staff* (Oxford: Oxfam).

Wilson-Grau, R. (2003) *Grantmaking: Opportunity and Risk Appraisal*, Novib Toolbox (The Hague: Novib Oxfam Netherlands).

— (2004) 'PPCs: Novib and Policy and Practice Changes, Concepts and Some Examples' (draft), 25 February (The Hague: Novib Oxfam Netherlands).

3 | The case of CARE International in Rwanda

ANDREW JONES

Adoption of a human rights approach to CARE's work would mean that we view the people we assist as rights holders, and not simply as benefici-aries or project participants. Our central aim – across all our programmes – would be to facilitate, in collaboration with others, a process of self-empowerment of poor, disenfranchised peoples and communities in order to help them pursue and achieve progressively their rights, broadly defined, as human beings. This central aim would not deny the importance of CARE's provision of basic supplies and services, often critical to livelihood preservation and recovery as well as longer-term development. Neverthe-less, across all CARE programmes, the provision of supplies and services would be thought of as a means to an end, and the end – the engagement of marginalized and vulnerable people in the realization of their rights – would be central to programme design, implementation and evaluation (CARE International statement, February 1999)

Over the past decade, many relief and development organizations have embraced and sought to integrate a human rights or rights-based approach (RBA) to their work. Such a shift reflects the growing recognition that development, at its core, is not about injecting resources and technical expertise to facilitate the delivery of basic social and economic services. Rather, it is about a much wider set of human conditions that enable people to live with dignity and to develop their full potential as human beings. This chapter is an attempt to present CARE's RBA integration process through the lens of its experience in Rwanda.

Rwanda is a country and society seeking to recover from a history of political and ethnic violence culminating in the 1994 genocide. The geno-cide had a devastating impact, leaving profound physical and psychological scars and reinforcing deep divisions in Rwandan society. A mere ten years later, the government and the population in general are faced with the overwhelming task of rebuilding, even as armed elements and sympath-izers of the previous, genocidal regime remain at large in the region and a constant threat to Rwanda's security.

In Rwanda, government has long been dominated by a select few to the detriment of the vast majority of the population. There is virtually no tradition of popular participation in public affairs. The freedoms of expression and association have long been suppressed by a heavy-handed state. Long-term institutionalized control (and often abuse) of power by a relative few has frustrated if not hijacked poor, marginalized Rwandans' development efforts. That said, the current government of Rwanda is making an effort through, for example, the poverty reduction and decentralization processes, to tolerate and even invite civil society participation and, to a limited degree, dissent. Most significantly, there is now some space for citizens, including women and youth, to participate in and shape development opportunities. Although the prevailing culture remains one of fear, distrust and silence, these are positive signs.

From needs to rights: a look at CARE's RBA

The wider CARE context From its origins delivering CARE packages to post-Second World War Europe, CARE International (or CI) currently comprises twelve member CAREs in the following countries: Australia, Austria, Canada, Denmark, France, Germany, Japan, the Netherlands, Norway, Thailand, the United Kingdom and the United States. CI's secretariat is in Brussels. The organization provides relief and development assistance in more than sixty-five countries across Asia, Africa, the Middle East, Eastern Europe, Latin America and the Caribbean.

At the same time as CARE was developing new mission and vision statements in the late 1990s, the organization also was exploring a human rights-based approach to its work. This stemmed from an internal push to become a more principled organization and reflected the broader community's efforts to address the shortcomings of apolitical humanitarian aid and micro-level economic and social development programming, which had yielded far too little in the way of lasting, systemic results.

CARE's RBA initiative started, informally, with high-level discussions reviewing our work, especially our emergency response efforts, from a human rights perspective. These more theoretical discussions led to four country-specific case studies, through which CARE staff in different parts of the world and in a range of operating environments explored the implications of a rights perspective for their work. By the late 1990s, the initiative was formalized, with a full-time staff person dedicated to increasing staff understanding of RBA, promoting field experimentation with a commitment to ongoing learning, adapting organizational policies and systems to incorporate RBA principles and on-the-ground learning, and developing strategic alliances with like-minded organizations worldwide. Since that time, a growing number of CARE country offices worldwide have experimented, more and more profoundly and systematically, with RBA in relief and development work.

Within CARE, we understand human rights holistically, as entitlements all people have to basic conditions supporting their efforts to live in peace and dignity and to develop their full potential as human beings. Those basic conditions span the spectrum of civil, political, economic, social and cultural rights. For CARE, as defined at a global conference in 2001, RBA means that:

1. We support poor and marginalized people's efforts to take control of their own lives and fulfil their rights, responsibilities and aspirations.
2. We stand in solidarity with poor and marginalized people whose rights are denied, adding our voice to theirs and holding ourselves accountable to them.
3. We hold others accountable for fulfilling their responsibilities towards poor and marginalized people.[1]
4. We oppose any discrimination based on sex/gender, race, nationality, ethnicity, class, religion, age, physical ability, caste or sexual orientation.
5. We examine and address the root causes of poverty and rights denial.
6. We promote non-violence in the democratic and just resolution of conflicts contributing to poverty and rights denial.
7. We work in concert with others to promote the human rights of poor and marginalized people.

These defining characteristics of RBA say little about practical implications, which depend on how an organization integrates in its operations a commitment to human rights.[2] One could argue that development organizations since long before the 1990s espoused principles such as participation and solidarity with the poor. What is really different about RBA, or is it just the latest packaging of good development work? Several important differences come to mind. First, the fact that such elements of good development practice become mandatory in a rights-based framework; there is nothing optional about participation when viewed as a human right, for example. RBA transforms relationships between governmental or development agencies and the recipients of their goods and services. RBA implies that development actors assume responsibility – morally if not legally – for the impact their assistance has on people's ability to realize their rights. Beyond that, three marked differences are worth highlighting.

First, RBA demands equal attention to process and outcomes. Process – in the form of genuine participation and relationships of accountability between poor people and responsible actors – represents, in and of itself, the achievement of a human rights outcome. Process also is essential to the long-term, institutionalized changes needed to ensure that other human rights and poverty reduction outcomes are sustained. Second, RBA deepens the focus on people who face discrimination and exclusion in their communities and societies, people whose rights are systematically denied. Development assistance through a rights lens focuses on fostering respect for their equal dignity and worth and on enhancing their opportunities in life. A critical part of this equation is their right to participate meaningfully in public affairs, and especially to hold their leaders to account. Third, RBA tells us that we have to tackle legal, policy and socio-cultural issues impeding development at the roots, both to live up to our commitment to advance human rights and to make major and lasting gains in poverty reduction.

These changes, if fully put into practice, are radically different from traditional, mainstream development approaches. CARE and many other (governmental and non-governmental) development actors have sought to ground their work in human rights principles and norms for the better part of a decade now. Even where the commitment to change is genuine, change tends to be evolutionary as such a paradigm shift cannot take place overnight.[3] Part of the explanation for this is that RBA calls for internal, organizational change, which is extremely difficult because it shines the spotlight on our own shortcomings in respecting and fostering human dignity and rights. Yet only by going down this 'house cleaning' path can we be effective role-models and agents for change externally.

CARE Rwanda's adoption of a rights-based approach In Rwanda, CARE developed a long-range strategic plan in late 2000 and early 2001. At that time, the country was emerging from a decade-long period of strife, preceding and following the genocide in 1994. CARE staff reflected on their traditional aid philosophy, approaches and results and agreed that CARE had to do what it could, in partnership and alliance with others, to tackle the underlying causes of poverty and social injustice in Rwanda. Otherwise, the organization risked accomplishing little and, even worse, becoming part of the problem.

The final versions of CARE Rwanda's mission and programme goal, as refined at the mid-term strategy review workshop in December 2003, are as follows:

CARE Rwanda's mission is to work alongside communities to enable them to overcome underlying and specific causes of poverty, achieve positive lasting change and live with dignity.

By the end of June 2006 (i.e. the end of the current 5-year strategic plan), poor and marginalized communities targeted by CARE programming will have identified and taken action to address specific and underlying causes of poverty and fulfil their rights in peaceful coexistence.

The staff went so far as to identify rights (defined as 'respect for the dignity of all people', 'solidarity with communities' and the promotion of social justice) as a core value of CARE Rwanda. On paper at least, RBA became a central paradigm for all our programming. Of course, translating commitments on paper to daily practice is the hard part, and we are currently struggling with this. The staff is overwhelmingly Rwandan and thus comes from a culture where conformity and acquiescence to authority are deeply engrained. Moreover, in spite of favourable policy developments in recent years, the reality on the ground is not conducive to diversity of civic thought and action. The state continues to view NGOs as essentially technical assistants and subcontractors in the shared endeavour of developing the Rwandan population.

In the following section, I will describe our strategy for integrating RBA to development within CARE Rwanda, followed by our experience to date.

CARE Rwanda's strategy for becoming a rights-based organization

Internal transformation CARE Rwanda's change strategy is predicated on the assumption that, in order to promote rights externally with any measure of credibility and success, we have to transform ourselves internally. The emphasis, externally, is on both empowering poor, marginalized groups and nurturing an environment enabling them to mobilize, express themselves freely and realize their rights. This is vastly different from traditional 'business as usual'. We thus have begun constructing a culture of rights at the workplace and, staff member by staff member, a heart-felt, personal commitment to advancing rights in our work. Without internal ownership of RBA, outward action is doomed to fail. The following objectives are guiding the change process:

1. Cultivate staff ownership of RBA, building on supporting values and norms in Rwandan culture/society and encouraging open discussion where there are tensions.
2. Weave basic and rights education, and support of the grassroots-level defence and pursuit of rights, into new programme and project designs.
3. Engage in policy dialogue at all levels with an emphasis on the commit-

ment of resources and creation of opportunities for poor, marginalized Rwandans to realize their rights to participation in public affairs, health, education and an adequate standard of living.

4. Strengthen partnerships and alliances with Rwandan and international organizations sharing similar objectives.

It is impossible to view CARE Rwanda's internal change process, through which local ownership of RBA is cultivated, as anything but a long-term one. The process has been characterized by widespread curiosity among staff and, over time, a growing enthusiasm among a core set of committed colleagues. One key driver of this commitment is the clear link certain staff have made to the violations of human dignity and rights that have underlain Rwanda's episodic ethnic violence, and most notably the 1994 genocide. Colleagues increasingly realize that without grappling with the underlying societal issues that foster division and exclusion, CARE cannot and will not achieve much in terms of contributing to Rwanda's sustainable development. They also see increasingly how human rights norms and standards challenge, with a universal legitimacy, generations of social and political discrimination and control, of resources and opportunities for advancement by a relative few in Rwanda. They want to see real change in Rwandan society and systems of governance, even as they are acutely aware of the risks associated with challenging the status quo and are thus cautious in how they proceed.

Of course, in a society where open criticism of authority remains taboo, outright resistance to this shift in CARE's directions has not been highly visible, although there undoubtedly are many who are uncomfortable about the change process, particularly those who are risk averse. They may go along with it, at a surface level, but are not genuinely part of it. To address this problem, a central element of CARE Rwanda's approach has been to facilitate local leadership of the process. Even with a programme director who served as CARE's global rights-based programming adviser prior to coming to Rwanda, or perhaps especially because of this, emphasis has been placed on supporting emerging leaders from among the Rwandan staff. Emerging leaders were those who showed the most interest in learning more about RBA and contributing to its integration within CARE Rwanda. Nurturing these seeds of change, CARE Rwanda has invested in such colleagues' conceptual understanding of RBA and development of such an approach for application in the Rwandan context. This has resulted in the formation of a corps of change agents (or 'ambassadors') who are themselves driving the process (and not merely following for reasons such as job security). At the end of the day, sceptics are much less likely *genuinely* to buy in to the change process on the basis of a foreigner's as opposed to a fellow Rwandan's appeals.[4]

With the emergence of a core group of Rwandan staff firmly behind the rights-based change process in CARE Rwanda, programme and project teams have engaged in a growing number of pilot initiatives to integrate rights analysis and action into efforts to combat poverty and social injustice. Experimentation ranged from new tools and approaches for poverty analysis and participatory programme design, monitoring and evaluation (DM and E), to non-traditional programme activities to complement our more traditional local-level assistance to community groups and service providers. Such new approaches are changing the way CARE defines and interacts with its primary constituency, towards greater focus on the poorest and most marginalized Rwandans and greater accountability for the results of its interventions. They also have brought us much more squarely into broader social and political arenas, well beyond the narrow confines of technical support to the health, agricultural, micro-finance and education 'sectors'. This is shifting CARE's relationships with civil society and with government.

I will focus the rest of this chapter on two practical changes to CARE Rwanda's programme DM and E brought about by RBA integration. These centre on how development assistance agencies (i) analyse the causes of poverty in programme planning/design processes and (ii) monitor and evaluate how they are doing. After presenting new approaches being tested by CARE Rwanda, I will close with observations on key challenges and opportunities for practitioners moving in the rights direction.

From purely technical solutions to socio-political action: rights-based analysis and design In Gikongoro Province in 2003, CARE Rwanda invested in a participatory, inclusive analysis of the underlying causes of poverty and rights deprivation. The objective was to go beyond the extensive data collection already undertaken for the government's development of its poverty reduction strategy, which was limited mainly to quantitative information and simple community rankings of priority needs. To do this, we applied our causal–responsibility analysis (CRA) tool, adapted from UNICEF (Jones 2000b). In brief, the tool links the analysis of causes of poverty to a human rights framework by identifying the rights issues underlying poverty and exploring the associated responsibilities and capabilities of key duty bearers. Such information is then used to design interventions that can help to bring about more responsible, rights-based action to address conditions of poverty.

In this case, the analysis uncovered a range of factors driving poverty in the province, including social discrimination and exclusion, limited educational and economic opportunities, and ineffectual, unaccountable governance. It also helped to shed light on key responsible actors and why they are not doing more to address the underlying issues, and thus generated ideas for rights-based programming in response. Table 3.1 provides a sense of the results generated in this case.

Application of the CRA tool is one tangible example of how RBA is changing our programme analysis and planning process to take into account and respond more explicitly and deliberately to the rights violations that create and perpetuate poverty and conflict.

So what has CARE Rwanda done to translate such analysis into action? We are currently looking to integrate this in-depth analysis, as much as possible, in our Gikongoro programme planning and design processes through a rights-based programme approach. A rights-based programme consists of a set of focused and mutually reinforcing activities – some project-based, some non-project-based; some carried out by CARE, many carried out by others – that are based on strong social analysis of underlying causes of poverty and social injustice and that, over time, lead towards the sustainable achievement of a common rights goal. Key elements of the definition are the following:

- activities are focused and mutually reinforcing, not scattered (as projects in a 'sector' sometimes are)
- many activities are projects, but some might not be (e.g. basic government programmes, advocacy efforts, mediation and dialogue efforts)
- CARE carries out only some of the activities; others are also important
- some activities within a programme may be relatively technical but these need to be combined with other efforts designed to contribute towards a more fundamental, rights-based goal
- strong social analysis informs the programme goal and its activities
- each programme must be custom-made for its own social and political environment
- the time-frame is longer than a project
- the goal is sustained change in the form of achieving a rights-based goal for poor, marginalized, and vulnerable groups (Ambler 2002)[5]

CARE Rwanda's Gikongoro programme is heavily focused on HIV/AIDS, with short-term, essentially emergency, funding behind it. What the CRA analysis is helping us to do is maintain a broader focus on social and political factors that prevent people living with HIV/AIDS (PLWHA) and AIDS widows and orphans from improving their conditions and frustrate

TABLE 3.1 Causal responsibility analysis in Gikongoro province

Underlying human rights-related causes of poverty	Potential actions in response
	Working with partners, empower poor and marginalized people and encourage and support government efforts to:
Governance issues: i.e. factors affecting the access to, and sharing of, power in the public sphere	• Promote free access to information on decision-making processes, especially planning and budgeting, at all levels, and make them more participatory and inclusive • Promote transparency and accountability of public officials and others in positions of power vis-à-vis the population
Economic opportunities: i.e. factors affecting people's ability and opportunity to generate income	• Enhance agricultural production and facilitate better access to markets (pro-poor and -marginalized land policy, road and communications networks, marketing associations/networks) • Facilitate better access to credit (savings and credit associations/societies, favourable regulatory environment) • Strengthen people's ability to cope with the environmental constraints affecting agriculture
Access to basic education: i.e. factors preventing or hindering children from getting basic education	• Promote understanding about, and enforcement of the government policy on universal primary education (addressing cultural values and norms standing in the way) • Address the issue of child labour • Promote understanding of family planning and effective access for all to family planning services
Social discrimination/exclusion: i.e. factors resulting in the marginalization of certain segments of the population from decision-making processes and the benefits of development and other resources in the province	• Promote tolerance and accommodation among all members of the population (addressing deep-seated discriminatory attitudes and stereotyping of certain groups, raising awareness on human rights and responsibilities, promoting equitable access to public resources and opportunities) • Promote transparency and accountability (vis-à-vis marginalized groups) of public officials and local leadership

their efforts to live with dignity and self-worth. Donor funding, not surprisingly, is concentrated on technical interventions to strengthen the health system, provide access to voluntary counselling, testing and anti-retroviral therapy for those PLWHA who qualify, and provide care and support to

The case of CARE

PLWHA and AIDS widows and orphans to alleviate their suffering. All of this is vitally important, but it does not address deeper societal issues related to ignorance about HIV/AIDS, stigma and discrimination against PLWHA and AIDS orphans, exploitation and exclusion from governance.

In developing a rights-based programme approach, CARE and its partners and allies are beginning to address these issues, even if funding is directed mainly at short-term health goals. How? CARE's rights-based response to HIV/AIDS extends, through community mapping and action planning[6] and the use of popular theatre and radio, to community awareness raising and dialogue on the conditions and expressed demands of PLWHA, widows and orphans and, through strengthening paralegal capacities and outreach, to the provision of legal aid services for those who have suffered abuses. Such efforts call for longer-term investments and new types of partnerships, but they are critical to defending personal security, engendering community inclusion and solidarity, and assisting marginalized groups' participation in public affairs. Importantly, they also can be sold to donors on the basis of their contribution to the achievement of mainly short-term health results.

From top-down to bottom-up accountability: rights-based monitoring In Gitarama Province, CARE Rwanda is experimenting with a participatory, interactive monitoring tool designed to provide a regular forum for the orphans and vulnerable children (OVC) we serve – approximately 2,250 child-headed households (CHH) across seven districts – to critique our work and to suggest new approaches and directions for our interventions. The pilot tool is designed for the children to hold CARE and others who are, or should be, providing assistance to account. A limited set of questions is asked every four months, confidentially and in a safe environment, of selected children involved in CARE's programme. CARE and local partner representatives will report back each time on how we have taken into account OVC feedback from previous gatherings in current approaches and future plans, with space made for them to critique the steps we have taken. What is unique about this approach is its emphasis on accountability; affording OVC regular opportunities for scrutiny of CARE's and others' actions and committing ourselves to respond, directly to them, is at least an initial attempt to share power and control over the OVC programme. The tool is grounded in a child rights perspective, which is pushing us to respect more fully children's right to be heard and, at the same time, raising our awareness on a broader range of living conditions associated with children's well-being.

In light of the fact that CARE's standard monitoring and evaluation system already collects periodic data on basic social services and economic indicators, we have focused data collection in this complementary pilot initiative on other factors pertaining to children's well-being, such as discrimination, protection and participation. That said, the tool preserves space for the orphans and vulnerable children to raise their own, self-identified priority issues. The first round of testing of this tool – carried out in June and July 2004 – brought out major issues that previously may have been suspected but never systematically tracked and acted upon. Table 3.2 illustrates key issues identified by the children themselves and provides a sense of how CARE is responding.

This pilot approach to monitoring and accounting for the results of our work with orphans and vulnerable children has provided direction to our staff and to local partners and volunteers, and plans are being made to test such an approach in CARE's other programmes across Rwanda.[7]

Challenges and opportunities for rights-based programming

RBA implies a whole new perspective on how international NGOs engage with national civil society and governments. Traditionally, CARE's local civil society partners served essentially as subcontractors and we paid attention mainly to whether they could carry out the required (by CARE) task and little else.[8] We are now looking more deliberately to get behind civil society partners that are genuinely representative of and accountable to the poorest, most marginalized Rwandans and, based on their constituents' priority problems and proposed solutions, are willing to speak out and act on their behalf. We understand this agenda to be central to our RBA and believe poor Rwandans will not be able to lift themselves out of poverty unless and until they can exercise such rights.

By 'speak out', I do not necessarily mean publicly or confrontationally, but with conviction and persistence none the less. This is a major issue in Rwanda, where all too often national CSOs are unwilling to express independent views or positions on public affairs for fear of being perceived to be 'political'.[9] Many such CSOs lack a grassroots base anyway and cannot speak genuinely on behalf of groups they supposedly represent.

An independent CSO has its own constituency and is committed to responding to and representing that constituency. It does not follow blindly what governments are doing but, on the basis of its constituents' views and demands, critically examines and engages governments with the ultimate aim of improving their Rwandan constituents' conditions.

In spite of the Rwandan government's efforts to encourage citizen participation, their appreciation for, indeed tolerance of, critical review is still limited, which affects the degree to which civil society asserts itself. On

TABLE 3.2 Accountability to orphans and vulnerable children in Gitarama Province

Major themes and recommendations	CARE's planned response
Belonging/community relations	
'They do not treat us like other children – they rebuke and beat us; we live alone and no one can protect us', teenage boy	
'They do not treat orphans as human beings; you wonder if you insulted God! In reality, they are jealous because we get assistance from CARE', girl head of household	• Organize, through the OVC programme's advisory committee, discussions with local leaders on vulnerability mapping
	• Develop specific criteria for determining the most vulnerable CHH
• Conduct vulnerability mapping exercises with communities, encouraging all to see OVC as a community problem to which they have to respond together	• Undertake detailed planning of vulnerability mapping exercises and carry them out
• Provide assistance to communities based on participatory analysis and agreement on the most vulnerable	• Organize meetings with donors to promote flexibility in programme implementation – a participatory process for the selection of beneficiaries requires a heavy investment of time and resources
Protection	
'After my parents' death, my paternal uncle took our banana plantation', teenage girl	
'I saw some boy running after a child, having [sexual] relations with her, and threatening that, if she says anything, he will kill her', child, under twelve	

- Conduct child rights training with local authorities and have them present their responsibilities to CHH
- Document cases of property and sexual abuse for advocacy to CHH
- Strengthen links with legal aid providers and facilitate access for victims of abuse
- Continue to sensitize OVC about their rights, the responsibilities of others, and legal recourses

Participation

'CARE involved us because we requested goats [for manure] and CARE gave them to us', boy, head of household

'They [local authorities] do not ask us to tell our problems; they take decisions for us', boy, head of household

- Consult OVC in design and implementation of all project activities
- Educate children on how to involve younger siblings in decision-making
- Hold discussions, in which children have a central voice, with local authorities and communities on the vulnerability of CHH

- Elaborate a child rights training module for CHH within psychosocial training already underway
- Continue child rights training for those authorities who have not yet received such training
- Create partnerships/networks for documenting and communicating abuses
- Initiate and facilitate discussions with responsible actors at different levels to establish procedures to protect CHH

- Organize meetings with CHH associations to discuss their ideas for sustainable development activities (reports to be shared with and taken into account by CARE staff, as much as feasible)
- Educate heads of CHH on the importance of communicating all information they receive through CARE's interventions to their younger siblings and of involving them in household decision-making
- Look to initiate and support mass media communications through which OVC themselves describe their lives and contemplate their futures
- Train local leaders in the rights of the child and help establish forums through which OVC's real needs and priorities are expressed and incorporated into local-level planning processes

TABLE 3.2 Accountability to orphans and vulnerable children in Gitarama Province (continued)

Major themes and recommendations	CARE's planned response
Empowerment	
'If CARE could put children into handicraft schools, we could find jobs ourselves because we want to solve our needs', boy, head of household	
'The authorities could request community assistance to build the houses that collapsed', boy, head of household	
• Continue to respond to immediate needs, strengthening community and government commitment and capacities, while initiating more long-term, sustainable interventions • Strengthen OVC capacities to resolve their own problems • Assist OVC to identify and contribute to addressing the underlying causes of their problems	• Continue food distribution while preparing all except the most vulnerable recipient CHH for phase-out in one year • In the meantime, provide small livestock and agricultural inputs, train CHH further in business literacy and micro-savings and loan (for micro-enterprise) activities, and expand activities designed to increase OVC access to basic education • Encourage and support CHH in the sustainable use of their resources (e.g. land) • Develop an approach/methodology to facilitate OVC identification of the causes of their problems and solutions • Apply the approach within associations of CHH and community volunteer mentors and follow it up with regular monitoring by OVC themselves

the one hand, President Kagame himself has recognized the role of civil society organizations as constructive critics of the government,[10] and, within certain boundaries, there is space for engaging in public affairs. CSOs have engaged in the PRSP process and in the development of national policies relating, for example, to land, education, including civic education, HIV/AIDS and orphans and vulnerable children. On the other hand, organizations pushing more aggressively[11] for changes in government policies, practices and plans, risk crossing the line between being 'constructive' critics and mere critics. If that line is deemed to be crossed, CSOs risk being labelled political opposition, or, even worse, 'divisionist'.[12] Of course, to protect the Rwandan people in a society still deeply scarred by what happened in 1994, the government has an obligation to regulate very tightly any genocidal forces operating in the country. A central challenge in Rwandan society is distinguishing between such extremists and Rwandans in general who, though diverse in their views, want to construct a better future for themselves and their country.

Looking ahead, Rwandans need to transform their largely ethnically-driven, negative perceptions of each other and the social division that festers as a result. An essential way forward in this regard is to open space for honest discussion among Rwandans and between Rwandans and their government on the state of affairs in the country. To nurture this, CARE is supporting civic education and promoting public dialogue and debate. For example, CARE is one of some forty organizations active in Rwanda's Peaceful Coexistence Network. The Coexistence Network was initiated by UNHCR, through its Imagine Coexistence Project, in 2000 and housed at CARE from mid-2002 until early 2004. The Network provides a forum for national and international NGOs, government officials, donors and researchers working in the field of peace and reconciliation to exchange experiences and ideas contributing to the reconstruction and consolidation of a peaceful society in Rwanda. Monthly meetings of the Network seek to create an environment marked by respect for divergent opinions and a spirit of trust and openness in the pursuit of mutual learning and action on behalf of peace and reconciliation, although progress in this direction has been slow, with some authorities showing little tolerance for criticism of government policy and practices.

Working with other Network members, CARE's intention is to foster such fora at decentralized levels, as a way to contribute to popular participation in public affairs, which remains a foreign concept to ordinary Rwandans and their leaders. The government-backed decentralization process offers a real opportunity to advance this vision, even as changing popular attitudes, perceptions and practices, grounded in generations of top-down, authoritarian rule will require a long-term, fundamental change process.

CARE's RBA does not preclude strong working relations with government; in fact, on the contrary, it underscores the importance of building such relations. Even as CARE Rwanda supports the (slowly) emerging civil society in the country, particularly groups representing poor, marginalized Rwandans, it is committed to raising the awareness and strengthening the capacities of public officials to fulfil their human rights and poverty reduction responsibilities. This translates into more regular, honest engagement on the conditions of poor, marginalized Rwandans and what actions need to be taken by the government, with assistance from CARE and others, to advance a culture of human rights and sustained progress towards rights realization and the reduction of poverty. Ultimately, RBA holds the potential for deeper, more meaningful, collaboration with government, at times seeking to persuade responsible authorities to do the right thing and, where mutual commitment is there, striving together to achieve shared goals.

CARE recognizes that poor people's realization of their human rights is a monumental, long-term challenge. RBA calls, necessarily, for a sustained, collective effort on the part of a range of concerned actors. Thus, CARE seeks to build coalitions and alliances for rights realization, as is being done currently with like-minded organizations – including government ministries (for gender and the promotion of the family, education, etc.) – dedicated to putting in place a rights-based strategy and action plan supporting the hundreds of thousands of orphans and vulnerable children in Rwanda.

Final reflections

What lessons can be gleaned from CARE Rwanda's experience integrating RBA? The most important overall lesson is that integrating RBA takes time, especially in a polarized society still struggling to overcome conflict and construct independent civic space. Even in a more favourable country environment, RBA integration is not easy. For one, major institutional funding of development NGOs comes through 'project' windows. NGOs like CARE implement a series of projects for their respective donors. Each project is a self-contained unit, with its particular design, budget and reporting requirements. The project-based system of development aid breeds tubularity, with little space for synergy and broader, more strategic thinking across interventions. It also breeds insularity, as different NGOs implement 'their' different projects largely in their own worlds. The result is that the kind of collective, multidimensional approaches needed to attack the roots of poverty, including the denial of rights, are difficult to piece together in practice. At another level, donor governments and their tax-paying constituents increasingly want to see immediate, tangible pay-offs from their investments. The result is pressure for rapid-fire results that generally discourage reflection and longer-term efforts to change the more fundamental structures and systems underlying persistent poverty and rights deprivation. All of these factors work against a rights-based programme approach. To place development programmes in a longer-term, rights framework requires transcending short-term timelines, 'output' (as opposed to impact) thinking and project boxes.

Above and beyond these broader, systemic issues, the Rwandan context is particularly resistant to rights-based change, in spite of not insignificant political will. Even as stated policies and priorities of the Rwandan government have changed in pro-rights and pro-poor directions in the last several years, deeply entrenched social and political systems and practices remain largely the same. Hierarchical leadership, passive acceptance of the status quo, and a culture of silence, rumours and mistrust, are not conducive to pro-rights change. Deep societal divisions colour every Rwandan's view of the world and choices about with whom to relate and how. Politically, they fuel government suspicion, thereby limiting civic space and at least the short-term prospects for participatory, rights-based development. Full adoption and effective implementation of RBA to development will take time, as well as considerable political acumen, diplomacy and personal conviction and courage in the Rwandan context.

Even while we recognize that change takes time and persistence, there are a few additional lessons to guide CARE and others' approaches. One key to success is to find and get behind progressive thinkers and change agents, both on the staff and in the wider society. The old maxim about strength in numbers is critical in contexts such as Rwanda, and real rights-based change can be moved forward only by passionate, bright and courageous people working together. Thus, efforts to build national staff commitment and coalitions and alliances among like-minded organizations are essential.

Another key to success is to exploit windows of opportunity furnished by the government. Rwanda has seen some very positive policy development over the past few years, including the PRSP, the democratization and decentralization policies, most provisions of the new constitution, and specific legislation covering women's rights and the rights and protection of children. This pro-rights and pro-poor legal and policy framework provides a solid basis from which to pursue rights-based development in Rwanda. One can debate the depth and breadth of government commitment to such policy developments, many of which came into being with a strong push and extensive technical assistance from the international donor community. Still, the legal and policy framework is in place to make real rights and poverty reduction progress. All too often, policies and laws are passed without adequate follow-up. Rights-based development organizations should help to focus everyone's attention on the commitments made in pro-poor, pro-rights legislation and encourage and assist, by demonstrating practical approaches that work, their fulfilment. Of course, one has to appreciate the magnitude of the task in a country like Rwanda; still, real if incremental progress towards rights realization should be expected by all involved.

Another key lesson from CARE Rwanda's experience is that lower-profile, more local-level actions to empower poor, marginalized people to develop their full potential and stand up for and contribute to their development are less threatening than higher-profile, national-level work on behalf of human rights and poverty reduction. This is especially true in countries with politically controlled environments. The point here is not so much that decentralized action is further from the radar screen of national governments but that major progress at national level cannot be constructed without a foundation – and a foundation can be built only from the bottom up, through long-term investments in changing social attitudes, perceptions and practices, and corresponding political institutions. Starting small is not an excuse for avoiding major, underlying causes of poverty. The ultimate aim of RBA has to be systemic change, independent of external support, that achieves lasting gains in human rights and poverty reduction.

Finally, no matter where NGOs/CSOs applying RBA choose to intervene, risk assessment and management become supremely important. CARE Rwanda's experience shows that transparency, regular communications and relationship building with leaders are essential. Proactive engagement helps to minimize misunderstandings, smooth over potential differences of opinion, and not just avoid trouble but strengthen shared commitment to rights and poverty reduction goals.

In conclusion, the pilot application of RBA is central to CARE Rwanda's change strategy, allowing us to test what works in practice. While the theory has been clear for some time now in CARE Rwanda and the wider development world, appropriate and workable ways for putting the theory into practice have been much harder to pinpoint. Experimentation leads to 'demonstration plots' that CARE staff and other development actors can observe and draw inspiration from, refining their thinking and future actions in the process.

Notes

1 CARE has taken the view that all development actors have an obligation to respect and foster human dignity and rights. Whereas state actors, including national governments and multilateral government agencies (i.e. the World Bank, European Union), have legal obligations to respect, protect and fulfil human rights, CARE's view is that, as moral beings, we are all obliged to respect each other's rights and to do our utmost to assist their protection and fulfilment. This reflects CARE's view that human rights represent more than just a legal code; more fundamentally, they represent an ethical framework for human relations.

2 It may be helpful to consider two approaches. The first could be termed a *'violations'* and the second a *'promotional'* approach. The former focuses on denouncing violations of human rights and on enforcement through legal remedies. The latter emphasizes positive ways to engage governments, important non-state actors, civil society organizations and poor marginalized communities themselves in the pursuit of rights through education, dialogue and advocacy. While both of these approaches are necessary, CARE generally is adopting the latter, promotional approach. In any case, CARE country offices worldwide are grappling, to one degree or another in a range of contexts, to put these characteristics into practice (Jones 2000a).

3 For many development agencies, a human rights approach has become central to their policies and plans in recent years. That said, the level of awareness and (especially) ownership of such approaches in the field varies considerably. On the whole, my sense is that official policy pronouncements from home offices in 'the North' barely filter down to decision-makers on the ground and thus scarcely influence their actions. In other words, changes on paper, even seemingly radical changes, can all too easily amount to the same wine in new wineskins.

4 How can I be so sure that emerging leaders are not simply following to gain the favour of senior management? My assertion is necessarily impressionistic and perhaps somewhat wishful; I have, after all, invested a lot of my time over the past couple years in this! That said, one development that supports the assertion is that I have observed ambassadors challenging CARE's internal policies and practices and pushing for them to be better aligned with human rights principles, which is a relatively confrontational and risky business. Such courage and energy would not be exhibited without heart-felt commitment.

5 For an abbreviated version developed for CARE Rwanda staff, see Jones (2004).

6 Community mapping refers to a participatory and inclusive process through which representatives from all segments of society – including government and especially vulnerable and marginalized groups – come together at local level to analyse the underlying causes of their HIV/AIDS-related vulnerabilities and the responsibilities they all have to address those causes. Action planning refers to the planning process that follows such analysis, through which various actors agree to intervene in complementary ways to reduce or at least mitigate their communities' vulnerability to the causes and consequences of HIV/AIDS.

7 The potential for advocacy based on the results of such monitoring efforts is clear and already being realized informally. CARE Rwanda also sees this as an opportunity to promote more systematic monitoring of OVC conditions by government at all levels.

8 This, of course, all too often reflects our own mere subcontractual relationship with donor agencies.

9 Even as an international NGO with member organizations predominantly in much freer, Northern societies, CARE is only slowly evolving to assert its independence from donor governments and challenge policies and practices that are detrimental to poor people around the world. The evolution in this direction is essential to our 'walking the talk'.

10 See, for example, Maina and Kibalam (2004: 71), citing an 8 August 2002 speech by President Kagame.

11 In other words, confrontationally – in this day and age in Rwanda, the government is not receptive to anything other than a low-profile, collaborative approach.

12 Rwanda's new constitution guarantees free thought, opinion and speech but, at the same time, forbids 'all propaganda of an ethnic, regional, racial *or divisive* character' (see Arts 34–35). What constitutes 'divisive propaganda' is left undefined. Rwandan CSOs alleged to be divisive are at great risk and inevitably have to curtail their activities. International agencies (including CARE) have been accused of contributing to ethnic division as well, for supporting allegedly divisive Rwandan groups.

References

Ambler, J. (2002) *The Programme Strategy Paper*, unpublished draft, November (CARE).

Jones, A. (2000a) 'Rights-based Relief and Development Assistance: An Essay on What It Means for CARE', in A. Frankovits and P. Earle (eds), *Working Together: The Human Rights-based Approach to Development Cooperation, Stockholm Workshop, 16–19 October 2000*, report prepared by the Human Rights Council of Australia for SIDA, the Swedish Ministry for Foreign Affairs and the Swedish NGO Foundation for Human Rights <www.hrca.org.au/activities.htm#Development>

— (2000b) *Rights Approach and Causal–Responsibility Analysis*, unpublished (CARE).

— (2004) *Guidelines for the Development of Rights-based Programmes*, unpublished (CARE Rwanda).

Maina, P. C. and E. Kibalama (eds) (2004) *Searching for Sense and Humanity: Civil Society and the Struggle for a Better Rwanda*, draft, report of a fact-finding mission, commissioned by SIDA (Kituo Cha Katiba – East African Centre for Constitutional Development).

4 | Rights in practice – assessing the impact of rights-based training in Uganda

PAMELA ASHANUT OKILLE

... as we let our own light shine, we unconsciously give other people permission to do the same. (President Nelson Mandela, inaugural speech, 1994)

There is increasing international attention focused on the importance of human rights to development, more specifically, a recognition that pure service delivery has not resulted in sustainable change, so there is a need to shift to a more demand-driven and rights-oriented approach. The idea of addressing human rights and bringing about lasting change in structures that contribute to the entrenchment of poverty is not new. However, there have been a few successful efforts to integrate these ideas into programmes and activities aimed at poverty reduction. There are some examples, but the challenge is to articulate and translate these so that they can be understood and made useful in various contexts.

In Uganda, as in other developing countries, key donors and the government have recognized the central role that human rights play in relation to poverty eradication and development. In response, various initiatives are being implemented to promote and generate discussion among civil society organizations and government agencies, on the relationship between human rights and development, and what this means in practice.

Between 2002 and 2004, eighty-six women and men attended a course entitled Applying Human Rights to Governance and Development. Developed by the Danish International Development Agency (DANIDA), through its Human Rights and Good Governance Programme (HUGGO) in Uganda, and the International Law Institute, Uganda (ILI-U), this course provides space for the participants to discuss the dual role of civil society – advocacy and service delivery – and to explore how these roles can be enhanced through the application of the rights-based approach (RBA) to development. The course targets civil society organizations (CSOs) that operate at district level, within a decentralized system of governance and therefore deals with realities at the local level. Recipients of this training include national CSOs, district-based CSOs and local government officials. The initial training was carried out in 2002, followed by a national training course in 2003 and district-based trainings in late 2003 and early 2004. The course is arranged under four modules that cover human rights (including national and international legal frameworks), civil society, the RBA to development, and CSO roles under the decentralization framework.

After three years of application, HUGGO and ILI-U decided to study the impact of the course. In addition to exploring the overall impact of the training and methodologies applied, the study also examines the participants' understandings of human rights and particularly RBA in practice, thus contributing to ongoing national and international discussions and debates on the efficacy of the approach. A study was thus commissioned in May 2004 to assist the exploration of the aforementioned issues. The methodology used was administration of a questionnaire and follow-up discussions/interviews, as well as a study of available documentation on the course.

The study and this chapter are a result of conversations and interactions with forty-nine women and men who work in east, west and central Uganda. The teachers, doctors, lawyers, accountants, NGO workers and journalists who experienced this training have given us the opportunity to share their lives, their work and to hear stories of their courage, perseverance and optimism. This chapter reflects these conversations and offers a glimpse of the impact that applying human rights can have, providing encouragement in a situation where most perceptions of the viability of rights are rather negative. It therefore offers insights on possibilities and opportunities to be built upon in future initiatives, and in so doing will inspire those who are doing human rights work to let their light shine too.[1]

Perceptions and understandings of human rights

In response to a question on specific new topics learnt, 58 per cent of the responses focused on the area of human rights. Of these, 72 per cent were exposed to learning in the area of international human rights instruments, including the African mechanisms (African Charter on Human and Peoples' Rights and its implementing organ the African Commission), for the first time. Of much interest were the enforcement mechanisms, and how relevant they are to the Ugandan context, as well as knowledge of instruments that the Ugandan government has ratified. Four responses identified new learning in linking the Ugandan constitution to international instruments, and the awareness that CSOs can appeal against human rights violations using the constitution and international instruments. One female participant expressed awareness and exposure to women's rights for the first time, as follows: 'As a woman, I did not know that there are rights for me.'

Fifty-two per cent of the respondents indicated that their perspectives of local government, specifically in the area of accountability, had changed, and that they now understood that local government officials as duty bearers had a high level of accountability. One respondent, specifically referring to accountability in planning and budgeting processes, stated that, '[w]e have the right to participate in budget processes; they [local government] should not plan for us'. Twenty-five per cent of these responses focused on a new perspective that local government officials should be considered as partners of CSOs, and highlighted the importance of local government and CSOs working together for development. One respondent stated: 'I thought that the local government had nothing to do with CSOs but now I know they need to work together for development.' Another 21 per cent emphasized the need for local governments to be more conscious of rights and to integrate the RBA to development in their work. Further changes in perspectives included the recognition of central government as a duty bearer and therefore as ultimately responsible for the rights of citizens.

Eighteen per cent of the responses mentioned that they had realized the importance of CSOs working together in order to attain their common objective of respect for human rights. Thirteen per cent of the responses on CSOs focused on the recognition of the importance of accountability of CSOs to their constituents.

Twelve per cent of the respondents indicated new topics directly related to the concept of the RBA to development. The distinction between duty bearers and rights holders was a new area. One response stated that '[h]uman rights need to be given priority to enhance development', and another that '[d]evelopment is people-oriented and so people should be consulted'. In response to questions that sought to explore their understanding and perception of RBA, the responses can be divided into seven main categories: (i) 13 per cent indicated that RBA highlighted the importance of participation, one respondent stating, 'I have understood the need to avoid token participation', and in terms of the relationship between rights and methodology for participation, '[I am] more sharpened on rights and how to approach the masses'; (ii) 6 per cent indicated that RBA highlighted the importance of participation in government development processes; (iii) 26 per cent responded that RBA means and requires increased consciousness of the rights of others and confidence to challenge rights violations; (iv) 37 per cent pointed out that RBA means human rights are part of development, and therefore, as one respondent stated '[d]evelopment strategies should not hinder human rights'; (v) 6 per cent linked RBA to the importance of dealing with political issues; (vi) service delivery was seen as an obligation, as one respondent commented, 'I come to realize that service delivery to the country is an obligation and a privilege so much that the country doesn't need to merit it, they deserve it by right, and no conditions should be applied'; (vii) RBA as information flow and advocacy.

The boxes below contain stories that capture some of the different perceptions and understandings.

Box 4.1 Rights at work

Nasta works with the AIDS Support Organization (TASO) in Mbale. The Mbale TASO branch is a model office in Uganda in terms of management and successful operations, and Nasta is proud to be one of the team that does so well. She told us that before she attended the ILI-U course she firmly believed, like many in NGOs, that what mattered was attainment of targets and outputs within a given time-frame. So, as the person in charge of the counselling section, she used to demand results from her staff without any concern for staff interests and issues. As a result, her relationship with her team was characterized by lack of openness and dialogue. However, after attending the course she has become more flexible in her approach to dealing with staff. She states: 'I appreciate RBA in relation to management and understand it this way, that as organizations run there is a framework within which they must view the people they work with. All the staff have rights, they are individuals in their own right – there are some slow performers, fast ones and others need to be motivated.' Nasta enjoys a better working relationship with her staff and strives to ensure that staff in all circumstances have the right to be heard.

Box 4.2 RBA and programming

Emmanuel is a member of the Rwenzori Anti-Corruption Coalition in western Uganda. In a discussion on his perception of RBA, he stated: 'I see the RBA as encompassing everybody and touching on basic rights such as that to food, shelter and health. The RBA helped me recognize that one is born with these rights and they are not given.' He further elaborated that 'because of the RBA training, I now know that before any development programme there is a need to identify the rights to be fulfilled and how people will benefit. After assessing the development programmes against the rights, the beneficiaries can determine whether the programme will help them or not.'

What has been done differently?

All the participants were affected differently by the course and applied the information gained in their lives and workplaces in accordance with their designated roles and responsibilities. Seventy-two per cent of respondents indicated that they had done something differently as a result of the training. Ultimately, the course was able to create shifts in the mind-sets and attitudes of the participants. These shifts have been manifested in the way they relate to their families, other people, their colleagues, duty bearers and their constituents.

For instance, 80 per cent of the respondents indicated a change in their attitudes towards their families, particularly their children and wives, who are now considered to have equal rights, notably the right to be heard. One particularly pointed out that '[r]ights and governance should start with the family', and another stated that he had realized that 'respect for individual rights can boost the self-esteem of each member of the family'.

Fourteen per cent mentioned increased confidence and capacity to train others in human rights-related issues, and 20 per cent indicated increased confidence to take action on matters of rights concern, including in the following instances: demanding a list of tender awards from the district administration; confronting police about corruption; helping people to come out of police custody without paying a bribe; resolving conflicts among women voters; and an increasing ability to demand one's own rights. Twenty-two per cent indicated changes in personal development that had led them into doing some things differently, such as acquiring email, reading more and attending more rights-related activities. Sixteen percent stated that they had generally increased interest in government programmes, while 28 per cent of the responses indicated things done differently in their organizations, with heavy emphasis on the use of participatory planning.

The examples in the boxes below (pp. 104–6) overlap with those cited above to indicate that changes were not just in perceptions, understandings and values, but also extended to changes in practice.

Challenges/obstacles to applying RBA

Since most of the respondents related the application of RBA at district level to their capacity and ability to influence and engage with local government officials, many of them (25 per cent) indicated the lack of commitment by local government as a key challenge. This is particularly reflected through the local government not having time for them because of a busy schedule and other commitments. It was specifically mentioned that 'local governments are too busy attending workshops on the Poverty Eradication Action Plan (PEAP), Local Government Development Plans (LGDP), etc.'.

Box 4.3 Improved dialogue and listening

Rosemary is the deputy head teacher of ADRA Primary School in Mbale. She stated that she has been able to apply the insights and knowledge from the course to her school situation through having more dialogue with the pupils, i.e. giving them a right to be heard. Formerly there was a communication gap between teachers and pupils. This is what Rosemary referred to as a 'more dictatorial approach to learning' in which 'you would sit on a teacher and the teacher would in turn sit on the children'. However, she has created more space and time to meet and discuss with teachers, who have in turn been more open to listening to their pupils and the result is that the children feel freer to express themselves. Rosemary understands RBA to be 'giving a platform to an individual and the individual knowing and exercising their rights towards sustainable development'.

Box 4.4 Applying RBA to policy and legislation

Bernard works at the Ministry of Gender, Labour and Social Development and attended the course in 2003. He has had various opportunities to use the information gained from the course since then in his work. One of his great achievements so far is his work in spearheading and ensuring the drafting of the proposed Equal Opportunities Bill and policy that are currently before cabinet. In his words, these documents are 'fully rights sensitive'. As a result of this and other contributions he has made on RBA, he has been co-opted on various policy task forces, most recently on the one drafting an adult literacy policy, and he is specifically charged with working on the policy guidelines and the policy and legal framework, all of which will need to be 'rights sensitive'.

Bernard has participated in and facilitated CSO training workshops on RBA, participated in radio talk shows and workshops on the right to health, and in a case study on best practices on RBA that assessed the work of his ministry. In his view, RBA is a tool that empowers individual and communities. He thinks the key ingredient to ensuring the application of RBA is to create paradigm shifts, so that people stop perceiving others as recipients of services, but as rights holders who have a say in what they are provided.

Box 4.5 RBA and women's rights

According to Margaret, a member of KALI (Karambi Action for Life Improvement), a community-based organization in Kabarole, western Uganda, 'the RBA opened my eyes to specific rights of women. I came to realize that rights are free and are for all.' Margaret is a local councillor and her efforts have mainly focused on advocating for the rights of children and women. When local council budgets are being drawn up, she ensures that issues of concern to women and children are included in the budget.[2]

She asserts: 'I am more confident and know that I should not be unduly harassed. For example, I have to ride a motorcycle to do my work and I used to be afraid of traffic policemen. After the training I now know that if a policeman demands to see my permit I have forty-eight hours within which to produce it and that I can present it at any police station. I have also been able to sensitize other motorists of this. I can challenge anyone who infringes on my rights. I have full capacity.'

Margaret also said that 'as a woman I have grown up knowing that when a man divorces you, all you can do is pack up your belongings and go. Now I know that women too have rights to property and can demand a share of the property. I will give you the example of a woman in my village who was married officially. After several years of marriage her husband decided to divorce her and send her away with nothing. I spoke to her about her rights and referred her to the constitution as well as helped her approach Legal Aid who are now assisting her present her case in court. I am confident she will win the case and get compensation from her husband.'

Another respondent mentioned that the leaders felt challenged by them and insinuated that they were politicking and interfering with their work. This was also alluded to by two other respondents who emphasized that they are perceived as people who were stirring up trouble as follows: 'Some local leaders are blaming us for opening the people's minds about human rights.' A female respondent mentioned that 'people complained that these women would be big-headed'.

Another group of respondents pointed to organizational barriers from bosses and workmates who do not appreciate RBA. This means that while they believe in ensuring that human rights are mainstreamed into their

---

Box 4.6 Using rights language

George, also a member of the Rwenzori Anti-Corruption Coalition, has been using 'rights language' in his interactions with the authorities and said that '[w]henever a policeman senses that you have some knowledge of your rights they will treat you with more respect and will not intimidate or harass you. For instance, whenever I ask a policeman, "Please officer, can I know your number?" he senses that he might get in trouble later if he is up to anything funny, and usually will not pursue a request for a bribe.'

George stated that he is also more confident in seeking justice. Recently, someone who didn't know how to drive drove into his aunt's house. The matter was reported to the police and the car impounded. However, both the car and driver were released and the police seemed to lose interest in the case. He has taken up this matter on behalf of his aunt and asked the police to ensure the case is followed up and his aunt compensated.

He believes RBA works, and says that 'we are now able to demand and assert our rights. We who were trained are even sensitizing others. The RBA should be improved by sensitizing others as well.'

---

organization's programmes, this is not a view shared by other members of the organization.

Twenty-three per cent of the respondents mentioned ignorance about human rights among people at the grassroots as a key challenge. One specifically mentioned that 'grassroots partners find it hard to conceptualize rights'. One participant pointed out that there is a 'not possible' attitude among the community. This is particularly challenging because members of the community need to appreciate the value of human rights before they can respect these rights, as well as demand the fulfilment of their rights.

It was also pointed out that it is difficult to get people to congregate and listen to messages on human rights because people do not gather unless they are assured of money for their transport or lunch. It is particularly challenging for the respondents who are keen to share the knowledge they acquired, and yet they do not have any funding for such costs.

Conclusion and recommendations

The training was relevant and has been able to influence attitudes and mind-sets which are at the centre of human rights work, i.e. the values and belief systems. People have been able to apply RBAs in their lives and work to varying degrees. The challenge is to provide support to sustain this momentum, and work on providing other people with the opportunity to experience and benefit from the training. Among the specific recommendations made for the course were the following:

1. The great interest and appreciation of the module on human rights legislation and enforcement mechanisms may indicate that the respondents have observed a way to enforce respect for human rights and hold duty bearers accountable for human rights. However, the judicial and social/political environment may not augur well for the justiciable approach, the training should therefore emphasize the search for alternatives, 'home-grown' alternative ways of ensuring accountability that can work within the participants' specific contexts.

2. The training should have a follow-up module that further explores the challenges of applying RBA. This module should build upon the participants' experiences in applying RBA. It should also include a component on power relations and how they are manifested, particularly in the relationship between local government and CSOs. The area of gender analysis can provide insights on how to analyse and address power relations.

3. Many of the respondents related RBA to participation, and more specifically participation of the grassroots, the most vulnerable and those who are often discriminated against. This may be an area worth exploring further through questions such as: Who are the poor and vulnerable in given situations? How are they identified? CARE International and the Community Development Resource Network, in Uganda, have carried out research in this area.

4. Not all the respondents participated in the action planning session of the training and, even then, no mechanism was put in place for review and follow up of these plans. ILI-U should consider providing follow-up support to trainees, and encourage participants from the same locality or working on similar issues to provide support to one another.

Notes

1 This chapter is an abbreviated version of a report of a study carried out for DANIDA HUGGO, and the ILU-U, entitled *Rights in Practice: Exploring the Possibilities and Opportunities that Applying RBA Presents* (September 2004).

2 Local councils consist of elected representatives and are a structure within the local government system.

5 | Using rights to address conflict – a valuable synergy

GHALIB GALANT AND MICHELLE PARLEVLIET

A hooded prisoner perched atop a crate with electric wires attached to his genitals; flies buzzing around the hungry mouth of a malnourished baby somewhere in Africa; international demonstrators squaring off to shielded police officers and water cannons in wealthy and well-developed streets; election posters urging the electorate to keep out the foreigners who steal 'our jobs', 'our houses', 'our women'; a youth launching a stone at a tank while a helicopter gunship hovers menacingly just out of reach; a spouse cowering in a corner amid shards of broken crockery while a baby's screams compete with the blaring radio; striking workers chanting demands for a living wage on a hot pavement while luxury sedans glide past in air-conditioned comfort.

These images of conflict beset us on a daily basis through various media. Despite their regularity, they can still disturb or make us think of ways to address the situation, especially if we work in development, humanitarian assistance, human rights or conflict management.[1] In the short term, human rights activists would seek to right injustice perpetrated against victims; conflict management practitioners would seek to end the physical violence and get the parties to talk with each other in order to find a mutually acceptable solution; and humanitarian actors would want to attend to the humanitarian needs of the displaced and affected.

Press them for their vision of a long-term solution, and, using different words perhaps, they are likely to paint a similar picture of conditions allowing people to live out their potential fully, in a society based on justice, equality and dignity. The human rights actor might emphasize the rule of law, a legitimate system of governance and full expression of individual and group rights. The conflict management practitioner might talk of a just peace where conflict is managed without resorting to violence, underlying causes are addressed and parties' needs and interests are met. The development worker might replace the humanitarian agent in the long term, highlighting the establishment of socio-economic conditions that allow human development to take place.

Thus, in different ways, these various actors may all work towards a long-term objective that could be called 'sustainable peace'. Locked within this notion are the absence of violence, the presence of healthy relationships, mechanisms to manage conflict constructively, socio-economic and political justice, and conditions for long-term development.

At times, a tension is perceived to exist between human rights and conflict management, especially in situations where rights have been breached. In such instances, the question may arise whether to prioritize upholding the law by holding those responsible for such breaches accountable for their actions by, for example, criminal prosecutions; or whether to focus on seeking to reconcile the interests of the parties concerned and find a solution acceptable to all, including those who violated rights standards.[2] Other tensions between human rights and conflict management may relate to actors' roles in and approaches to conflict situations. For example, it would be difficult to act as an independent mediator or facilitator in a conflict situation, trying to facilitate dialogue and eventually agreement between parties, if one were at the same time also criticizing one of the parties involved. The advocacy, lobbying and speaking out that is often part and parcel of human rights work, may not be easily reconciled with the independence and impartiality sought by conflict management practitioners in conflict situations, based on the desire to be accepted as credible and legitimate interveners by the parties involved.

Notwithstanding these possible tensions, this chapter will focus on the relationship between human rights and conflict management based on the idea that actors in these areas have a common interest in promoting sustainable peace with justice.[3] Other intersections suggested above – with development and humanitarian assistance – also merit examination but are beyond the scope of this chapter. The chapter will explore how an understanding of human rights and their impact on conflict may make conflict management interventions both more effective and more sustainable.[4] This chapter is based on the work and publications of the Human Rights and Conflict Management Programme (HRCMP) of the South Africa-based Centre for Conflict Resolution (CCR) (Parlevliet 2002, 2004; Maloka 2002).

We will first consider six analytical propositions about the relationship between human rights and conflict management, which form a conceptual framework for our efforts to link these two fields in theory and practice. Afterwards, we will discuss different dimensions of rights that assist in operationalizing a rights-based approach to conflict management. Three case studies will serve as illustrations of how the ideas have been applied in practice.

Six propositions[5]

1. *Human rights abuses are both symptoms and causes of violent conflict* Violent and destructive conflict can lead to gross human rights violations, yet can also result from a sustained denial of human rights over a period of time. In other words, human rights abuses can be both causes and consequences, or symptoms, of violent conflict. The relevance of the distinction between rights violations as causes or symptoms is that it helps those seeking to intervene in their identification of the problem to be addressed and the desired outcome. If human rights violations *result from* destructive conflict, the objective is to protect people from further abuses; the outcome pursued is the cessation of hostilities and an end to physical violence. If, however, rights violations are *causing* such conflict, the main objective of activities by both human rights and conflict management actors is to reduce the level of structural violence through the transformation of the structural, systemic conditions that give rise to violent conflict in society. The outcome would entail the presence of political and socio-economic equality, and the development of mechanisms that can manage conflict in non-violent, constructive ways.

2. *A sustained denial of human rights is a structural cause of high-intensity conflict because basic human needs are not met* From a conflict management perspective, a denial of human rights over a period of time may lead to destructive conflict because it involves the frustration of basic human needs. Defined differently in various disciplines, basic human needs are seen in conflict management as universal motivations that are an integral part of human beings and are both material and non-material. Relating to security, welfare, identity and freedom, human needs are generally non-negotiable. They are fundamental to human survival, subsistence and development, which means that people will seek to meet those needs – preferably peacefully but, in certain circumstances, possibly violently (Burton 1990).

Human needs, such as subsistence, security and participation, can be satisfied through human rights; the implementation of rights ensures that people's needs are met (Galtung and Wirak 1977.) If people's needs are consistently not fulfilled through a sustained denial of their rights, it can become a structural cause of violent conflict because the frustration of needs tends to be embedded in structures of governance, in terms of how the state is organized, institutions operate and society functions.[6]

The potential to enhance and deepen analysis of structural, systemic factors that underlie societal or communal instability and violence, that are invisible at first sight, can thus inform the focus and design of an intervention and one's choice of strategies. The relationship between rights and needs may also prompt a conflict management practitioner to consider what needs are at stake for the parties in conflict, and how developing a rights framework would allow for those needs to be satisfied.

3. *Institutionalized respect for human rights and the structural accommodation of diversity is a primary form of conflict prevention* If the sustained denial of rights can be a structural cause of high-intensity conflict, it follows that a sustained protection of rights is essential for addressing or pre-empting structural risk factors. Institutionalizing respect for rights may entail, for example, the inclusion of a Bill of Rights in the constitution, securing the independence of the judiciary, establishing an independent human rights commission, facilitating equal access to employment, education and healthcare and so on.

Accommodating diversity warrants specific attention in this regard, considering the central role of identity in intra-state conflicts – identity is often a primary point round which protagonists mobilize (Nathan 2000). Accommodation of diversity must go beyond mere recognition of the formal equality between various groups in society. Non-discrimination must take into account the relative position of the people or groups in order to effect substantive equality.

This proposition thus highlights the value of human rights standards and institutions as tools for conflict management and prevention. Institutionalizing respect for rights also generally means that mechanisms are developed within the state and society that can manage conflict constructively.

4. *The prescriptive approach of human rights actors must be combined with the facilitative approach of conflict management practitioners for the effective and sustainable resolution of intra-state conflict* The human rights perspective tends to be concerned with substantive issues related to the distribution of political power and economic resources, security and identity. In the context of negotiation and conflict management processes, this generally translates into a prescriptive approach towards the outcome or product of negotiations: it must be in line with human rights standards and must embrace constitutionalism and the legal protection of rights. Conflict management practitioners, on the other hand, generally adopt a more facilitative approach towards the outcome. They tend to focus more on a particular kind of process – one that is aimed at establishing dialogue, developing relationships and building trust between the parties. This is based on an awareness that the quality, legitimacy and sustainability of the outcome depends on the process used to achieve it.

Contrary to those who see the relationship between conflict management and human rights as an irreconcilable tension, this proposition underscores the complementary nature of both perspectives. In intervention processes, both outcome and process should be given due consideration – one needs to be conscious of the type of outcome to be pursued, and the type of process that will support it.

5. *Conflict management can function as an alternative to litigation in dealing with rights-related conflicts* Within conflict management, different approaches for dealing with conflict may be distinguished. A widely used categorization is that of power-based, rights-based and interest-based approaches to conflict. The first approach entails the exercise of power over a weaker party; the second is based on the use of standards of justice and fairness such as an organization's or society's laws, norms and values to determine who is right or the legitimacy of a party's claim; and the third approach seeks to reconcile the interests, needs and differences of parties through negotiation and consensus (Ury et al. 1988: 7–15). Each of these types of approaches has certain advantages and disadvantages.

In addressing rights-related conflicts, we tend to think immediately of rights-based methods, and litigation is indeed a primary strategy to ensure that human rights are protected. However, interest-based methods such as mediation and negotiation can also assist parties to reach lasting solutions that are respectful of rights. They may also facilitate balancing conflicting rights; if the rights of parties are in conflict, such processes can assist in reaching outcomes that meet both parties' needs and interests while remaining within a rights framework.

This proposition highlights how litigation and mediation can be seen as options on a *spectrum of conflict management processes* available to interveners concerned with addressing rights-related conflict. It implies that, in each case, actors must carefully consider the different approaches available and determine which is most suitable.

6. *Whereas human rights and justice are per se non-negotiable, the application and interpretation of rights and justice are negotiable within the context of a negotiated settlement* Human rights and justice are often seen as absolute concepts. Rights reflect internationally and/or nationally agreed-upon norms of behaviour between individuals, groups of people, and between the state and its citizens; they set the parameters for the management of conflict. However, within this framework, there is great scope for variation in how rights are realized, in terms of, for example, the form of government and constitutional arrangements.

The relevance of this proposition is that it highlights how implementation of rights may differ from context to context, even if the fundamental rights standards remain the same across the board. Thus, working within a human rights framework allows for the specific political, historical and cultural conditions to be taken into account in designing mechanisms for protecting rights and constructive conflict management in local contexts.

Synergy between human rights and conflict management The above propositions underscore the relevance of looking at human rights and conflict management in conjunction. They suggest that a synergy exists between human rights and conflict management perspectives and approaches that can strengthen efforts geared towards long-term sustainable peace as insights, skills and practices from the one field can strengthen activities in the other field. Conflict management practitioners can benefit from the rights perspective in terms of deepening their analysis of conflict situations, the delineation of what is possible in a particular context in terms of the rights framework, and the focus on structuring long-term and systemic solutions. Thus, grasping the human rights dimension in conflicts can help to make conflict management more sustainable. At the same time, human rights actors can derive value from conflict management by developing an awareness of the importance of process and the range of approaches available to address conflict, including interest-based approaches, and by developing skills to engage with parties in a constructive, non-adversarial way. Clearly, within a human rights framework, there is much scope for dialogue, negotiation and accommodation in dealing with conflicts.

These propositions, moreover, do not hold true only for large-scale conflict, even though they are easily illustrated with reference to intense conflict situations such as Rwanda, the Democratic Republic of Congo, Sudan, Bosnia, Iraq and Afghanistan. The ideas contained in them are also relevant for smaller-scale, community-based conflict or in working with particular bodies that operate at the intersection of human rights and conflict management, such as national human rights commissions, ombudsman's offices, or non-governmental organizations involved in rights monitoring and crisis intervention.[7] Also, in working with this conceptual framework over a period of time, we have come to realize that a narrow, legalistic interpretation of rights is insufficient to capture in real, practical terms the importance of rights for conflict management; it provides little guidance for operationalizing how rights can be integrated meaningfully in conflict management processes. Subsequently, in exploring with different audiences how rights affect them beyond being an abstract notion, we have discerned a number of dimensions of rights that seem useful in making rights practically relevant. They help us think about and plan our interventions in a more structured and strategic way (Parlevliet 2004).

Dimensions of rights in addressing conflict

Rights as rules This is the most obvious way to think of rights. Rights as rules can be found in a constitution, legislation, contracts, agreements, even in something as tenuous as custom and practice. When it is claimed that a substantive right has been violated, it is this dimension of rights which is being referred to.

Rights as rules provide the framework within which interactions between people take place. By being part of a local, national or international community, we have accepted that a certain rules framework exists and that it is better in the long term that collectively we obey them for the stability of the society of which we are a part. Consequently, these rules must frame the interventions that practitioners undertake. In order for any settlement of issues to last and not be open to challenge, it must fall within the legal framework (the rules). This applies even if parties themselves may be comfortable with a solution that does not uphold these rules. As noted above, breaches of this rules framework may lead to further conflict, because they risk rendering certain actions or processes illegitimate, as the invasion of Iraq illustrates. The rules framework might also point to the range of possible solutions within specific conflict situations as rights standards often delineate for parties the allowable solutions – while still permitting parties to fashion their own solution(s) within those parameters.

The rules dimension of rights thus highlights the need to take the substantive rights of parties into account in conflict management processes. Often, conflict management practitioners in communal conflicts have little regard for or knowledge of the range of options that the rules allow. Parties in conflict may not understand the full range and scope of their rights and may make demands or decisions without fully exploring all their options or realizing the limitations of their rights. A conflict management practitioner should be sufficiently aware of the rights options or, alternatively, s/he should be aware enough to draw in other actors who can apprise parties of their substantive rights. Another practical implication of the rules dimension of rights is that it suggests a possible outcome of a conflict management process: the development of a set of rules to guide the interaction between parties or to facilitate (joint) problem-solving in difficult situations. This may entail, for example, a code of conduct, or a policy regarding particular issues of concern. In other words, this dimension of rights points to the need to be aware of the standards that are in place, to enhance such awareness among parties where necessary,[8] and possibly to put standards in place where they do not exist.

Rights as structures and institutions Flowing from the second and third propositions discussed above, this dimension of rights relates to the structural division of power and resources in a society and the mechanisms or institutions that exist to manage conflicts linked to this distribution. It emphasizes the need to address structural, underlying causes of conflict in intervention processes. Conflict management is not so much about containing or mitigating a problematic situation but, rather, it is about trying to transform a situation in terms of the objective (and subjective) conditions that put parties at loggerheads. This involves considering who has power and resources, what kind, how these are exercised and accessed, and the long-term consequences thereof. Where an unequal and unjust distribution of power and resources lies at the root of the conflict between parties, redress must be found.

In order to live beyond the confines of legislation or a constitution, rights need institutions (including policies) to support and facilitate the orderly expression of rights and secure remedies. Having well-functioning institutions builds trust in the overall system, which means that outcomes generally will be respected and accepted. A sustained protection of parties' rights to equality and justice becomes an integral part of the context in which they function and forms the fabric of their relationship. It also points to the need to develop mechanisms that assist in the orderly expression of conflict, which may be of both an informal and formal nature. Those structures – courts, commissions, community or street committees – become a conduit for the resolution of disputes, often through consensual or constructive means.

Rights as relationships Human rights fundamentally involve relationships: relationships between the state and individuals and/or groups of citizens, and relationships between individuals and groups themselves. Rights are concerned with how people ought to be treated so that their dignity and integrity remain intact and that they can fulfil their full potential. Rights standards thus are a means to construct a certain type of public relationship, based on justice, equality, fairness and dignity. Historically, the human rights perspective has mostly concentrated on the vertical relationship between the state and the individual, because of the state's duty to protect and promote rights. It is, however, increasingly acknowledged that rights are also relevant in horizontal relationships between persons. Rights exist in a social context where people's rights come with responsibilities; some modern constitutions recognize these responsibilities formally.

The relationship dimension of human rights highlights the need to make the development of healthy relationships – vertical and horizontal – an integral part of conflict management processes. Vertically, this entails addressing structural concerns that impact on the relationship between state and citizens (or, in a local context, between authority and subordinates); horizontally, it relates to repairing or transforming the interaction between parties to alter negative attitudes, perceptions and behaviours between them. A conflict management process must facilitate an understanding of parties' responsibilities towards themselves, their context and others, so that each party can develop an appreciation of the other's humanity, dignity and perspective. Parties also need to become aware of their interdependence. This focus on the horizontal relationship between parties has long been the pursuit of conflict management practitioners.

There is a temporal aspect to the relationship dimension, because relationships, by their very nature, have a past, present, and if handled well, a future. This means that the conflict management practitioner working within a rights framework should be mindful that past events are acknowledged and dealt with before working towards a sustainable future.[9]

Rights as processes Finally, for rights to enjoy the fullest legitimacy, supported by appropriate institutions in healthy relationships, they still need good processes to ensure that parties own the solution to their conflict. Earlier we saw how process is an important concern of conflict management practitioners, based on the recognition that the quality of a process affects the validity and sustainability of the outcome of that process. The process dimension of rights highlights the need for conflict management practitioners to give meaning to universal human rights and values by embedding them within the processes they facilitate, so that these reflect such values. Values such as involvement and ownership, participation and equal voice, must permeate the process for parties to remain committed. Giving effect to human rights values through intervention processes can also assist parties in developing a practical understanding of rights – for example, the importance of respect for diversity and the need for protecting weaker or marginalized parties and ensuring that their voices are heard.

Further, this dimension of rights also underscores the importance of choosing the most appropriate process for the resolution of a particular conflict. Conflicts do not come in a one-size-fits-all or, rather, one-process-fits-all configuration. What the appropriate process is will depend on the context, the rights and interests at stake, the prevailing traditional and cultural values, the relationship(s) between the parties, even the abilities of the intervener. Nevertheless, it is important that there be a suite of processes available, which parties understand and then exercise their choice.

Coherence, clarity and integrity Important in this rights-based, multidimensional approach to conflict management is the notion that all of the above must cohere and be considered as a whole. In order to build sustainable peace, the framework of rights must frame relationships that are respectful, dignified, interdependent, fair and equal. Indeed, these rights must ensure that those values are imprinted on the very structures of society and community in the way power is expressed, access to the resources within the community is granted, and participation in public life is allowed and fostered. Where rights or related values are violated, a range of possibilities must exist to address them. Moreover, the institutions and processes available for doing so should be legitimate and credible.

Interventions are thus likely to consist of a range of strategies and activities which address different aspects of a conflict situation. As issues of structure and relationships are intertwined in the evolution of a particular conflict, efforts to transform conflict into sustainable outcomes and relations must be multi-faceted yet coherent. This endorses the idea that interventions are not necessarily the domain of a solitary figure (Lederach 1997). Different actors can take responsibility for different aspects and roles, provided that there is some communication, collaboration and coordination to ensure that all efforts hang together and that there is synergy.

Consequently, an imperative in a rights-based approach to conflict management is ensuring role *clarity* and role *integrity.* Different actors in an intervention process may play different roles, and where one actor is called upon to play various roles, his or her primary role should not be compromised. This is, however, not to argue that all advocacy is precluded for those involved in conflict management – it depends on the kind of advocacy in which one engages. Ron Kraybill (1992) usefully distinguishes between four kinds of advocacy: process, party, outcome and values.[10] A rights-based approach to conflict management helps practitioners to appreciate the kinds of advocacy available to them, and calls on them to be passionate process and values advocates. It also allows for practitioners to work for an outcome, not pre-determined by him/her, but one that fits within a rights framework. Not only should the outcome as far as possible satisfy all the parties, it should also remain respectful of fundamental human rights and values. In other words, certain types of advocacy can be combined with acting in facilitative roles; the imperative here is ensuring that like roles and values are linked, and that combining contradictory roles and values is avoided.

How does it work in practice?

Three case studies are explored below, each of which engages with aspects of the rights–conflict relationship and conceptualization mapped out above. The first example, Mambo High, focuses most directly on the four dimensions of rights used in addressing conflict; the second, eviction from an informal squatter settlement, tackles challenges faced by the approach, especially where conflict is related to extreme poverty and material need; and the third, about work with Zimbabwean churches, explores the dynamics of a single actor trying to combine different roles, necessitated by their interest in both peace and justice.

The case of Mambo High[11] Pieter Mambo High School is located in a sprawling, impoverished 'coloured' township outside a major South African city. The area is infamous for the number of gangs it has spawned among disaffected youth. Violence, alcoholism, drug abuse and crime are rife. Political change in the country has gradually changed the racial composition of the school as more Africans apply. Despite the dire economic and social conditions, the school has become known for academic excellence and successes in various sports. Many achievements have occurred under the leadership of the principal, who seeks to make the school a leading one in the province. Over time, however, Mambo High has become replete with conflict. The staff feel aggrieved about various issues, including the selection of prefects, admission of black learners, flawed decision-making processes and the principal's managerial style, perceived as intimidating, humiliating and authoritarian. Other issues relate to alleged gender and racial insensitivity on the part of the principal, and his use of corporal punishment (a practice outlawed by recent legislation but still practised frequently by educators intent on maintaining discipline). The principal, on the other hand, perceives his teachers to be lazy and unwilling to give their all. The situation at the school eventually comes to a head and external interveners are called in.

The situation above describes one not unfamiliar to many practitioners. A cursory evaluation would suggest different kinds of conflict. Relationships are strained; decision-making is problematic; parties share little in terms of values although they have much in common; the degree of information-sharing and the quality of that information is contentious; parties feel undervalued, misunderstood, undermined and disrespected.

When we asked a group of seasoned conflict resolution practitioners in a training session to analyse this case and propose a way forward, they were quick to design a process that would gather more information and open up dialogue between the various parties. Rebuilding the relationships and getting the parties into some kind of process seemed to be of paramount importance. The fact that a legal and rights framework existed was acknowledged but not taken into account in any substantial way; it was considered to be 'out there' but as of no direct consequence to the intervention. The possibility of conflict management training for the staff and the principal was suggested as a way to ensure sustainability of any solution reached. Little attention, however, was devoted to the question of how to improve the functioning of systems in the school to allow for greater sharing of responsibility, power and decision-making, with a view to enhancing the school's performance and developing a vision shared by all.

In the actual intervention, using the frameworks outlined above, the Centre for Conflict Resolution (CCR) interveners sought to address all dimensions of rights. In terms of the rules dimension, it was realized that the school is located in a context delineated by the Education Department's policies, national legislation and the constitution. These are the instruments that create the rights enjoyed by all parties and constitute the parameters within which a solution must be sought – the rules applicable. Where those rules had been breached, action needed to be taken if only for all parties to understand that breaches bear consequences and that the rules apply to everyone. Thus, discrimination against educators and potential learners as well as the corporal punishment meted out needed attention. The process to be used was influenced by the rules framework and the need to reach a constructive solution – under South African labour legislation, discrimination charges can be addressed through mediation and, if that fails, through arbitration or adjudication.[12] Similarly, instances of corporal punishment might require some disciplinary action against the principal, utilizing the department's own internal mechanisms.

Under the normal reporting process utilized by CCR, the Education Department was made aware of the allegations of misconduct. It was subsequently up to the department to gather any evidence to substantiate the allegations and decide on any disciplinary action to be taken.[13] Separately, the interveners realized that, as part of the intervention process, some explanation was necessary for all parties of their rights and obligations within the South African legal framework. Someone from the department's internal staff, charged with overseeing policy implementation, was engaged to this extent. A briefing of this nature could have been provided by the interveners themselves, but in the heated emotional climate, this might have compromised their impartiality in some parties' eyes.

Certain rights violations had occurred because the relationships between the principal and the staff were particularly frayed. Awareness of the relationships dimension made the interveners realize that dealing only with the breaches of the rules might provide respite from the issues – at least for some time – while instilling a sense of vindication among the teacher corps (and a sense of alienation on the principal's part). However, to prevent recurrence of similar issues, relationships and the hurt experienced by everyone had to be addressed. Mechanisms also needed to be put in place so that the parties would be able to resolve future disputes by themselves; parties had to address the question of how to relate to each other in future. To this end, a workshop involving all staff aimed at relearning how to engage with each other and focusing on constructive communication was arranged. A code of conduct was developed and adopted in this workshop to guide the interaction among staff, including the principal. In this way, efforts were made to rebuild the relationships on the foundation of human dignity and respect for all and to develop a common frame of reference for treating self and others. During this process, moreover, common interests were explored so that, in the long term, the school's overarching vision and values would be acknowledged and people would agree on how to realize this.

Also in terms of the structures and institutions dimension, the interveners realized early on that the deeper, more difficult, issues to tackle were the structural conditions at the school and how these fed into the conflict. Such structural issues are often difficult to address properly because they may lie beyond the control of the parties and/or efforts to address these may require resources that parties may be unwilling or unable to provide (time, money, human resources). Both factors were present to some degree in the case of Mambo High. Regulations regarding school governing bodies and appointment procedures could not be altered by the parties. In terms of resources, the profile and prominence of the school had motivated the Education Department to allocate some resources to the effective resolution of this conflict, but this was limited in light of the many other schools in the province needing additional resources. This had an impact on the scope, scale and structuring of the intervention.

Clearly, the staff felt disempowered because their opinion and contributions were not taken seriously and they had lost faith in the school's governance structures. Those structures needed overhauling and restructuring so as to facilitate participation and enhance the legitimacy and correct use of such structures. As part of the intervention process, elections were held for staff representatives to the various structures, and discussion was encouraged on the functioning of these structures. Attention was also paid to the feedback and communication mechanisms to and from these bodies. The interveners recommended that the principal's management style be modified through executive coaching and training while clarifying expectations around teachers' influence on decision-making and developing their understanding of the role and responsibilities of the principal.

Throughout the intervention, it was important, as interveners, to remain critically aware of the process as it unfolded and of the parties in holding both accountable to the fundamental values of justice, equality and dignity that inform our practice. Appreciation of the process dimension was especially evident in how the interveners treated the various parties and process suggestions made. Processes recommended to parties in conflict had to be appropriate to the context; the recommended and agreed-upon redress needed to be appropriate to the situation.

Overall, the rights-based approach to conflict management outlined in this chapter added depth to the interveners' analysis of the situation; to the manner in which they dealt with the conflict; and to the range of possible and implementable solutions. Approaching the intervention from a rights basis prompted them to consider more than just the relationship challenges, which are often a primary focus for interveners coming from a conflict management perspective and highlight classical strategies such as helping parties to communicate and understand each other's point of view. It provided some analytical tools with which to approach the situation, and challenged the interveners to remember the broader framework so as to make the intervention efforts effective and sustainable.

Parties were challenged to look at the situation in a comprehensive manner, and therein lay the greatest challenge: moving the parties beyond their focus on the visible conflicts and the immediate satisfaction of their needs to a long-term, sustainable solution. Parties were focused on their own strongly held positions and opinions on what should happen. Getting them to focus on meeting everyone's underlying needs was a challenge and could happen only once they started seeing some change in their immediate conditions; developing an appreciation of everyone's humanity and dignity was an important part of this process.

While the dimensions have been applied here in relation to a localized conflict, we believe that they have wider application and might also be useful for considering interventions in larger conflict situations. The principles remain the same although their application and the challenges may change depending on the complexity of the situation.

Eviction from an informal settlement In January 2001, local South Africans from two squatter communities near Cape Town forcefully evicted people of foreign descent living in their midst. Those evicted, mostly Angolans and Namibians, lost their houses and belongings through arson and other forms of destruction. They were also subjected to harassment and assault while being chased out of the informal settlements, and were threatened with more violence should they try to return. Yet many of them were married to South African citizens and/or had valid residence permits; some had been naturalized. Whether or not this qualified them to live in the settlements was of no particular concern to the South Africans; their priority was to get those considered 'foreigners' out. Once the latter had found refuge at the police station, the local municipality requested CCR to intervene and facilitate a lasting solution to the conflict. The case also came to the Centre from another direction: several evictees had submitted complaints about violations of their human rights to the South African Human Rights Commission (HRC). After some initial fact-finding, the HRC concluded that the complaints might be best dealt with through some kind of facilitated process between the various parties involved. It felt that the value of classical human rights strategies in dealing with this conflict was limited: lobbying, documenting the abuse, highlighting any flaws in the police response to the matter, possibly preparing a case for litigation and then monitoring its progress through the court system and calling for justice would all be legitimate but were unlikely to secure a sustainable resolution of this conflict. While geared towards upholding the rule of law, protecting fundamental rights and sending a clear signal about unacceptable behaviour, this approach could well fuel resentment among the local squatter residents and increase their hostility to those deemed 'foreign'. Chances were slim that it would assist the evictees to return to the areas or to shift local attitudes and perceptions about their presence and their right to be there. The HRC hoped that a facilitated process, on the other hand, could work in this direction, while also developing an understanding among all involved about rights and responsibilities.

The intervention team had to consider how to balance these different imperatives. In addition, criminal charges had been laid by a few evictees for destruction and theft of property. The pending court case and the allegations of human rights violations inflamed members of the South African settlement communities; with regard to the latter, they vehemently objected to any claim of xenophobia levelled against them. The question thus arose of how not to further alienate the South Africans while not downplaying the treatment to which the supposed 'foreigners' had been subjected. The moment the latter issue would be raised, the South Africans would get defensive and threaten to leave the intervention; yet the moment there was mention of not placing the alleged rights violations explicitly on the agenda for talks between the parties, the 'foreigners' would object and suggest that that would amount to further victimization. The team agreed with the HRC that the intervention should facilitate some understanding of the rights of all living in South Africa, including people of foreign descent. At the same time, its information-gathering and analysis highlighted that underlying the violent outburst of the South African residents was intense frustration and anger about the lack of delivery in the settlements of basic services such as water and electricity; access to housing was severely limited and there was little police presence to deal with law and order. Overall, thus, key questions or issues arising in the intervention were: (i) how to raise issues of human rights in the intervention, when to raise them, and who should do that; and (ii) how to deal with the larger rights context and the degree to which the limited realization of social and economic rights fed into the actual situation of violent conflict that had prompted the intervention.

With regard to the first issue, the intervention team decided to refrain from using the term 'xenophobia' in the initial stages of the intervention, to help the foreigners understand why this was done, and to work with the South Africans to make clear that issues of rights, dignity and security had to be included in the mediation process – concerns of both parties had to be raised. This also involved explaining the role of the intervention team, what it could and could not do; for example, the team could not interfere with the criminal proceedings of the court case, nor would it suggest that charges be dropped. Much time was also spent explaining the intervention process, so as to facilitate understanding of the principles underlying it (voluntary nature, joint problem-solving, parties come up with their own solution) and to build trust in the relationship between the parties and the interveners. This then assisted in creating space where those evicted could themselves raise their concerns about the violations of their rights, and how the violations had affected them. At a later stage in the intervention process, moreover, an education officer of the HRC was invited to provide an information session about rights and responsibilities in the South African context. By that time, the concerns of the South African residents relating to housing, water, etc. had also been placed in a rights context, so that rights had become highlighted as a matter for everybody, not just for others.

In terms of the second issue, it was clear that the intervention would need to address the underlying issues. To this extent, the intervention team engaged in discussions with local authorities to get clarity on issues of delivery and development. An agreement was brokered between the squatter community and the local police station about increased patrols.

There were, however, clear limitations to what the team could do to facilitate movement on the need to sort out housing and services in the relevant areas, because of the extent to which these were embedded in larger political and bureaucratic processes. The interveners then concentrated on facilitating interaction between the residents in the informal settlements, civic organizations and local government officials, with a view to increasing the flow of information, improving relationships between the relevant actors and getting the issues higher on the political agenda. To some extent, this approach allowed for collaboration between the two original conflict parties, as they engaged with government officials on matters of common concern. Overall, however, little substantial progress could be made on addressing the structural conditions feeding into the particular conflict situation at hand because of the multitude of issues and dynamics involved. Nevertheless, placing rights in a larger context and as related to basic human needs was useful in highlighting both the responsibility of authorities and the conflict implications of lack of delivery.

While working to place structural issues of delivery and development higher on the agenda may have had a positive impact in the short term, or in relation to this particular situation, there might be a drawback in what this means for the overall allocation of resources – whether it feeds into ad hoc, reactive decision-making on the political level rather than a systemic approach to development and delivery. It also raises the question to what extent the negative behaviour of a party is inadvertently promoted, or condoned. A few months after this case, another group of people, deemed 'Zimbabweans', were chased out of another informal settlement, this time in Johannesburg. The conditions in the settlement were similar to, if not worse than, the ones the Centre had dealt with in Cape Town. The upheaval and press coverage raised by this eviction meant that, suddenly, much attention was devoted to this settlement. Resources were found to improve the settlement and its infrastructure. The violent outburst of the South African squatters thus produced results for those who lived there. It left the intervention team wondering whether the Cape Town situation had set a precedent, and how further cases of this nature could be avoided.

Zimbabwean churches The Centre's work with a group of Zimbabwean churches was of a different nature. Here, the Centre was asked to assist the churches to think through the difficulties that faced them as they tried to work towards peace with justice in local communities. Aside from the difficulty of operating in an increasingly repressive environment with limited, if any, resources, it transpired that a key challenge was balancing different roles.[14] The churches' commitment to justice led them to assist victims of violence, denounce human rights abuse and call for accountability. Their interest in peace, on the other hand, made them want to intervene in local conflict situations and prompted them to facilitate dialogue between different actors in the local context, including war veterans, youth militia, security forces and local communities. The more active they were on the justice front, the less they were able to act effectively on peace because they were perceived as biased by one side or the other. When trying to engage with actors engaged in committing violence, they experienced pressure from citizens to stand up for what was 'right' and 'just' and take a stand on the violence and repression. As a result, they were torn in different directions, as some in the churches prioritized one stance, and others gave preference to the other.

The facilitators assisted the group in identifying the range of roles they were playing in their local communities, and to analyse the merits and limitations of each role.[15] Discussions were held about which roles were more or less easily combined with one another and which churches (and individual clergy and lay ministers) were more geared towards particular roles than others. Issues of role clarity and integrity came up, and the churches started realizing that the question was perhaps not one of pursuing one *or* the other but, rather, how to balance different roles and how to ensure that an effective division of labour was developed with coordination and communication mechanisms.

Conclusion

Human rights and conflict situations are inextricably linked. Efforts to transform destructive conflict into sustainable outcomes and relationships must be multifaceted and coherent. This requires a synergy between the prescriptive human rights approach with its emphasis on structure, vertical relationships and the rights framework, with the facilitative approach of conflict management that focuses on the process and relationship(s) between the parties. The propositions made in this chapter on the relationship between human rights and conflict management and the four dimensions of rights – rules, structures and institutions, relationships and processes – provide a framework for understanding the complex nature of conflict, analysing particular situations and deciding on appropriate approaches. They may also provide practitioners with some tools with which to consider, design and implement interventions. A rights-based approach to conflict management does not present any easy solutions or answers to the dilemmas and questions we face – in fact, it may raise new, or additional, ones. Nevertheless, our experience is that approaching conflict management from a rights-based perspective does allow for a different appreciation of the challenges that face us as we seek to address conflict involving issues of human rights and human dignity.

Notes

1 The use of the term 'conflict management' in this chapter rather than 'conflict resolution' is based on the awareness that conflict is a normal and inevitable part of life. As a social and political phenomenon, it cannot be eradicated; conflict will always form part of our experience. Hence, it is not so much a matter of 'resolving' conflict, but rather of 'managing' conflict. 'Conflict management' is thus used here as a generic term encompassing a wide range of approaches and processes to handle conflict, including the transformation of conflict situations. Thus, the term is here *not* used in the sense of 'mitigating' or 'containing' conflict.

2 Of course, much depends on the specific circumstances of situations and the type and scale of abuses committed. In cases of large-scale violent conflict, this dilemma is reflected in the 'peace vs justice' debate on whether to pursue peace as the basis of justice, or whether to secure justice as the foundation for lasting peace.

3 For a more in-depth discussion of possible differences between the fields of human rights and conflict management, see Parlevliet (2002: 10–12). The argument is made that even though differences between the fields relate to goals, values, roles, focus and strategies, human rights and conflict management need not be mutually exclusive and may be far more complementary than contradictory.

4 It should be noted that this chapter considers the relationship between rights and conflict management only in one direction (namely, a rights-based approach to conflict management) and not the other direction (a conflict management approach to human rights).

5 These six propositions are drawn from Parlevliet (2002), where they are analysed and discussed in more depth.

6 Relevant here is the analysis of Kofi Annan, the United Nations Secretary General, who identifies four 'key structural risk factors that fuel violent conflict': *inequity* (disparities among identity groups), *inequality* (policies and practices that institutionalize discrimination), *injustice* (lack of the rule of law, ineffective and unfair law enforcement, inequitable representation in institutions serving the rule of law) and *insecurity* (lack of accountable and transparent governance and human security) (Annan 1998: 3, para. 12). Each of these relates to human rights and entails the frustration of certain human needs.

7 These are some of the organizations CCR's Human Rights and Conflict Management Programme (HRCMP) has worked with since 1999. In South Africa, this includes (but is not limited to): the Human Rights Commission, the Independent Complaints Directorate, the Office of the Inspecting Judge; and the Public Protector's Office. Outside South Africa, the HRCMP has worked with Tanzania's newly established Commission on Human Rights and Good Governance, a loose network of churches in Zimbabwe, the Northern Ireland Parades Commission and so on.

8 In our practice we have found that enhancing awareness of standards

may in fact entail promoting a common understanding of them within an organization or context.

9 It is beyond the scope of this chapter to deal with the various theoretical and philosophical concerns raised by the question of how to deal adequately with the past, and whether it is necessary to achieve peace, justice and reconciliation. The question of dealing with the past relates to societies emerging from a period of intense, violent conflict, and is also relevant in the context of inter-personal or inter-communal conflict involving abuse, suffering and violation of respect, dignity and integrity.

10 A *party advocate* promotes a particular party's interests; an *outcome advocate* pursues a specific outcome which is considered desirable by the intervener without regard to who happens to benefit from it. In the case of a *process* or *values advocate*, however, neither a specific party nor a specific outcome is promoted, but rather a particular way of deciding things or getting things done; or concepts or principles like democracy, transparency, the rule of law and justice are championed. The distinction between these four types of advocacy has proven very useful in our work, because the question of advocacy is often raised as a primary challenge in pursuing a rights-based approach to conflict management. To what extent can practitioners adopt roles relating to justice and empowerment? Is advocacy, 'taking a stance', by definition impossible for conflict management practitioners, and what would that mean for efforts to be rights-based?

11 The discussion in this section is not exhaustive. Certain elements that should be taken into account in designing an intervention have not been discussed (such as the impact of outside stakeholder needs and interests in the matter – parents, learners and the school governing body would need to be involved in the resolution process). Space limitations do not permit a fuller exploration of these other dimensions.

12 This scenario is based on an actual case and is therefore located within a specific national legal framework that allows for a range of processes to take place and places particular emphasis on interest-based methods of resolving disputes. South African legislation allows for the overarching objective of finding a lasting solution to play a role in the selection of the process. In other words, the intervention process and interests of the parties can easily be aligned because the legal context creates space for parties to fashion their own solutions in line with their interests. In other contexts, where breaches of rights must be addressed through prosecution, a tension may arise between two imperatives: upholding the law on the one hand (which may lead to a hardening of positions and to an exacerbation of the conflict), and finding a constructive solution that meets the parties' interests on the other. This dilemma has particularly played itself out in the international arena in relation to questions of accountability for gross human rights violations.

13 It should be noted that a conflict management intervener can and should utilize the rules framework, but generally does not act in an 'enforcer' capacity. This situation also raises the possibility that an intervention could be halted for a period for evidence-gathering purposes, which may negatively affect the momentum of the intervention process and the commitment of parties.

14 CCR's work with the group of churches also involved other aspects, such as developing basic conflict resolution knowledge and skills, strategies for crisis intervention, violence monitoring, managing fear and so on; here, particular attention is devoted to the question of roles because of its particular relevance from a human rights/conflict management perspective, and because this was the original request that prompted the assistance to the churches. Work with an inter-denominational forum of churches in one of Zimbabwe's provinces was conducted over a seven-month period during 2002–03.

15 The group identified five roles, which they related to Jesus: the prayer (seeking spiritual guidance and intervention, but refraining from taking any specific action by oneself); the prophet (advocating for what is right); the pastor (facilitating dialogue between different parties); the teacher (educating others about the world, norms and values); and the shepherd (counselling and supporting others).

References

Annan, K. (1998) *The Causes of Conflict and the Promotion of Durable Peace and Sustainable Development in Africa, Report of the Secretary-General to the United Nations Security Council*, Document A/52/871-S/1998/318 (New York: United Nations).

Burton, J. (1990) *Conflict: Resolution and Prevention* (London: Macmillan).

Galtung, J. and A. H. Wirak (1977) 'Human Needs and Human Rights: A Theoretical Approach', *Bulletin of Peace Proposals*, 8: 251–8.

Kraybill, R. (1992) 'The Illusion of Neutrality', *Track Two*, 1 (3) November: 13–14 (Cape Town: Centre for Conflict Resolution).

Lederach, J. P. (1997) *Building Peace: Sustainable Reconciliation in Divided Societies* (Washington, DC: United States Institute of Peace).

Maloka, V. (2002) 'Conflict or Cooperation? Building Bridges between Human Rights and Conflict Management', paper presented at conference hosted by Héritiers de la Justice and the Centre for Conflict Resolution on Reconstruction of the DRC, August 2003, Bukavu, DRC (publication forthcoming).

Nathan, L. (2000) 'The Four Horsemen of the Apocalypse: The Structural Causes of Conflict in Africa', *Peace and Change*, 25 (2) April: 188–207.

Parlevliet, M. B. (2002) 'Bridging the Divide. Exploring the Relationship between Human Rights and Conflict Management', Occasional Paper, *Track Two*, 11 (1) March (Cape Town: Centre for Conflict Resolution).

— (2004) 'Icebergs and the Impossible: Human Rights and Conflict Resolution in Post-Settlement Peacebuilding', in E. Babbit and E. Lutz (eds), *Human Rights and Conflict Resolution in Context*, Fletcher School of Law and Diplomacy (publication forthcoming).

Ury, W. L., J. M. Brett and S. B. Goldberg (1988) *Getting Disputes Resolved: Designing Systems to Cut the Costs of Conflict* (San Francisco, CA: Jossey-Bass).

TWO | **Case studies: Latin America, Asia and Europe**

6 | Combating infant malnutrition – an experience of networking in the social struggle for the human right to food and sustainable nutrition

MARTA ANTUNES AND JORGE O. ROMANO

[T]he persistence of hunger and malnutrition in a country so powerful and rich in economic resources as Brazil should not be tolerated ... [I]t should be possible to ensure the right to food of all Brazilians. (Ziegler 2003: 27)

As Sen (1999) points out, hunger is a process in which people do not have access to enough food; it is not necessarily related to availability of food. This is particularly relevant to the Brazilian case, where the average person consumes 2,100 kcal/person/day (Ziegler 2003; FASE 2003), and where, according to the Food and Agriculture Organization (FAO), there are 2,960 kcal/person/day *available*,[1] almost as much as the average consumed in developed countries (3,020) that face serious problems with obesity.

Brazil has signed a number of international treaties[2] committing itself to fulfil progressively the human right to food for all Brazilians. National legislation now guarantees that right to children, but there are still more than 22 million Brazilians suffering malnutrition or severe hunger.

In this chapter we analyse the experience of a networking organization engaged in the social struggle for the human right to food and sustainable nutrition ('Mutirão')[3] that started in the urban municipality of São João de Meriti in the metropolitan region of Baixada Fluminense, in the state of Rio de Janeiro, Brazil, and developed into a struggle at state and national levels. The municipality of São João de Meriti is characterized by poverty, hunger and the absence of the state, and marked by the effects of Brazil's urban crisis.

The urban crisis in Brazil: an overview

Structural adjustment policies, combined with changes in modes of production caused by innovations in technology, have had a profound impact on Brazilian metropolitan areas, where poverty has both grown and deepened. In 1940 approximately 80 per cent of the Brazilian population lived in rural areas. Sixty years later, 81.2 per cent (138 million out of 170) live in urban areas. Two aspects of this process highlight the so-called urban crisis: the growth of large and medium-sized cities; and the growth of marginalized areas within and around these cities, with an increased growth of slums but with no equivalent growth in urban infrastructure.

The process of urbanization of the Brazilian population reflects the economic model that has been adopted by the political elite in Brazil. This model promotes conservative modernization of agriculture, thus expelling rural workers from the countryside to the cities; and instals a type of industrial modernization that creates a rise in urban unemployment and the growth of the informal sector. The consequences of this approach have become increasingly clear over the years and now pose a serious danger to the food security of the urban poor.

One of the most notable results of urbanization is the growth of peripheral areas of population. Twenty years ago, a third of the population of Brazil's largest cities lived on their periphery. Now the figure stands at almost a half. In the last nine years, 717 new *favelas* (slums) appeared across Brazil. In the *favelas* and other marginalized areas there is little or no access to health, education, sanitation or transport services, thus increasing the disparities between the centre and the periphery, and aggravating the population's food security problems.

It is in the *favelas* and peripheral areas that, with differing levels of intensity, the characteristics and social systems linked to structural and systemic conflict manifest themselves, generally in the following three ways:

1. Through traditional political patron–client relationships. These relationships focus on the elites and populist or conservative leaders who simultaneously maintain power structures and prevent the formation of autonomous poor people's organizations. This is the manner in which, historically, these poor populations have managed to have their demands for public services, benefits (social security, education, health), employment and housing met, albeit only partially. It is through this type of relationship that, paradoxically, public institutions have a presence in the *favelas* and peripheral areas of the cities.

2. Through relationships with a 'master' figure. Since the mid-1980s, and principally in the 1990s, this role has been taken over by drug gang bosses and their organizations (for example, *Comando Vermelho* [Red Command] and *Terceiro Comando* [Third Command] in Rio). These bosses are often the providers of collective public goods in marginalized areas, doing so privately or in a coercive manner. They provide their own forms of security and justice as well as attending to other demands, often from individuals. In exchange, poor populations owe them loyalty and cover for their illegal activities and often become involved in the consumption of drugs.

In these two forms of unequal relationships, rights are treated as favours, precluding the possibility of citizenship building. With the privatization of services such as water, human waste disposal and electricity, dependence on patrons or bosses tends to increase for those without income. The power of local bosses increases with the growth of the informal market and the 'privatization' of public spaces and rights.

3. A third way of gaining access to public services and basic needs is collective action through organizations formed by community members, focusing on solidarity, lobbying and pressure on local government. The tradition of showing solidarity through mutual aid has broken down over the last decade with the weakening of the social fabric among poor communities due to the activities of drug gangs, political clientelism, the 'absence' of the state and the accelerated growth of peripheral areas.

These three means of securing public and collective goods and services are open to poor people in *favelas* and peripheral areas in a simultaneous and conflicting, but not mutually exclusive, way. This means that residents in these areas can have access to these differing systems of social organization, although choice is limited by the violent, marginalized and insecure context where structural and systemic conflicts abound.

Reflections on the urban crisis in São João de Meriti

São João de Meriti, a city of 34 square kilometres, constitutes, along with seven other cities, part of the Baixada Fluminense, an area integral to the metropolitan area of Rio de Janeiro. This area houses the greatest number of urban problems in the state.

São João de Meriti's population of 425,772 has a housing deficit of 9,483 units. Fifteen per cent of families (16,000) pay more than 30 per cent of their earnings in rent. Around 52 per cent of homes are inadequate or deficient and 16 per cent of them are overcrowded (more than one family). The sanitation infrastructure is seriously deficient. Approximately 50,000 children live in families that earn less than half the minimum wage. Children under six suffer from respiratory illnesses, contagious infections, malnutrition, and the absence of nursery and pre-schools essential to their development. There is a high infant mortality rate. Many children aged between seven and fourteen years have already left school and are thrown into the labour market in order to contribute to the family income.

The local political class has controlled the region for fifty years and maintains a patron–client relationship with the poor population. This political class, instead of ensuring the right to food, gives mere crumbs in a relationship of domination and control.

ActionAid's approach

In its strategy to fight poverty, ActionAid Brazil, a member of ActionAid International, uses both a rights-based approach (RBA) and empowerment as complementary approaches. In Brazil, civil society has a strong prejudice against these approaches due to their relationship to social actors responsible for instigating and maintaining the poverty cycle. Nevertheless, civil society uses elements from both approaches, allowing for an interesting dialogue between ActionAid Brazil and its partners.

> In general, Brazilian social movements and NGOs operationalize rights, participation and power as dimensions of the same political process – the fight for citizenship. To overcome poverty and social inequalities means, in this perspective, to guarantee and to expand rights in the excluded sectors. In order for this to occur it is necessary to confront the relations of power and domination that drive processes of exclusion which is only possible if society mobilizes and becomes a protagonist in the fight for citizenship. (Pereira et al. 2003: 3)

ActionAid Brazil's approach, then, is one of fighting for citizenship, comprising elements of both RBA and empowerment approaches. Within this, grassroots and social movements are fundamental actors for social mobilization and in the fight for citizenship.

ActionAid Brazil's work with partner organizations has three aims: (i) to foster the active participation of impoverished and marginalized populations at the grassroots level, encouraging them to form or join social movements; (ii) to facilitate the horizontal connection of social movements by forming networks and coalitions at the local, national and international levels; (iii) to promote social movements' capacity to influence public policies, primarily through their autonomous participation in public spaces, but also through democratizing access to social, economic, natural and cultural resources, and expanding the spaces available for popular participation and social control. It is by these means that impoverished people will be able to fight for their rights – by being the agent of their own development process.

The legitimacy of their fight is not only based on international and national human rights law; social movements have gone beyond traditional rights to establish new rights such as the collective ownership of land and access to natural resources independent of property. However, ActionAid Brazil's understanding is that having a right established in law is only one of the steps necessary to fulfil that right. The constant process of empowerment of grassroots and social movements and the resulting changes in power relations and social control are essential to ensure that the right is enforced.

The experience of Mutirão in combating infant malnutrition in São João de Meriti

ActionAid Brazil encouraged its partner organizations to use empowerment methodologies with the poorest among the populations in which they already worked through the creation of a Special Fund for the Empowerment of the Poorest. The Centre for Aritistic and Cultural Training (Casa da Cultura), the Association for Educational and Social Assistance (FASE) and the Council of Community Organizations of São João de Meriti (ABM) accepted the challenge and proposed a project to empower the poorest to participate in the struggle for the right to food and sustainable nutrition, denied to most children in the region. In this project, they took as a point of departure the previous experiences of empowerment process in community groups such as Catholic Church groups,[4] Baptist and Evangelical Church groups, neighbourhood and cultural associations and social movements.

The strategy used by Mutirão to deal with the denial of the human right to food was to start by emphasizing this denial at the local level, focusing on children under the age of five.[5] Mutirão's methodology consisted then of integrating base action – through direct assistance of malnourished children and their families – with strong socio-political mobilization around the right to food and sustainable nutrition, fighting for malnourished children and their families' access to existing public services and goods, and thereby establishing permanent public policies that effectively combat malnutrition.

The first stage of the process – institutional organization – consisted of identifying and mobilizing the most active organizations in the city. The goals were to instigate a debate around the problem of infant malnutrition and strategies for the fight, and to organize an administration that would maintain and expand Mutirão. This administration was composed of representatives of ABM, the Catholic Church, the Baptist Church, FASE and the Casa da Cultura, supported by national and international NGOs including ActionAid Brazil.

The aim of the second stage was to ensure participation in the process by community-based organizations (CBOs) such as churches, neighbourhood groups, cultural associations and community centres. A number of meetings followed in several communities in São João de Meriti, with the goal of presenting Muritão's proposal and recruiting volunteers to form the *mutirões* (local organizations carrying forward Muritão's work). It was thus that more than 400 volunteers grouped into fifty-four *mutirões* extending throughout the city. A training course followed in which the problem of malnutrition was articulated and explained, involving both clinical and political aspects.

Official statistics relating to malnutrition are neither precise nor reliable.[6] Therefore, the goal of the third stage was to produce a more accurate diagnosis. This initiative was presented not just as a way of identifying cases of malnutrition, but also to raise public awareness of the problem.

Between December 2001 and January 2002, the *mutirões* weighed 5,930 children under five and found that, in São João de Meriti, 19.6 per cent were at nutritional risk (on the threshold of malnutrition) and a further 6.6 per cent had acute malnutrition (in need of immediate medical attention); a figure greater than the Brazilian average (5.7 per cent). This survey also found that the great majority of children at nutritional risk or acutely malnourished are from low-income families with no access to any kind of government assistance programme (Silva 2004; Ziegler 2003).

The objective of the fourth stage was to move from the emergency dimension of malnutrition to the structural dimension through public policy propositions. It consisted of elaborating the City Plan to Combat Mother–Infant Malnutrition and promoting and discussing it in public spaces of participation. The City Plan comprises a number of propositions in the field of public policy – municipal, state and federal – and social mobilization that aims to eradicate malnutrition and to ensure the right to adequate food for thousands of children in the city.

Through the City Plan, and in possession of the real figures for malnutrition in the city and the package of proposals, *mutirões* visited a number of city council offices, including the mayor's office, the public ministry and the children's custody court. The goal of this action was to recruit public officials, to respond to the serious malnutrition in the city and to put pressure on the public institutions.

The fifth step was the creation of a task force to deal with the emergency dimension of the problem. Within the provisions of the City Plan, children with nutritional problems identified by the research were attended to as emergency cases by doctors, nutritionists and city social assistants. These cases were immediately registered in the ICCN – Incentive for the Combat of Nutritional Needs (today extinct and replaced by the Alimentation Fund). This registration allows them to receive monthly supplies of milk and oil and to have their weight monitored by the health unit. Some families also became beneficiaries of city assistance programmes.

Achievements, setbacks and challenges

Mutirão has had quite a successful beginning, especially considering its short existence (two years) and the power relations within the conservative sectors of local politics that work against it. Since the announcement by Brazilian President Lula of his intention to combat hunger, the problem has gained greater visibility at the national level, occupying an important space in the media. Mutirão's methodology has been replicated in diverse cities throughout Rio de Janeiro and other states.

Local level In São João de Meriti the elites have had control over local power for more than fifty years. Their power is maintained and reproduced by the practices of 'clientelism' and paternalism, giving favours to the poor in exchange for loyalty, votes and submission.

This power imbalance makes it difficult for Mutirão to influence public policy at local level. Given that altering established power relations is a slow and difficult process, we consider it a positive impact that the actions of Mutirão are starting to 'trouble' the local political class.

Despite the difficulties, Mutirão was able to pressure local government and emergency measures are being developed by the municipality. The visit of Jean Ziegler, UN Special Rapporteur on the Right to Food, raised the visibility of the food insecurity problem affecting São João de Meriti through media coverage of his visit to the region and his report on Brazil (Ziegler 2003).

The first achievement was the agreement reached between the municipal government and Mutirão. Through this, a doctor is sent to the task force in each community who monitors the weight of the children. Malnourished children are sent to health posts and families are assigned to federal and municipal programmes (such as grants). This was considered a major achievement because, for the first time, these families could see the presence of the public authorities in their community.

Another important achievement of this movement was to put pressure on the municipality to hold a Municipal Conference on Food Security.[7] From an institutional point of view there were achievements: new actors, more networking among actors and new spaces of participation. This posed the challenge of giving capacity-building training and empowering the new actors to enable them to occupy the new participatory spaces that had been opened.

An extremely important impact was awareness raising among families on their right to food and sustainable nutrition: breaking 'clientelistic' links with local politicians that gave rise to eternal debts and the maintenance of their power. People started to struggle for their rights, becoming actors in their own development, empowering themselves through their participation in the movement. This led to the strengthening of São João de Meriti's CBOs, which organized themselves into a network with actors from local, state and national levels. In 2004 Mutirão was in a phase of growing institutionalization, with elected and functioning coordinators.

In the state sphere, the main challenge relates to the true incorporation of food security as a dimension of public policy by following the actions proposed by Mutirão in the City Plan.

In the civil society sphere, we find important challenges for the future, relating to the need to further empower the families with whom Mutirão work and in moving from emergency actions to more structural ones. It is also crucial to strengthen the links between local, state and national civil society organizations that fight for the right to food in order to increase pressure on the state and attain social control over its actions, to exchange knowledge and experiences and to strengthen all the actors in this struggle.

State level When analysing achievements at state level we must keep in mind two different periods: the first with a favourable and more progressive state government (Benedita da Silva's) and the second with a more populist state government (Rosangela Mateus'). Under the former, Mutirão achieved at state level what was not achieved at the local level – its protest action and rights claims were transformed into a reference model for public policy with Programme *Crescer* (to grow): 'In less than six months, Programme *Crescer* weighed more than 33,000 children aged 0 and 5, and more than 10,000 were given milk and oil and medical assistance' (Silva 2004: 62–3).

Despite this, political circumstances changed for *Crescer* when the more favourable political group left power. In 2003, a new programme appeared – Citizen-Check (*Cheque-Cidadão*) – which had the characteristics of a populist programme and was able to destroy and disband the work of the organizations in Mutirão.

The major differences between the two programmes concern the criteria of inclusion. In *Crescer* the children at nutritional risk were monitored by the state government and received a nutrition ticket for milk and oil; the Citizen-Check, however, ignored Mutirão proposals and defined other criteria to benefit families (for example, according to income level), with the possibility of inserting their 'clients' as beneficiaries of the programme.

Through the national NGOs that form part of the Mutirão, especially FASE, the movement was able to put pressure on the state government of Rio de Janeiro to insert the right to food and sustainable nutrition into its agenda. This was achieved by the state Conferences on Food Security, which took place only under pressure from national NGOs and social movements working in the state of Rio de Janeiro.

Due to the spaces opened by this process for civil society to participate in defining public policy, at local and state level, FASE is communicating with other NGOs that act at state level and in universities to work as an advisory group to the social movements and CBOs, in order to produce a common agenda for pressure at local level.

National level At this level there are also two distinct political periods, first with President Fernando Henrique Cardoso (FHC) and the second with President Luiz Inácio Lula da Silva (Lula). FHC government social policies focused on several income transfer programmes (school-grant, food-grant, gas-ticket), with no specific focus on the right to food security. Jean Ziegler criticized the efforts of this government towards the progressive realization of the right to food:

> Although Brazil has initiated innovative programmes to combat poverty and hunger ... [t]he Special Rapporteur believes that the Government of Brazil has not fully met the obligation to spend 'the maximum available resources' on the progressive realization of the right to food, and has not taken enough action to protect against violations of the right to food.
> (Ziegler 2003: 2)

In Lula's government the struggle against hunger was announced as a national priority, and the main social programme of this government is Zero-Hunger (*Fome-Zero*). This programme consists of more than fifty activities that work on two fronts: emergency and structural dimensions of hunger.[8] Activities in the rural and urban areas emphasize the active participation of the local communities with civil society involved in monitoring the programme.[9]

A recent change in the programme was the unification of all income transfer programmes into a 'family-grant', incorporating the families that were already recipients of the existing transfer programmes (created at the time of the previous government) and aiming to include more families based on their income level.

FASE and Mutirão have an important role as intermediaries between federal and local government on the introduction of family-grants in São João de Meriti. The aim is to prevent the programme from doing only income-transfer and to combine it with structural measures that change life in the region. 'It is crucial that the programme discuss with the Mayors' Association of Baixada Fluminense a development agenda for the region that broadens the offers of employment and income, as well as basic infrastructure' (interview with Delmar Silva).

Another achievement was to change the criteria for inclusion in the programme in Baixada Fluminense. Discussions with the Minister for Food Security and Fighting Hunger, and with the local government, focused on recognizing families to whom the right to food is denied and registering them with the programme. This has been partially incorporated by the public authorities at the community and federal levels. Moreover, the National Conference on Food Security, in which FASE participated, was very important as it incorporated some of the demands of Mutirão into the food security agenda at federal level.

Conclusion: some lessons learned

The experiences analysed in this chapter demonstrate the importance of ActionAid Brazil's strategy in the fight for rights. This strategy gives voice to poor and marginalized populations through the use of mediators with different roles: (i) CBOs with the legitimacy and capacity to mobilize families locally; (ii) churches' representatives who have access to government authorities, multilateral organizations (e.g. the UN) and the press; (iii) NGOs with state and national presence; and (iv) INGOs, like ActionAid Brazil, with experience in the fight for rights, empowerment and CBO networking, and able to provide the small and necessary finance and strategic support to make activities take off.

ActionAid Brazil has learned two important lessons from the Mutirão experience for future work in the fight for rights. One concerns the important role of media coverage in giving visibility to the struggle and applying pressure to public power; the other relates to the importance of a political environment that is amenable to the implementation and enforcement of new and existing rights.

'Having a strategy towards the use of media as an instrument in the struggle for rights is crucial, it's the way to reach visibility and public opinion,' stated Delmar. The importance of the media's role in giving visibility to the struggle for rights became clear after Jean Ziegler's visit to São João de Meriti in March 2002. He came to Brazil to monitor progress towards ending hunger, a commitment made by the FHC government during the World Summit in 1996. ActionAid Brazil coordinated Ziegler's visit to São João de Meriti, and gave press advice to the Mutirão.

During his visit, Ziegler received a report on child malnutrition prepared by members of Mutirão, and made the following statement to the press: 'I came to Brazil to check if this country is fulfilling the duty of fighting hunger. Now I realize it isn't.' This statement gave international, national and local visibility to the issue of hunger and malnutrition among children in Brazil and pressured the FHC government that was congratulating itself on fulfilling that commitment through its charity-based programmes. The need to respond to this statement led the federal government to put pressure on the local authorities and to support Mutirão with local programmes to combat malnutrition.

Political analysis of forces inside governments, especially those forces unfavourable to the rights of people in a state of poverty and exclusion, is crucial in the fight for rights. It is clear that the achievements of Mutirão are related to the existing correlation of forces within the government between more progressive sectors that try to strengthen citizenship, and other groups that, although aware of poverty and exclusion, prefer more populist practices that do not favour participation and maintain patron–client links.

Thus, in Brazil, the problem is not a lack of mobilization of civil society actors; and, since the opening of governments to civil society participation through councils, neither is the greatest problem the lack of incorporation of public policy proposals. The biggest problem in the fight for existing or new rights is how to consolidate these policies as government practices and obligations, in order not to depend on politically favourable governments. The different achievements at local, state and national level in terms of incorporation of the City Plan as public policy show the importance of the political environment. It was not enough to demonstrate visibly the denial of rights and find solutions at state level, because these were incorporated only by favourable governments and soon abandoned by unfavourable ones.

The state in Brazil has been appropriated by traditional elites that use resources and policies for their own benefit while giving the appearance of a formal democracy. In order to achieve and exercise their rights fully, not as clients, beneficiaries or consumers, but as agents, the fight for rights will continue day by day, with mobilization and active pressure of the population, organized in CBOs, social movements or NGOs.

As the state remains a field of dispute, different forces within it open different spaces for the incorporation of initiatives, such as the one analysed, into public policies. ActionAid Brazil's strategy is one of analysing power in order to orientate civil society efforts in the fight for rights.

It is crucial that participatory spaces at the councils (local, state and federal) and others such as those created during the conferences on food security are institutionalized and their decision-making power defined, so that they become independent of the political power of the day. However, social control within these spaces is crucial and for that civil society actors must act in concert with jointly constructed political platforms.

The case of Mutirão is one of many examples of mobilization experiences that instigate public policies which then die without notice due to changes in political forces – disappearing for ever from official political memory, but not from the popular memory of those who participated in the experience. In the Mutirão experience the seed was sown in the memory of the communities involved. Food security is no longer seen as a favour bestowed by political elites or as a private issue of individual survival, but as a right. This means rising to a different stage in the continuous fight for citizenship among the population of São João de Meriti. With Mutirão and its increasing visibility, the failure of the local power to incorporate the proposals of the City Plan is being criticized by more and more people. What was seen as a favour (creating debts) is becoming recognized as a right that must be claimed from the authorities, since the population now considers that these authorities have a duty to fulfil the right to food.

Notes

1 The minimum recommended kcal/person/day is 1,900 and the average recommended is 2,350 (Ziegler 2003: 22).

2 Brazil has ratified, without reservation, the main treaties related to the right to food. Brazil signed the International Covenant on Economic, Social and Cultural Rights, the most important human rights instrument concerning the right to food (Article 11). It is also committed to a number of other treaties relevant to this right including: the International Covenant on Civil and Political Rights (Article 6), the Convention on the Elimination of All Forms of Discrimination Against Women (Articles 12 and 14), and the Additional Protocol to the American Convention on Human Rights (Article 12) (Ziegler 2003).

3 We have decided not to translate *mutirão* into English for lack of a word that captures the social, ideological and political dimensions it carries in Portuguese. A rough translation is 'joint-effort group'.

4 Some of these church groups emerged in the historical process that began in the 1960s with the Ecclesiastic Base Communities (CBEs) and was consolidated in 1969.

5 Malnourishment, especially during pregnancy and in the first two years of life, is responsible for infant mortality, increases vulnerability to infection and impedes development of the nervous system. Difficulties in learning, repeating and abandoning school may be consequences of infant malnourishment, reproducing in the long term the vicious circle of poverty and illness. According to Silva (2003), quoting data from the Ministry of Health, the infant mortality rate is 37 per million, and approximately 55 per cent of these deaths are caused directly or indirectly by malnutrition. In absolute terms, it is estimated that 57,000 children below the age of one die annually due to malnutrition.

6 According to the state government of Rio de Janeiro, in 2002 around 17 per cent of children up to the age of five from Baixada Fluminense were malnourished or at severe nutritional risk.

7 With the election of Lula as President and his declared intention to fight hunger as the first priority of his government, food security appeared as a national issue for civil society and for the state at all levels. As part of Programme Zero-Hunger, municipal and state conferences on food security were instigated by the federal government. Their main objective was to give input

to a National Conference on Food Security where state and civil society met to define food security policy guidelines for the future. Nevertheless, not every state or municipality held/participated in these conferences.

8 Some of these actions are: food and nutritional education, support to food self-consumption, school alimentation, support to family farmers and to the creation of cooperatives, food banks, food-cards and popular restaurants.

9 The National Food Security Council (Consea), was created in 1993 and became one of the first spaces where civil society and government were able to meet and design public policies. The FHC government was unreceptive to such collaboration. In 2003 President Lula declared food security and nutrition a priority and reanimated Consea (Chequer 2004).

References

Chequer, J. (2004) 'Dever cumprido, trabalho pela frente', *Jornal da Cidadania* (Journal of Citizenship), 122, April/May.

FASE (Association for Educational and Social Assistance) (2003) *Mutirão contra a fome a desnutrição infantil da Baixada Fluminense: multiplique!* (Rio de Janeiro: FASE).

Pereira Jr, A., M. Antunes and J. O. Romano (2003) *Linking Rights and Participation: Brazilian Country Study*, May (Rio de Janeiro: ActionAid Brasil).

Sen, A. (1999) *Poverty and Famines: An Essay on Entitlement and Deprivation* (Lisbon: Terramar).

Silva, D. J. C. (2004) *Mutirão de combate à desnutrição materno-infantil: uma experiência de luta pelo direito à alimentação e nutrição*, April, Revista de Segurança Alimentar.

Ziegler, J. (2003) *The Right to Food: Mission to Brazil*, report submitted by the Special Rapporteur on the Right to Food in accordance with Commission on Human Rights resolution 2000/10, UN Doc. E/CN.4/2003/54/Add.1, United Nations <www.unhchr.ch/Huridocda/Huridoca.nsf/0/b7a109d9387b c99dc1256cc6004doc57?Opendocument>.

Interviews

Hélio Porto, FASE, 11 April 2003
Delmar Silva, FASE, 21 May 2004

7 | Rights, development and democracy: a perspective from India

SUPRIYA AKERKAR

Background: human rights in the Indian context

The rights-based approach to development is not an entirely new concept. Rooted in the concept of human rights – a notion upheld by the United Nations in its various conventions – this approach affirms that every human being on this earth has an equal right to live a life of dignity and to develop his/her full abilities and participate in his/her own development. The Indian constitution provides a framework to enforce these rights under various articles which protect the fundamental rights of all citizens irrespective of caste, class, gender or any other social status. The right to equality and liberty are some of the basic civil and political rights guaranteed in the constitution. The fundamental right to life guaranteed in the Indian constitution has since been interpreted to include social and economic rights through progressive judicial decisions. However, vast sections of the Indian population continue to be discriminated against and prevented from enjoying these rights. The reasons are several, including the need for fair laws which promote human rights; the failure to enforce progressive laws; the lack of accountability of the state towards its citizens in guaranteeing basic service delivery; and the continuing exclusion of certain classes and social groups from access to the basic resources that sustain life such as land, forests, water or government entitlements.

Today in India, several groups work at the macro- or meso-levels. For example, several networks specifically look into changes in the law so as to expand civil and political rights. Other organizations undertake policy research and campaign around social, economic and other issues, such as natural resources or socially marginalized communities.

Traditionally, the space for the micro-level action in India was occupied by left-wing parties which, in the 1960s and 1970s, through the mobilization of peasants and workers, aided land reform and established minimum wages in different parts of the country. However, the 1980s saw a decline in parties from the traditional Left and an increase in non-government, non-party-political processes. Mass organizations pioneered the right to information in the country as the democratic right of every citizen to ensure better and transparent governance as well as to check corruption in

public life. Several other non-party-political formations or mass organizations continued to work with marginalized groups such as *Dalits* (formerly
known as 'untouchables') or *adivasis* (tribal peoples) on issues such as
land reform and other social and economic rights. This period saw the
rise of non-government organizations (NGOs) and some vibrant action by
civil society groups both at the meso- and micro-levels.

Critical debates resulted in leftist parties sometimes taking a very
anti-NGO stance, seeing them as the stooges of imperialist forces. Some
very right-wing NGOs emerged which today do relief and rehabilitation
work among marginalized sections of society while supporting communal
hatred. In other words, the term 'NGO' in India is no longer associated
only with progressive liberal groups, but with organizations of all kinds of
moorings from left-centric to conservative to right-wing organizations.

It is within this wider context that this chapter will look into the discourse and practice of rights-based approaches to development, specifically
that of international NGOs such as ActionAid, in the Indian context. As an
international aid NGO, ActionAid has in recent years changed its analysis
and understanding of poverty to one that sees it as a result of processes
of marginalization and exclusion.

ActionAid India and the rights-based approach

Founded in 1972, ActionAid India in its early phase supported institu-
tion-based childcare. With child sponsorship as the sole funding source,
ActionAid India concentrated on welfare activities such as subsidizing the
food, clothing and educational costs of children in hostels – work mainly
carried out by voluntary organizations. The second phase of its work, from
1981 to 1985, saw a greater emphasis on education and AAI developed
distinctive competence in this area. There was also some attempt to graft
community development activities on to the education programmes.

The third phase of work, from 1986 to 1991, focused on integrated
rural development, the most significant change being a move towards a
long-term, multi-sectoral attack on poverty at the community level, in fewer
locations but with a substantial amount of money available per capita
to bring about measurable reductions in poverty (ActionAid India 1993:
18–19). In 1993 the organization first articulated a vision that marked a
shift from the project-based approach to a rights-based approach. Reflecting on its achievements and weaknesses, the first country strategy paper
(CSP-I) says:

> The most important lacuna in ActionAid India's work is the almost exclu-
> sive focus on the micro-project action at the rural community level ... and

the assumption that village communities operate in a more or less closed system. The real problem however lies in the excessive thrust on action without adequate and truly integrated framework of analysis of the fundamental causes of poverty. (ActionAid India 1993: 20)

This critique translated into the new mission statement: 'ActionAid India exists to facilitate the empowerment of the poor in the process of social development.' As facilitator, AAI was to concentrate on building the capacity of the institutions of the poor, partner NGOs and other agents of change. Empowerment was articulated as enabling the poor to gain and keep control over the development process. Facilitating empowerment also meant 'taking sides with the poor' – a phrase that was to influence AAI's later work in significant ways. AAI also defined poverty at that time as a 'lack of access to, and control over, the social, economic and political resources required to meet basic human needs with dignity'. The next five years (1993–97) saw more micro-level, geographically confined programmes (termed development areas) with a commitment to long-term support over ten years.

The CSP-II 1998–2003 prepared in 1998 continued with this thrust and in 2000 the India Country Programme released a mid-term country position paper called 'Taking Sides'. The Taking Sides document argued for a rights-based approach to identify chronic and systematic denial of rights through close interaction with people suffering from these denials through a Freirian processes of conscientization, which enables people to reflect on their own social reality, reasons for poverty and powerlessness so that they can take social action against it. It also resolved to take sides unambiguously with the poor: to influence state laws and policies in favour of the poor and the marginalized, to ensure community accountability and transparency, to strengthen democratic processes, to build people's institutions and to establish partnerships with like-minded NGOs. It resolved to work with the most vulnerable among these groups who faced the denial of multiple rights (ActionAid India 2000). The India Country Programme in 2004 undertook a review of its work and began formulating its CSP-III for the next five years.

The more recent debates around development have also influenced ActionAid India's rights-based approach. Amartya Sen argues that poverty is the deprivation of basic capabilities and not merely a lack of income. Sen emphasizes the importance of choice, with development manifested as a process of expanding the real freedoms that people enjoy. He argues that free agency is itself a constitutive part of development and itself contributes to the strengthening of free agencies of other kinds. However, the relation between individual freedom and the achievement of social development goes beyond the constitutive connection: what people can achieve is influenced by economic opportunities, political liberties, social powers and the advantages of good health, basic education and the encouragement of initiative. Freedom also includes the liberty to participate in social choice and in making public decisions that impel the progress of these opportunities (Sen 2000: 3–5).

As the experiences highlighted in this chapter will show, AAI's rights-based approach has in its own way contributed to the expansion of democratic spaces within India. It has influenced this by affirming and supporting: (i) the right to development; (ii) the right to participatory and deliberative democracy; (iii) civil society action which upholds political alliances that further public policy and practice in the interests of marginalized sections of society; and (iv) organizations representing vulnerable and socially marginalized groups in society. By focusing on the human rights of the vulnerable, ActionAid India and its partners have qualitatively widened the concept of citizenship and real freedoms.

Two experiences will illustrate the above: (i) the response to emergency situations in Gujarat; and (ii) the Bolangir initiative to combat drought.

Response to emergency situations in Gujarat

One year after the Gujarat earthquake of 26 January 2001, thousands of people continued to be homeless in spite of the *crores* (10 million) of rupees that were pumped into the government and development organizations in the district. In response, in January 2002, the people of the Kutch district of Gujarat sat in *dharna* (protest) in front of the administration offices in different parts of Kutch until they received their compensation. They were also demanding more transparency in the ways in which compensation amounts were calculated – people were not even informed of the outcome of damage assessments of their homes.

The protest was launched by Lok Adhikar Manch (People's Rights Forum), an organization formed by the aggrieved people of Kutch, particularly the poor and the socially marginalized who did not have the influence to ensure their fair share of compensation. Lok Adhikar Manch was supported by a network of organizations connected with Sneh Samudaya (Community of Love), which was formed after the earthquake and supported by ActionAid through funds from the Disaster Emergency Committee based in the UK.

Sneh Samudaya was formed in the Kutch district to support those affected in three ways: psycho-social support to cope with the disaster; help with claiming entitlement rights from the state; and assistance in rebuilding lives and a better Kutch. This was done by training grassroots volunteers to act as lay counsellors and rights activists, thus enabling people to have new hope and to rebuild a new life. The volunteers of Sneh Samudaya, many of whom were socially disadvantaged, had achieved a great deal of success: along with psycho-social healing, they enabled affected people to organize themselves and fight for the rights required for rehabilitation.

In February 2002, as the ActionAid team and partner organizations[1] were discussing the Lok Adhikar Manch protest, news arrived of the outbreak of communal violence in Ahmedabad and other parts of Gujarat, in which minority Muslims were under attack after a train was set on fire in Godhra leading to a number of deaths. Bleak TV and radio reports revealed that parts of Ahmedabad and other areas of Gujarat were being burned down, and that there was a curfew in most of Ahmedabad and throughout the state. Fortunately, there were few such incidents in Kutch, although it too was gripped by tension. Along with other colleagues, ActionAid staff reached Ahmedabad two days after the outbreak of violence. In the days that followed, a small number of non-government groups came together under the umbrella of Citizens' Initiative (an alliance of non-government organizations in Gujarat) and responded to this human-made disaster. As part of this alliance, ActionAid participated in relief activities, reaching out to the thousands of minority Muslims made homeless and now staying in relief camps. The Gujarat state had failed in its duty to protect the right to life of innocent women, children and men. While the plundering continued, the state looked the other way and people were left to fend for themselves in the relief camps. Later, the report of the National Human Rights Commission highlighted the state's inaction and its culpability in the spread of communal violence.

Although this tragedy struck Gujarat just one year after the Kutch earthquake, few national or international organizations came forward to help the victims the way they had during the earthquake. Responding to Gujarat's communal violence meant taking a political position against a fascist and communal alliance and in defence of secularism and democracy. Not many aid and non-government agencies were willing to do that, as such positioning also meant opposing the openly right-wing state government of Gujarat. It was in this politically charged atmosphere that ActionAid facilitated the formation of Aman Samudaya (Community for Peace) along the lines of Sneh Samudaya earlier formed in Kutch and Sneh Abhiyan (Campaign of Love) formed after the cyclone in Orissa in 1999.

Aman Samudaya was housed in Citizens' Initiative and, after an initial wave of humanitarian relief to the people in the camps, hoped to rebuild the secular fabric of society, ensure justice to the victims of the communal violence and give psycho-social support to the victims. Like Sneh Samudaya and Sneh Abhiyan, it hoped to intervene in the fractured society by building a group of volunteers called Aman Pathiks ('travellers on the road for peace'). Only, this time, the restoration of secular society would need healing of a different kind, and therefore it was decided that the Aman Pathiks must come from different religious backgrounds. They would work together to rebuild the community and stand for peace and justice.

The initial days of Aman Samudaya and Citizens' Initiative were full of relief work and facilitating fact-finding teams to report the truth while the state government of Gujarat tried to hide its partisan role in the violence. One of the early reports was that of the then Country Director of Action-Aid India, Harsh Mander, which gave an account of the brutality of the communal violence and the state's openly partisan role in it. Published in a national newspaper, it generated a response from a large section of civil society and also among politicians in different parts of the country. Such articles, along with the reports of fact-finding teams, gave different versions of reality and influenced public debate and opinion, thus assuming a central role in restoring secular society and pressuring the state to ensure justice for the victims. In the months to come, the Aman Pathiks, many of whom had lost loved ones in the violence, engaged fearlessly on these issues. They were given training in legal issues, psycho-social counselling and peace building. Meetings were continuously held to learn of and respond to emerging situations in the relief camps.

Supported by ActionAid, Aman Samudaya provided support that included, but also reached beyond, physical assistance. So, when the Gujarat state forcibly closed the relief camps, the Aman Pathiks built interim shelters for the victims. When the state gave people meagre compensation for property lost, they, along with the people, lodged protests and fought for their rightful share. When the state failed to lodge correct First Information Reports (FIRs), they and several volunteers of Citizens' Initiative worked to get accurate FIRs filed in the police stations. When false accusations were made against innocent people, efforts were made in court to get them bail. When minority Muslims faced economic boycott and lost their jobs, the Aman Pathiks took their cases to the labour commissioner for justice.

Alongside this work, peace-building efforts focused on inter-faith community meetings in Ahmedabad and parts of rural Gujarat. The challenge here was to change the mental borders imprinted in the minds of different religious communities. Mental borders could be healed only through the touch of those who believed in compassion and humanity. Sharif's story (see Box 7.1) represents the experiences of several Aman Pathiks.

Box 7.1 Enabling healing

During the rainy season of 2002, Sharif visited Dani limda to give tarpaulins to families whose houses were damaged in the communal attacks. Sharif found that while most of the damaged houses in the area belonged to Muslims, one damaged house belonged to a Hindu family. The lone house belonged to one Shiv Narayan Bhai who lived with his old mother and wife. When Sharif reached his house, neighbours accompanying him said, 'This is not a Muslim house, it belongs to a Hindu. Don't go in.' But Sharif went in and started talking to Shiv Narayan Bhai.

During the conversation, Shiv Narayan Bhai asked Sharif, 'You are a Muslim, so you will only help Muslims, won't you?'

Sharif told him, 'It is not that we only help Muslims. We help all those in distress, be they Muslim or Hindu.'

A tarpaulin was given to Shiv Narayan Bhai too. Shiv Narayan Bhai then said, 'You are the first Muslim who is helping a Hindu since the communal violence broke out and my house was damaged.'

Sharif told him, 'True, I am a Muslim, but I am an *insaan* [human being] first.'

The inter-faith community meetings led to the formation of Shanti (peace committees) in sensitive parts of Ahmedabad. When one of the senior right-wing leaders held a meeting in rural Gujarat with the aim of spreading communal distrust, Aman Pathiks a few kilometres away held a meeting of people of different faiths, distributing roses as a mark of peace and harmony. In this way, the Aman Pathiks were changing the discourse of communal hatred into a discourse of communal harmony in everyday life, upholding the pluralist values central to democracy and affirming universal human rights.

Sporting and other events were organized that would lead to an intermingling of different faiths and to celebrations of festivals of different faiths. Resources were mobilized to restore livelihoods. Widows were enabled to access state pensions. Support was also leveraged from other organizations to ensure that children of single parents were able to stay in school.

For several Aman Pathiks, the Aman Samudaya was a transforming experience. Their confidence increased and several of them who had never before questioned the police or state functionaries were empowered enough to question them and fight for justice, ensuring that the perpetrators of the communal crimes were punished. Today, along with other Citizens' Initiative volunteers, they continue to support witnesses to the communal violence as they seek justice through legal, moral and other avenues. The legal struggle of the victims of communal violence for justice continues today in Gujarat.

Four years later, the work in Kutch, Gujarat, has taken new forms. The agitation of Lok Adhikar Manch led to the government sharing the survey results of damaged property and to several thousand people receiving compensation. Organizations fighting injustices against people with disabilities and single women are at the forefront of the struggle for a new, more humane and disability-friendly Kutch. An impact evaluation of Kutch a year ago showed that the earlier, caste-based power relations had changed. Social inequities continue in some ways, but the earlier, all-pervasive, caste-based domination has changed for ever.

The Bolangir initiative to combat drought

Bolangir district is in Orissa, an eastern state in India. The Bolangir initiative started as an emergency response to drought in 1997 with six local organizations. As ActionAid and its local partners started relief work, they soon realized the need for long-term intervention. In 1998 ActionAid performed a participatory study of the drought, demonstrating that it was not just the result of lack of rainfall, but also a failure of entitlement, revealing heavy indebtedness and landlessness among poor *Dalits* and other vulnerable groups in the district.[2] In spite of land reform laws, a small number of persons of higher caste continued to own most of the land.

Without an adequate livelihood, *Dalits* in particular, but also other socially marginalized groups, borrow money and migrate on a large scale to the neighbouring state of Andhra Pradesh to work in the brick kilns in Hyderabad. More than 1 *lakh* (100,000) people migrate out of Bolangir every year in search of work in neighbouring states. The migrating people are trafficked in distressing conditions and live a life of semi-bondage at the brick kiln, receiving almost half the minimum wage and suffering constant ill health and hunger. The ActionAid study showed for the first time that the drought in Bolangir was not a result of natural calamity such as lack of rainfall – highlighted by the fact that only certain people (*Dalits*, tribals and other lower castes) migrate for work. It showed that drought and migration were a consequence of skewed development processes that marginalized certain sections of people, namely those who lack access to livelihood resources, government social security and entitlements which could enable them to cope with hunger. They instead had to rely upon the patronage of wealthier sections in the villages and nearby towns – who used their vulnerability to acquire surplus wealth by acting as contractors and landlords. In the light of this understanding, a new network of non-government organizations, called CADMB (Collective Action for Drought Mitigation in Bolangir), was formed, supported by ActionAid and committed to combating the effects of drought.

From 1998 to 2004, CADMB grew from a network of six to eighteen organizations including ActionAid India. The foundation of CADMB is teams of village-level development workers. In 1999, while deepening their understanding of the causes of drought and migration, these teams developed Lok Yojana (People's Plan) through participatory planning methods (using a combination of Participatory Rural Appraisal [PRA] tools and Freirian-inspired techniques that encourage people to analyse their own reality) in 371 villages to influence the development plans in their villages. The People's Plan was adopted by the *Gram Panchayats* (elected village bodies mandated by the constitution of India) and later became the basis for negotiation with district administrations. The Plan aimed to mobilize youths, women and socially marginalized groups in the villages to assert their rights and access their entitlements, such as social security provisions meant for the poor in the village. Elected village committees federated at the district level and took up different issues that affected their food security. In several villages women, through their self-help groups, prevented money-lending and the forced acquisition of lands. At the district level, labour societies of migrant labourers were formed to secure government contract work in the villages – such as the construction of buildings and roads – otherwise given to the larger contractors from outside the community. This has reduced migration in certain periods. However, the large contractors have also organized themselves together into bogus labour cooperatives, taking work away from labour societies. The struggle against such cooperatives continues.

CADMB also works on projects such as forming grain banks in the village, giving emergency medical help through *gram kosh* (village cash support) to vulnerable persons including single women, old persons, people with disabilities and landless labourers, overseen by the village development committees. Village education committees have been formed to persuade the district administration to open 'bridge' schools during the times that labourers migrate to ensure that their children's education does not suffer. In addition, the village-level and district-level committees have started monitoring the movement of the migrant labourers to force the district administration to accept the fact of large-scale migration. In spite of the Inter State Migration Act which regulates human trafficking, much of the migration goes unregistered by the district labour commissioner's office, so although more than 100,000 people migrate out to work, official statistics record only a few hundred people. Keeping village *panchayat* (committee) registers has therefore been a lobbying method employed by CADMB and the people's organization to advocate for waged work, bridge schools and implementation of Bolangir's migrant labour laws. There have been some gains, but the struggle of the people of Bolangir for the right to life with dignity and without hunger continues.

Learning from experience: the strategic links between a rights-based approach and human development

The above experiences show that in its work ActionAid has offered a different version of reality from the dominant paradigms. In Gujarat, through its own reports as well as by facilitating other fact-finding reports, it showed that the communal violence was not the result of some 'natural' passion on the part of a section of an enraged population, but rather that the state had played a systemic role. In the earthquake situation, ActionAid's analysis showed that vulnerable groups in society had been excluded from the rehabilitation process – against the dominant analysis which assumed that all sections of the Kutch population were equally affected and therefore needed an equal response from the state. In Bolangir, ActionAid's analysis showed different reasons for drought and migration from the dominant explanations that emphasized natural forces such as rainfall. Foucault recognized that knowledge and power are closely related. By offering different constructions of reality, ActionAid enabled *different kinds of actions* to change that reality. These different kinds of actions are social, political, economic and legal and include a variety of strategies: use of law, organization building, community mobilization, forming larger coalition alliances, research and other campaign methods.

Sen's freedom-centred view of development is very much an agent-oriented view. With adequate social opportunities, individuals can effectively shape their own destiny and help each other. They need not be seen as passive recipients of the benefits of development programmes (Sen 2000: 11). Using this notion, ActionAid's approach shows that it can successfully combine a service delivery approach with a rights-based approach – the latter aiming to empower the socially marginalized and vulnerable. This is achieved when the transfer of aid is made in a transparent manner – that is, after the community has analysed their reality and developed an alternative development vision for themselves. Further, community-based volunteers who had insight into community dynamics and whose perspective and capacities were built through training ensured that in most cases the beneficiaries belonged to the socially vulnerable groups and were selected on the basis of need. Grain bank support, or emergency medical support, membership of credit groups and livelihood support were given in this way. At the same time, these village-level organizations and community-level volunteers continued to struggle with the state and other vested interests in the society for the basic rights of the vulnerable. Thus the successful combination of service delivery and the rights-based approach was made possible due to the *mobilization of agency* of people belonging to the socially disadvantaged sections of the community in the form of village-level organizations or as community-based volunteers. ActionAid thus worked with notions of empowerment and empowered agency to promote equity and justice.

A rights-based approach uses a *more dynamic construction of notions of vulnerability*. While in Kutch and Bolangir the *Dalits* and other economically and socially marginalized groups were the vulnerable social groups, historically marginalized from development processes, the Gujarat communal violence showed a different face of vulnerability where the Gujarat state's lack of respect for universal human rights, justice and the impartial rule of law became a threat to the fabric of Indian democracy. In this scenario, ActionAid, along with other civil society organizations, sought to protect the rights of minority Muslims in Gujarat. Further, as civil society itself became vulnerable to the right-wing discourse of hatred, ActionAid sought to work with the different religious groups to ensure healing and affirm pluralist society – central to any participatory and inclusive democracy.

Lastly, by embracing coalition politics where ActionAid not only acted as a donor organization but also as a part of larger civil society networks such as Citizen's Initiative or CADMB (themselves an alliance of civil society organizations based on common goals), it was able to influence the micro- as well as the macro-environment in the interests of the marginalized sections it represented. Traditionally, given the lack of state accountability or its inability to access life-sustaining resources, poor people in India typically used their social networks or continued in patron–client relationships vis-à-vis the dominant sections of society (as seen in Bolangir) or the state to sustain themselves. ActionAid's work with the poor and their organizations shows an emergence of *new kinds of social network* or relationships that enable poor people to secure their rights.

These four sets of development practices – (i) offering different constructions of reality, thus enabling different kinds of actions; (ii) mobilization of people's agency, namely that of socially marginalized and disadvantaged groups; (iii) dynamic notions of vulnerability; and (iv) new kinds of social networks – form some of the core components of the rights-based approach of ActionAid India, and are a new form of emancipatory politics to which development organizations such as ActionAid have contributed.

Notes

I remain grateful to my colleagues from Gujarat and Orissa whose inter-action has influenced many of the ideas stated above. Special thanks are due to the Sneh Karmis, the Aman Pathiks, Harsh Mander and AmarJyoti Nayak, colleagues with whom I share memories of difficult times during our response to the Kutch earthquake and the communal violence in Gujarat.

1 ActionAid's partners here are the Behavioural Science Centre, Marag and Prayas in Rapar taluka of Kutch district.

2 The pioneering study by Amartya Sen and Jean Drèze, *Hunger and Public Action* (1989), highlights the connections between hunger, famines and lack of entitlements.

References

ActionAid India (1993) *Strategy Paper 1993–1997* (Bangalore: ActionAid India).
— (2000) *2000–2003 Taking Sides: Updated Country Strategy Paper* (New Delhi: ActionAid India).
Sen, A. (2000) *Development as Freedom* (New York: Knopf).
Sen, A. and J. Drèze (1989) *Hunger and Public Action* (Oxford: Oxford University Press).

Rights, development and democracy

155

8 | Children's participation, civil rights and power

JOACHIM THEIS AND CLAIRE O'KANE

Children's charities have undergone profound changes over the past fifteen years as many of them have morphed into children's rights organizations. This chapter provides an overview of the emergence of children's rights approaches and the changes that have occurred as a result of the recognition of children's rights and their contribution to society. The example of child clubs in Nepal illustrates the evolution of children's participation as a force for transformation in communities and organizations. The case study analyses the challenges that have emerged as a result of children's participation and empowerment. The chapter concludes by outlining some fundamental obligations of all development agencies for children and their rights.

Child rights and the evolution of children's participation

Children as social actors Until the early 1990s, child welfare agencies treated children largely as immature, passive and vulnerable beings in need of protection and services. Children[1] were seen as unfinished adults. Accordingly, studies about children rarely involved children themselves. Adults were assumed to know what was best for children and consulting children was generally considered a waste of time.

This view of children was challenged by the UN Convention on the Rights of the Child (CRC)[2] and by new thinking and research about children.[3] A number of influential publications about childhood confronted widely held assumptions about children and recognized children's social and economic contributions to their families, communities, schools and society at large. These publications contributed to the establishment of childhood as an independent area of social science research and the founding of childhood studies centres in many parts of the world.

The recognition of children as active participants in society had a profound impact on child welfare organizations. Agencies began to question their assumptions about children and to take children's views seriously. Researching children's competencies and their social and economic contributions opened new perspectives on children and their roles in society.

Children as rights holders The Convention on the Rights of the Child (CRC) is the first human rights treaty to explicitly to assert children's civil rights. Every child has the right to information, to express his or her views, be involved in decisions affecting him or her and form or join associations. Children's participation is not about a select few children 'representing' other children at special child participation events or activities. Children have the right to participate in the family, in schools, child welfare institutions, orphanages, the media, in the community and at national and international levels.

Participation is an instrument to realize other rights. The rights to information, expression, decision-making and association affirm children as rights holders. They are instruments for demanding and realizing children's rights to survival, development, protection and participation. In situations where children are denied their 'participation rights', other rights, such as the right to life, health, education or protection, are also denied. Conversely, children who lack birth registration, are hungry, are exploited or abused, face major obstacles when they want to exercise their participation rights.

Participation transforms the power relations between children and adults, challenges authoritarian structures and affirms children's capacity to influence families, communities and institutions. Participation is a process that builds new relationships between children and adults. It requires mutual respect and trust and a long-term and sustained commitment. Children develop communication and participation skills over time. Adults who work with children improve their understanding of children's situation and recognize their contributions to family and society.

Save the Children is one of a growing number of development agencies promoting children's participation. Efforts have concentrated on:

- developing the capacity of adults (government officials, NGOs, community members, teachers, academics, media) to facilitate children's participation and to take children's views seriously
- developing the capacity of girls and boys to access information, to strengthen their life skills, to assert their rights in respectful ways and to build partnerships with key adult duty bearers
- broadening the space for children's involvement in decision-making, access to information and opportunities to form associations in their communities, schools, at home and in the broader policy arena
- developing tools, guidance materials, practice standards and child-friendly information to promote ethical, quality child participation practice

- organizing and supporting processes which create strategic opportunities for children's genuine participation in national, regional and global policy fora
- strengthening constituencies for children's rights by providing financial support for the development of civil society organizations (including child-led organizations) and networks

Quality standards of children's participation Considering the power imbalance between adults and children, a focus on ethical practice is essential to avoid tokenism and manipulative practice when empowering girls and boys as active citizens. Challenging entrenched power relations is inherently risky. Protecting children is particularly important where children are in the front line of social and political struggles. This poses a dilemma for child rights advocates who are supporting children's empowerment and participation. The success of the child clubs in Nepal, for example, has attracted the attention of Maoist rebels. According to some reports, rebels have used child clubs as recruiting grounds. This brings into sharp focus the responsibility of child rights agencies to consider the ethical implications of promoting children's participation.

To improve the quality and consistency of children's involvement, Save the Children has developed a set of quality standards for children's participation, which are being promoted across child rights organizations. They are grouped under the following headings:

- an ethical approach: transparency and honesty
- children's participation is relevant and voluntary
- a child-friendly, enabling environment
- equality and equity in participation
- staff are effective and confident
- participation promotes the safety and protection of children
- ensuring follow-up and evaluation

Case study: child clubs in Nepal

'Before we had a child club I didn't have the confidence to express myself. Even my own family didn't expect me to have a view. However, since being a part of the club I feel like I am a human being with views to contribute and I feel confident in doing so.' Boy, member of child club

Background The first child clubs were established in Nepal by Plan International in 1991. Other agencies, such as ActionAid and Save the Children (Norway, US, UK) followed a few years later. Part of the driving force behind the emergence of child clubs was the growing acknowledgement of children's roles in society. Many child clubs emerged out of Child-to-Child initiatives (involving children in decision-making) for health education, waste management and environmental protection. Others came out of child rights education, monitoring and reporting initiatives (Save the Children Norway), or the establishment of children's groups as part of participatory research studies (ActionAid). Still other clubs developed through diffusion from neighbouring villages with children themselves asking for a club. Another route was through the influence of a children's radio programme.

Currently, about 3,000 child clubs are operating across Nepal in hill communities, rural plains and urban areas. Tens of thousands of girls and boys aged between eight and seventeen from different ethnic and socio-economic backgrounds are members of child clubs. Members hold regular (usually weekly) meetings to share their views and organize activities which are of interest to them.[4]

The objectives of the child clubs are:

- to develop children's leadership and life skills
- to create opportunities for children to explore and develop their talents
- to raise children's awareness of their rights
- to create a forum for children to discuss the issues that are important to them

Child clubs are diverse. Some clubs are school-based and focus on improving their school environment. There are community-based clubs which include children who are in and out of school and focus on improving the child rights situation in their own community. Some clubs focus on sports, others raise money to support those in need in their community, or use the money to pay for poor children's school books. There are other groups that focus on particular issues, such as girls' rights or environmental protection. Activities initiated by children's clubs in schools and communities include:

- school libraries
- publication of wall magazines and school newsletters
- interaction programme with teachers and parents
- awareness-raising programmes, rallies and street drama on discrimination between boys and girls, children's rights, drug and alcohol use, HIV/AIDS, polio, vitamin deficiencies and other socially relevant issues
- door-to-door programmes on child abuse, exploitation and trafficking
- financial support and care for children with disabilities and other underprivileged children
- village clean-up campaigns and reforestation programmes
- encouraging children to enrol in school

Box 8.1 Example of Bhowani child club, Eastern Nepal

Bhowani child club started in 1997 with support from a local organ-ization and Save the Children US. The club has approximately eighty members: fifty boys and thirty girls aged between eight and eighteen years old. The girls face more discrimination and thus have been en-couraged less by parents to become club members. The children meet at least once a month, sometimes more often. They maintain a registra-tion book, a book of minutes and a visitors' book. Club members pay a 2-rupee (1 UK penny) membership fee per month. They have raised additional funds from the local community to build a child club build-ing (constructed in the local style). The children have also established a children's library inside their club.

The children feel that they have benefited considerably from being part of their child club: they have gained much information about their rights. Through drama, speeches and other programmes they have raised awareness of children's rights in their village. They have raised various issues such as school enrolment, birth registration, child abuse, child marriage and trafficking, health and sanitation (e.g. vaccinations, diarrhoea).

The children feel that their child club has brought about much change locally. The children have learned that they have their own views and they are increasingly recognized within the family and village as people with opinions and suggestions. The club members helped establish a Village Development Committee (VDC) level network of child clubs that meet once a month to share their experiences with children from other clubs.

The children are also anxious to develop better relations with higher officials in the VDC so that children's rights concerns could be addressed in a serious manner. The children feel that the VDC and district level officials do not yet take children or child clubs seriously. They are keen to find solutions to the challenges that they face and to build meaningful partnerships with the adult authorities at higher levels. The children feel that further training in communication will help them to be taken more seriously by adults. They are also seeking funds for visiting other child clubs in the country to share experiences and to learn from others.

- debates, quizzes, games and competitions (art, song, dance and sports)
- fundraising and income-generation activities
- training workshops on child rights, leadership, public speaking, street theatre, environmental protection etc.
- networking and coordination with other clubs, organizations and offices

The example in Box 8.1 illustrates how a child club may become engaged in a range of different activities within and beyond its local community.

Achievements[5] Child clubs have enrolled working children in school, monitored school drop-out, prevented early child marriage, child trafficking and other forms of exploitation, and taken action to secure justice for child workers and other groups of marginalized children and their families.[6] Children contributed to Nepal's five-year plans and to the country's CRC report, through an inclusive process supported by Save the Children and the government of Nepal.

IMPACT ON ADULT–CHILD RELATIONSHIPS. Child clubs have had far-reaching effects on the relationship between children and adults in communities. Adults have accepted children's and young people's participation and their involvement in local governance. They have also accepted the increased participation of girls. The high degree of participation by their children is the strongest indicator of acceptance by parents. In this sense, there is a remarkably high degree of support for the clubs from parents. Many parents also directly support the children's clubs by attending meetings; sharing their ideas and experiences; helping in the planning of action programmes; networking with village institutions; supporting the games, cultural programme and competitions and sometimes providing financial help. Through their organized participation in local governance, girls and boys have gained recognition for their contributions and are being accepted as partners for change. Adults who were patriarchal and gender insensitive have accepted their responsibilities for children's rights. Some have even become advocates for the rights of children.

RELATIONS WITH GOVERNMENT. Village Development Committees, the local-level governing bodies, are responsible for education, health and other basic services. They are also responsible for helping children's development. In August 2001, after a long struggle for the legal recognition of children's organizations,[7] the Supreme Court of Nepal granted child clubs the right to register their organizations. Basing its decision on Article 15 of the CRC (right to association), the Supreme Court set a historic precedent both nationally and globally for children's rights. Other significant developments in recent years were the establishment of district-level child club networks and the forming of stronger partnerships with VDCs and District Child Welfare Boards (DCWB). This has increased children's influence on village- and local government-level decisions on issues concerning children. In Surkhet district, for example, the DCWB includes child representatives and in Siraha district the child club network is seeking official registration in the VDC.

IMPACT ON CHILDREN. Children have been encouraged to come together and express their opinions. This has made boys and girls more confident and more articulate in discussing and addressing their concerns. Children have improved their organization, coordination, leadership and networking skills. Children are better able to negotiate and to convince adults and are able to communicate their concerns through different media, such as street drama, wall magazines and journalism. Children are able to put forward their views and concerns in adult fora. They have lost their fears and gained confidence while dealing with adult officials, such as the VDC chairman. Children are able to explore options and find solutions to their problems and those of the community. Over time, the number of girls in leadership positions has increased. Children have become more aware of excluded groups and are making greater efforts to ensure that clubs and participation initiatives include children with disabilities, younger children, both girls and boys.

IMPACT ON ORGANIZATIONS. Initially, NGOs supported child participation 'projects'. Now children's participation is integral to programmes and is being encouraged at every stage of the programme cycle. Some organizations, such as Save the Children, have begun to involve children in staff recruitment. Increasingly, agencies are collaborating to advance opportunities for children's participation.

In 1998, Save the Children Norway and US commissioned a study to assess the situation of child clubs in Nepal. The participatory research, conducted with over 140 child clubs, provided valuable insights into democratic processes in the clubs and their relations with adult institutions. The study made detailed recommendations for:

- strengthening the self-management and sustainability of the clubs, and for making them more democratic and inclusive by improving membership and the involvement of girls and children with disabilities
- strengthening the support of child clubs by communities, districts, local and international NGOs through networking and capacity development

- improving support for child clubs by government agencies at village, district and national levels by registering child clubs, including representatives of child clubs in meetings and committees, financially supporting clubs and by providing meeting space for child clubs

Prompted by these recommendations, ten NGOs formed the Consortium of Organizations Working for Child Clubs in 1999. By September 2002, the Consortium had twenty-eight full and four observer members supporting 1,868 child clubs with a combined membership of about 63,200 children. The Consortium aims to promote children's citizenship rights and the children's movement in Nepal by strengthening and extending child clubs.

Organizations supporting child clubs are working together to increase the effectiveness of their advocacy and to improve the quality of their support. Among others, the Consortium is:

- establishing a code of conduct for stakeholders working with child clubs
- facilitating the network of child clubs
- providing a platform for lobbying the government for legislative change relating to the registration of child clubs
- improving the quality and reducing the cost of capacity development of member agencies
- providing a focal point for donor funding and technical assistance to child clubs

An adult coordinator manages the Consortium with funding from Save the Children. In 2003, a fifteen-member children's advisory board was set up which includes girls, boys and children with disabilities from child clubs from every region of Nepal. The child advisory board meets twice a year to review and provide input for the Consortium's annual programme plan. Efforts are underway to develop child facilitators to complement the adult facilitators.

Challenges Child clubs are facing many obstacles. At the same time they are posing challenges for adults, for public officials and for support organizations.

VALUES AND ATTITUDES TOWARDS CHILDREN. Despite the progress made towards greater child participation, much remains to be done to change adult attitudes. In Nepal, children are expected to obey their parents and teachers; they are not encouraged to question adults. Some parents and teachers do not believe in the abilities and potential of child club members and do not let them expand and grow. Some people consider

163

child participation as a foreign idea that has been brought from the outside by international NGOs, rather than a local initiative. The experience of the child clubs has shown that it is important not to take an approach which is overly negative or confrontational. Children participating in public life have to be respectful of adults and community traditions. In order to reduce tension it helps to present positive examples of child participation and emphasize good cultural practices rather than focusing on the negative, to design policies which minimize conflicts, and to engage families and communities in work with children.

POWER RELATIONS BETWEEN CHILDREN AND ADULTS. These have a major impact on child clubs. In many situations resources do not reach child clubs because adult organizations give children's organizations lower priority. In other situations, adults may try to influence child clubs to represent the concerns of adults rather than children's own agenda. In some communities, prominent adults have used child clubs to reproduce local power structures and to pursue their own political agendas. Most parents know little about the clubs and would benefit from an introduction to the philosophy of the clubs and the kinds of non-directive support they need to flourish.

CONTROL, DEMOCRACY AND POWER IN CHILD CLUBS. Some child clubs are more democratic than others. In some clubs leadership has been monopolized by a few children, thereby excluding others from the opportunity to develop skills, acquire knowledge and make decisions. Such clubs represent the views of the executive members of the club rather than those of its membership base. Rarely do members of child clubs get equal opportunities to participate in training, workshops and seminars outside their communities. In 1995, the Jhapa child club developed guidelines to ensure representation from *Dalit* children. However, no *Dalit* children were elected in the first round. In the re-run, a girl and a boy from the *Dalit* community were elected. Ongoing efforts are required to ensure that girls, children of lower castes, younger children and children with disabilities are not marginalized or excluded in the clubs. To promote broad and equitable participation and fair representation in the child clubs, children have conducted campaigns to educate families and communities about child clubs, and have organized membership drives to involve more marginalized children in family, community and government affairs. It has been important to prevent adults from setting criteria for children's selection and to provide space for children to question the structures and procedures of the child clubs.

OVERBURDENING CHILDREN. Club activities require time and may conflict with other responsibilities, such as school, work and family obligations. Some children are not able to take part in club activities because of lack of time. Child clubs have developed several strategies to deal with such conflicts:

- changing the participation approach and preventing adults from imposing their views on what children should do
- lobbying family members to free up children's time for club activities
- rotating club leadership reduces time commitments and creates equal opportunities for all children
- developing children's abilities to identify priorities and to work on one or two issues at a time
- promoting children's participation as part of school activities and the campaign for universal education
- enabling children to explore ways to reduce their workload

CHANGING ROLE OF ADULTS. Child clubs are very dynamic. As children become more experienced and better organized in leading their own initiatives, the role of supportive adults changes. This requires flexibility and a learning approach from the supporting organizations.

CHILDREN BECOME ADULTS – GRADUATION STRATEGIES. Children become older and as the most experienced members of the clubs enter adulthood they have to be replaced by younger children to keep the movement alive. Graduation strategies are needed to ensure a constructive role for 'graduated' members.

CHILD CLUBS AS A DEVELOPMENT FASHION. It has become something of a fashion for NGOs to establish child clubs in Nepal. Some NGOs are competing to establish the largest number of child clubs. Inevitably, child clubs are under-resourced and lack proper facilitation. Such attitudes do little to ensure the quality of children's participation.

MAOIST REBELS. In recent years, Maoist rebels have emerged as a new threat for child clubs and their members. Aside from the general effects of the ongoing civil conflict on communities, some members of the student wing of the Maoist party are targeting child clubs to recruit rebels, especially among the leaders of child clubs and among older, graduated members. These children are targeted because they have some education, are vocal, have acquired leadership skills, are able to articulate their rights and identify social injustices. In brief, they are empowered. Another tactic is to abduct children from communities and schools. To avoid abductions, many children are forced to leave their villages and seek refuge in towns.

The child clubs in Nepal show how children's participation can be a force for transformation in communities and in organizations. Child clubs foster processes of change among children, adults and organizations. Transforming power relations between adults and children requires a long, gradual process of changing adult attitudes, behaviour, institutional approaches and procedures.[8] Child clubs represent significant efforts to create a culture of listening and responding to the views of girls and boys. They contribute to overcoming resistance to children's and young people's participation and are a democratizing force that promotes greater equality and tolerance in communities.

Over time, clubs are becoming more political with children's involvement in village decisions. Most child rights issues, such as poverty and access to quality education, are political issues. They involve power relations and distribution of resources. To realize children's rights requires that children have a right to have a say in all decisions that affect them. Children should have full information and access to local governance and national governance decision-making procedures. Children's voices should be heard within the political arena so that more effective programmes and policies can be made. At the same time, child clubs need to be able to protect themselves from some of the negative effects of party politics. The protection of children who are involved in public decision-making has become particularly acute in light of the conflict between Maoist rebels and security forces in Nepal.

As child clubs evolve, they are increasingly influencing agency thinking and approaches. They are challenging organizations to accept children as social actors and their involvement in decisions, establishing standards, and setting up permanent structures and mechanisms for child participation.

Save the Children is one of a growing number of international organizations that support child-led organizations and children's civil rights. Helping children to develop and strengthen their own organizations, initiatives and networks is an effective strategy to empower children to develop as active citizens in society. Through their own associations children have highlighted a range of children's rights violations, and have made their parents, communities, media, government officials and institutions take notice of their views.

Organizational implications and commitment to children's participation In practice, promoting children's participation in society, programming and within agencies can be challenging for adult organizations. Adults who are not empowered to participate in agency decisions find it difficult to work with children in empowering, non-discriminatory ways. Children's participation challenges agency hierarchies and exposes gaps in transparency and in organizational processes that are inimical to children's involvement.

Despite these challenges, children's participation offers rich opportunities for organizational learning and change. Agencies have to develop new ways of working with children, build the capacity of staff and management, and establish an organizational environment, policies, processes and procedures that support children's participation.[9] It requires a fundamental change in organizational culture and strong support from senior management and from project staff. This needs long-term organizational commitment and a learning approach (Kirby et al. 2003: 7).

Mainstreaming children's rights Children and their rights are affected by government policies and budget decisions, by World Bank loans and IMF policy prescriptions, by World Trade Organization rules, and by the programmes of donors, UN agencies and NGOs. However, few mainstream development agencies and government departments pay much attention to children. Working with children and for their rights remains, to a large extent, the exclusive domain of child welfare and children's rights organizations. While no development agency can afford to ignore gender issues, many continue to leave children's issues to child-focused organizations.

Children's rights organizations have an obligation to mainstream children's rights and children's participation and share their experiences with the wider development and human rights communities. They have a responsibility to monitor and analyse the impact of economic policies on children and to ensure that children's rights and concerns are taken into account by policy-makers.

Children are not just the concern of child-focused agencies and departments. All development and human rights organizations have obligations towards children. To conclude, we provide an illustrative rather than comprehensive list of steps every agency can take to address children's concerns and to promote their rights:

Listen to and consult children
- listen to children and respect their views and opinions
- recognize and demonstrate children's social, economic and cultural contributions to their families, communities and societies
- consult children in all matters that concern them
- promote children's right to be heard (listening to children) in the family, in schools, in the media and in society

Analyse the situation of children

- analyse the situation of children, not just of women and men
- analyse budgets and public expenditures to show the amounts of resources allocated for children (disaggregate data by age and gender)

Assess impact on children (not just on women and men)

- analyse the impact of economic and social policies on children and ensure that children's rights and concerns are taken into account by policy-makers
- assess the impact of programme work on children
- involve children in programme reviews and evaluations to gather their feedback on programme performance

Involve children in decisions that affect them

- involve children in planning and implementation
- involve children in recruitment of staff working with children

Ensure children's access to information

- produce and disseminate child-friendly versions of important programme documents
- promote children's access to information in families, schools and media (e.g. about HIV/AIDS, sexuality)

Support children to organize themselves For example, in student councils, children's clubs or unions of child workers.

Recognize differences between children Children are a very diverse group, their needs and views differing greatly depending on age, gender and abilities.

- Disaggregate all information about and from children by age, gender and other relevant factors (e.g. ethnicity, caste, wealth status of parents). Use consistent age ranges to allow for comparisons across agencies and research studies.
- In research, treat children as individuals (unit of analysis), not just as part of the household. Analyse intra-household differences in the allocation of work and the distribution of resources to highlight differences in the situations of girls and boys of different ages.
- Produce child-friendly documents for different groups of children according to their age, ability and language requirements.

Include all children

- Confront discrimination and promote equity and inclusion of all children in programmes, families, schools, communities and services. This includes children of all age groups, girls and boys, children with dis-

Analyse the situation of children

Theis and O'Kane | 8

abilities, ethnic minority children, working children, poor children and other groups of children.

Protect children

- Establish child protection policies and ensure the safety of all children involved in programmes and research.
- Promote child protection policies in partner agencies, institutions and departments.

Notes

We would like to acknowledge Save the Children colleagues working in Nepal for their support in developing this chapter, particularly Chandrika Khatiwada.

1 Children are defined as human beings below the age of eighteen.

2 The CRC was adopted by the United Nations in 1989. It is the most widely ratified human rights convention in the world.

3 See in particular publications by James and Prout (1997), James et al. (1998) and Corsaro (1997).

4 Save the Children (Japan, Norway, UK, US) played a key role in supporting the development of child clubs in Nepal.

5 From a Save the Children workshop for Save the Children and its partners in Nepal, February 2002.

6 See O'Kane (2003).

7 Ibid.

8 Seeing children as social actors in their own right, with their own individual identities, thoughts and feelings.

9 Full acceptance may develop over time through a learning process in which adults and children work together, with adults coming to recognize children's immense potential and to share power.

References

Corsaro, W. A. (1997) *The Sociology of Childhood* (Thousand Oaks, CA: Pine Forge Press).

James, A. and A. Prout (eds) (1997) *Constructing and Reconstructing Childhood, Contemporary Issues in the Sociological Study of Childhood*, 2nd edn (London: Falmer Press).

James, A., C. Jenks and A. Prout (1998) *Theorizing Childhood* (Cambridge: Polity Press).

Kirby, P., C. Lanyon, K. Cronin and R. Sinclair (2003) *Building a Culture of Participation: Involving Children and Young People in Policy, Service Planning, Delivery and Evaluation*, Handbook (Nottingham: Department for Education and Skills) <www.cypu.gov.uk/corporate/participation>

O'Kane, C. (2003) *Children and Young People as Citizens: Partners for Social Change* (Kathmandu, Nepal: Save the Children, South and Central Asia).

Save the Children (2000) *Children and Participation: Research, Monitoring and Evaluation with Children and Young People* (London: Save the Children UK). <www.savethechildren.org.uk>

Save the Children Alliance (2002) *Child Rights Programming: How to Apply Rights-based Approaches in Programming*, Handbook for International Save the Children Alliance Members (Save the Children).

Websites on Nepal child clubs:

Consortium of Organizations Working for Child Clubs: <www.childclubs consortium.org.np>

Global Action Nepal: <www.gannepal.org>

Save the Children Alliance: <www.savechildren-alliance.org.np>

9 | Reforms that benefit poor people – practical solutions and dilemmas of rights-based approaches to legal and justice reform

AMPARO TOMAS

Introduction: legal and justice reform

Since the 1960s there has been a common belief that financial and other forms of support to the justice system of developing countries will somehow help to reduce poverty.[1] This cause–effect relationship between justice reforms and poverty reduction was initially conceived in indirect terms, through the mediation of the market. Early projects in the 1960s and 1970s under the so-called Law and Development movement viewed law as an instrument for engineering societies. The main assumption was that law and justice matter in development because they can help either to 'free' the market or to hold it under the control of the state. Mainstream development practice proposed a particular model (Western-based, particularly in the USA) as the one that could help produce 'modernization'. 'Underdeveloped' countries should thus pattern their justice systems on Western legal frameworks, as they were key for economic growth, and economic growth is the recipe for eradicating poverty. Policy statements underlying projects in the 1980s and 1990s ascribed a similar economic potential not to the 'law' in particular, but to the 'rule of law' more generally (US Agency for International Development [USAID], Asian Development Bank [ADB]).

However, development programmes on law and justice have traditionally had a weak knowledge base (Carrothers 2003). Consequently, it has been difficult to predict the potential impact of aid programmes, or to solve questions of prioritization of reforms. Weakness in the knowledge base of justice programmes derives from three main factors: (i) some theoretical assumptions underlying reform strategies (for instance, that they contribute to economic growth and good governance) are insufficiently corroborated by evidence; (ii) there is a lack of sufficient understanding of how change occurs within and through the justice system, and of how reform programmes can contribute to such change; and (iii) adequate qualitative parameters for assessing programs and projects are not available.

Development approaches to justice reform have traditionally underestimated the complex social processes involved in rule-making and institutional development. This has resulted in an overemphasis on formal institutions (courts, lawyers, prosecutors, police) and in a tendency to export Western legal models. Much justice-related development work takes for granted that law and institutions provide opportunity, empowerment and security, through which they promote economic growth and reduce poverty (World Bank 2002). However, laws and institutions cannot provide security and opportunity by themselves; it is the application of those laws and the actual functioning of those institutions that can. Therefore, the question is not only whether particular laws or institutions exist or how they appear, but rather how laws and institutions relate to people and how people perceive, use, change and develop them. This lack of understanding of change is reinforced by a tendency to ignore or underestimate the importance of the processes of development in general. As a consequence, there has been a tendency to overestimate the impact of programme results – for example, the potential of training as a tool for attitudinal change, or the impact of improvements in court management and administration. More importantly, the potential of the justice system to sustain and reinforce discrimination (and therefore poverty) has been overlooked.

Development programmes have shown a traditional preference for quantitative assessments, in line with a primary focus on the 'efficiency' of the justice system. Some quantitative indicators have been developed, particularly with regard to formal justice systems (for example, ratio judges/population, case disposition rate, salaries and fees). However, traditional parameters for designing and assessing justice reform programmes have proved inadequate in two ways: (i) it is difficult to assess the positive or negative impact of programmes on poor people's lives; and (ii) the definition of 'fair and effective' justice risks being subjected to elite capture. Practical and meaningful indicators for justice programmes are scarce. As Messick (1999) notes, the proxies used for judicial system performance are often questionable (for example, 'entrepreneurs' perception of the political risk involved in conducting business in a given country').

All development actors agree that justice programmes also need qualitative indicators. However, while there is a minimum consensus around possible features of efficiency (for example, time and economic costs involved), there is much less consensus and understanding on what is the meaning of 'quality' in the justice process. This increases the risk of definitions being 'captured' by those involved in programme decision-making, usually development agency personnel and government officials.

Dealing with power: human rights as tools in development assistance

New approaches to law and justice are part of a larger paradigmatic shift in development assistance. Since the end of the 1990s, the arrival of 'rights-based' and 'empowerment' approaches has increased interest in legal and justice issues. This is also being favoured by a growing concern for the accountability dimensions in development, and the fact that the justice system is a primary accountability mechanism in many countries. Thus, over the past decade development funding to the justice sector has substantially increased.[2]

Under the influence of rights-based approaches, development agencies such as the Canadian International Development Agency (CIDA), the UK Department for International Development (DFID) and United Nations Development Programme (UNDP) explicitly mention human rights as values they promote through legal and justice reform. It is believed human rights principles and standards (for example, fair trial, freedom from torture or independence of the judiciary) can provide qualitative parameters to assess efficiency, legitimacy and fairness of justice processes (UNDP 2004). On the other hand, human rights can also help to identify new areas for reform. For instance, new approaches to enforcement seek not only more effective systems, but also sentences that put reparation before retribution, alternatives to prosecution and prison that are more humane and cost-effective, and the improvement of prison conditions in line with minimum international standards (DFID 2002).

Importantly, rights are used instrumentally as well as normatively in justice programmes. For example, UNDP (2004) uses human rights norms as a means to reduce the extent of 'elite capture' in reform programmes. This is based on the recognition that it is usually government officials, legal professionals and development agency personnel who have a much greater capacity to influence decisions than the poor. Thus it is they who define the understanding of 'fair and effective' justice in particular situations. The use of human rights standards in this context, the argument goes, can provide reform programmes with a minimum scope for accountability *that is not exclusively defined by those from whom accountability is to be demanded*. From this perspective, human rights are seen not only as legal tools to transform the justice system, but also as political tools to achieve more structural changes. Human rights fill a void that is seen at the root of development failure: a platform to demand accountability. As Anderson (2003) puts it, they provide a language to give voice to the grievances of the poor in a state-legitimated vocabulary. Therefore according to the defenders of rights-based perspectives, human rights can support two movements

173

– legal and political – that reinforce each other and contribute to more effective strategies for change.[3]

Together with providing qualitative parameters on justice, a rights-based approach addresses some traditional dilemmas in reform programmes. Causal relationships between justice and poverty become easier to observe at the micro- and macro-levels. A rights-based approach facilitates the analysis of how justice systems deal with poverty-related inequalities, and thus the extent to which they may be 'biased' against the poor. Recent research conducted by UNDP in countries such as Indonesia, Nepal and the Philippines indicates that poor and marginalized groups face significant obstacles to benefiting from formally recognized rights; these obstacles (low income, weak awareness, knowledge and organization, vulnerability to risks and threats, etc.) are a direct consequence of poverty, and an expression of poverty itself. Furthermore, justice systems are not neutral: laws can be biased against the poor and other groups, such as women and indigenous people, and often are. Reform programmes are therefore increasingly including issues such as 'access to justice' and 'legal empowerment'.[4] This reveals an explicit attempt to develop poor people's capacities to demand justice and use justice remedies, rather than simply strengthening the institutional ability of justice providers. There is also a growing recognition of the function that civil society participation can play in improving overall accountability in the system, for example, through using independent citizen groups as control mechanisms for appointments and promotions.[5] For instance, in Guatemala UNDP assisted in the establishment of Defensorias Indigenas, a group that provides legal assistance to indigenous people, as well as a civil society network to improve oversight of military and police forces.

The scope of development programmes is expanding to include both formal and informal justice, the latter entailing customary and other non-state mechanisms (DFID 2002; UNDP 2004). Greater attention to informal justice is not just a consequence of their unexplored potential for the poor: it is also an attempt to improve the efficiency of reforms. Research has shown that projects must take the presence of informal mechanisms into account, or otherwise they could backfire (Messick 1999). As Upham (2002) puts it, 'not only are formal legal systems expensive in terms of the capital and talent necessary to operate them effectively, but such transplants may displace valuable indigenous institutions'. These are precisely the institutions that the poor use more often and tend to prefer. Furthermore, recent UNDP research in Nepal[6] shows how, in situations of internal conflict, formal justice systems such as courts and police are the first to weaken. They may be attacked simultaneously from the outside by the insurgents' alternative justice system (for example, so-called Maoist People's Courts), as well as from within the state institutional system, by falling increasingly under the authority of the army. As a result, people retreat to informal means of dispute resolution, even for cases that would otherwise have ended in court. As the conflict goes on, informal justice systems may also weaken as a consequence of internal displacement, or become functionally displaced by both sides in the conflict. Eventually, people retreat from the justice system altogether, seeking other avenues in the search for remedies, such as revenge, alcoholism or religion. More generally, rights-based approaches stress the existence of direct connections between lack of access to legal remedies and deterioration in people's well-being. As a consequence, they tend to highlight the cross-cutting implications of justice reforms for other development issues (for example, health, education). Therefore access to justice strategies, particularly with regard to supporting the legal capacities of the poor, can be 'integrated' into different programmes (for example, environment, local governance, micro-credit), although these types of strategies are considerably more advanced among NGOs than in official development assistance.

Human rights as a guide for action: between evidence and faith

Rights-based approaches to justice reform attempt to focus on direct connections between access to legal remedies and the production and reproduction of deprivation. For instance, a person subjected to torture may be unable to work as a consequence of physical and mental damage; a farmer whose land has been grabbed with impunity by a powerful landlord may fall into poverty. This causal relationship is easier to observe empirically than the relationship between 'rule of law' and economic growth, and as a result more evidence is slowly being gathered.

Using a rights-based approach has also allowed the identification of practical connections between justice, human rights and conflict. For instance, the UNDP Nepal research mentioned above highlights how perceptions on the 'legitimacy' of non-state justice systems, including those of insurgent groups, are highly dependent on the extent to which these systems address grievances related to abuses of power at public and private levels (such as corruption or domestic violence). In Nepal, the Maoist People's Courts were sometimes initially welcomed by poor populations precisely because they were dealing with the type of grievances that formal courts had long ignored. At the same time, such initial legitimacy may be progressively eroded as a consequence of violations of human rights in the justice process (for example, the right to defence or inhuman and degrading punishment). Moreover, while rights-based perspectives prioritize people's

175

own solutions to the problems they face, rights-based justice assessments show that those solutions are not always in line with human rights. The UNDP research illustrates how justice providers may violate human rights to surmount obstacles that arise (for example, the police may use torture as a standard investigation procedure in the absence of investigation skills and equipment). In a context of conflict, people's solutions (for example, vigilantism, revenge) may exacerbate violence.

As with previous approaches, the problem with more recent perspectives seems to be an insufficient understanding of how change occurs within and through the justice system, and of how reform programmes can contribute to such a change. There is also little understanding of the role that human rights may play in that process. This makes it difficult to solve questions of prioritization. As Anderson (2003) states, the formal recognition of a particular right is not enough; rights also need to be seized from below by active individuals and groups in civil society. This is how they become tools for social and political change. This is rarely recognized by more institutional perspectives on human rights, and little is known about how to support this process effectively through development assistance.

NGOs in the developing world are coming up with innovative rights-based strategies in this regard. For example, an organization of urban poor women in Jakarta (Voices of Mother Concern) sought to assess and set indicators on economic, social and cultural rights in their communities through a process that involved oral history methods and used poor women themselves as lead researchers.[7] Through the use of human rights categories, poor people were better able to identify the scope of accountability with regard to critical problems in health, food and education and to understand specific accountabilities that existed both on the part of poor people themselves, and with regard to government and local authorities. Lessons from this experience point to the value of human rights as tools that can help poor people understand the socio-political as well as economic dimensions of the problems they face. This can help to 'empower' people to deal with such problems more effectively, by providing a platform to demand accountability from the authorities. At the same time, the process has allowed solutions to be identified that can be undertaken by the community itself to help its most marginalized members – for example, through inclusion in social networks and self-help schemes.

Understanding change is important as justice reforms can threaten those with a stake in the status quo and therefore are likely to encounter powerful resistance. For instance, the bar can be an important source of opposition to reforms, which may threaten lawyers' incomes and their monopoly over certain tasks. Inefficient legal and judicial systems can also provide opportunities for rent-seeking by attorneys, judges and court personnel, and corruption may benefit those who can afford it.

Current debates on the perceived tension between justice 'as a right' and justice 'for poverty reduction' illustrate difficulties for prioritization arising from limited knowledge of change. The argument states that, in particular contexts, pursuing justice at any cost may hamper important development goals. A classic example appears in post-conflict situations with regard to transitional justice (for example, through special human rights tribunals or international courts). It is perceived that 'justice as a right' can stall the peace process and produce new outbreaks in the conflict, with a corresponding impact on poverty and human development. On the other hand, defenders of justice 'as a right' claim that ignoring human rights violations will jeopardize results in the long term, by perpetuating the root causes of conflict and by adding new ones.

The reality is that current knowledge is still insufficient to sustain conclusively either position. Some evaluations of justice-related assistance seem to support the human rights argument.[8] However, it is not possible to make a calculus of short-term and long-term benefits and costs with regard to poverty and other development issues, simply because our state of knowledge does not enable reliable prediction as to the outcome of possible scenarios. Traditional perspectives cannot settle the question, and recent ones give a normative solution based on the victim's right to justice.

There is, however, a stronger knowledge base on the importance of justice 'as a right' during a conflict situation. UNDP research in Nepal shows that a deterioration of human rights in the justice system exacerbates conflict. It also shows that the justice system is not sufficient to give people the full sense of justice they demand and, moreover, that perceptions of users and providers of justice are different. Justice providers tend to have a more 'formalistic' approach, stressing the formal adherence to facts, law and tradition. On the other hand, users tend to relate 'justice' to the notion of remedy or satisfaction. These remedies may be available through the justice system (for example, financial compensation), but often fall partly beyond its reach. For instance, 'justice' for a victim of rape or torture may also imply being able to forget and move forwards, or to obtain the community's recognition.

Having developed the problems associated with an insufficient understanding of change at some length, it is important to recognize that there are at least three further critical areas where rights-based approaches to justice reform face a shortage of knowledge:

1. How to deal with informal and traditional justice systems.

2. How to identify the most important risks and vulnerabilities and deal with them.
3. How to implement a normative approach based on human rights in a context of legal pluralism.

Knowledge gaps with regard to informal justice systems Although recent perspectives on justice reform underline the importance of traditional systems of justice, little is known about how to support them in the most effective manner, or about how they interplay with formal systems. Development itself can affect the mix of formal and informal mechanisms in an economy (Messick 1999). Often the line between formal and informal mechanisms is not clear, and in some cases a hybrid system appears. As explained above, UNDP research in Nepal indicates that conflict situations bring informal systems of dispute resolution to the forefront, as people increasingly retreat from collapsing institutions of justice. However, the Nepal case study also shows that interfaces between state and non-state systems exist even in situations of internal conflict. In this regard, the role of administrative and local agencies (and not only of courts) may be key. For instance, the Maoists still refer to local administration agencies to enforce decisions resulting from informal 'People's Courts' (for example, to issue land titles in line with a land dispute settlement), even when such authorities objectively belong to the opposite side in the conflict.

Challenges to identifying critical vulnerabilities and risks Recent rights-based approaches to justice reform present certain problems of focus. Policies and programmes increasingly seek to impact on 'poor and disadvantaged' people and not only on the poor. However, beyond income poverty and gender there is little understanding of other 'disadvantages' in the context of justice. It is thus difficult to identify who are the 'most disadvantaged' groups that require priority attention. This risks the notion of 'disadvantage' becoming another development mantra.

The notion of 'disadvantage' is a relative concept – a person is always 'disadvantaged' with respect to someone or something. It is likely that disadvantaged groups include categories based on general grounds of discrimination, such as gender or ethnicity (for example, low-caste persons that simultaneously are women and live with HIV/AIDs), but general categories are useful only as a broad guidance. 'Disadvantage' refers to a greater vulnerability to particular risks. The functioning of a justice system has inherent risks involved, such as substantial financial loss, eventual non-implementation of decisions, insults and harassment, or social ostracism. Thus, if we want to find out who may be the groups at a greater disadvantage

– that is, those with greater exposure to risks – it is important first to identify the risks involved in a particular situation. When used this way, the notion of 'disadvantage' may shed light on the actual results of discrimination in the process of justice, so that the processes of discrimination can be understood and targeted. In the Nepal example mentioned above, UNDP research found that 'disadvantaged' groups are likely to vary within the same country, depending on the context. The risks associated with formal justice systems (such as courts and police) mean that people who live in situations of high insecurity (such as the poor) tend to prefer solving their disputes through more informal means. Similarly, not everybody is exposed to the same risks: for instance, wealthy Brahmin women are highly exposed to social ostracism when using courts for divorce or rape cases, but less exposed than men from lower castes to falling into poverty as a consequence of court expenses. On the other hand, situations of conflict exacerbate risks, thus impacting more on groups who were already very vulnerable within the system. Conflict situations also produce additional risks, such as physical threats from both sides, that put new groups of people in a disadvantaged position when seeking justice.

Finally, there is also insufficient knowledge about what type of prevention and coping strategies are being used by both users and providers of justice to respond to the risks implicit in the processes of justice. Identifying and building on local solutions are important if simplistic legal and institutional transplants are to be avoided. After all, human rights are perceived by many (including in the West) as a Western creation. Many conclude from this that methods for realizing human rights should also follow Western models. However, non-Western cultures have a lot to offer in the human rights field – for instance, with regard to providing special protection to elderly populations, or to stressing individual and collective accountabilities in the realization of human rights.

Challenges to using human rights as operational tools in justice programmes Rights-based approaches are explicit about the qualitative dimensions of 'justice' and use a normative framework based on human rights. However, the reality is that establishing qualitative parameters that can be operationalized in development is not simple. Definitions of accessible justice vary from society to society, and often within different groups in a society. This poses two main dilemmas: (i) whether human rights standards may prevail over people's perceptions when contradictions arise; and (ii) whether human rights standards can be meaningfully 'adapted' to reflect local conditions.

With regard to the first question, it should be noted that human rights are useful in development processes to the extent that they help to protect people from abuses of power. Sometimes human rights standards in the field of justice are insufficient to provide adequate protection (for example, with regard to legal aid in civil cases, or with regard to adequate standards for traditional justice systems). At the same time, there is a tendency to overlook the existence of multiple normative levels in the society (international laws, constitution, traditional norms, informal 'living' law, etc.). When these are recognized, hierarchic relationships among them are assumed normatively and often do not corresponded to reality. It is necessary to understand what specific social relationships are regulated by different normative levels and whether international human rights standards are meaningful in that context. For instance, 'independence' is not necessarily useful in the context of informal justice systems, where kinship is critical.

On the other hand, perceptions and understanding of justice depend on the context, but there is no clear guidance on how to ground international standards on specific social, cultural, economic and political conditions. For instance, what should be the time limit for the disposition of cases or how much should a police officer earn? Even defenders of the binding nature of human rights as legal norms recognize these should be 'adapted' to local contexts to be meaningful (UNDP 2004). It is not clear, however, how adaptation is to take place – who should define the local standards and benchmarks reflecting particular human rights? Agencies such as UNDP talk of the participation of claim holders and duty bearers in defining local standards; however, such statements tend to reflect aspirations rather than development realities.

Conclusion: structural obstacles to development assistance

Even if new approaches to justice reform are able to overcome the theoretical and empirical challenges mentioned above, the extent to which they can substantially influence current development practice faces other types of challenges.

The practical implications of a greater emphasis on process are not yet fully clear. For example, agencies such as the World Bank and UNDP have come to recognize a participatory process as critical for successful legal reform. However, the practical understanding of participation in this context refers to supporting parliamentary hearings and commentaries on draft legislation. There are doubts whether consultations on externally drafted legislation can amount to a 'participatory legal process'; but even if this is assumed to be the case, such approaches overlook the fact that those who lack the necessary capacities to form and express an informed opinion (for example, because they lack information or organization) cannot 'participate' on equal terms, and therefore are unlikely to influence the process to the same extent. It is thus not surprising that the focus of justice-related development programmes has remained on formal institutions, and predominantly those where lawyers play a role.

At the same time, a human rights approach brings to light the conflicting dimensions of development. It is important to acknowledge that implementing a rights-based approach may cause conflict – for instance when both claim holders and duty bearers are involved in defining the extent of accountability and particular local standards. Similarly, resistance to the empowerment of marginalized people through donor-supported programmes may be strong at different levels – including in donor agencies themselves. To implement a rights-based approach, official assistance needs to provide stronger support to social movements and informal actors in the justice system. Given scarcity of resources, this implies less support to formal actors and government personnel, who may be reluctant to support this process.

Some incentives in development assistance discourage the implementation of a rights-based approach. For instance, while there is growing pressure for 'results' in development cooperation, these are generally understood merely as financial delivery targets and the production of tangible, quantitatively measurable outputs. Time and financial constraints, and a general aversion to risk are powerful obstacles to following 'empowering' processes in development cooperation. There also seems to be an inadequate understanding of the meaning of 'sustainability' in development assistance, particularly in the context of justice. For instance, while it is understood that delays and miscarriages in justice can affect businesses and thus hamper economic development, for the poor they are even more urgent matters. They can jeopardize their livelihoods and even their lives. Programme 'sustainability' should thus be understood beyond institutional terms, to look at the sustainability of 'impact' achieved in people's lives – for example, through legal aid that allows a person to obtain a legal remedy to protect his/her well-being, or prioritizing the elimination of torture.

Moreover, the learning capacity in development assistance appears too weak. The limitations of strategies such as legal transplants, training or institutional strengthening have been apparent for a long time. As Carrothers (2003) remembers, lessons are available, but they are not being learned. Some argue that there is a reluctance to change the basic premises in the light of evidence (McAuslan 1997); that is, that the Western model is the legal framework necessary for development as it establishes clear and predictable rules, and that this model can be transferred. Others stress the influence of improper incentives such as pressure for quick results and financial delivery within short time-frames. As Golub (2003) puts it, the reality is often that 'the dominant paradigm can consume large amounts of money and that this is considered a good thing'.

The critical obstacle, however, is a contradictory situation: while development assistance uses a rights-based approach to strengthen accountability at the national and local levels, accountability of development agencies and donors at those levels is weak or non-existent. Corruption and nepotism may occur in the same agencies that advocate for their elimination in national governments and non-governmental organizations. Selection of partners, hiring of national and international experts and design of project activities (for example, 'study tours') often respond to the personal interests of the decision-makers involved rather than to the realities of the problem being addressed. Despite official policy statements having become increasingly 'rights-based', people continue to have little means to access the critical information necessary to curb corrupt and other 'unethical' practices in development assistance, to assess the potential negative impact of development projects, or to get adequate remedies when they occur.

Thus, while rights-based approaches to justice reform are grounded on empirical causalities and have an explicit focus on the poor and can be linked to other development issues, the normative and instrumental implications are still being contested in development practice. Even as new perspectives help to answer some critical questions posed by justice reform processes, they also create new ones. Difficulties in generating practical knowledge and in absorbing the lessons of the past are still urgent challenges in justice-related assistance. More importantly, the existence of structural obstacles to development cooperation seem to leave little opportunity for the 'reinvention' of current development practice.

Notes

1 This chapter refers to the 'justice system' as the set of rules, processes, institutions, individuals and other actors *formally and informally* involved in demanding and/or providing one or more of the following services: dispute resolution; decisions, penalties and other legal remedies for grievances among two or more parties; legal control of political action; and provision of authoritative interpretations of the law.

2 For instance, justice and human rights represented around 40 per cent of the global UNDP's Governance Trust Fund allocation in 2002.

3 Anderson (2003) refers to the term 'rights revolutions' that some analysts have used to describe patterns of governance in which constitutional or human rights become an important vehicle for political struggle on the part of groups seeking more egalitarian outcomes. He argues that new approaches need to take into consideration the experience of previous law movements in developing countries such as Indonesia to lobby for the legal control of state

power. Law movements are most successful when the demands for individual rights, judicial autonomy and institutional controls over political authority are expressed in a moral language grounded in the history and culture of the society.

4 Legal empowerment is the result of greater access to justice; that is, 'the use of legal services and related development activities to increase disadvantaged populations' control over their lives' (Golub 2003).

5 This emphasis on the monitoring role of civil society is connected to a greater interest in 'reputation' as a powerful tool for accountability. Anderson argues it is possible to mobilize systems that put pressure on reputation. The media and NGOs, for example, can be mobilized to monitor the implementation or enforcement of judicial decisions. UNDP in the Asia Pacific advocates for supporting the role of NGOs and the media in monitoring the justice process (UNDP). Messick (1999) observes that reputation plays an important role in economic transactions, and that informal systems for the enforcement of contracts based on reputation have proven effective.

6 See UNDP Nepal report, 'Access to Justice During Armed Conflict in Nepal: Obstacles to Access to Justice and Responses to them in a Context of Armed Conflict', May 2005.

7 The project was facilitated by a local human rights NGO (ELSAM) and partly funded by Forum Asia. Project information is available at <elsam@nusa.or.id> or at <advokasi@indosat.net.id>

8 Blair and Hansen's (1994) USAID-commissioned study of rule of law assistance in six Latin American and Asian countries advises against a 'legal system strengthening/institution building strategy unless a number of elements already are in place in a country'. These include the absence of rampant corruption in its justice system and the absence of major human rights violations in the society. Where such abuses are prevalent, they argue against any legal and justice reform assistance.

References

Anderson, M. R. (2003) *Access to Justice and Legal Process: Making Legal Institutions Responsive to Poor People in LDCs*, Institute of Development Studies (IDS) Working Paper 178.

Blair, H. and G. Hansen (1994) *Weighing in on the Scales of Justice: Strategic Approaches for Donor-Supported Rule of Law Programs*, Program and Operations Assessment Report 7 (Washington, DC: US Agency for International Development).

Carrothers, T. (2003) *Promoting the Rule of Law Abroad: The Problem of Knowledge*, Carnegie Endowment for International Peace, Working Paper 34, Rule of Law series, January.

DFID (2002) *Safety, Security and Accessible Justice: Putting Policy into Practice*, July (London: DFID).

Golub, S. (2003) *Beyond the Rule of Law Orthodoxy: The Legal Empowerment Alternative*, Carnegie Endowment for International Peace, Working Paper 4, Rule of Law series.

McAuslan, P. (1997) 'Law, Governance and the Development of the Market: Practical Problems and Possible Solutions', in J. Faundez (ed.), *Good Governance and Law: Legal and Institutional Reform in Developing Countries* (New York: St Martin's Press).

Messick, R. E. (1999) 'Judicial Reform and Economic Development: A Survey of the Issues', *World Bank Research Observer*, 14 (1): 1,117–36.

UNDP (2004) 'Access to Justice Practice Note', March <www.undp.org/governance/docs/A2J%20PN%20Final.doc>

Upham, F. (2002) *Mythmaking and the Rule of Law Orthodoxy*, Carnegie Endowment for International Peace, Working Paper 30, Rule of Law series, September.

World Bank (2002) *Legal and Judicial Reform, Strategic Directions*, Legal Vice Presidency, World Bank.

10 | New foundations? Human rights and peace-building in Northern Ireland

NEIL JARMAN

The extensive coverage of the conflict in Northern Ireland over the past thirty years largely obscures the fact that the descent into violence from 1968 onwards was one outcome of an extensive campaign against discrimination by the state against the Catholic population and for equal rights for all citizens of Northern Ireland. Ireland was divided into two states in 1921 following a successful military uprising against British rule. While the larger part of the island of Ireland was given independence, the industrial north-east area was retained as part of the United Kingdom. The boundaries of Northern Ireland were drawn to ensure that it included a large majority of the Protestant population of Ireland and that the Protestant Unionist community would be in a large majority in Northern Ireland. This process of demographic engineering also meant that Protestant Unionist political parties would dominate every government between 1921 and 1972, when the devolved administration in Northern Ireland was suspended by Westminster. Over the course of that fifty-year period there was extensive discrimination against the Catholic Nationalist population, particularly in regard to voting rights, opportunities for employment and access to public housing. This Unionist domination was underpinned by the presence of an overwhelmingly Protestant police force, the Royal Ulster Constabulary (RUC), which could draw on extensive emergency legislation to restrict any potential challenges to the social and political order.

Eventually, this discrimination led to the emergence of a formal campaign for equality and, in 1966, to the creation of the Northern Ireland Civil Rights Association (NICRA), which modelled itself on the civil rights movement in the USA (Purdie 1990). The NICRA organized a variety of protests and direct action events to highlight its demands. Protests were frequently confronted by Protestant groups and constrained by the police and in many cases ended in violence. The civil rights movement drew upon a broad range of individuals and organizations for its support and, on occasion, responded to the opposition from Protestant groups by challenging some of the many commemorative parades by bodies such as the Orange Order and the Apprentice Boys of Derry. Opposition to a major Apprentice Boys parade in Derry in August 1969 led to extensive riots in the city, which soon spread to Belfast. The RUC struggled to regain control and the British army was sent on to the streets to restore order. Attempts by the British government to respond to the worst of the discrimination were now considered by Catholics to be too little, too late. Tensions increased and hostilities degenerated into more violent conflict. By 1971 the Provisional Irish Republican Army (IRA) had established itself as the principal agent of the Catholic working class and, while numerous attempts to develop political solutions failed, militarized violence dominated Northern Irish politics for the next twenty-three years.

Over the duration of the Troubles there were significant legal changes (e.g. fair employment legislation) and a variety of political and policy reforms (e.g. removal of housing allocation from political control) that aimed to address many of the inequalities of the previous regime. But over the same period there were also many claims of human rights abuses, particularly by members of the security forces towards members of Republican groups and the Nationalist community more generally. There were also claims of continued inequitable treatment of the two main communities and of a lack of respect given to aspects of Nationalist culture more generally within Northern Ireland. In this regard, the complaints of abuse of rights were made primarily by members of the Catholic community, but they were made against both the state and the Protestant community more generally. Human rights were thus acknowledged as an important issue on the political agenda, but they also came to be regarded as primarily a part of the Nationalist agenda.

The Protestant Unionist community had always identified closely with the state, and organizations such as the Orange Order looked back to the ideas of the Glorious Revolution of 1688 and the conceptualization of 'civil and religious liberties for all'. Unionists generally considered claims of human rights abuses made against the security forces as politically motivated actions rather than legitimate complaints. This feeling of bias was reinforced by the fact that human rights groups in Northern Ireland focused specifically on actions by the state, and in particular by the security forces, while refusing to comment on the activities of the paramilitary groups. The human rights community in Northern Ireland thus maintained the traditional line in regarding human rights as a relationship between the state and the individual, and did not accept that non-state actors had the capacity to abuse human rights. Human rights were thus readily incorporated as a key element of the Nationalist agenda, while for Unionists they were considered at best a marginal issue and were regarded with suspicion. The primary focus was thus very clearly on the vertical pole of rights as a relationship between state and individual, and although there was some recognition of inequalities of treatment and respect between communities (what became named as 'parity of esteem' in the peace negotiations), such horizontal relationships were regarded as a secondary and minor matter.

The declaration of the paramilitary ceasefires in 1994 and the consequent reduction in the level of political violence provided the space for political discussions aimed at establishing a new democratic regime in Northern Ireland. The significance of human rights issues to the peace process surfaced almost immediately, and in a somewhat unexpected manner, with the eruption in 1995 of a number of disputes over the routes taken by a number of 'Orange' parades. Protestant organizations such as the Orange Order and the Apprentice Boys of Derry hold a large number of commemorative and celebratory parades every year (Jarman 1997; Bryan 2000), some of which pass through or near Catholic Nationalist areas. Such parades were often regarded as hostile invasions by residents and many required a large police presence to ensure the safe passage of the marchers. There had been opposition to such parades in many areas over the years, but in most cases the police had supported the right of the marchers to follow their 'traditional route', rather than uphold the complaints of local residents. This was one example of how the Nationalist community felt doubly discriminated against: the police overrode their objections to what were perceived as provocative Orange parades, but they also stopped many Nationalist parades because they were regarded as too provocative (Jarman and Bryan 2000). The annual cycle of parades thus fostered a sense of inequality of treatment towards the two communities and was a recurrent reminder to the wider Catholic Nationalist population that the police were biased towards their community and not simply to the radical Republican elements within.

However, changes soon became evident when a series of protests was launched by Nationalist groups across Northern Ireland in 1995 and a number of key parades were subsequently re-routed by the police away from Nationalist areas (Jarman and Bryan 1996). The disputes rapidly became one of the key political topics and discussions over human rights became a prominent feature of the public debate about the future of Northern Ireland (Hadden and Donnelly 1997). The difference now was that both Nationalist and Unionist communities used the language of rights and each side claimed that its rights were being infringed by the actions of the other. Respect for, and protection of, human rights were thus rapidly acknowledged as key elements of any new dispensation, and were subsequently prominent in the Belfast Agreement, signed in April 1998 (Harvey 2001; Mageean 1997). In the Agreement, the political signatories 'affirmed their commitment to the mutual respect, the civil rights and the religious liberties of everyone in the community' (para. 1, 16; Rights, Safeguards and Equality of Opportunity), while the document also committed the British government to incorporate the European Convention on Human Rights (ECHR) into Northern Irish law, to develop a Bill of Rights for Northern Ireland and to establish a Human Rights Commission (para. 4, 16–17). In the assessment of two leading human rights activists from the Committee on the Administration of Justice (CAJ), the commitments in the Agreement across a range of topics illustrated how human rights had moved 'from the margins to the mainstream' (Mageean and O'Brien 1999).

Although human rights were accepted as an essential part of the larger political agenda under the Agreement, it was arguably a less prominent issue in the public domain. However, one issue in which demands for rights did impact on the wider public was in the disputes over parades, where the nature of freedom of assembly became a hotly contested topic (Jarman and Bryan 1998; Jarman et al. 1998). The disputes over parades highlighted two key issues that are addressed in the remainder of this chapter. First, the importance of human rights for policing and the role of the police, as an agent of the state, in protecting human rights for all. Second, the challenge for the two main communities to find a way of respecting each other's rights. The manner in which these two issues have been played out over the past eight years in many ways mirrors the wider political transition. The transition from the conflict of the Troubles to the negotiations of the peace process has involved a shift of focus from the politics of force to a rights-based agenda. Similarly, the reform of policing has seen a change from a highly paramilitarized force to a service where human rights are presented as the 'golden thread' of the organization. And the culture of parading has begun to change from a tradition that drew upon differentials of power, to one that acknowledges and respects difference. This transition has not been completed in any of the domains, but remains a work that is actively in progress.

Policing and human rights

There has been extensive criticism of the abuse of human rights by police officers in Northern Ireland since the formation of the Royal Ulster Constabulary in 1922. Prior to the beginning of the Troubles, much of this was couched in the language of civil rights and was related to the partisan nature of the RUC, which was always overwhelmingly Protestant in composition, and its relationship to the Protestant state (Farrell 1980; Ryder 2000; Weitzer 1995). Throughout the twenty-five years of conflict, from 1969 to 1994, numerous accusations were made of abuses of human rights committed by the various sections of the security forces to and by various human rights bodies. These related to such matters as the treatment of people who were subject to internment, procedures at the various holding centres, shoot-to-kill practices, the use of the emergency legislation, rights to silence, collusion between police officers and members of paramilitary groups, and low-level harassment of the Nationalist community (McVeigh 1994; Ni Aolain 2000; Walsh 2000). Although the United Kingdom government has been found in breach of human rights standards in a number of cases, accusations of abuse were widely countered by reference to the ongoing 'terrorist' campaign. For many in government, in the security forces, the media and within the general population, an undue focus on human rights was regarded as something of a luxury which would have to wait for a different political climate.

Policing both before and during the Troubles was a highly contentious subject, with Nationalists overwhelmingly hostile to the RUC as a result of years of heavy-handed policing practices, while Unionists staunchly defended the force, which they regarded as having protected Northern Ireland from terrorism. The need for reform of policing was regarded by many as an essential component of any peace process and any new political regime, although parties differed over the scale of such reform. While much of the attention focused on the need to attract recruits from the Catholic community and thus increase the wider legitimacy of the police, there was also growing focus on the centrality of human rights issues to any reformed police and the importance of increasing the accountability of the new structures to the wider civil society (O'Rawe and Moore 1997). The disputes over parades focused interest on the importance of human rights for policing by drawing attention to the often complex role that the police have to play in managing public order. But the disputes also raised concerns over alleged police abuse of human rights during the management of public disorder (CAJ 1996; Human Rights Watch 1997). Many of these were related to the use of force, while others concerned restrictions on freedom of movement, sectarian abuse by the police and the general lack of accountability for police actions. Some of these issues, such as the use of plastic bullets, had been widely raised before, but others were being aired for the first time, and were contingent on the new political context, the peace process and the attempts to establish an acceptable future political structure. As such, these issues served to broaden the debate both about the role of human rights in a new society and the centrality of human rights to future policing practices. These concerns were eventually reflected in the prominence given to human rights in the Belfast Agreement, signed on Good Friday 1998.

New foundations?

The Belfast Agreement provided for the establishment of an independent commission given the task of drawing up proposals for the reform of policing. The report of the Independent Commission on Policing in Northern Ireland (the Patten Report) was published in September 1999. It set out 175 recommendations that it hoped would set the standards for policing in the new Northern Ireland. A key element of the report, and therefore of its vision for a new police service, was the assertion that policing and human rights are inextricably linked and this was given emphasis by the fact that the first group of recommendations in the Patten Report focused on human rights. To explain this prominence, the Commission asserted that it was doing no more than representing the widely held views of the people of Northern Ireland: 'Our consultations showed clear agreement across the communities in Northern Ireland that people want the police to protect their human rights from infringement by others, and to respect their human rights in the exercise of their duty' (Patten Report 1999: 18: 4.1).

The report also drew on the work of Ralph Crawshaw (1995) and acknowledged his assertion that there was a perceived tension between human rights and policing that can lead police officers to be concerned that an emphasis on human rights limits their ability to enforce the law (see also Crawshaw et al. 1998). However, Patten emphasized that, '[t]here should be no conflict between human rights and policing. Policing means protecting human rights' (Patten Report 1999: 18: 4.1). The report states that it should be made clear that there is no fundamental contradiction here but, rather, '(u)pholding human rights and upholding the law should be one and the same thing' (Patten Report 1999: 18: 4.3). The authors state that the police have a responsibility to uphold human rights and the rule of law and if they disregard human rights they serve only to undermine the rule of law. While the report refrains from making judgements about the culpability of the RUC for past 'inattention' or 'abuse' of human rights, it does stress that future relationships with local communities will inevitably be damaged, and policing will be less effective, if human rights are disregarded. For Patten, paying greater attention to the positive protection of human rights was therefore one way to help legitimize any future police service in the public eye.

The Patten Report made seven recommendations related to the integration of human rights into policing culture. The first general recommendation stated: 'There should be a comprehensive programme of action to focus policing in Northern Ireland on a human rights based approach' (Patten Report 1999: 107). The report continued by recommending that there should be a new oath for all police officers; a new code of ethics and codes of practice, which reflected the ECHR; that all police personnel should be trained in the fundamental principles and standards of human rights; and that individual officers should be appraised as to the impact this has on the performance of their duty. The report also recommended that a lawyer with human rights expertise be appointed to the police legal services department and that overall police performance in respect of human rights should be monitored by the proposed new Policing Board. It was thus clearly hoped that emphasizing the centrality of human rights would increase the transparency of policing practice of individual police officers and provide a framework through which to address issues of accountability at an institutional level.

While there was a clear focus on the need for police practice to conform to human rights norms and standards, it was also recognized that in order to build confidence in the new body, which would be called the Police Service of Northern Ireland (PSNI), it should be reviewed and monitored by a broad range of independent bodies who would hold the new service publicly to account. These bodies included, among others, the Independent Oversight Commissioner, who was responsible for monitoring the implementation of the recommendations of the Patten Report; the Northern Ireland Policing Board, which has overall responsibility for policing matters and to which the Chief Constable is accountable; the Police Ombudsman for Northern Ireland, who is responsible for investigating all complaints made against the police; and the Northern Ireland Human Rights Commission.

These various bodies have published a wide range of reports that address the role that respect for human rights has been given within the PSNI. The Oversight Commissioner published his eleventh detailed report on the implementation of the Patten recommendations in September 2004. This report noted that each of the seven key recommendations had been implemented or was in the process of being addressed. Among these, the Commissioner noted the work of the Policing Board in drafting a new code of ethics, based on the ECHR, and a human rights monitoring plan which will form the basis for a regular evaluation of activities across the full range of policing practice. While noting the progress that had been made, the Oversight Commissioner did express concerns over issues of training provision and the evaluation of the impact that the human rights training had had on police officer practice. These concerns are addressed in more detail by the Northern Ireland Human Rights Commission, which has undertaken three reviews of different facets of the overall human rights training programme (NIHRC 2002, 2004a, 2004b). The Human Rights Commission acknowledges the work done by the PSNI to date, but also argues

191

that this needs to be taken further and more fully embedded within the overall structures of the organization. Finally, the Police Ombudsman has monitored police use of force and published two reports on the use of baton rounds (2002) and batons (2003). These noted that although the use of baton rounds on the seven cases investigated was 'fully justified and proportionate', there was concern at the apparent ready recourse to the use of police batons.

The evidence from the various monitoring bodies (and it should be noted that the PSNI is probably publicly scrutinized more extensively than any other police body) indicates that considerable work has been done in developing an institutional culture of human rights and that there has also been some recognizable impact in policing on the ground. For example, although there have been ongoing public order problems in many areas of Northern Ireland, the police have not fired a baton round/plastic bullet since September 2002, but rather have focused on building relations with community-based organizations to try to reduce the potential for disorder. This is not to claim that policing is now perfect, or that human rights are at the core of police practice and thinking (see O'Rawe 2003 for a critical review of the police reform process), but rather that it now has a higher profile than before and that there is greater awareness of the need to monitor the development of the reform process. However, there is also recognition that this will be a longer, slower and less complete process than some would have liked and many had hoped for.

Parades

The disputes over parades and parade routes raised two connected but distinct questions related to human rights issues. First, how does one adjudicate between competing claims when different parties claim that the assertion of the other's rights impedes their own? Second, who should decide on such competing claims? Neither of these two questions has any clear and obvious answer, both illustrate how although rights can be clearly established on paper, in practice they are subject to the rigours of political manoeuvre and negotiation. Furthermore, they highlighted the difficulty of adjudicating between competing claims of rights, and emphasize the need to develop a broad political culture in which rights, respect and responsibilities sit in some form of balance.

Initially the disputes over marches were regarded as a relatively minor matter and an issue that could be resolved by dialogue and compromise at a local level. However, although regular attempts have been made to encourage marchers and protesters to engage in a mediation process, a satisfactory compromise was only rarely achieved. More frequently suspicion, mistrust, fear and hostility proved sufficient barriers to any open discussion, while the persistent uncertainties of the trajectory of the political process further undermined people's willingness to talk across the boundaries. It was thus increasingly left to the police to deal with the competing claims and demands through the use of public order legislation. Whether there was a right to march or not was thus often determined by who could mobilize the biggest crowd and provide the biggest threat to public order. This was regarded by many as an unsatisfactory solution and it was argued that it should not be within the remit of a police force to attempt to adjudicate on what was as much a human rights issue as a public order issue (Jarman and Bryan 1996).

The issue came to a head in July 1996 when the police banned the Drumcree Orange Order parade in Portadown from returning along its favoured route and insisted the men walk a different way home. A similar decision the previous year had been resolved after two days with a compromise. But the 1996 decision was met with street protests and rioting across Northern Ireland by Unionists who objected to the ban. As the violence increased, the police reversed their initial decision and the parade was allowed to complete its original route. This, in turn, led to rioting in Nationalist areas in the north. There was widespread condemnation of both the violence and the belief that the police had been seen to give in to the threat of escalating violence. The rule of law had been all too visibly undermined and the police lost considerable credibility within both the Nationalist community and among large sections of the Unionist community.

In response to the continued violence and disorder, the government set up the Independent Review of Parades and Marches. Their report in January 1997 recommended that an independent Parades Commission should be given responsibility for dealing with disputes over parades (North Report 1997). The Commission's powers and responsibilities were set out in the Public Processions (Northern Ireland) Act 1998, which replaced large sections of the 1987 Public Order (NI) Act. This has meant that the focus for making determinations was now on issues of human rights and social responsibilities rather than the blunter instrument of public order (Jarman 1999). This new approach has since been further underpinned by the incorporation of the ECHR into United Kingdom domestic legislation with the introduction of the Human Rights Act in October 2000. However, the practical working of the legislation and the need to find a balance between claims of different rights has meant that concerns for public order are still a factor considered by the Commission and that many of their eventual determinations are strongly contested by one of the rival parties. The police were not initially supportive of the formation of the Parades Commission

New foundations?

because they were concerned that this would mean a loss of some control and authority over public events. However, that view soon changed. The Commission has in fact reduced pressure on the police, as they now simply have to enforce a decision made by another agency, whereas in the past the police often had both to make contentious decisions over conflicting claims of human rights and then police the events as well.

The Commission has thus had mixed success in attempting to resolve the disputes. It has had some degree of success in improving the climate around parades and, in many areas, its determinations have established a new status quo, which, if this has not resolved the disputes, has nevertheless helped to reduce tension and the potential for violence. Its Code of Conduct has been used to raise awareness among the various actors of their wider social responsibilities and the Commission has also supported the development of a training programme for stewards, which has helped raise standards of behaviour and reduce the potential for disorder at public events. However, the Commission has been less successful in encouraging the parties to engage in mediation to reach a mutually agreed resolution, largely because the Orange Order has refused to recognize the Commission as a legitimate body or to engage with those who oppose their parades. It has therefore proved impossible to establish the processes of mediation and dialogue between the conflicting parties that are considered necessary to establish a degree of understanding and respect for each other's perspectives.

The introduction of the Human Rights Act in October 2000 has yet to provide any significant guidance over the ongoing disputes. None of the aggrieved parties has sought to take its claims to court, but rather has preferred to continue to assert its claim to their rights without risking judicial scrutiny of such claims. In large part this is due to the fact that the European Court of Human Rights has generally upheld the right of the state to limit freedom of assembly if there is any potential for violence or public disorder (Hamilton et al. 2001). This in turn suggests that while human rights principles may help to sustain and underpin some arguments, any long-term resolution of these disputes is going to require a sustained programme of mediation with the various organizations rather than a series of legal cases pursued through the courts.

The one case where a dispute has been relatively successfully addressed has been in Derry, where parades by the Apprentice Boys have been contested by Nationalists since the late nineteenth century (Fraser 2000). When the current cycle of disputes began in 1995, the Apprentice Boys' parade around the ancient city walls soon became one of the most controversial in Northern Ireland. It is in fact the only parade to have been banned completely in recent years after the Secretary of State intervened due to the fear of violence in August 1996. The parade is particularly important for Unionists because of the historical symbolism of the Siege of Derry in 1688–89, while for Nationalists the event recalls the long history of domination and discrimination by Unionists in the city. However, while there is a history of suspicion and mistrust, both communities feel a deep sense of belonging, perhaps unlike anywhere else in Northern Ireland. Furthermore, in recent years there have been considerable efforts to build a common future, to share political power, to regenerate the commercial heart of Derry and encourage tourism. Violent rioting in the city in 1996 threatened to undermine such efforts and this led to pressures from a broad section of the business and political leadership to push the conflicting parties to find a compromise that would both acknowledge the rights of both communities and also lead to the recognition of those rights by the other party. While in all other locations the loyal (Unionist) orders have refused to negotiate with those groups who were organizing protests, ostensibly because of the role of ex-IRA members in the protests, there was considerable pressure in Derry to find a local accommodation.

A breakthrough came in August 1997 when, following intensive 'proximity' talks, Nationalists announced they would cancel their formal protest on the day of the parade, while the Apprentice Boys organized a pageant prior to the parade, to emphasize the historical importance of the event (Kelly 1998). This was the first of a series of events over the following years in which each side slowly acknowledged both the rights of the other community and the importance of encouraging the rejuvenation of the wider city. These included the steady development of the Apprentice Boys festival as a cultural event, an exertion of greater control by marchers and protesters over the crowds they brought on to the streets, closer links between the police and marchers to improve crowd control, and the decision to change the date of one of the two main marches in the city to reduce its impact on Christmas shopping. Individually, these were all minor events, but together they acknowledged a growing mutual respect and recognition that each side in the dispute had rights. On one hand, the right to parade, and on the other, the right to protest, and also that each side had to respect the expression of those rights by the other side. Furthermore, each side also implicitly acknowledged its social responsibilities to the wider city and its population; thus while the parades and the protests have continued, the scale of disorder has been limited, and while tensions recur each year, the expectation is that they will be addressed by discussion and debate rather than by the use of force or the introduction of the riot police.

Conclusion

Over the duration of the transitional period since the paramilitary cease-fires of 1994, human rights have moved towards the centre of the stage in Northern Ireland. This process has not been without difficulties and has not been fully supported by all parties. For example, the government has been accused of failing adequately to resource the institutions established to protect human rights, the Human Rights Commission has been accused of bias by Unionists and of weakness by Nationalists, and progress on a draft Bill of Rights has been extremely slow. But if one acknowledges these difficulties, then one must also acknowledge the fact that some considerable progress has been made and many more individuals and groups are using knowledge and the language of rights to present their arguments and demands.

The two areas discussed in this chapter are both examples of the imperfect development of a rights culture as part of the peace-building process in Northern Ireland. In neither case is the culture of rights fully and securely embedded. There is suspicion that, for many police officers, human rights is still a hoop to be jumped through, rather than a valuable tool of the job, while for many community-based organizations there is still a feeling that rights are a scarce commodity and if 'they' are claiming them, then 'we' must be losing them. But the cases of police reform and the reforms to the management of parades indicate something of the positive change that has been achieved: that rights are now a part of the mainstream political agenda and that rights must be acknowledged as a factor both in relations between citizen and state and also between citizens of different communities. As such, this is a move forward from a position where use of force was more widely seen as the centre of any form of practical adjudication in disputes between police and community or between neighbouring communities.

A start has been made but, as with the peace process itself, it is a long road to travel and progress is often slow. Northern Ireland is currently in a state of political transition. It is no longer a society in conflict, but nor is it a post-conflict society. The transition is a time to make change, to monitor change and build the new institutions and relationships that will help consolidate the new political regime. Human rights are now established as one element of the peace-building process, but one that will need to be nurtured, supported, encouraged, monitored and sustained over the coming years to ensure that a culture of human rights is firmly established as a feature of Northern Irish social and political life.

References

Belfast Agreement (1998) Office of the First Minister and Deputy First Minister. <www.ofmdfmni.gov.uk/publications/ba.htm>

Bryan, D. (2000) *Orange Parades: The Politics of Ritual, Tradition and Control* (London: Pluto Press).

CAJ (Committee on the Administration of Justice) (1996) *The Misrule of Law: A Report on the Policing of Events During the Summer of 1996 in Northern Ireland* (Belfast: CAJ).

Crawshaw, R. (1995) 'Human Rights, the Rule of Law and Policing', in Council of Europe (ed.), *Human Rights and the Police: Seminar Proceedings* (Strasbourg: Council of Europe).

Crawshaw, R., B. Devlin and T. Williamson (1998) *Human Rights and Policing: Standards for Good Behaviour and a Strategy for Change* (The Hague: Kluwer Law International).

Farrell, M. (1980) *Northern Ireland: The Orange State* (London: Pluto Press).

Fraser, T. G. (2000) 'The Apprentice Boys and the Relief of Derry Parades', in T. G. Fraser (ed.), *The Irish Parading Tradition: Following the Drum* (London: Macmillan).

Hadden, T. and A. Donnelly (1997) *The Legal Control of Marches in Northern Ireland* (Belfast: Community Relations Council).

Hamilton, M., N. Jarman and D. Bryan (2001) *Parades, Protests and Policing: A Human Rights Framework* (Belfast: Northern Ireland Human Rights Commission).

Harvey, C. (ed.) (2001) *Human Rights, Equality and Democratic Renewal in Northern Ireland* (Oxford and Portland: Hart Publishing).

Human Rights Watch (1997) *To Serve without Favor: Policing, Human Rights and Accountability in Northern Ireland* (New York: HRW).

Jarman, N. (1997) *Material Conflicts: Parades and Visual Displays in Northern Ireland* (Oxford: Berg).

— (1999) 'Regulating Rights and Managing Public Order: Parade Disputes and the Peace Process 1995–1998', *Fordham International Law Journal*, 22 (4).

Jarman, N. and D. Bryan (1996) *Parade and Protest: A Discussion of Parading Disputes in Northern Ireland* (Coleraine: Centre for the Study of Conflict).

— (1998) *From Riots to Rights: Nationalist Parades in the North of Ireland* (Coleraine: Centre for the Study of Conflict).

— (2000) 'Green Parades in an Orange State: Nationalist and Republican Commemorations and Demonstrations from Partition to the Troubles, 1920–1970', in T. G. Fraser (ed.), *The Irish Parading Tradition: Following the Drum* (London: Macmillan).

Jarman, N., D. Bryan, N. Caleyron and C. de Rosa (1998) *Politics in Public: Freedom of Assembly and the Right to Protest* (Belfast: Democratic Dialogue).

Kelly, G. (1998) *Mediation in Practice* (Derry/Londonderry: INCORE).

McVeigh, R. (1994) *Harassment: It's Part of Life Here … Survey of Young People's Attitudes to and Experiences of Harassment by the Security Forces* (Belfast CAJ).

New foundations?

Mageean, P. (1997) 'Human Rights and the Peace Process in Northern Ireland', *Critical Criminology*, 8 (1).

Mageean, P. and M. O'Brien (1999) 'From the Margins to the Mainstream: Human Rights and the Good Friday Agreement', *Fordham International Law Journal*, 22 (4).

Moore, L. (1999) 'Policing and Change in Northern Ireland: The Centrality of Human Rights', *Fordham International Law Journal*, 22 (4).

Ni Aolain, F. (2000) *The Politics of Force: Conflict Management and State Violence in Northern Ireland* (Belfast: Blackstaff Press).

NIHRC (Northern Ireland Human Rights Commission) (2002) *An Evaluation of Human Rights Training for Student Police Officers in the Police Service of Northern Ireland* (Belfast: NIHRC).

— (2004a) *Human Rights in Police Training 3: Probationer Constables and Student Officers* (Belfast: NIHRC).

— (2004b) *Human Rights in Police Training 4: Course for All* (Belfast: NIHRC).

North Report (1997) *Report of the Independent Review of Parades and Marches* (Belfast: Stationery Office).

O'Rawe, M. (2003) 'Transitional Policing Arrangements in Northern Ireland: The Can't and Won't of the Change Dialectic', *Fordham International Law Journal*, 26 (4).

O'Rawe, M. and L. Moore (1997) *Human Rights on Duty: Principles for Better Policing – International Lessons for Northern Ireland* (Belfast: CAJ).

Patten Report (1999) *A New Beginning: Policing in Northern Ireland: The Report of the Independent Commission on Policing for Northern Ireland* (Belfast: Stationery Office).

Police Ombudsman for Northern Ireland (2002) *Baton Rounds Report* (Belfast: OPONI).

— (2003) *A Study of Complaints Involving the Use of Batons by the Police in Northern Ireland* (Belfast: OPONI).

Purdie, B. (1990) *Politics in the Streets: The Origins of the Civil Rights Movement in Northern Ireland* (Belfast: Blackstaff Press).

Ryder, C. (2000) *The RUC 1922–2000: A Force Under Fire* (London: Arrow).

Walsh, D. (2000) *Bloody Sunday and the Rule of Law in Northern Ireland* (Dublin: Gill and Macmillan).

Weitzer, R. (1995) *Policing Under Fire: Ethnic Conflict and Police Community Relations in Northern Ireland* (New York: SUNY Press).

THREE | **Current challenges**

11 | Rights-based responses to aid politicization in Afghanistan

PAUL O'BRIEN

The spiral of aid politicization has seen another revolution since 2001. Afghanistan and Iraq have crystallized the inseparability of aid and politics in the world's hot-spots. While the rules of classic humanitarianism may still apply in 'forgotten emergencies', NGOs can no longer expect to be given the humanitarian space to serve people apolitically in contexts like Afghanistan and Iraq, where, for better or worse, the rules of international aid policy are increasingly being written.

This chapter accepts the politicization of aid in such contexts as a given and asks what NGOs ought to do about it. First, it explores what NGOs really mean by 'aid politicization', and then considers why rights-based approaches offer humanitarians a principled response to this phenomenon. Looking at aid politicization in Afghanistan, it considers how rights-based NGOs responded to two dimensions of aid politicization: the role of the military in humanitarian action and the funding environment. It concludes that a rights-based lens made a real difference to NGOs both in terms of approach and in terms of impact. The chapter closes by drawing some more general lessons from the recent experience of incorporating rights into humanitarianism and reconstruction in Afghanistan.

What does 'aid politicization' mean?

The allocation of aid is always driven by political objectives. The expenditure of public funds must always be justified in political terms. Even for humanitarian field workers, there are core political values that guide what they do and why they do it. No matter how altruistic the motivation or urgent the need, regardless of who benefits, politics lies at the core of every aid decision. So why is 'aid politicization' even a matter for discussion? Because as long as it has existed, the aid community has used the term 'politics' in two very different ways. In the vernacular of most aid workers, our work is necessarily 'political' with a small 'p', but never 'Political' with a big 'P'. Whether the distinction is real or misperceived, it profoundly informs the self-perception of most NGOs.

What do aid workers mean when they claim their work is 'political' but not 'Political'? Having listened to this discussion in many different fora over the past few years, I have come to believe that they mean, in short, that aid is and should be informed by certain political values that are shared by intended beneficiaries, warring parties, and donors,[1] but aid should not be subject to or used in furtherance of partisan 'Political' agendas that divide any of these constituencies, either internally or from each other.[2]

This notion of higher shared political values has informed humanitarian intervention from its earliest days. Modern-day humanitarian action was born on Napoleonic battlefields. Having witnessed the horrific aftermath of Solferino, Henri Dunant called for new principles and new actors to protect wounded soldiers who were *'hors de combat'*, and so the Red Cross movement was born. Dunant's vision survived because he convinced warring parties to accept the difference between their short-term political and military aims of winning the conflict, and the longer-term political and military visions over which those conflicts were fought. By forging agreement over the ethical difference between killing a fighting soldier on the one hand and murdering non-combatants on the other, he created the 'humanitarian space' for his Red Cross to tend the wounded of both sides without favouring one or the other. At the heart of Dunant's success was the shared acceptance by states of common values that superseded the short-term military goals of the warring parties. Those common values – that war should have rules and should be fought between combatant soldiers – were profoundly 'p'olitical. But because they were values that did not trigger partisan disagreement, they were not seen as Political in the big 'P' sense of the word.

As humanitarian law and action evolved from saving wounded soldiers to the protection of civilians in armed conflict, so too did the concept of political neutrality.[3] Today, humanitarian space means much more than protection for battlefield medics; it claims, in its most ambitious form, to guarantee aid actors access to people in need in any life-threatening situation.

At each stage in its evolution, humanitarianism has forged and then relied upon consensus on core *political* values: people in need should be protected from life-threatening harm (the principle of humanity); aid should be distributed solely according to need (the principle of impartiality). To guarantee the fulfilment of the humanity and impartiality principles, aid implementers should be both independent and neutral between partisan political actors.[4] Are 'humanity', 'impartiality', 'independence' and 'neutrality' political values? Most certainly. Politics, at its essence, is the process through which resources and power are allocated and used.[5] Through such a lens, all aid work is profoundly political in its goals and its implications. Aid seeks to channel resources and power in a certain direction and in a certain way – towards those in dire need to alleviate suffering and to help them fend off future vulnerability. What could be a more political goal than redistributing the resources of one country to fight extreme poverty in another?

Ask most relief workers operating in conflict settings which 'side' they favour, and most will tell you they favour no side at all. But ask them whether they are politically aligned with oppressive power-brokers in conflict with each other, or with those oppressed on both sides of a conflict, and most will claim solidarity with the latter. Even those organizations that cherish their apolitical roots most fervently are inclined towards 'pro-poor politics'.

If all aid is already politically driven, what does 'aid politicization' mean, if anything? In reality, it refers to the allocation of resources on general political principles around which consensus does *not* exist. When aid is used in non-consensual circumstances to achieve partisan political objectives, it moves from the small 'p' to the big 'P'. As later sections of this chapter will show, that is precisely what has happened in Afghanistan since the fall of the Taliban. Because aid is being used in Afghanistan to achieve political goals over which there is diminishing consensus, concerns over aid politicization are growing.

Responding to aid politicization through rights

There was a time when the integrity of humanitarian agencies was beyond question. Challenging the narcissism of the 1980s, NGOs gave us back our social conscience by appealing to higher political values. When they borrowed from the 1960s rhetoric of Martin Luther King Jnr and John F. Kennedy to remind the world of our common humanity, the world responded. The Ethiopian famine of 1985 was a zenith of sorts, as the genius of Bob Geldof's Band Aid tapped into the humanity principle, global compassion and people power.

Since then, however, in places like Somalia, Cambodia, Bosnia, Kosovo, Rwanda and East Timor, the aid community has struggled to communicate those universal political values that can mobilize mass support and action. By the 1990s, people wanted to know why the grand development project was failing, why endemic poverty survived. Northern governments were questioning the larger impact of development as corrupt regimes siphoned off aid dollars with entrepreneurial efficiency. Journalists, overwhelmed by compassion fatigue, wrote countless stories of NGO mismanagement. Jaded assistance workers reflected upon how it had all gone wrong.

Battered by those critiques, many international NGOs decided that a course change was necessary. They didn't want to be accused of naïvely applying Band-Aids to dying patients. They wanted to move from inadequately treating symptoms to getting at the underlying causes of poverty and suffering. If their programmes were putting people in danger, they wanted to find out how, and to take steps to minimize unintended harms. If unending cycles of conflict were robbing generations of hope, then NGOs would promote peace through advocacy and 'peacebuilding' programmes. If corrupt regimes were impoverishing their peoples, NGOs would mobilize communities to protect their rights, and pressure the outside world to act. If rich donor nations were not living up to their rhetoric or responsibilities to poorer countries, NGOs would use their moral authority and ground knowledge to educate donors, and if necessary embarrass them into action.

In other words, these NGOs wanted to move towards 'new humanitarianism'. While preserving their right to serve communities aPolitically (capital 'P') in non-partisan ways, new humanitarians believed that NGOs had to become more politically astute, and even take on the political causes and symptoms of endemic poverty and suffering (small 'p').

To explain and organize their new thinking, new humanitarians turned to human rights. Through the 1990s, many of the larger NGOs either reaffirmed and expanded a prior commitment to promote human rights, or integrated 'rights-based approaches' into their thinking for the first time.[6] Human rights principles were the perfect vehicle for new humanitarians. At a time when NGO integrity was being challenged, human rights offered the highest and most universally accepted political principles. They were, by definition, applicable to everyone. Any root cause of poverty and suffering worth addressing could be explained in human rights terms. Any call to political action would be stronger if couched in terms of human rights and responsibilities.

In the late 1990s a powerful constituency formed to challenge the move towards new humanitarianism. It started in British humanitarian policy think-tanks like the Overseas Development Institute, and the Institute for Politics and International Studies in Leeds. More recently, it was joined by American commentators such as David Rieff who wrote the influential book, *A Bed for the Night: Humanitarianism in Crisis* (2002). In sum, thinkers like Rieff, Mark Duffield (2001), Joanna Macrae and Nick Leader (2001), and Fiona Fox (2001) believe that new humanitarians have tried but failed to adapt effectively to the politicization of aid.

In *Global Governance and the New Wars*, Mark Duffield notes a marked 'radicalization of the politics of development', and concludes that NGOs are losing their sense of proportion and humility (2001: 15). Rights-based NGOs are fooling themselves and others if they think they can address egregious human rights violations, mitigate conflict through new trans-formative tools, shift the balance of power between discordant groups or change deeply held attitudes, beliefs and values, he concludes.

By adopting a 'consequentialist ethical framework' (ibid., p. 75),[7] NGOs now claim a greater capacity to do good than we have any basis to assert, Duffield believes. Simply because badly conceived aid can entrench wars does not mean that, in the right hands, aid can also end war. 'New humanitarianism', with its promise to minimize its negative side effects, strengthen peace and prevent conflict, is a phoney. Duffield concludes that humanitarians should give up this shell game and get back to providing life-saving services, whenever and wherever they can, simply because it is the right thing to do, and it is all they know how to do. Consequential-ist ethics will always fail, Duffield contends, because humanitarians have neither the will nor the capacity to understand and respond to the real consequences of their actions. They are too self-serving, too predisposed to accommodate those who threaten them, too beholden to obsolete notions of a mechanistic construct of the world to comprehend the realities of emerging political complexes and their role in them.

Better, as David Rieff argues, to provide the suffering with 'a bed for the night' than an empty promise that we could never fulfil. Their competency, their reason for being, is not to address the world's great problems. NGOs will never bring peace to Afghanistan, end human rights abuses by warlords, or stamp out government corruption; but if only they would stay true to their roots, they could mitigate the worst excesses of human cruelty and remain a relevant force for good, whatever twists and turns Afghanistan might take. Rights-based humanitarianism, with its institutionalization of compassion tied to legal standards that it can rarely meet, may have gone too far, and 'may never recover' (Rieff 2002: 302).

How did NGOs get themselves into this mess? Duffield believes that for too long NGOs have been driven by the simplistic cause and effect logic of Newtonian physics. We assume that a given amount of inputs combined with a given amount of energy would produce given outcomes. He argues that NGOs have yet to adopt new scientific thinking, which describes the world organically rather than mechanistically. Whereas machines create predetermined outcomes, organic systems are concerned with self-renewal, and, as such, are more than the sum of their distinct parts. Duffield con-cludes that NGOs are prone to see complex political emergencies like Afghanistan as states of nature that can be understood and ameliorated through mechanistic problem-solving. Instead, NGOs needed to acknow-ledge the reality of 'emerging political complexes' where fluid systems of actors and relationships play off each other politically, militarily and economically, and determine humanitarian well-being in ways beyond the conceptual capacity of humanitarian agencies.

By Duffield's analysis, Afghanistan is an 'emerging political complex' *par excellence*. Gone is the ruthless simplicity of the Taliban. The new Afghan government is a multi-headed temptress with some players more progressive than many NGOs, and others who would happily evict all international NGOs, and divide Afghanistan into a feudal pie. Gone is donor indifference and media naïveté – every donor has an agenda, every story needs a twist. Gone, too, is the monopoly of compassion and humanitarian competence that not-for-profits once exercised in Afghanistan. On the heels of all the new money come an array of profit-oriented contractors, national and foreign, who threaten NGOs with their 'doubtlessness' and 'deliverables', not to mention the military, who have gone from engaging in the odd 'hearts and minds' humanitarian project to seeking a central coordination role in the overall assistance effort. The new Afghanistan is complex indeed.

Will the adoption of rights-based approaches help NGOs deal with this complexity? Duffield says no. He argues that by interpreting human rights in moral rather than legal terms, NGOs have coopted human rights principles without changing their behaviour. As Duffield concludes, 'it is not a case of reforming the NGO to address human rights, but the reverse: it is the aid agency reforming its concept of human rights to bring it in line with the work that it already does' (2001: 222).

Duffield's challenge is a serious one: if all NGOs do is retool their vocabularies and now talk about 'addressing rights' rather than meeting needs, they will not only fail to grasp the import of a rights-based approach, but they will remain unprepared to face the politicization of aid. What Duffield and other new humanitarians fail to understand, however, is the nature of organizational change and how much rights-based thinking has actually transformed the identity of self-proclaimed rights-based NGOs.

In *Global Governance*, Duffield falls victim, at the last hurdle, to the challenge he identified at the outset – the need to understand that the world rarely works in simple, linear, cause-and-effect patterns. Rather, organizations change like organisms, over time and when a multitude of forces come together. Instead of seeing organizational change as a process of systemic development, Duffield faults NGOs that have adopted human rights and new humanitarianism for not changing overnight into radically different creatures. He expected a flick of the switch to usher in a new reality. And so he fails to examine how NGOs have actually responded in concrete ways to the politicization of aid by adopting more principled methods. In sum, the frugality of Duffield's analysis sells new humanitarianism short.

As institutional organisms, agencies that adopt new humanitarianism are already transforming themselves and will continue to do so. In aiming to take responsibility for the consequences of their work, and in holding others responsible also, they are having a real and meaningful impact on the contexts in which they work. Certainly they can do more, but to argue that new humanitarianism can already be judged a failure is off the mark.

Why are human rights-based approaches such a powerful and relevant response to the politicization of aid? Because aid politicization, properly understood, is the use of aid for increasingly partisan political objectives. Whereas aid allocation is by nature a political act, what distinguishes today's reality are the growing lack of consensus over aid decision-making, and the lack of consensus over the role of humanitarianism in complex crises. Donors no longer claim the high moral ground of pure humanitarian motives; they are less and less shy about their partisan political objectives in their use of aid funds; the military want to use humanitarian aid to achieve military objectives, anti-Western militants see NGOs as political proxies for their donors and therefore legitimate targets.

For much of the last fifty years, when donors responded to humanitarian crises they promoted a political vision of the world which was increasingly shared by the world's policy-makers: people should not be allowed to suffer when adequate global resources are available to help them; parties to conflict should ensure that innocent civilians are protected on all sides; when people are suffering, resources should be allocated according to need alone. Consensus over such political premises created the humanitarian space in which the aid community functioned.

Since 11 September 2001, Western policy-makers, and the United States in particular, have struggled to forge the kinds of consensus that seem larger than partisan 'Politics'. In Afghanistan, lines were quickly drawn and policy-makers wanted to know whose side NGOs were on: were we for or against the 'war on terror'? Did we support the new Afghanistan over the Taliban legacy? Faced with the horror of New York, NGO pretensions at moral neutrality would have appeared like weakness. But explicitly supporting the 'war on terror' would have cut us, once and for all, from our humanitarian roots. Faced with the polarization of global politics, NGOs had to find a way to situate themselves.

This was where rights-based approaches offered NGOs a choice other than classic humanitarianism on the one hand and partisan political co-option on the other. Whereas the case for classic humanitarianism – 'let us function because we have no political agenda other than saving lives' – has lost its utility for donors and its credibility for anti-Western forces, the value-laden perspective of the rights-based new humanitarian may be what is required to survive in such contexts. The rights-based humanitarian commits to protecting the human rights of the people she serves. Recognizing her minimal role in the fulfilment of those rights, she advocates systematically with policy-makers to stop rights denial and promote rights protection. She does not claim to be apolitical – her very political goal is the fulfilment of the economic, social, cultural, political and civil rights of the people she serves – but she is not partisan either. She can stand before the Afghan government and its international donors and say, 'I will work with you, in so far as your goals and my human rights goals coincide. But as soon as those goals diverge, I will hold you responsible.' She can stand before anti-government forces or sceptical communities and say: 'I may work with the government, but I am not here for them. I am here for you, and your human rights protection.' Of course, what she says will mean little if actions do not follow – always the test for rights-promoting aspirants. But the promise and potential of human rights is that when actions *do* follow words, they can offer hope for new consensus based on the rights of the people that all parties claim to represent.

The following examples review the specific case of Afghanistan and assess whether NGOs that adopted a rights-based approach managed to translate words to action and, in so doing, to stand up to the increasing challenge of aid politicization.

The Afghanistan case study

On 8 September 2003, five Afghan NGO workers were travelling towards their field office in southern Afghanistan's Ghazni province when they were stopped by a group of armed men. Identifying themselves as Taliban, thee men said, 'You were warned about working for NGOs', and then executed four of the aid workers, shooting the fifth in the leg four times.[8] Fifteen days later, two more NGO workers were murdered on a road in Helmand province.[9] On 27 September, a letter was posted on the door of a CARE field office in Ghazni at 11 a.m., which translated as follows:

- Separate yourselves from the Jewish and Christian community
- Cut your relations with the present transitional government
- Cut your relations with the NGOs and other aid agencies
- Don't take part in the funeral ceremony of the people working in foreign NGOs while killed ...
- In case of any disagreement with the above points, people will face the expected bad result.

In the next week, another CARE sub-office in Ghazni was shelled by a rocket.[10] That month, there were twenty-two separate violent attacks on NGOs, mostly in southern Afghanistan, mostly politically motivated.[11] From March 2003 to December 2004, thirty-three aid workers were killed and hundreds more injured. In June 2004, after five of their staff were murdered, Médecins Sans Frontières (MSF) shut down all its programmes and withdrew from Afghanistan. If aid workers ever hoped that claims of political neutrality would shield them from harm, that hope died in Afghanistan in 2003 and 2004. For anti-government forces, they had become legitimate targets. For international donors and the government, they were political agents in a much larger game, with much greater stakes than poverty alleviation and the short-term relief of suffering.

The September 2003 attacks sent shock-waves through the NGO community. There had been a growing pattern of attacks through the previous year, but the executions had taken insecurity to a new level.[12] At a standing-room-only emergency meeting on 2 October 2003 NGOs discussed the new environment. There was strong consensus on the cause of the targeting: the widely shared perception that NGOs had become part of two related political projects – the winning of the international war on terror and extending the influence of the Karzai government.

NGOs initially discussed whether they should even aim for political neutrality on these issues when faced with an internationally supported government on the one hand, and militant extremists on the other. While there was no sympathy for the Taliban, there was also growing doubt about the legitimacy of these two political projects. The Karzai government was born of a pragmatic political accommodation at Bonn that left it populated with human rights abusers and private militia leaders, and it had shown a questionable ability to clean itself up.[13] While most communities rejected the Taliban and still trusted promises of future support from the Afghan government, not all did. Increasingly, by late 2003, southern Pashtun communities where NGOs worked were feeling alienated by the central authorities. Similarly, the war on terror in Afghanistan had been conducted in ways that had unnecessarily alienated southern Pashtun leaders and the communities they represented.[14]

NGOs faced a dilemma: if the consensus over these two political projects continued to dissipate, and southern communities saw themselves on the wrong side of a partisan political project, their relationship with these communities might be damaged, irrevocably. At that emergency meeting, NGOs discussed whether insecurity had become so bad as to demand a mass suspension of NGO activities in the South. The unanimous decision was no. If they pulled out en masse, they might never re-establish the trust of communities on which they relied so much. Through the Mujahadeen civil wars, through the Taliban years, the source of their legitimacy and effectiveness was the faith of communities that NGOs had their interests at heart, and they proved that by staying with them through insecure times. In return, communities helped to protect NGOs and to facilitate their work, even when it conflicted with government policies.[15]

That meeting revealed a major challenge for NGOs. For years they had relied upon political agnosticism so as to avoid the stigma of political partisanship. They treated poverty as an economic problem, and offered the kinds of economic solutions that they could deliver. But now they were losing the sanctuary of ignorance, as it became increasingly obvious that Afghanistan's problems were profoundly political. Whether they liked it or not, some NGOs felt they would have to define themselves politically, or withdraw from the country to preserve their staff's safety and their organizational integrity.

Most NGOs accepted the politicization of the Afghan context reluctantly. Perhaps NGO recalcitrance reflected a refusal to come to terms with their own marginalization post-Taliban. In the land of the one-eyed Taliban, the politically blind truly were kings.[16] Humanitarian funders had the only money available,[17] and insisted that NGOs maintained an arm's-length relationship with the Taliban.[18] The assistance community, for its own part, enjoyed the power that such independence gave it, becoming a de facto shadow government that delivered many of the social services that the Taliban were unable or unwilling to provide.

When the world came to Afghanistan post-Taliban, power and donor interest transferred to the new interim government. As money became available not just for humanitarian activities but for reconstruction, NGOs did not adjust easily. When asked to participate in explicitly political or security related exercises, such as election awareness raising, participating in the emergency Loya Jirga that elected the Transitional Administration, NGOs balked, fearing that too close an alignment to the Karzai regime would jeopardize their relationships with communities. Many NGOs continued to argue that reconstruction aid should be delivered 'neutrally, impartially and independently', but were now on shaky ground.

Why were NGOs holding on to claims of political agnosticism long after the Afghanistan project had moved from pure humanitarianism (if it ever was)? Perhaps it was really true, as Duffield and Rieff claim, that NGOs had neither the capacity nor the will to think about the new political context they were in. Some who saw the change that had happened still refused to distinguish between higher political principles like good governance, which they should have fought for, and promoting one set of government actors and partisan political ideas, which they could legitimately argue was beyond their mandate. Perhaps they feared being misinterpreted as anti-governmental rather than non-governmental.

But not all NGOs felt this way. Increasingly in policy conversations, NGOs recognized that if they were to survive current trends in aid politicization, they needed new principles upon which to ground their actions and decisions. This chapter argues that human rights provided some NGOs with just such a foundation. The next section offers a review of how some NGOs demonstrated in Afghanistan, with mixed results, that getting political and using a rights framework to do so makes sense. It does this by looking at two different dimensions to aid politicization: the militarization of aid and the politicized allocation of aid.

The civil–military dilemma No issue has brought home the politicization of aid in Afghanistan more explicitly than the intermingling of military and assistance goals by international policy-makers. Even before the war against the Taliban was over, it was clear that Afghanistan would be a template for the militarization of aid. As Bob Woodward noted in *Bush at War* (2002), the coalition's decision to air-drop both bombs and humanitarian packages in the autumn of 2001 was motivated, above all, by military goals and the desire to make allies of ordinary Afghans. There was almost no calculus, public or private, of how effectively those packages would relieve suffering compared with supporting professional humanitarian agencies (for example, the UN's World Food Programme). NGOs argued that those packages might end up doing more harm than good to ordinary Afghans,[19] but they did so equivocally, and their nuanced messages failed to catch the ears of policy-makers and an international public who wanted a quick victory in Afghanistan.

In December 2002, at a meeting with NGOs, senior USAID officials revealed their plans to co-locate with US-led military teams to strengthen the overall coordination of US-donated aid. The officials made clear that the aim of this initiative, like that of all US efforts in Afghanistan, was to win the 'war on terror'. When they acknowledged that aid coordination would be used as one weapon in this fight, I raised the obvious dilemma: if NGOs participated in this effort, they would be taking United States funding in order to help achieve a military objective, not a humanitarian one, and I asked what advice the US government had for us in resolving this dilemma. One official replied, 'I feel like I'm in that Casablanca scene when the guy whispers, "Do you know that there is gambling going on in the casino?"' He did not think there was a real dilemma at all.

He would have been surprised, therefore, at the strong NGO reaction to the new military-aid concept they were proposing – what is now known as the 'Provincial Reconstruction Team' concept or 'PRT'.[20] The first PRTs were US-led and brought together soldiers (usually fewer than 100), civil affairs officers, political representatives from the Department of State and USAID representatives.[21] They were explicitly mandated to use reconstruction aid to local communities to improve security and strengthen the writ of the Karzai government.[22]

At their conception, PRTs were mooted as the way to fill a clear coordination gap ensuring that aid was delivered quickly to people in need. The United Nations and NGOs reacted strongly, arguing that the military had neither the capacity nor the mandate to coordinate aid. More importantly, they were fearful that the organizing principle of aid delivery would become the war on terror, and not sustainable impact for ordinary Afghans. The 'coordination' claim was soon dropped by the military, but debate on the PRTs continued for much of the next year.[23] Both sets of humanitarian actors argued that PRTs should focus more on security and engage less in direct reconstruction, which unnecessarily and dangerously blurred the line between the military and civilians and was designed for short-term visibility, not long-term impact.

Although the military retracted proposals that the PRTs coordinate aid, they did not accept arguments on the need for a clear separation between military and civilian-led aid. Nor did they accept the distinction that civilian humanitarians wanted to make between 'reconstruction work' on the one hand and 'security work' on the other. They saw the two sides of the PRT mission as interdependent with reconstruction playing a key part in the promotion of security.[24] While NGOs recognized the relationship, they urged the PRTs to emphasize security, and to reconceive themselves as 'Provincial Security or Stabalization Teams'.

The reaction of policy-makers in both Afghanistan and the United States was negative. President Karzai wanted the PRTs to keep their name. Already sensitive about being perceived as a US puppet, he hoped to limit foreign troop presence. Wanting to play down the weakness of his own security forces, he also liked that they were called 'reconstruction' teams.[25] Meanwhile, US Secretary of Defense, Donald Rumsfeld, needing a military victory to present to the US public, was declaring Afghanistan largely at peace by May 2003, and was referring to PRTs as, 'the best thing that can be done to ultimately provide security in Afghanistan'.[26]

A rights-based response to the civil–military dilemma The first time most NGOs heard of PRTs, they reacted strongly and negatively. At first, NGOs mostly argued that the military were unnecessarily stepping into humanitarian activity, a decision that would blur the distinction between them and civilian humanitarians and ultimately put NGO workers at risk.[27] But these arguments fell on unsympathetic ears. PRT supporters implied the NGOs were 'whining' and argued there was more than enough need to go around. Even the United Nations thought NGOs were arguing for little more than the protection of their business interests. 'NGOs do not have a monopoly on humanitarianism,' one UN official told me. In a large meeting of donors and government in March 2003, US Ambassador Robert Finn recalled how his father had provided life-saving aid to civilians in the Second World War, and that there was a long tradition of soldiers helping people. 'Soldiers want to do good too,' he said.

To borrow a metaphor from Hugo Slim, NGOs appeared to some like a jester who wanted a monopoly on humour in the court of public opinion. Like a good joke, humanitarianism was something everyone valued, yet NGOs seemed to be saying, 'because we do this for a living, we don't want anyone else to do it'. What NGOs tried and failed to do early on was to take up Slim's challenge of proving why certain types of humour *should* be the sole preserve of the court jester. As Slim points out:

> At his or her best, the humanitarian in war is also a liminal figure who can tread where others cannot tread ... He [or she] must have no political interest so as to be beyond suspicion. The clown can only mock the King because he has no desire to be King ... So it is with humanitarians who can introduce resources into a war because they have no desire to win it. (Slim 2003)

Slim challenged NGOs to explain their PRT positions through arguments and principles that stood for more than self-preservation. The position he offered to NGOs, however, was one they were initially unwilling to take: that they had no desire to be part of the winning political side in the current war for power in Afghanistan. If they had taken up Slim's challenge, they would have argued that there was still a real political conflict in Afghanistan, and its outcome was uncertain, and therefore aid should be delivered only by dedicated neutralists. If the Karzai government fell, NGOs would need access to people in need, and the PRTs, by associating humanitarianism with a particular political standpoint, were jeopardizing that access. But NGOs chose, in large part, not to focus on that argument. Mostly they avoided highlighting the fragility of the political project, at least in part, because they did not want it to fail.

Instead, NGOs took another path, not based on their humanitarian authority, but grounded in notions of rights and responsibilities. And so, they aimed to highlight what the Afghan population actually deserved in terms of human security, and to get policy-makers to live up to their security-related promises.

While NGOs did not explicitly rely upon human rights or humanitarian law,[28] they did aim to focus discussions on the rights and responsibilities of the stakeholders in ways that they would not have done ten or even five years before. Through the first half of 2002, international NGOs were the only public voice challenging the international community to deliver on their security-related promises to ordinary Afghans.[29] Rather than tinkering with the PRT concept, NGOs urged the international community to provide Afghans with an adequately sized peacekeeping force. They pointed out that, while other contexts such as Bosnia, Kosovo, East Timor and Rwanda had seen an average of one peacekeeper for every sixty-five people, PRT members – the only international forces outside Kabul mandated to improve security for Afghans – numbered one for every 100,000 Afghans (CARE 2003). In July 2003, more than 100 NGOs signed a joint statement challenging the PRT concept and seeking to refocus policy discussions on security for ordinary Afghans.

When the NGOs challenged policy-makers that the PRTs were not providing adequate human security for Afghans, there was little disagreement. Even the PRTs themselves conceded that their role was not to keep peace directly, to protect civilians, to disarm militias or intervene militarily between fighting factions. They recognized that while militias were growing stronger and fighting with each other, injuring civilians, they were powerless to intervene directly. While poppy cultivation and heroin production were growing exponentially, they simply did not have the mandate or resources to interfere. They had no official 'reach back' capacity to call upon the 'war fighting' coalition forces, and operated under different chains of command that met only at the highest levels. In reality, their mandate was restricted to negotiation, intelligence gathering, small reconstruction projects and other forms of 'hearts and minds' work for the central government and the coalition.

Publicizing these constraints, NGOs argued that the PRTs, instead of addressing the deteriorating security situation, were more focused on how they would be perceived internationally. With fewer than 300 soldiers operational in September 2003, Western policy-makers could talk about soldiers on the ground helping Afghans in different parts of the country, and rest assured that they were not overly depleting their treasuries or putting large forces in harm's way, as a peacekeeping force might. They could point to how PRTs were helping not just to bring security, but to rebuild Afghanistan (even though the current PRT budget is less than one-thousandth of Afghanistan's reconstruction needs).[30] As Barnett Rubin argued to the United States House of Representatives Committee on International Relations:

NGOs have criticized the PRTs for confusing the role of the military and assistance providers and hence failing both to provide security and to promote reconstruction ... [L]ike many other proposals for reconstruction, security, and other goals in Afghanistan, the proposal for PRTs seems largely dictated by what donor countries are willing to do, for reasons other that what it would require to achieve their alleged goals in Afghanistan. (Rubin et al. 2003)

It was with relief, therefore, that NGOs received news from NATO[31] and then the United Nations Security Council[32] that the expansion of the International Security Assistance Force (ISAF) outside Kabul would ultimately be authorized. After almost two years of advocacy, ISAF expansion ('the issue that would not go away')[33] would finally happen. When presenting their reasons for expansion, NATO explicitly made reference to repeated NGO advocacy.[34]

In the end, the NGO victory may have been somewhat pyrrhic. When NGOs heard that the initial expansion would be a German-led 450-strong PRT to Kunduz, they feared that, once again, public relations had prevailed over the security rights of ordinary Afghans. Kunduz was one of Afghanistan's safest provinces by far.[35] The only real threat to security in Kunduz was the growing poppy trade, but the German PRT was not mandated to engage in getting the narcotics trade under control in its area.

Throughout 2004, when NATO's PRT expansion stalled and those that did come did not take on issues such as drugs and local commanders, NGOs continued to protest that the security rights of ordinary Afghans were not being met. US NGOs met with Pentagon and State Department officials on this issue on numerous occasions. In hundreds of stories published in international media outlets, they challenged Western policy-makers to live up to their security-related promises to Afghans.[36] In October 2004, just prior to the national elections, the Human Rights Research and Advocacy Consortium (HRRAC) published a report entitled *Take the Guns Away* (Thorold et al. 2004), which argued that international security forces had largely abdicated their responsibility to bring real security to ordinary Afghans.

Whereas NGOs had little or no success in shifting coalition or NATO policy when they appealed to traditional humanitarian values of separation between civilian- and military-led humanitarian responses, they were able to make progress when they situated their efforts in the security rights of ordinary Afghans. While some classic humanitarian NGOs believed that advocating for ISAF expansion compromised NGOs' neutrality, rights-based NGOs were able to engage fully in the debate over the security rights of

Afghans, without being perceived to be proxies for donors. By arguing that the international military had to do more to take on drug lords and warlords, as well as holding them responsible when the war on terror led to civilian casualties, NGOs situated themselves as loyal, not to the partisan political objectives of either the military or the anti-government forces, but to the security rights of the Afghan citizenry.

The funding dilemma Even before 9/11, the White House was signalling a shift towards using aid more overtly for political goals.[37] For too long, in the administration's view, the misuse of aid capital had squandered precious political capital abroad. In May 2001, USAID boss Andrew Natsios made his views clear: 'As a great power, I believe America's foreign assistance both serves to accomplish our foreign policy objectives, and expresses the deep humanitarian instincts of the American People.' USAID, he went on, is a 'key foreign policy instrument' and concluded that: 'Foreign assistance is an important tool for the President and the Secretary of State to further America's interests' (Rieff 2002: 237–8).

Of course, aid politicization did not begin with Afghanistan,[38] but as the first context in which significant aid was called for post-9/11, it remains a key marker. It was the template for the war on terror, and US policy-makers wanted to demonstrate that aid would protect Afghan civilians even as their political masters would be held accountable.

Yet the sums promised to Afghanistan were never based upon assessments of what Afghans actually needed. In January 2002 in Tokyo,[39] donors pledged $4.5 billion with five donors promising more than the United States.[40] These sums promised only a fraction of Afghanistan's real needs (as NGOs pointed out repeatedly). More worrying still, they diminished significantly over time. Instead of going up as Afghanistan's absorptive capacity increased and its economy went into gear, pledges dropped from $1.8 billion a year for 2002 to less than $400 million for 2006 (see CARE 2002; CARE International and the Center for International Cooperation 2003: 4).[41]

As the Iraq situation became more complicated, however, the need for real progress in Afghanistan increased, and the USA went from being one aid donor among many to the dominant force in terms of resources committed.[42] For the first two years of the Afghan financial calendar (from March 2002 to March 2004), the United States spent $1.47 billion dollars, more than any other donor.[43] In September 2003, when George Bush requested $87 billion for Iraq and Afghanistan, he asked for $20 billion (for Iraq) and $1.2 billion (for Afghanistan) for reconstruction. While this sum provided only a fraction of Afghanistan's actual reconstruction needs, it was impressive none the less, particularly as it was made in the middle of a US fiscal year.

In the Congressional debates following Bush's request, however, the issue of greatest contention was not the $65.5 billion portion allocated to military assistance, but the $21.5 billion requested for reconstruction assistance. Why did Iraq and Afghanistan deserve so much when needs were so great elsewhere? With the United States in an economic downturn, why were social services being promised to Afghanistan and Iraq (e.g. health-care) when those same services were not universally available in the United States? As the political consensus over the use of aid dissipated, accusations of aid politicization grew. The hefty reconstruction bill in Afghanistan and Iraq was characterized as little more than political appeasement – the price that had to be paid for a failed foreign policy.

A rights-based response to the funding dilemma Traditionally, when humanitarian organizations have spoken about the allocation of resources, they have used the moral force of suffering humanity to garner resources for their own programming. Fundraising appeals tugged heartstrings to urge the Western public to give what they could to people in need, and did so with increasing effectiveness. In Afghanistan, CARE adopted a different approach. Rather than asking the giving public to 'give what they could' and to give it to CARE, they situated their arguments in a larger political framework of rights and responsibilities, and argued that more discretionary funds should be channelled through the state system to build up internal capacity.

Promises had been made by policy-makers to Afghans. 'To the Afghan people we make this commitment,' Tony Blair had said: 'The conflict will not be the end. We will not walk away, as the outside world has done so many times before.' With the war won, President Bush evoked the Marshall Plan in promising the Afghan people a better life, and European and other policy-makers followed suit.

Recalling those promises, CARE argued in a well publicized policy brief entitled *Rebuilding Afghanistan: A Little Less Talk, a Lot More Action* (2002), that the donors' Tokyo 2002 commitment of $4.5 billion had drastically underestimated needs in Afghanistan, and was an abdication of donor responsibilities. Analysing aid expenditures from four other contexts (Kosovo, Bosnia, Rwanda and East Timor), CARE found aid spending levels had averaged out at $250 per person per year. A similar commitment to Afghanistan would have promised more than $27 billion over five years.[44] The government of Afghanistan agreed with CARE's analysis and publicized it in meetings with policy-makers, even posting this information on its website.[45]

The Center for International Cooperation in New York, probably the most influential independent Western think-tank working on Afghanistan post-Taliban, summarized CARE's analysis for the House of Representatives.[46] The brief also argued that too much funding was being controlled by donors and the assistance community, and not enough funding (18 per cent) was under the government's discretionary control. If the donors wanted to help the Afghan authorities take control of the reconstruction process in their country, they had to invest more funding through the government.

Over the course of the next year, CARE continued to press its concerns with donors in Kabul, Washington and Europe, and was invited by the Afghan government to attend the August 2003 donor conference. Having heard one donor after another refer to their progress against their Tokyo pledges, CARE called upon donors to move from supply-driven donor patterns to engaging in an objective assessment of real needs in Afghanistan, and to measure their contributions against *that* objective. In other words, CARE was urging donors to move from a charity mind-set to recognizing the rights of Afghans and fulfilling their responsibilities accordingly. While they did not couch their argument in international legal obligations, their approach was profoundly rights-oriented and profoundly political.

In late 2003, CARE refocused its efforts on the Afghan government and argued that if the government was going to shift the donor community from its traditional supply-driven approach towards fulfilling its responsibilities to Afghans, the government would have to articulate exactly what those responsibilities were. Whether these arguments fell upon ears already prepared to make the case for demand-driven rights-based aid, or influenced the Afghan government's decisions, is not known. What is clear is that the Afghan government, through the publication of *Securing Afghanistan's Future* in April 2004, radically reconfigured their relationship to donors towards a responsibility model of giving. By setting clear rights-based benchmarks for donors, through the Millennium Development Goals, the Afghan government held donors responsible for living up to their promises, and significantly outpaced expectations of donor contributions to Afghanistan as a result.[47]

Lessons learned for rights-based approaches in Afghanistan

The following lessons aim to reflect on the politicization of aid and offer some ways forward for NGOs.

NGO advocacy does matter Mark Duffield and David Rieff criticize NGOs for engaging in politics from two different standpoints, but both are wrong for the same reason. Duffield believes NGOs have got it wrong conceptually, and claims that they think in too linear and limited a manner to understand how the world really works – organically and systemically. Our rights-based consequentialist ethical framework will let us down in the end, he believes, because we don't have the capacity to get our heads around it. Rieff's critique is more experiential. A decade of following humanitarian interventions taught him that what may work for NGO headquarters does not necessarily work in the field. He aimed to offer a dose of reality to humanitarians. What he wants for humanitarians is rediscovered humility, but what he may ultimately contribute to is a failure of responsibility.

What both authors fail to acknowledge is the nature of political influence. It is particularly surprising that Duffield does not recognize this, as he clearly understands that political bodies are systemic organisms that change dynamically as different forces are brought to bear upon them. Politics and policies do not change in linear ways. Nor do human rights conditions. Single causes do not yield given political or rights effects. But it is precisely because the world works this way that NGOs *must* engage in political and rights debate. Because policy changes occur when forces from a host of different sources form a critical and influential mass, and those influences can come from any source willing to speak up, then the more political NGOs become, the more influence they will have. Perhaps they will never determine the fate of humanitarianism or human rights in Afghanistan or anywhere else, but they can certainly influence those fields by becoming more political.

The political influence of particular NGOs in the US context is readily apparent, and US policy-makers know this. As Andrew Natsios said to NGO leaders:

> Your donors get educated about what goes on in the Third World through your newsletters and your magazines. I asked to get a calculation once, when I was with World Vision, and when I added it all up, I think I came up with 6 million American families receive on a regular basis news from the Third World from the NGO community. I don't know what the size of *Newsweek* is, but I bet it compares favorably with the larger NGO publications. You are a major way that people connect with people in the developing world. (Natsios 2003)

Many of those 6 million publications offer a political vision of global poverty that would resonate with the philosophies of Gandhi, Martin Luther King Jnr and John F. Kennedy, all of whom refused to localize politics.

Perhaps NGO pressure was not the sole reason ISAF forces chose to expand beyond Kabul in 2003. Perhaps it was not the sole reason that the USA chose to multiply its annual funding commitments six-fold from

January 2002 to September 2003. But that does not mean that NGO voices went unheard on these issues, or that they had no influence at all. Rieff wonders whether NGO efforts to promote human rights have 'kept a single jackboot out of a single human face' in Afghanistan or anywhere else. But unless he believes that additional forces and funding won't make a whit of difference to the rights of Afghans, or unless he is sure that these policies would have moved ahead without the countless meetings between NGOs and policy-makers in Kabul, Washington and European capitals, and without the thousands of international media stories in which NGOs drew attention to these problems, his case ultimately fails.

In *A Bed for the Night*, David Rieff (2002: 265) concludes: 'What Afghanistan demonstrated was that humanitarianism was too important a matter to be left to humanitarians (from the donor perspective).'[48] What he fails to recognize is that certain political visions are too important to be left to politicians.

Rights-based approaches can and should influence the 'war on terror' US policy towards the war on terror has become clear since 2001: it involves the use of both hard military power and soft power in the form of humanitarian aid and post-conflict reconstruction. It is also clear that post-conflict reconstruction requires both hardware (physical infrastructure) and software – the human and institutional capacity necessary to turn investments into long-term political stability and equitable economic prosperity.

Since 2001, the international community's challenge in Afghanistan has been the use of its soft power, not hard power. While the military effort to defeat anti-government forces has gone relatively well, reconstruction efforts have faced huge challenges – none more so than the development of the human and institutional capacity to manage the reconstruction effort. In other words, supporting Afghanistan's software continues to represent a major barrier to post-conflict reconstruction, and therefore to the war on terror.

Why does a rights-based lens help NGOs to engage in such an analysis? Unlike classic humanitarianism, which accepts the inevitability of conflict, and has little to say about post-conflict reconstruction, a human rights approach situates NGOs as advocates for the use of soft power in the so-called war on terror. Not only do human rights, in totality, represent the preconditions for sustainable peace, they demand that post-conflict reconstruction policies focus on the human rights of civilians – not just the political and security rights, but the economic, social, cultural rights as well, and they propose a standard to which those reconstruction efforts ought to be held.

Additionally, human rights advocacy can focus policy-makers on the software dimensions of soft power. Human rights, after all, concern the measurement of outcomes in human terms, and are often more effective when they focus on institutional responsibilities. In 2004, for example, the Human Rights Research and Advocacy Consortium in Afghanistan published a brief on education which held both the government and the donor community accountable for failing to focus on the human and institutional capacity required to provide quality education to Afghan children. The brief argued that too much emphasis had gone into the hardware – the erection of empty school buildings – and not enough focus had been given to the quality of education and to ensuring educational outcomes.

The war on terror will continue to stimulate public policy debate on the appropriate balance both between hard power and soft power and between hardware and software. If NGOs are to live up to their rights-based calling, they will engage fully in that debate in favour of the use of soft power and to ensure that outcomes are measured in terms of human rights promotion.

NGOs and funding When asked by a senior Department of Defense official about NGOs' views on PRTs, I suggested that NGO views broke down into three groups. There were the classic humanitarians who wanted nothing to do with the PRTs, and certainly would not engage in discussions with them on how to improve their performance.[49] There were smaller NGOs desperate for funding and happy to work with the PRTs as a much needed source of income.[50] And then in the middle were a number of NGOs which were willing to talk with the PRTs, at least in coordination and strategy meetings (if not in joint 'humanitarian projects') and seek to modify their behaviour. When I suggested that these 'moderate' NGOs were few in number – probably no more than a dozen – and perhaps not worth their attention, the Department of Defense official was quick to remind me, with a glimmer of irritation, that those NGOs exercised a disproportionate influence in policy discussions.

Large humanitarian NGOs coming from a US perspective are even fewer in number. In 2000, one-quarter of the US government's development aid went to four NGOs: CARE, Catholic Relief Services, Save the Children and World Vision (Stoddard 2003: 32). Together with the International Rescue Committee and Mercy Corps, both of which have large programmes in Afghanistan, these six NGOs exert considerable influence in Afghanistan.

The four secular NGOs have engaged heavily in high-profile policy advocacy in Afghanistan since the fall of the Taliban and, in doing so, have challenged the notion that this is something that US NGOs just do not do seriously.[51] Abby Stoddard (2002) describes NGOs with American roots as having a 'Wilsonian' notion of humanitarianism, while European NGOs remain closer to the 'Dunantian' paradigm. Stoddard concludes that their organizational philosophies and fundraising mechanisms still reflect those different histories. Wilsonian NGOs, she suggests, are more likely to see themselves as ambassadors for American public values, and are far less concerned about the 'non-' in non-governmental. They might not be so shocked by the syllogism David Rieff sees in USAID's new policies: 'Humanitarian aid is good, the United States is good; therefore why shouldn't the two be twinned?' (Rieff 2002: 238). Europe's Dunantian NGOs, however, are much more concerned about the separation between humanitarianism and the state, Stoddard argues. As a result, the ratio of government funding to private giving is much larger for American NGOs than for their European counterparts.[52]

The strong pull of these roots should not be underestimated. US NGOs aiming for the high political ground of human rights must also respect their origins and protect their institutional viability. Truly redefining themselves in rights terms will be almost impossible if they do not find a way financially to support that redefinition. Unlike European counterparts such as Oxfam and MSF, US NGOs do not appear to see their policy advocacy work as an adequately powerful breadwinner yet. They have tended to fundraise through more traditional heart-string-pulling methods and advocate through separate divisions in both Washington and their headquarters.

If this bifurcation remains the case, it will spell doom for rights-based approaches in US NGOs, for they cannot significantly expand advocacy work if it runs at a loss, while biting the US government hand that feeds them. The hope is that in truly grasping the compelling power of rights approaches, these NGOs will position themselves philosophically and financially for the new century and these new political times.

Along with everything else that has changed post 9/11, so have the political interests of the American public. Foreign policy plays a much greater part in the political mind-set of America today than it did three years ago. Americans are looking for voices to help them make sense of the world, voices that they can trust, whose political interests are clear. If American NGOs are willing to step into global politics they can become a trusted voice for pro-poor policy, pro-human rights policy change in the United States.

This does not mean that they will have to abandon all forms of US government financial support. Even MSF, the most independent and 'Dunantist' of the NGOs, maintains 30 per cent levels of public to private support (Stoddard 2002: 29). But it may mean they will have to reduce significantly their reliance on public support.

Rights-based approaches are particularly relevant in 'Type A' contexts
When NGOs sought to bring their global institutional identities to Afghan-

istan in 2001, they quickly found themselves in conflict with both donors and the government. New rules were being made in Afghanistan. Since 2001, it has become increasingly clear that humanitarian contexts divide broadly into two categories. In many of today's forgotten crises, the traditional rules of humanitarianism still apply. Claims of neutrality and impartiality between warring factions still create humanitarian space. In highly politicized contexts such as Afghanistan and Iraq, however, classic humanitarianism has been profoundly challenged. It may well be the case that, in years to come, humanitarianism will require very different postures in 'loud' emergencies or, as some label them, 'Type A' emergencies (Feinstein International Famine Center 2003).

The Afghanistan experience since 2001 demonstrates the value of a rights-based lens in highly politicized contexts. That lens gave NGOs the ability to define and affirm their own values when faced with competing political demands. When many believed that being non-governmental amounted to being anti-governmental, human rights allowed them to define what they stood for in the affirmative. Rights-based NGOs were not there to support the Karzai government, but to support good governance. They were not there as proxies for the donor community but as implementing partners who would work together with donors only in so far as their shared agenda protected and promoted the rights of the people they served. Adhering to human rights allowed NGOs to parse through difficult policy choices on when they should speak out and when they should not, when they should accept funding and when they should turn it down.

The phenomenon of aid politicization did not begin with Afghanistan – there has been a series of crises in the last twenty years that have garnered the world's political attention. Nevertheless the trend is clear, and as it is increasingly likely that more 'Type A' complex crises will arise in future, the need for rights-based capacity to respond effectively in those contexts will grow ever stronger.

Adopting rights-based approaches will ultimately have costs Too many organizations that adopted rights-based approaches in rhetoric have been unwilling to back that rhetorical commitment with resources. For the most part, NGOs engaging in policy advocacy in Afghanistan did so largely by adding to the already overburdened workloads of their operational programmers and senior management. As a result, their ability to sustain systematic analysis and advocacy was severely limited. Programmers expected to apply rights-based lens to their interventions were largely challenged to do so as a normal part of improving programme quality.

NGOs like CARE that did decide to allocate significant resources to policy analysis and advocacy found that, initially, they had to draw on their donations from private donors, a luxury that very few NGOs can afford. Over time, however, CARE was able to turn to institutional donors for more than 50 per cent of their advocacy funding. Regardless, it was clear that policy analysis and advocacy require specific human and financial resources.

Rights-based approaches not only require investment; they may also require a willingness to put existing investments at risk. Too often NGOs in Afghanistan thought they were expected to make the transition to promoting human rights at *no* cost to their core business. While they understood it was now politically correct to talk about 'rights' rather than 'needs', they also believed they were expected, above all, to protect the economic and political security of their organizations, and the relationships upon which that security is founded. Many staff concluded, as a result, that when adopting these new directions, they were expected to use 'judgement' and 'experience' to find win–win solutions in every situation.

Rights work, though, is not always about win–win solutions. A basic premise of rights work is that poverty and social injustice are not an accident. Poverty, as Gandhi said, is a 'form of violence', for which someone is responsible. One simply cannot meaningfully influence policy decisions without stepping on toes. Policy problems almost always exist because someone with influence profits. Discrimination prevails, not out of ignorance of alternatives but because someone gains from marginalizing others.

NGOs will not confront inescapable adversaries until they genuinely threaten the interests of those adversaries. Such individuals and institutions are always happy to let NGOs spin their wheels unless and until those wheels run over their interests. Rights work has a huge potential to become a public relations exercise that does not fundamentally challenge the root causes of poverty. Our commitment to rights work becomes clear only when those challenges arise, and we have to choose how we respond.

If certain costs are unavoidable, then NGOs must learn to integrate those costs into their planning and organizational cultures. More importantly, they must work out how to align their commitment to human rights with their economic survival. While CARE found that rights-based advocacy in Afghanistan was costly in the short term, they also found out that it had a positive impact on CARE's profile both in Afghanistan and internationally. There were concerns that constantly challenging US foreign policy would have consequences for CARE's relationship with its major donor, USAID, and that challenging the Afghan government would compromise our ability to function in country – but those concerns proved groundless. CARE's advocacy was accepted for what it was, both in Kabul and in Washington:

a good faith effort to focus policy-makers on the human rights of ordinary Afghans. That is not to say that its rights-based advocacy was risk-free. Some of CARE's public critiques, that members of the Afghan government were participating in the drug economy, and that the US government was responding inadequately on the human security of Afghans and long-term reconstruction, no doubt irritated policy-makers. But increasingly, over a two-year period, both sets of policy-makers appeared to expect and accept such positions from the NGO world.

Conclusion

The assistance community has been presented with an inescapable dilemma – aid has been politicized. We cannot continue with business as usual, occupying a middle ground that tinkers with apolitical neutrality, and tinkers with rights. We must go one way or the other. This chapter has tried to show, through the Afghanistan experience, that it may indeed be time for NGOs to accept fully the frightening burden and inspiring possibility of becoming true rights-based organizations.

Notes

From November 2001 to August 2004, Paul O'Brien was the Advocacy Co-ordinator for CARE Afghanistan. The views expressed in this chapter are his alone and do not necessarily reflect the views of CARE.

1 Those political values include, for example, the obligation to facilitate the allocation of life-saving resources to the innocent in conflict situations. The consensus around this political value forms the basis for humanitarianism.

2 It is not just NGOs that instinctively use the same 'political' terminology to differentiate between the negative connotations of political partisanship on the one hand, and higher shared political goals on the other. In May 2003, USAID head, Andrew Natsios, told NGOs that they needed to let communities in Afghanistan know when USAID was supporting their programmes. He then commented: 'Now some of you may say, "Well, you're being political." It's not political. Karzai, if he falls, we're in big trouble. I don't have to tell all of you what's going to happen. It does affect the survival of the central government if the people in the villages do not believe the central government is being responsive to their needs.' What Natsios meant when he said, 'It's not political', was that his reasoning was not based on partisan political considerations such as the political standing of the current US administration. Instead, he justified his thinking in much more serious political terms – the very survival of the Afghan state (Natsios 2003).

3 Humanitarian action and law incorporated protection for civilians only in the Geneva Conventions (1949). Until then, it had focused exclusively on the protection of non-combatant soldiers. Perhaps the changed nature of warfare, from the First World World War trench battles to the urban carpet-bombing of the Second World War, demanded such an evolution.

4 The humanitarian community continues to debate the relevance of such principles. The Good Humanitarian Donorship initiative was launched at an international meeting on 15 and 16 June 2003 in Stockholm where donor governments, UN agencies, the International Red Cross and Red Crescent movement, and other organizations involved in humanitarian action gathered to promote the principles of good humanitarian donorship (see Humanitarian Practice Network 2003: 9).

5 Classic humanitarians may take issue with this understanding of politics, for their whole argument is that there is a realm of political activity that lies, and should always lie, beyond the reach of the aid community. For them, politics is essentially and exclusively the art of government, and is by definition a partisan act.

6 CARE, for example, began intensively to explore a commitment to rights-based approaches in 1998, and systematically amended their organizational vision and mission in the following three years.

7 By 'consequentialist' Duffield means that NGOs now claim to be able to understand and even measure the outcomes of their interventions, both positive and negative, and to determine the ethical nature of their response based on that analysis. An NGO might conclude, using such a framework, that saving one person today would lead to killing more people tomorrow and therefore choose not to act as a result. It is such a calculus that profoundly disturbs commentators such as Duffield and Rieff.

8 The men were working for an international NGO, the Danish Committee for Aid to Afghan Refugees (DACAAR). They were travelling in a local hire vehicle towards the DACAAR field office in Makur village, Ab Band district, Ghazni province, Afghanistan. See ANSO (10 September 2003).

9 The victims worked for VARA, an Afghan NGO. They were murdered while driving on the Delaram–Kandahar road by gunmen in a passing vehicle. Security reports at the time concluded it was a Taliban attack. See ANSO (24 September 2003).

10 CARE was the organization, and the sub-office was in Rashidan district in Ghazni province. The letter was reported in ANSO (28 September 2003).

11 CARE has been monitoring security incidents against the assistance community. See CARE International and the Center for International Cooperation (2003).

12 From August to December 2002, there were five attacks. In the next four months, there were twenty-six attacks, and from May until August 2003, there were sixty-two attacks. See CARE International and the Center for International Cooperation (2003).

13 It would be wrong to say that the Karzai administration has made no progress on this front. As Antonio Guistossi points out: 'Hamid Karzai and his circle of pro-western allies within the transitional administration ... have been carrying out a slow but steady confrontation with the main warlords, trying to limit the warlords' power and increase their own. Because of Karzai group's limited resources and the unwillingness of its international patrons to commit much of their own, this has not been an open confrontation. There have

been no decisive clashes, rather an ongoing arm-twisting over the balance of power within the administration and within the state' (Guistossi 2003).

14 Much of this was ascribed to a lack of sensitivity by US coalition forces about local conditions and local politics, allowing them to be manipulated by local actors. As one American diplomat acknowledged: 'We're not the British, we're not the Raj, we don't do colonialism well, we don't understand this local tribal politics stuff' (see International Crisis Group 2003: 20–1).

15 Despite Taliban edicts forbidding female education, for example, many NGOs worked closely with southern communities to school their girls.

16 A word twist too hard to resist. The Taliban's leader was the one-eyed Mullah Omar.

17 The two most influential were the United States Office of Foreign Disaster Assistance (OFDA), and the European Community's Humanitarian Office (ECHO).

18 For an in-depth analysis of NGO positions during the Taliban years, see O'Brien (2004).

19 The campaign focused on both the cost of the Humanitarian Daily Rations (HDRs), and the fact that because the HDRs were the same colour as cluster bombs, they could cause unintentional fatal injury to civilians, especially children.

20 The PRT concept was first publicly mooted to NGOs in meetings in Kabul and Washington in December 2002. At the time it was called the Joint Regional Team or JRT, but took on the 'reconstruction' label when the Afghan government objected to the use of the word 'regional'.

21 The first US-led PRTs were located in the provinces of Paktia, Kunduz and Bamyan. They were followed by a British PRT, deployed to the northern city of Mazar-e-Sharif.

22 Their initial budget of $12 million came from the Department of Defense, and restricted the projects they could do to basic social services such as schools, health clinics and wells. The fund was known as the ODHACA fund. Subsequent budgets may be drawn from USAID and other funding.

23 That debate went on behind closed doors for the United Nations, and both privately and publicly by NGOs. Through much of 2003, operational NGOs were the only voices publicly criticizing the PRT concept.

24 That was the argument made to me by a senior US policy-maker in Kabul in September 2003.

25 When I asked senior US officials in Kabul whether the name could not be changed to Provincial Stabilization or Security Teams, they said that President Karzai insisted on keeping the name.

26 Donald Rumsfeld, speaking at a press briefing, 26 April 2003.

27 Different NGOs have different policies on military engagement in humanitarian action. By far the largest constituency are those who acknowledge the necessity for such action in very limited circumstances, where lives are at risk and civilians do not have the capacity to respond.

28 The Afghan government is obliged, under the International Conven-

tion for Civil and Political Rights (1976), to provide security for its citizens. Arguably, Common Article III of the Geneva Conventions also applied, as the conflict with the Taliban was showing signs of becoming an internal armed conflict, with the Taliban exerting de facto military control over some of the countryside, at least as far as NGOs were concerned.

29 The first public position paper on the PRTs was from Agency Coordinating Body for Afghan Relief (2003).

30 The $12 million was allocated for US fiscal year 2003, which runs until 30 September 2003. Reconstruction needs are now estimated by the Afghan government at $30 billion (CARE 2003).

31 'NATO nations have agreed on a political basis for a possible expansion of the mission beyond Kabul ... But they did not decide that they would expand. They agreed on the basis' (NATO spokesperson quoted in IRIN 2003).

32 UN Security Council Resolution 1510 (2003), adopted unanimously on 13 October 2003, 'authorizes expansion of the mandate of the International Security Assistance Force to allow it, as resources permit, to support the Afghan Transitional Authority and its successors in the maintenance of security in areas of Afghanistan outside of Kabul and its environs'.

33 This was how one senior UN policy-maker described ISAF expansion, providing a backhanded compliment to the dogged persistence of NGO advocacy on this issue.

34 In repeated Powerpoint presentations, NATO referenced a statement sent to them by CARE and IRC calling for NATO to do more to ensure the security of ordinary Afghans.

35 Sixteen of Afghanistan's thirty-two provinces had large areas deemed high risk for assistance work. Three more were medium risk. Another five had seen constant factional fighting. Only eight provinces were relatively secure, most were in the north and north-east. One was Kunduz.

36 CARE alone contributed to more than thirty TV and radio stories and 150 print stories in Western media calling for greater international support for security in Afghanistan. Many of those stories were 'wire publications that went to papers all over the US'. Many stories challenged the PRTs as a successful model.

37 Pre-9/11, the trend had been moving away from impartial giving according to need (judged a failure) towards incentive-driven aid (blacklisting pariah states and investing heavily in/rewarding success stories).

38 US policies have see-sawed with respect to the political use of aid. In the early days of modern aid policy (post-Second World War), 'Washington was unapologetic about the use of aid for political purposes. Later however, a conceptual line was drawn between long term development assistance and life-saving emergency relief, and relief activities took on a mantle of neutrality' (Stoddard 2002).

39 Tokyo maintains a show of multilateralism that continues to embarrass the US-led Iraqi efforts by contrast.

40 The USA promised $297 million; the Europeans combined promised $2.1 billion, the World Bank $570 million, the Iranians $560 million, the

Japanese $500 billion and the Asia Development Bank $500 million (see CARE 2002).

41 This pattern of giving conflicts with a recent World Bank study of sixty-two different countries which showed that post-conflict economies go through aid-related growth spurts after several years of peace. The study concluded: 'from the perspective of effective use of aid for economic recovery, aid volumes should gradually build up during the first few years of peace, and gradually revert to normal levels after around a decade' (Collier and Hoeffler 2002: 3).

42 It remains debatable whether aid to Afghanistan has been hurt or helped by Iraq. On the one hand, some felt that the greater the political problems of Iraq, the more important it was for the proponents of the war on terror that Afghanistan was a success story.

43 Within this time-frame, other key donors expected to spend more than $100 million are: European Union, $1.3 billion; Japan, $500 million; Canada, $166 million; and the World Bank, $103 million.

44 Key US policy-makers argued much the same point. US Senator Joseph Biden (2002) wrote: 'To date, total international pledges – about $5 billion – have fallen far short of that legacy and well below the $20 billion-plus that most experts believe Afghanistan will need to build a self-sustaining future. All of us have to do better, faster.'

45 Foreign Minister Abdullah Abdullah and Finance Minister Ashraf Ghani used these figures publicly on numerous occasions. Government position papers can be found at <www.dad.af>

46 Barnett Rubin submitted the following paper to the House Committee on International Relations on 19 June 2003 (Rubin et al. 2003).

47 *Securing Afghanistan's Future* led to Afghanistan receiving more than $8.2 billion in pledges for three years. These kinds of multi-year pledges significantly outstripped donors' initial post-conflict pledges, almost unheard of in donor giving patterns.

48 Rieff was not arguing that humanitarianism should fall under government control. He was merely making the point that governments increasingly felt that humanitarian action was too valuable a political tool to be abdicated to NGOs.

49 MSF was probably the strongest member of this school in post-Taliban Afghanistan.

50 Most, but not all, of these NGOs were smaller Afghan NGOs, some of which came into existence simply to execute a specific contract. With more than 1,800 NGOs registering with the Afghan Ministry of Planning between 2002 and 2003, the 'not-for-profit' credentials of many of these briefcase NGOs is suspect.

51 The two religious-based NGOs, Catholic Relief Services and World Vision, the former employer of Andrew Natsios, have been relatively quiet with respect to Afghanistan, perhaps because of their religious roots. Both organizations have vocal advocacy campaigns in other contexts such as Sudan, Colombia and the West Bank/Gaza for World Vision and the Africa Rising

Campaign for CRS. See <www.worldvision.org/worldvision/wvususfo.nsf/
stable/globalissues_homepage> and <www.catholicreliefservices.org/
get_involved/advocacy/index.cfm> respectively. IRC has led collective NGO
campaigns to expand ISAF and address security; Mercy Corps has testified
before the Senate Foreign Relations Committee on Afghanistan; CARE have
issued policy briefs and advocated in Washington and elsewhere on security
and reconstruction; and Save the Children has been one of the most consistent NGO policy voices in and on Afghanistan over the past ten years. All have
engaged in collective advocacy efforts.

52 'The major secular US NGOs could not operate at their current level
without funding from the US government. CARE and Save the Children US
receive close to half of their funding through the US government; over 70
per cent of the International Rescue Committee (IRC)'s funding comes from
public sources. To be able regularly to refuse government dollars, these
agencies would have to reduce radically the size of their organizations. The
private funding raised by Save the Children US, for example, 'would not be
sufficient to support significant programming by any one of its individual
country field offices if its public funding were to disappear' (Stoddard
2002: 29).

References

Agency Coordinating Body for Afghan Relief (2003) 'NGO Position Paper Concerning the Provincial Reconstruction Teams' (15 January) <www.careusa.
org/newsroom/specialreports/afghanistan/01152003_ngorec.pdf>

ANSO (Afghanistan Non-Governmental Security Office) (2003) *Reports*, 37 and
38 (September).

Biden, J. R. (2002) 'A Commitment to Afghan Security', *Boston Globe*, 28 June.

CARE (2002) 'Rebuilding Afghanistan: A Little Less Talk, a Lot More Action',
7 October.

— (2003) 'A New Year's Resolution to Keep: Secure a Lasting Peace in Afghanistan', Policy Brief 2, 13 January.

CARE International and the Center for International Cooperation (2003)
'Good Intentions Will Not Pave the Path to Peace', Afghanistan Policy Brief,
15 September <www.careusa.org/newsroom/specialreports/
afghanistan/09152003_afghanistanbrief.pdf>

Collier, P. and A. Hoeffler (2002) 'Aid, Policy and Growth in Post-Conflict
Societies, World Bank Conflict Prevention and Reconstruction Unit', May
<http://econ.worldbank.org/files/15710_CollierHoefflerAidPostConflict.
pdf>

Duffield, M. (2001) *Global Governance and the New Wars: The Merging of Development and Security* (London: Zed Books).

Feinstein International Famine Center (2003) *The Future of Humanitarian
Crises, the Future of Humanitarian Action: Implications of Iraq and Other
Recent Crises*, Workshop Report, Friedman School of Nutrition Science and
Policy, Tufts University, 9 October.

Fox, F. (2001) 'New Humanitarianism: Does It Provide a Moral Banner for the 21st Century?' *Disasters*, 25: 275–89.

Government of Afghanistan (2004) 'Securing Afghanistan's Future' 2004 <www.af>

Guistossi, A. (2003) *Respectable Warlords: The Politics of State Building in Post Taliban Afghanistan*, Working Paper 33, Development Research Center, LSE, September.

Humanitarian Practice Network (2003) *Humanitarian Exchange* magazine, 24, (July/August) <www.odihpn.org>

Human Rights Research and Advocacy Consortium (2004) 'Report Card: Progress on Compulsory Education (Grades 1–9)', March (Afghanistan). <www.afghanadvocacy.org/documents/EducationBriefEnglish.pdf>

International Crisis Group (2003) 'Afghanistan: The Problem of Pashtun Alienation', *Asia Report*, 62 (Kabul/Brussels), 5 August. <www.icg.org/home/getfile.cfm?id=319andtid=1641>

IRIN (UN Integrated Regional Information Networks) (2003) 'Afghanistan: NATO Takes Step Towards Possible Expansion Outside Kabul' (Ankara) 6 October. <www.irinnews.org/report.asp?ReportID=37033andSelectRegion=Central_AsiaandSelectCountry=AFGHANISTAN>

Macrae, J. and N. Leader (2001) 'Apples, Pears and Porridge: The Origins and Impact of the Search for "Coherence" between Humanitarian and Political Responses to Chronic Political Emergencies', *Disasters*, 25: 290–307.

Natsios, A. S. (2001) Testimony of Andrew Natsios, Administrator, USAID, before the House Appropriations Committee, Subcommittee on Foreign Operations, 17 May, Washington, DC. <www.usaid.gov/press/spe_test/testimony/2001/ty010517.html>

— (2003) Speech given to USAID InterAction Forum closing plenary session, 21 May. <www.usaid.gov/press/speeches/2003/sp030521.html>

O'Brien, P. (2004) 'Old Woods, New Paths and Diverging Choices for NGOs', in A. Donini, N. Niland and K. Wemester (eds), *Nation-Building Unravelled? Aid, Peace and Justice in Afghanistan* (Bloomfield CT: Kumarian Press).

Rieff, D. (2002) *A Bed for the Night: Humanitarianism in Crisis* (New York: Simon and Schuster).

Rubin, B. R., H. Hamidzada and A. Stoddard (2003) 'Through the Fog of Peace Building: Evaluating the Reconstruction of Afghanistan', Center for International Cooperation policy paper (June). <www.nyu.edu/pages/cic/conflict/ conflict_project2.html>

Slim, H. (2003) 'Humanitarianism with Borders? NGOs, Belligerent Military Forces and Humanitarian Action', paper presented at an International Council of Voluntary Agencies Conference on NGOs in a Changing World Order: Dilemmas and Challenges, Geneva, February 2003. <www.icva.ch/cgi-bin/browse.pl?doc=doc00000935> The full text of the paper can be found in the *Journal of Humanitarian Assistance* at <www.jha.ac>

Stoddard, A. (2002) 'Trends in US Humanitarian Policy', in J. Macrae (ed.), *The New Humanitarianisms: A Review of Trends in Global Humanitarian Action*,

Humanitarian Policy Group Report, 11: 39–50 (London, April). <www.odi.org.uk/hpg/papers/hpgreport11.pdf>

— (2003) 'Humanitarian NGOs: Challenges and Trends', in J. Macrae and A. Harmer (eds), *Humanitarian Action and the 'Global War on Terror': A Review of Trends and Issues*, Humanitarian Policy Group Report, 14: 25–36 (London, July). <www.odi.org.uk/hpg/papers/hpgreport14.pdf>

Thorold, C., H. Natiq and S. Aviel (2004) 'Take the Guns Away: Afghan Voices on Security and Elections', Human Rights Research and Advocacy Consortium (September). <www.afghanadvocacy.org/documents/TaketheGunsAwayEnglish.pdf>

Woodward, R. (2002) *Bush at War* (New York: Simon and Schuster).

12 | Rights as struggle – towards a more just and humane world

HARSH MANDER

This chapter argues that rights-based approaches are an essential element in the struggle for a more just and humane world. By contrast with earlier service delivery approaches, which achieved much but also had many shortcomings, rights bring the root causes of impoverishment to the centre of development and force a focus on the needs of the very poorest. Starting from a critique of service delivery, the features of rights-based practice are examined, defined in terms of solidarity with the poorest and a struggle from below. Central to this understanding is the active agency of the repressed in assessing their own needs and finding their own solutions to their own problems. However, the essential role of the state is also acknowledged, revealing a crucial question: what is the effect of neo-liberalism, good governance and the rule of law, and what alternative role for the state should be sought?

Service delivery approaches

It was during the 1970s that the basic needs discourse came to dominate development theory and practice, closely linked to the manifest failure of the 'trickle-down' public policies of focusing on economic growth to overcome poverty, adopted by most post-colonial national governments. Growing inequality, both within and between nations, and the alarming rise in both absolute and relative poverty, led to concern amid social policy analysts and activists regarding redistributive aspects of development. In many countries, reluctance by the state to address structural causes of poverty, such as through instruments like land reforms, led to governments adopting a softer approach of 'poverty alleviation', mainly through the expansion of micro-credit, supplemented in some countries by employment in public works, and progressively increasing the access of the poor to their basic needs, such as food, water, health and education. However, the majority of official efforts were riddled by several failures, of inappropriate design, low resources and corrupt and unaccountable delivery mechanisms. The NGO sector expanded in many of these countries, seeking to address the resultant failures by governments to extend micro-credit, promote livelihoods, extend healthcare and education and fulfil basic needs, by establishing its own more sensitive local mechanisms for the delivery of these services.

Before proceeding further, it is important to point out that when this chapter refers to NGOs, it addresses itself to a wide diversity of non-state non-profit groups and organizations which primarily rely on externally mobilized (including, but not necessarily exclusively, foreign) funds. The spectrum of people's organizations, cooperatives, trade unions and social movements that are frequently membership-based and locally accountable, functioning substantially on the basis of voluntarism and locally raised resources both from members and supporters, rarely made the delivery of services their primary goal, and pursued difficult journeys of organizing and struggling with dispossessed people for securing their legal and moral rights, long before funded NGOs discovered this path. Another necessary disclaimer is that any attempts to generalize about NGOs are perilous, in a sector of such enormous diversity both globally and within nations, and in theory and practice, and there will be several significant exceptions to every observation made in this chapter.

The service delivery approach to addressing the basic needs of disadvantaged people did achieve significant successes, mainly in local contexts, in assisting people in poverty to achieve better lives. The fact that these efforts were located in frequently difficult, even unreached areas, and were deeply sensitive to the needs of underprivileged groups, was a value in itself, for the suffering and deprivation that they attended to. It would be unjust to underestimate the contributions of NGOs in situations of extreme distress, as in disasters and famines, or chronic and unattended marginalization, such as of disabled or other impoverished people.

Service delivery approaches also helped pilot and build models, which influenced development policy, by providing demonstrations of success and innovation. They also implicitly or directly challenged public policy, and extended on occasion valuable professional advice to the state. In India, almost all significant government programmes to overcome poverty or address basic needs can be traced for their initial inspiration, or subsequent enrichment, to NGO experiments. In Bangladesh, NGOs have almost substituted the state in the social sector. What is more, by demonstrating what was possible in the delivery of services, service delivery approaches indirectly strengthened people's understanding of their entitlements to basic services in relation to the state. An often unacknowledged contribution of this phase of NGO activism has also been that it educated and sensitized in many countries large numbers of middle-class youth, who even if they migrated later to other mainstream professions, always carried the seeds of learning and sensitivity from their initial local NGO experience.

234

There was considerable value during this phase in the application and popularization of participatory development techniques, through which people were involved for the first time, outside the ambit of radical movements, in considering their collective destiny and ways in which it might be changed.

However, these mainstream NGO endeavours (lumped together by several analysts as the 'service delivery approach' but actually reflecting a diversity of approaches) were increasingly subject to searching criticism, including from within, of both their actual contributions and their philosophical and political underpinnings. One body of criticism flowed from the stubbornly small scale of the operations and aspirations that typically characterized NGOs (although once again there were notable exceptions such as in Bangladesh). It was often argued that even if their efforts were more successful than those of government, they often proved of little significance in positively influencing public policy and action, because the efforts of individual small NGOs covered so small an area and were so talent-intensive that their experiences and achievements were not relevant to the immeasurably larger challenges that confronted government. However, we have already observed that small-scale efforts were often pilot initiatives that guided larger government efforts, and therefore these were important in their indirect influence, despite the limitations of their direct reach.

A much more grave charge of service delivery NGOs is that this approach frequently neglected the issues of power and structural injustice, which actually led to the denial of rights. Using a powerful metaphor, Wayne Ellwood (quoted in Korten 1990) writes: 'If you see a baby drowning, you jump to save it; and if you see a second and a third, you do the same. Soon you are so busy saving drowning babies, you never look up to see there is someone there throwing these babies in the river.'

Streeten (1984) argues that it is not at all clear whether the basic needs approach mobilizes the power of the poor to improve their situation radically or whether it reinforces the existing oppressive order. In an even more trenchant critique of this approach, Firoze Manji (1998) suggests that NGOs through their espousal of such politically 'neutral' strategies of development have contributed to the 'depoliticization' of poverty. He feels that, in so doing, they have become 'an integral component of the political economy of under-development' and that 'they are now part of a system that contributes to the reproduction of impoverishment'. He describes many such NGOs as 'mere sub-contractors' for the provision of social services which would mitigate the effects of structural adjustment for the 'vulnerable' or 'poorest of the poor'.

235

This is a harsh and probably over-generalized critique of 'service delivery' NGOs. We have observed ways that they have been and continue to be relevant to improving the lives of poor people. Yet there are elements of truth that several of them have contributed to a 'techno-managerial' view of poverty, an approach that implies that poverty can be overcome simply with better-managed schemes and technology, not by addressing basic sources of injustice. They tacitly overlook that these sources are located in structured injustices, domination, oppression and the denial of rights. This applies even to the way participatory methods have been often reduced to technical instruments rather than genuinely democratizing the control of impoverished people over decisions related to their own lives, or enhancing the accountability to them of both the state and NGOs themselves.

The growing consensus is that it is impossible to address sustainably basic needs without enforcing basic rights. For example, Sen (1981) that even in acute circumstances such as famines, it is not the shortage of food that causes famines, but the lack of effective access to and ownership of food. Ferguson (1999) argues that viewing people as the site of needs, rather than as active choice-making agents, has influenced social policy (and NGO practice) to treat people as passive targets for technocratic top-down processes. People have not been regarded as empowered to participate in and influence the decision-making processes, in the household as well as formal public arenas, which shape their lives.

Nancy Fraser (1989) critiques conventional welfare approaches on the ground by pointing out that typically it is policy-makers and experts who define needs, not the people whose needs are being addressed. She shows how this in effect reinforces stereotypes such as gender roles, and this perpetuates injustice. She therefore affirms that the identification of needs itself is a political process, and should be seen as such. Our capacity to view people not merely as 'sites of want' but as active agents with entitlements, moves us into the territory of the 'rights mode'. As Manji puts it:

> there is no 'neutral' ground, no 'no-man's land' in the process of development ... The choice is thus a stark one: either play the role (unwittingly or otherwise) of reinforcing those social relations that reproduce impoverishment, injustice, and conflict. Or, make the choice to play a positive role in supporting those processes in society that will overturn those social relations. (Manji 1998)

Rights-based approaches to development

Rights may be defined as a justiciable claim, on legal or moral grounds, to have or obtain something, or to act in a certain way. In other words, rights are entitlements that are backed by legal or moral principles. Amartya Sen (1981) defines entitlements as enforceable claims on the delivery of goods, services or protection by specific others. The growing recognition of human rights since the turn of the twentieth century has helped it evolve from vague, diffuse aspirational statements and assertions to increasingly lucid and unambiguous enunciations in international and national statutory documents. However, both the enforcement and enforceability of many of these rights, especially by nation-states, remains uneven, and is typically particularly weak for the social, economic and cultural rights of citizens.

There are different dimensions in which rights, and their denial, can be analysed. On one axis may be groups whose rights are systematically denied, be they agricultural workers, indigenous people, industrial workers, *Dalits*, women, disabled people, the homeless and so on. On a second axis we can look at the problem in terms of the content of rights that have been denied, such as the rights to livelihood, to dignity, to choose an occupation, to shelter and so on. And since rights are often legal and may or may not be enforced by the state, a third axis of rights is the right to good governance, in relation both to the denied groups and the substantive content of the rights that are sought to be enforced. This variation is not merely of academic interest; it has close bearing on the nature of analysis and the agglomeration of interventions that emerge in a specific context.

If rights are the legally or morally sanctioned entitlement of people, what are rights-based approaches to development? The Overseas Development Institute (1999) has attempted the following definition:

> A rights-based approach to development sets the achievement of human rights as an objective of development. It uses thinking about human rights as the scaffolding of development policy. It invokes the international apparatus of human rights accountability in support of development action. In all of these, it is concerned not just with civil and political (CP) rights (the right to trial, not to be tortured), but also with economic, social and cultural (ESC) rights (the right to food, housing, a job).

There are some problems with this definition. Most importantly, rights approaches may or may not invoke international covenants for the achievements of its objectives. They may derive strength and legitimacy instead

237

from various other sources such as national law, socially acknowledged ethical principles of equity and justice, or from the organization and struggles of people's organizations. This definition is also based on a problematic premise that there is a set of human rights that are universally acknowledged. Shivji argues that:

> Rights should not be theorised as 'legal rights' ... which implies both a static and an absolutist paradigm, in the sense of an entitlement or claim, but a means of struggle. In that sense it is akin to righteousness rather than right. Seen as a means of struggle, 'right' is therefore not a standard granted as charity from above, but a standard-bearer around which people rally for the struggle from below. (Shivji 1989: 3)

In seeing a rights approach in this way, it is important to note that it is not defined by excluding service provision, but only that it does not regard the addressing of immediate suffering as an end in itself. There would be many instances, particularly in cases of extreme and chronic marginalization and vulnerability, such as of homelessness, of street children, of victims of violence, or survivors of natural or human-made disasters, where immediate suffering must be addressed even during the processes of more fundamental interventions for engaging people in defining and securing these rights and accountability from the state. But what characterizes the rights approach, as we will observe, is that even while it may mitigate people's distress, it regards as the most important task assisting in the process of identifying and addressing the basic causes of this distress.

There are other non-negotiable principles in the rights approach, elaborated in subsequent sections, which are equally relevant for service delivery. Both can be stirred by an unambiguous and open taking of sides in favour of those people whose rights are most denied. Both can also be built on the conviction that no service can be delivered, no need addressed, no injustice remedied, without the active agency of the person whose needs are to be addressed, whose rights are to be restored.

Since the rights approach is based centrally on the concept of entitlements, it also necessarily involves close engagement with the state, to influence the recognition and enforcement of entitlements. Here, once again, the importance of piloting innovative service delivery modes to influence public policy continues to be relevant. However, whereas these features can characterize service delivery, they are essential to any approach to civil society engagement that is founded on people's rights. In subsequent sections, we will elaborate what elements we believe to be non-negotiable to the diversity of rights-based approaches.

Features of rights-based approaches: addressing causes of impoverishment

As stated, it is misleading and problematic to speak of the rights-based approach, because this seems to suggest that there is a settled theory and uniform practice related to rights-based development. In fact, on the contrary, this is an unfolding area of civil society and state action, diverse, evolving and continuously contested. In these circumstances, it would be hazardous to try to abstract some essential features of rights-based approaches. If I still attempt to do so, it is in the spirit of recording the outcomes of my own present quests and observations in this area, with no claims of certitude, and inviting interrogation, challenge and contestation, to strengthen our collective ongoing search for ways to be more meaningful and useful in efforts towards a more just and humane world.

The first distinct feature of rights-based approaches lies in the recognition of the structural causes of people's impoverishment, of the fact that their condition is the outcome of the active denial of their rights and entitlements by social, economic and political structures and processes. Upendra Baxi (1988) rejects the words 'poverty' and 'poor' because they are passive and tend to normalize what ought to be centrally problematic. He substitutes the word 'impoverished' because,

> impoverishment is a dynamic process of public decision-making in which it is considered just, right and fair that some people may become or stay impoverished. These decisions are made by people who hold public power; and it is a mistake to think that only politicians hold this power, although they manifest it supremely and dramatically. Judges, bureaucrats, economists and other human science specialists, media persons and public opinionators, activists and intelligentsia, among others. (Baxi 1988: vi)

According to him, 'both the state policies and our innumerable daily actions decide who, how many, to what extent, for how long, and with what cost shall become or remain impoverished' (ibid., p. vii).

There is also wide reliance in the recent literature on the notion of 'social exclusion'. Beall and Clert (2000) point out that the reason for this wide and less than rigorous application is that, 'in its colloquial and political usage, the concept of social exclusion has tremendous resonance and is very compelling'. Whereas concepts such as poverty, vulnerability, deprivation and inequality do not necessarily impute causality, a social exclusion framework implies not only that a person or persons are being excluded but that someone or something 'is doing the excluding' (De Haan 1998). This points up another key dimension of the social exclusion perspective as we understand it and that is that it is relational, deriving from social relations, invariably founded on differences in status or power (Beall and Clert 2000).

Similarly, the word 'marginalization' suggests that there is a core and a periphery, and that 'marginalized' people are those who are actively denied access to the core. The importance of these perspectives is that poverty is not perceived to be a mere attribute of certain categories of people. Instead, it is seen as something that is actively done to people. It is not what they are, but what they have been made. It is interesting that the ex-untouchables of India have discarded the appellation given to them by Gandhi – *harijan*, meaning 'children of God' – which they regard as patronizing. They prefer *Dalit*, which means 'one who is crushed' – because the term implies that they have been oppressed, and it has therefore acquired a cultural context of assertion and anger. In this sense, the terms 'exclusion' and 'marginalization' are useful.

This recognition of the primarily political nature of people's impoverishment necessarily also entails a rejection of essentially techno-managerial solutions, such as of micro-credit or the more efficient delivery of public services, for this to be overcome. All rights-based approaches therefore require both an analysis of what has led to the conditions of people's deprivation and dispossession, what their rights are and how these have been denied, and of the political processes for them to be able to access and claim these rights.

Amid both the theorists and practitioners of rights-based approaches, one encounters today an acknowledgement of the extremely complex nature of poverty, which is seen to manifest itself in a dense range of overlapping and interwoven economic, political and social deprivations. These include not just economic deprivation in all its forms – assetlessness, denial of just wages, insecure, underpaid, exploitative employment or unemployment, low income levels, hunger, poor health, insecurity, physical and psychological hardship – but also social exclusion, degradation and discrimination, and political powerlessness and disarticulation. Once again, this implies that strategies to combat and overcome poverty need to address not just the manifest outcomes of economic deprivation, but also the forces that produce and reproduce this deprivation, and, what is more, gender, caste, race and a range of other forms of social discrimination, and the denial of effective political power of impoverished groups.

Many of these analyses of impoverishment and class oppression derive from and build on sturdy Marxist roots. Feminist and civil rights movements, as well as anti-colonial struggles and struggles of oppressed groups such as *Dalits* (in India), indigenous people and ethnic minorities, together have contributed further to our understanding of the burdens of patriarchy, racism, ethnic and caste discrimination. Collins (1991: 225) writes of 'interlocking systems of oppression' involving race, class, gender, age, sexual orientation, religion and ethnicity. She could have added caste and physical abilities. She sees a matrix of interlocking axes of oppression, but establishes that the overarching relationship is one of domination.

Sen's (1992) seminal contribution has been that he brought to centre-stage of the poverty discourse the notions of choice and freedoms. He states that what is very important for assessing a person's situation are the real freedoms that a person enjoys to do this or that. He suggests that a person's well-being may be seen in terms of a set of interrelated functioning. These can vary from basic functioning, such as having enough food and shelter, to more sophisticated ones such as achieving self-esteem and contributing to the community. A person's capabilities represent the freedom to achieve functioning that she has reason to value, or in other words to achieve the kind of life to which she aspires. Primary goods like income are possible means to achieve freedom or well-being, whereas capabilities are the substantive freedoms that a person enjoys to pursue valued life-plans. In this sense, capabilities represent real choices.

Insights such as these have assisted development practitioners to understand the complex matrix of factors that lead to impoverishment, exclusion and powerlessness. One major set of factors is economic, mainly lack of control over the means of production, land, capital, natural resources, credit and so on. But a large number of disabilities are also social and cultural, related often to stigma and prejudice. Thus, for instance, a person with leprosy, which is today medically fully curable, is routinely denied contact with the immediate family and community, and the right to work. Examples when such chances have been restored reveal, if such revelation was necessary, that they are capable of at least as much productive work as a comparable person without the stigma.[1]

Some impoverishment may also be the direct outcome of state policy and law itself. To take a few examples, there is often no legal recourse by which a very poor person in a city in India can obtain shelter, therefore they are pushed into a twilight zone of perennial insecurity and criminalization. People displaced by big development projects are also marginalized as the direct outcome of state policy. The point that is being made is that the apparently low capabilities of very marginalized groups do not arise frequently from their own intrinsic and irrevocable biological infirmities, but in fact in many cases these infirmities are externally imposed by social and governance arrangements themselves.

Such an understanding of poverty as the outcome of the active denial of people's rights implies a rejection of understanding 'development' as a neutral process, and instead an acknowledgement of its political content. Rights-based approaches therefore contain an implicit logic of clearly taking sides with groups suffering from injustice in terms of chronic and structured denial of rights. It requires extending direct or indirect support to processes that seek to combat or overcome the sources that produce or reproduce such injustice, and which lead to the restoration of rights to groups that have been historically and systematically deprived of these rights.

This role of rights-based approaches, of extending solidarity, has been effectively delineated by Manji (1998) as follows:

> Solidarity is not about fighting other people's battles. It is about establishing cooperation between different constituencies on the basis on mutual self-respect and concerns about the injustices suffered by each. It is about taking sides in the face of injustice or the processes that reproduce injustice. It is not built on sympathy or charity or the portrayal of others as objects of pity. It is not about fundraising to run your projects overseas, but raising funds that others can use to fight their own battles. It is about taking actions within one's own terrain that will enhance the capacity of others to succeed in their fight against injustice.

The essential active agency of the oppressed

In terms of processes, a rights-based approach would of necessity, as we have observed, involve the identification of the chronic and systematic denials of rights of impoverished, excluded and oppressed people, an analysis of the sources and causes of such denials, and active solidarity with the oppressed.

The next crucial feature of rights approaches hinges on who does the analysis, because the resultant remedies, such as services or redistributive measures, would flow from the outcomes of this analysis. In this section, we will argue that the processes of diagnosing the sources of impoverishment and rights denial, and of needs that legitimately should be addressed, would derive authenticity only if these are undertaken centrally (although not necessarily exclusively) by those people and groups who suffer from the denial of rights in the first place.

In other words, neither rights nor justice can be given to a passive and inert group of people. Sustainable justice requires their central and active agency in all processes connected with identifying, accessing and securing their rights. Rights approaches therefore are by their very nature profoundly democratic, if they are authentic. They require authentic processes by which such groups acquire consciousness of their oppressed situation and the causes of this situation, and by which they themselves both identify and advocate for the enforcement of their rights, and develop strategies to resist, combat and seek to overcome the situations created by the denial of their rights.

It is entirely feasible for the lives of disadvantaged people to improve through the more effective delivery of services by the state or NGOs, even in situations in which people are excluded from the planning, implementation and monitoring of these services, and are mere recipients. However, without the active agency of the people themselves, not merely as recipients of state or NGO services but as active partners in all that the state and other agencies do in relation to people's lives, 'sustainable' or enduring justice that addresses and reverses the causes of their rights denials cannot be achieved.

The first challenge is the defining of what people's needs are, and how these can best be addressed. Typically, this is done by state authorities, professionals and even many NGOs, without any genuine egalitarian consultation with the people whose needs are sought to be addressed by these services. What they tend to overlook is that people are not mere inert sites of those services based on needs identified and regarded as appropriate by the state, NGOs or professionals; on the contrary, people are active agents who must actively establish the nature and content of their needs, and utilize services for the fulfilment of their potential and enjoyment of substantial freedoms.

Services are only a means, not an end. When we recognize these people as ends in themselves, we are not talking about their rights merely of physical survival. We recognize physical, economic, political, social and cultural barriers that deny these persons the power, the substantive freedoms, to make real choices about their own lives. A just set of social and state arrangements would seek to create and protect spaces for the full enjoyment of these substantive freedoms. It is only then that each person would have the space, and the freedom, to achieve full human potential.

When confronted with a person's set of problems, the state, and many NGOs and professionals, search typically for a scheme into which the problems can be slotted. They tend to respond overwhelmingly in terms of programmes, departments, plans, funds and so on, rather than in terms of the person's own assessment of her needs, aspirations and unfulfilled potential. In this implied denial, and the alienation of people from both their problem and their potential, not only the bureaucracy but also professionals, academics and NGOs frequently contribute.

In an extremely sensitive critique of the American social-welfare system, Fraser establishes how welfare practices implicitly reinforce sexist gendered interpretations of women's needs and roles. Those families are constructed as 'normal' and socially desirable which are headed by (usually white) male breadwinners. Implicit also is that the appropriate role for a woman is that of home-maker, and welfare must assist women to fulfil this role especially when they live in what are constructed as 'defective (i.e. female-headed) families: '[S]ocial welfare programs provide more than material aid: they also provide clients, and the public at large, with a tacit but powerful map of normative, differentially valued gender roles and gendered needs' (Fraser 1989: 9).

The same surely applies to all welfare programmes for excluded and stigmatized people, which tend to assist them as passive recipients while reinforcing the social and cultural beliefs that cause or strengthen their exclusion. Thus, people who live by begging, street children, homeless people, women victims of violence and sex-workers are all provided 'services' by the state or NGOs which are located entirely in what the state (or NGOs and professionals) regard as their needs; never what they themselves aspire to. Fraser powerfully argues that the establishment of the 'needs' of any group like women must be recognized as political, and the struggle to establish needs must be fought primarily by those with the needs, rather than the welfare-givers or the experts. This would apply to all those marginalized groups which have 'special needs' that lay claim to state support.

In concrete terms, let us take the example of a person with disabilities. State policy for a monthly dole, or protection in state semi-custodial institutions, may be sufficient for the physical survival of the person. Access to healthcare may even ensure the correction of reversible biological disabilities, and also the availability of aids and appliances, which facilitate mobility and communication. But the person may still be denied entry into schools and institutions of higher learning. She may be denied employment. She may be restrained from getting married and having a family. Even in day-to-day life, she may not be able to access public places such as cinemas and libraries, because of architectural barriers. She may not be ceded the opportunity to contribute to society, participate in community life, fight elections and so on. Therefore, the state may ensure her physical survival, but she remains without real freedoms, behind the walls of an institution or in her home, unfulfilled, dependent, without dignity, and unable to develop and contribute her full potential.[2]

By contrast, we therefore envisage a state response in a just society which goes well beyond the parameters of conventional welfare, and which in fact may on occasion even contradict conventional devices of welfare such as doles and institutions. We are seeking instead a caring state, which we see in terms of a state that consistently, sustainably and on its own initiative provides protection and support to marginalized people. State support is extended in such a manner that it is deeply sensitive to their needs and aspirations, enhances their dignity and self-reliance and above all enables people to exercise free choice over their own lives.

It is important to stress that we are not denying the importance of the state's responsibility for providing services, even less to absolve the state from this major and largely unmet responsibility. We are only trying to distance ourselves from the widespread belief, which prevails particularly in relation to marginalized people, but also in relation generally to people at large, that the state's responsibilities end even with the providing of essential life-sustaining or life-enhancing services.[3]

Even in the best of state responses, people are converted into inert and passive recipients of the state's services (or equally those of professionals and NGOs). When people are perceived to be weak or less 'abled' in any way, and in situations of disasters, this tendency is further heightened, sometimes with cataclysmic results.[4]

A possible alternate paradigm would be one in which NGOs, professionals and the state start with the acknowledgement that people are necessary, in fact primary partners, individually as well as through their own organizations, in any process of assessing their own needs and finding solutions to their own problems. In such a paradigm, the whole process of achieving solutions itself becomes empowering. The role of the state would clearly extend well beyond the providing of services. It would involve first the recognition, protection and effective enforcement of people's entitlements. It would further be to acknowledge, create, nurture, provide resources for, and actively support, all efforts by people and their organizations for the solution of their own problems.

Whereas the struggle to overcome injustice and restore rights must be undertaken centrally by oppressed groups, there are many roles that an external facilitating and support agency can play. The specific roles must be clearly identified in local contexts, in close discussions with the groups in question. However, some possible roles that may be relevant are listed below:

- expressions of solidarity (already referred to in the preceding section) in terms of unambiguously taking sides in support of the group of people who are denied rights
- assisting in processes which Paulo Freire described as 'conscientization', which involve the construction of awareness of one's oppressed situation and its causes, and the conviction that this oppression can and should end, and the resolve to organize to overcome this oppression collectively

245

- assistance in fighting legal battles to restore rights
- support to peaceful resistance and struggle
- assistance in attempting to influence state law and policy and their implementation for the restoration of rights
- assistance in building or establishing linkages with larger networks or other groups working on related issues
- assistance in access to relevant information and technologies
- support to activists from the groups suffering denial of rights working on these processes
- delivery of services that help sustain the groups suffering denial of rights during the period in which these various processes have an impact.

'Good governance' and the role of the state

Another essential feature of rights-based approaches is the affirmation that the state is the primary agency for the enforcement of people's rights, security and well-being, for ensuring their just and adequate access to social services and other public goods, and for securing redistributive justice. This affirmation and defence of the critical role of the state gain importance because of the contemporary hegemony of neo-liberal perspectives of a limited and retreating state, supportive of and even subservient to the interests of the market.

The state may be defined as a set of institutions with the legitimate powers of coercion and a monopoly over binding rule-making. These powers are exercised over a defined territory and population. Throughout history and across continents, states have variously assumed responsibilities for defence, taxation, resolution of conflicts and providing basic public goods such as roads and irrigation. The twentieth century saw an unprecedented growth, both in theory and practice, of the size, functions and reach of the state, whether influenced by Keynesian remedies to address market failures, or Marxist class analysis of the state and the abolition of private property, or the emergence of new nations that shed colonial bondage and longed to bridge centuries of suppression through activist state action, or the blossoming of the welfare state.

What is new since the turn of the 1990s is an altered perception of the role of the state, under the seismic global impact of the collapse of the Soviet Union and the Berlin Wall, and with these the demise of the great experiment, unprecedented in human history, of overarching comprehensive centralized state planning. From its ruins, economic frontiers between nations blurred, and countries across the planet were drawn rapidly, almost inexorably, into an integrated global economy. A single economic orthodoxy swept the nations of world, of market-led economic growth and the neo-liberal policies of structural adjustment that were powerfully promoted by international financial lending institutions.

The policies and practices of national and local governments were critical even in the past to the destinies of poor people, but it is significant that good governance remained peripheral to the development discourse and practice, until such time as it became a critical concern for transnational capital. This is noteworthy also because the underlying, usually unstated, assumption in the contemporary dominant 'good governance' discourse is that what is 'good', or 'sound' or 'effective' governance from the perspective of private businesses would automatically be good in most cases for all sections of people, including impoverished and disadvantaged social groups. There is occasional acknowledgement that some people may just fall through the cracks in market-led economic development, but this is seen merely as an unfortunate by-product of an essentially healthy and benign economic process.

It is perilous to regard 'good governance' as a politically neutral category, requiring merely a bundle of institutional reforms, economic policies and techno-managerial interventions (Arora in Chaturvedi 1999). The problem is not just with suggesting that a common set of policy prescriptions would be beneficial to countries of such enormous political, economic and historical diversity. Possibly even more problematic is the implied suggestion that what is 'good' governance for one section of the population would also be 'good' for all others. What is good for business – and indeed, even within this, for international capital and the large, formal sector – is assumed to be good also for poor and socially disadvantaged people, for farmers and workers, for small informal local producers, for women, for children, for indigenous populations, for minorities, for persons with physical or social disabilities and so on.

Rights-based approaches instead start with a premise that governance is 'good' only to the extent that it benefits the social groups who are impoverished, oppressed and socially vulnerable and excluded. There may be some elements of governance that may benefit all sections of a society and, if these are identified and demonstrated, they would be supported. But in the event of a conflict of interests, if a policy, law or governance practice benefits one section of the population and harms another, then only that policy, law or practice would qualify as 'good governance' which sustainably benefits those sections of society which are most impoverished, oppressed, excluded and vulnerable.

In its influential *World Development Report 1997*, the twentieth in its annual series, the World Bank chose to focus on its perceptions of 'the role and effectiveness of the state: what the state should do, how it should do it, and how it can do it better in a rapidly changing world' (World Bank 1997: iii). The report stresses repeatedly that its renewed focus on governance involves an agenda not for an uncritical strengthening of the state's role but, instead, for redefining of its responsibilities and measures for enhancing its capabilities and effectiveness.

A dominant theme in this neo-liberal paradigm is of a smaller, leaner state, which shares its responsibilities with the private sector. *The World Development Report 1997*, for instance, lays stress on 'knowing the state's limits' (World Bank 1997: 6), and acknowledging that the state need not be the sole provider of public goods like infrastructure and social services. The World Bank stresses the desirability of 'a smaller state equipped with a professional, accountable bureaucracy that can provide an "enabling environment" for private sector-led growth, to discharge effectively core functions such as economic management, and to pursue sustained poverty reduction' (World Bank 1994: xvi). It regards the role of the state primarily to act 'not as a direct provider of growth but as a partner, catalyst, and facilitator' (World Bank 1997: 1). Service delivery NGOs may not explicitly subscribe to neo-liberal convictions about a retreating state, and most of them do not, but by substituting the state in the delivery of services, they unwittingly may contribute to enabling the state to abdicate its responsibility to defend the civil, political, social, economic and cultural rights of all people.

The renewed stress on the rule of law in the neo-liberal paradigm of good governance derives from the fact that markets cannot function in an uncertain and insecure environment. They require the stability and predictability of the rule of law. Even in highly market-oriented societies, it is only the government that can lay down the rules required for markets to function most efficiently, and to intervene when markets break down (McLean 1987). If the state does not have effective and reliable institutions not only to make rules but also to enforce them, to protect property rights, enforce contracts and maintain law and order, private investment will suffer greatly (Eggerton 1990). From these considerations emerge clearly what are perceived by neo-liberals to be the essential building blocks of a sound foundation of law: protection of life and property from criminal acts, property rights such as land titling, laws governing private contracts and securities markets, the protection of intellectual property, and competition law restraints on arbitrary actions by government officials, and a fair and predictable judicial system.

The stress on the rule of law on the surface may seem unexceptionable, because it seems reasonable to assume that the rule of law automatically yields justice. In reality, this may not always be the case; in some instances, even the reverse may be true. The law in a market economy is expected primarily to protect property rights, but what about the rights of people without property? The neo-liberal project in many countries contains an essential component of diluting worker protection laws, whether in terms of job security or statutory minimum wages, because this is seen as an impediment to investment. Even property rights are selectively protected, because land acquisition laws that enable to state to expropriate private lands for large projects are upheld. Therefore, it is clear that from the perspective of rights, law may in fact damage the interests of people whose rights are denied, and for them justice rather than the rule of law is the critical need. Law may act against justice, in several ways: (i) some laws are themselves anti-poor; (ii) laws may be neutral, but their enforcement acts against the poor; (iii) pro-poor laws may selectively not be enforced.

I introduce an extensive quote from the Gujarat Legal Aid Committee which points out that formal 'equality before law' is unlikely to yield justice in situations of vast social and economic inequality:

> Equality of justice requires first, a fair and just substantive law and secondly, an even-handed administration of that law ... Ehrlich suggests that *de jure* equality may actually accentuate de facto inequality. He argues that, 'the more the rich and the poor are dealt according to the same legal proposition, the more the advantage of the rich is increased'. This kind of discrimination is far more dangerous because it is not so apparent and easy to detect except when its consequences are analyzed in the light of sociological data. Inequality in such cases stems from a failure of the law to take into account the differential capacity of the rich and the poor to avail of the benefits which the law provides. (Menon in Baxi 1988: 351)

The report illustrates this with the law of contract:

> There is so much inequality in the bargaining power that the poor are especially disadvantaged as against the rich. They lack information, training, experience and economic resources to bargain on equal terms with those who are more fortunately placed. But justice stands blindfold, equally indifferent to the identity of either party, and in the result it is the stronger which is able to tip the scales. In such circumstances, equality before the law is only an illusory equality and the very neutrality of the law comes an instrument of inequality, for it differs to the power of the strong party. (ibid., pp. 351–2)

It is true that the experiment of centralized state planning for growth and equity appears lost in the rubble of the Berlin Wall. Likewise, state activism in countries of the South did not measure up to the needs and aspirations of its deprived populations. However, the inference that is so influentially being promoted does not automatically follow: that interventionist states were not needed, that vulnerable people must depend on markets and the private sector, or even NGOs, to redeem their living standards and secure them social justice. If stubborn and pervasive impoverishment and social discrimination are to be addressed, it cannot be assumed that this will be achieved by mainstream economic policies that either aggravate or are at best neutral to the problem, with merely the subsidiary adjunct of antidotes of social insurance and social assistance.

Even in the era in which they were perceived as central to state responsibility and from which governments derived both their legitimacy and popularity, these social assistance programmes could not make an adequate dent in poverty in most countries. At a time when these programmes have been relegated to the periphery of political and economic discourse, and funding has been cut back under the impact of fiscal austerity, they are even less likely to make an impact on poverty.

In order to dismantle the legacy of impoverishment and discrimination, not only does this have to be reclaimed from the periphery to which it has been exiled to become the core of government action in these countries; it also requires strong redistributive measures such as land reforms, access to and control of forest and water resources by poor communities, food and work as legal entitlements, budgetary reallocations to benefit poor people, legal and judicial reforms for the poor, and their access to mainstream financial resources. None of this can be left to markets, and all of this requires vibrant, strong, interventionist states with high legitimacy and authority but also with genuine accountability.

In an illuminating debate about the appropriate role of the state in the context of liberalization in India, Dreze and Sen argue that it is not a question of more or less government, but of the type of governance. They stress its role mainly in advancing human capabilities and effective freedoms, not merely as a means to greater economic growth, but because human beings should be valued as ends in themselves, and the advancement of human capabilities should be the objective of social and political organization. The specific agenda that they recommend includes expansion of basic education, healthcare and social security, population policy, land reform, local democracy, women's rights, sound environmental policies and a credible legal system.

Strong activist states are necessary but not sufficient conditions for poor and marginalized people to secure justice and good governance. States are perennially contested institutions, which can be expected to act in the interests of people living in poverty, only to the extent that these people can influence and coerce it to do so. They can do this in a variety of ways including: by directly participating in governance (planning, implementation and evaluation); by enforcing accountability for both expenditures and outcomes through measures such as people's audits, right to information legislation, budget analysis and report cards; and through poor people's own organizations and social movements.

Conclusion

Rights-based approaches maintain that the only feasible way of ensuring justice and good governance from the state is for people to exercise direct control over a significant part of the levers of strong and accountable governments. In other words, as we have observed, there can be no justice without the active agency of the people themselves, not merely as recipients of state or NGO services but as active partners in all that the state and other agencies do in relation to people's lives.

A possible alternate paradigm would be one in which the state starts with ·the acknowledgement that people are necessary, in fact primary partners, individually as well as through their own organizations, in any process of assessing their own needs and finding solutions to their own problems. In such a paradigm, the whole process of achieving solutions itself becomes empowering. The role of the state would clearly extend well beyond the providing of services. It would involve first the recognition, protection and effective enforcement of people's entitlements. It would further be to acknowledge, create, nurture, provide resources for, and actively support, all efforts by people and their organizations for the solution of their own problems.

It is important to emphasize that we are not arguing for a reduced, but rather an altered role of the state, one that recognizes and supports people's real freedoms, and is supportive of people's own action. The state would then assist people to achieve solutions that are based on their own assessment of their needs, promote their self-reliance and dignity, and the fulfilment of their own potential.

In summary, then, the rights approach involves the processes by which people whose rights are severely and chronically denied are able sustainably to secure justice and the restoration of their rights. It involves clearly taking sides with those whose rights are denied, and partnering their own efforts to identify the sources of these denials and their struggles to secure their entitlements and alter public policy in their favour. It is the active solidarity of dispossessed women and men, boys and girls, with persons and organizations that join hands, in the centuries-old journey for a more just and humane world.

Notes

1 See for instance the account 'The Secret Wounds of Jatin' in Mander (2001). Baba Amte, India's leading social worker who spent a lifetime working with leprosy-cured persons, gave them a powerful slogan: It is not your charity that we want; we seek only a chance.

2 It is pertinent that the profound and persistent denial of rights of marginalized groups has been neglected almost completely, not only by the state but even by civil rights groups, the organized Left, the press and the academic mainstream.

3 In formulating the insights of this paragraph, I was particularly aided by a discussion with Dr R. Srinivasa Murthy, NIMHANS, Bangalore.

4 The result of the exclusion of people who are in great distress from the solution of their own problems may be illustrated by experiences in the aftermath of the Bhopal gas disaster of 1984. The Indian government through the Bhopal Gas Leak Disaster (Processing of Claims) Act in March 1985 arrogated to itself sole powers to represent the victims in the civil litigation against Union Carbide. The law specifically denied the survivors the right to seek their own entitlements. On behalf of the victims the Indian government filed a suit for compensation of more than US $3 billion in the Federal Court of the Southern District of New York. The case was returned in May 1986 to the Indian courts on grounds of forum non-convenience, under the condition that Union Carbide would submit to their jurisdiction. On 14 February 1989 in a sudden departure from the matter of interim relief which it was deliberating, the Supreme Court passed an order approving the settlement that had been reached between the government of India and Union Carbide without the knowledge of the claimants of Bhopal. According to the terms of the settlement, in exchange for payment of US $470 million the Corporation was to be absolved of all liabilities, criminal cases against the company and its officials were to be extinguished and the Indian government was to defend the Corporation in the event of future suits. The settlement sum, nearly one-seventh of the damages initially claimed by the government, while being far below international standards is also lower than the standards set by the Indian Railways for railway accidents. Moreover, the extinction of criminal liabilities in a civil suit was unprecedented in Indian jurisprudence. This was only the first of a series of incidents, which continue to the present day, in which the survivors feel that their rights have been denied by the intervention of the state, but they are powerless to defend their own rights. (See also 'After Bhopal' in Mander 2001.)

References

Baxi, U. (1988) 'Law and Poverty', in U. Baxi (ed.), *Critical Essays* (Bombay: N. M. Tripathi Private).

Beall, J. and C. Clert (2000) *Social Exclusion and Globalisation: Implications for Social Policy and Urban Governance*, Department of Social Policy, London School of Economics, Monograph prepared for the African Technical Families – Macroeconomics 2, World Bank, April.

Chaturvedi, T. N. (1999) *Towards Good Governance* (New Delhi: Indian Institute of Public Administration).

De Haan, A. (1998) 'Social Exclusion: An Alternative Concept for the Study of Deprivation?' *IDS Bulletin*, 29 (1): 10.

Eggerton, T. (1990) *Economic Behaviour and Institutions* (New York: Cambridge University Press).

Ferguson, C. (1999) *Global Social Policy Principles: Human Rights and Social Justice* (London: Department for International Development).

Fraser, N. (1989) *Unruly Practices: Power, Discourse and Gender in Contemporary Social Theory* (Cambridge: Polity Press).

Freire, P. (1985) *The Politics of Education: Culture, Power and Liberation*, trans. D. Macedo (London: Macmillan).

Korten D.C. (1990) *Getting to the 21st Century* (Delhi: IBH).

McClean, I. (1987) *Public Choice: An Introduction* (Oxford: Blackwell).

Mander, H. (2001) *Unheard Voices: Stories of Forgotten Lives* (New Delhi: Penguin India).

Manji, F. (1998) 'Depoliticisation of Poverty', in *Development and Rights* (Oxford: Oxfam). <www.developmentinpractice.org/readers/rights/intro.htm>

Menon, N. R. M. (1988) 'Legal Aid and Justice for the Poor in Law and Poverty', in U. Baxi (ed.), *Critical Essays* (Bombay: N. M. Tripathi Private).

Sen, A. (1981) *Poverty and Famines: An Essay on Entitlements and Deprivation* (Delhi: Oxford University Press).

Sen, A. K. (1992) *Inequality Re-examined* (Oxford: Oxford University Press).

Shivji, I. (1989) 'The Pitfalls of the Debate on Democracy', *CODESRIA Bulletin*, 2.

Streeten, P. (ed.) (1984) *Beyond Adjustment: The Asian Experience* (Washington, DC: IMF).

World Bank (1994) *Development in Practice: Governance: The World Bank's Experience*, May (Washington, DC: World Bank).

— (1997) *World Development Report 1997: The State in a Changing World* (Oxford: Oxford University Press).

13 | Linking rights and culture – implictions for rights-based approaches

JONATHAN ENSOR

The meaning of a rights-based approach is inevitably dependent on an understanding of what 'rights' are. Straightforwardly, rights can be understood to be those requirements laid out in documents such as the International Covenant on Civil and Political Rights or the African Charter on Human and Peoples' Rights. Such international standards provide a common benchmark against which inter- and non-governmental organizations can judge behaviour and offer a mechanism for redressing the power imbalance in the relationship between a state and its citizens. Moreover, the achievement of such rights is understood by rights-based organizations to be central to securing human dignity, overcoming poverty and resolving conflict. While accepting the foregoing, the aim of this chapter is to demonstrate that a broader and deeper understanding of rights is important for rights-based approaches to be successful. More specifically, the aim is, first, to build an understanding of the relationship between rights and culture, and, second, to propose that this understanding demonstrates that an appreciation of identity and culture should in fact be at the heart of rights-based approaches.[1] The result is a framework for a mode of rights-based practice that focuses on the process of individual and communal change.

Introduction

Within the Western liberal consensus, human rights thinking has been dominated by the rights of individuals.[2] However, the role of culture and communities has been advanced from two platforms. Within rights theory, group or collective rights have long been suggested to address needs that are perceived to be inadequately provided for, or ignored by, individual rights. Liberalism, on the other hand, has been directly challenged by the communitarian school, which charges liberals with undermining communities and failing to recognize that the 'self' is embedded in communal commitments and values (Buchanan 1989: 852–3). The convergence of the communitarian view of society with the problem of collective rights has led to a substantial body of literature that reassesses the role of communities in modern liberal thought and contests the association of liberalism with individualism. In this view the meaning of individual freedom is deter-mined by the characteristics of a society, impacting on the aspirations, goals and the self-respect of individuals and shaping their understanding of a good life.

For those interested in understanding how rights-based approaches can be made relevant in different communities and cultures, a significant question arises: how can a theory of rights adequately account for the close relationship between an individual and the culture within which she or he exists? The purpose of this chapter is to propose an understanding of the meaning of rights that incorporates this relationship and, as a result, offers insight to those seeking to apply rights in practice. This understand-ing, referred to here as a 'cultural theory of rights', holds that individual interests underpin rights and *explicitly* acknowledges the relationship between those interests and the broader social environment. Thus, rights protect individual interests that have been culturally framed. However, the enforcement of rights also fosters a society that reflects their content. Therefore, where rights reflect a consensus on aspects of individual well-being that are of particular importance, they serve to protect not only the individual interest but also the society that shaped those interests. This understanding has important implications. Current views of rights-based approaches, as expressed in policy documents and studies, have little or no direct reference to culture or community. A representative summary is offered by the conclusions of a review of Danish rights-based aid policy (Sano 2000: 751): 'A focus on protection of individuals and groups against power exertion ... a focus on non-discrimination, equal opportunity and participation ... a focus on enabling support that allows individuals and groups to lead a life in dignity, free of poverty, with access to certain mini-mum standards of living, health, water, and education.'

The emphasis on participation comes closest to acknowledging the need to consider rights in their local context. Indeed, considerations of culture and context can form part of good programming practice; however, few go so far as to recognize the need to 'fully consider how identity is drawn into claim-making processes, and [how] rights may be articulated in ways that are different from international conventions and legislation' (Fisher and Acre 2003: 8).[3] These issues are at the heart of the implications of the cultural theory of rights and this chapter aims to demonstrate that rights-based approaches, properly understood, relate to them directly. The cultural theory of rights challenges those using rights-based approaches in practice to include an understanding of the integral role that culture plays in the well-being of the individual. If a rights-based approach is adopted by an agency, they must consider whether they are imposing a version of the 'good life' that resonates with their own (often Western, liberal) principles, rather than with the social norms that define the interests of the recipients; whether, indeed, they are knowingly or unknowingly imposing 'another form of Eurocentric violence which seeks to normalise a self-serving social vision' (Mohan and Holland 2001: 177). This is an essential step not only for an intervention to be morally acceptable, but also if it is to be successful in embedding social change.

The next two sections develop the notion of the cultural theory of rights from understandings of groups, communities and individuals, and the so-called 'interest' theory of rights. Having developed an understanding of the relationship between rights and culture, this is next contrasted with policy statements from two rights-based organisations – Oxfam and ActionAid – and considered in relation to power analysis. In the final two sections, the implications of the cultural theory for rights-based interventions are considered in more detail, noting in particular the likelihood of rights being manifested differently when considered in different places or at different times, and that power relationships and cultural practices are often important factors in individual well-being. Rather than challenging these social factors directly, a rights-based approach can therefore seek to work in sympathy with them, aiming to effect change from within rather than imposing change from without. Thus, an alternative mode of rights-based practice is proposed, from first principles, which offers a mechanism for constructive engagement in circumstances where the challenging or confrontational mode, often associated with the enforcement of legal rights, is inappropriate or may be ineffective. The final section considers rights-based approaches in practice, demonstrating via case studies how the implications of the cultural theory have been successfully operationalized in NGOs working in different cultural contexts.

Individual and community

In this chapter, communities and groups are repeatedly referred to in order to establish the nature of individual freedom and well-being, and the context that is implicit, yet rarely referred to, when rights are talked of. However, if the nature of culture, community and identity is to be discussed, it is first necessary to establish the nature of groups. Two points should be considered paramount. First, the comments presented in this section are equally applicable to those supporting or running rights-based programmes as they are to the communities or partners that are the beneficiaries. Second, a thesis of static and unchanging groups is not being suggested by this work. The idea of the 'naturalness of ethnicity' (Smith 1980: 85), in which groups are fixed entities that share a common 'primordial' ancestry, gained considerable favour in the colonial period. However, the reality tends to be more complex. In Africa, for example, Ranger (1999: 13) points out that the popular nineteenth-century societal signifiers such as language, belief and kinship 'had no necessary connection with ethnicity at all'. Instead, groups shared diverse languages, while individuals and households exhibited significant 'spatial mobility' as they migrated and traded across regions. Indeed, rather than fixed ethnic groups, Ranger (ibid., p. 18) suggests that it is more reasonable to speak of 'regional cultures' in pre-colonial Africa, in which individuals shared many identities defined by the various aspects of their ritualistic and economic lives. The missionaries and early colonialists, however, sought to identify bounded communities in order to understand the newly 'discovered' populations, while fixed social structures would later ease the administration of trade. The identification of 'partner' groups from among the supposed ethnic communities was a preferred method to facilitate indirect rule, and thus ethnicity emerged as an economic or political structure (Bowen 1996: 6).

The objective analysis such as that offered by Ranger is common to the 'social constructionist' approach to identity, in which groups emerge primarily as a result of environmental and political factors. As J. and J. Comaroff (1992: 61) explain: 'where "ascribed" cultural differences rationalise structures of inequality, ethnicity takes on a cogent existential reality. It is this process of reification that gives it the appearance of being an autonomous factor in the ordering of the social world.' Constructionist analysis reveals that a common culture, in terms of shared social norms, language and so forth, is not a necessary prerequisite for group creation, but becomes 'important for providing *post facto* content to group identity' (Horowitz 1985: 66–7).[4] Objectively, therefore, identity may be created, heightened or realized by discriminatory or differential law, forced migration or displacement, distinctive physical characteristics, or other external factors (Cohen 1999: 7–9). In each of these cases, the groups concerned may have little or no ethnic or cultural commonality in the primordial sense, but, significantly, the individuals may *subjectively* define themselves in these terms. Moreover, the sense of group identity may be reinforced among communities that are disenfranchised, face competition for resources, or are threatened by physical danger. Thus, while group identity may be socially constructed and therefore historically contingent, it retains real and important significance none the less. As Cohen suggests: 'it would be very foolish ... to ignore the fact that many individuals strongly believe that ethnic allegiances are part of their core identity and have to be defended on a life or death basis' (ibid., p. 10).

The foregoing represents an argument for a middle ground in the debate between primordialists and social constructionists, in which identity is acknowledged as constructed and therefore transient, yet remains a factor that may assume great significance for the individual. In contemporary liberal thought, this reality has been forced onto the agenda by the communitarian critique, and by persistent claims for collective rights. As Buchanan (1989: 882) observes, the communitarians 'have made a strong case for taking the value of community seriously and hence for recognising limitations on the value of autonomy and of exclusively individualistic conceptions of well-being'. In response, Will Kymlicka and Joseph Raz in particular have sought to clarify the nature of the relationship between the individual and their cultural community.[5] In this aspect of their work, the existence of a group or community is assumed, and may relate to ethnic groups, indigenous peoples, or other minorities.[6] Rather than addressing the processes of group formation, their focus is on the dependency of the individual on community, and thus on the importance of groups from the perspective of their contemporary role rather than for their historical foundation.

Raz (1988: 289–94, 307–13) considers the nature of communal living in terms of personal well-being, which he deconstructs via *goals* and *social forms*. A person's goals are important to Raz's analysis because well-being is considered from the point of view of the individual (ibid., p. 289). Different from the biological needs of climate, food and so forth, goals, incorporating plans, relationships, ambitions, etc., are consciously held and play a significant role in the actions and reactions of the individual. Thus, 'improving the well-being of a person can normally only be done through his goals. If they are bad for him the way to help him is to get him to change them, and not to frustrate their realization' (ibid., p. 291). Social forms, defined as shared beliefs, folklore, culture, collectively shared metaphors and the like, pervade an individual's decisions, such that 'a person's well-being depends to a large extent on success in socially defined and determined pursuits and activities' (ibid., p. 309). Thus, 'a person can have a comprehensive goal only if it is based on existing social forms, i.e. on forms of behaviour which are widely practiced in his society'.[7] Which is to say that goals cannot be selected by an individual in a purely objective manner; the important aspects of one's life are deemed so with reference to communal context, or social forms. Thus 'engaging in the same activities will ... have a different significance in the life of the individual depending on the social practices and attitudes to such activities' (ibid., p. 311).

Raz's model allows analysis of the mechanisms of social interaction and personal well-being. Importantly, the structure of goals and social forms demonstrates the interconnectivity of the individual and society, and thus helps to place the importance of individual autonomy in context. Kymlicka offers broadly similar analysis, but starting with Rawlsian 'self-respect' in order to ground goals. Self-respect is important in order to 'see value in our activities', and, thus, 'isn't so much a part of someone's rational plan of life, but rather a *precondition* of it' (Kymlicka 1989: 189; emphasis in original). Goals, therefore, are constrained to those activities that are consistent with self-respect. However, the range of options in which we may 'see value' is limited by the cultural 'context of choice'. Analogous to social forms, the context of choice determines the importance of our actions, as those actions 'only have meaning to us because they are identified as having significance by our *culture*, because they fit into some pattern of activities which can be culturally recognised as a way of leading one's life' (ibid.; emphasis in original). The phrasing here is evocative of Raz but, interestingly, Kymlicka offers empirical evidence to demonstrate the interdependence of the individual and society. First, noting that language is the medium through which the value and significance of activities is judged and communicated, Kymlicka (ibid., p. 193) cites Fishman (1972; emphasis in original) to demonstrate that language is a 'marker of ... societal goals' and thus 'itself *is* content, a referent for loyalties and animosities'. Thus the non-neutral nature of language realizes social and historical judgements of value. Second, the practice by oppressive regimes of attacking identity and culture provides evidence of the importance of cultural heritage in providing individuals with 'emotional security and personal strength' (Kymlicka 1989: 193). This second issue points to the power of identity politics, and is the complement of the subjective sense of group membership that is heightened when communities are placed under threat (Cohen 1999: 7–9).

Kymlicka summarizes his overall conception as 'how freedom of choice is dependent on social practices, cultural meanings, and a shared language'. Accordingly, '[o]ur capacity to form and revise a conception of the good is intimately tied to our membership in a societal culture, since the context of individual choice is the range of options passed down to us by our culture' (Kymlicka 1995: 126). Both Kymlicka and Raz, therefore, offer a view of autonomy that is shaped and constrained by society. However, by referring to the behaviour of authoritarian regimes towards groups, Kymlicka also identifies how the importance of community changes in different circumstances. While both Kymlicka and Raz develop the notion of how culture and identity form an inevitable part of ostensibly autonomous decisions and actions, it is also apparent that, in times of threat, identity may be manipulated either to mobilize or to undermine group resistance. Thus culture, community and identity are, at all times, playing either an explicit or implicit role in shaping our lives.

A cultural theory of rights

The previous section has aimed to establish the importance of the cultural context within which individuals, and their rights, are situated. However, conventional liberal interpretations of rights have focused on the individual as an autonomous agent, with little or no reference to the broader community.[8] While not challenging individual rights, the aim here is to outline a theory of rights that necessarily *includes* an account of culture and community, therefore demonstrating that an exclusively individualistic interpretation is but one conception of rights. The following definition of rights is assumed: '"X has a right" if and only if X can have rights, and, other things being equal, an aspect of X's well-being (his interest) is a sufficient reason for holding some other person(s) to be under a duty' (Raz 1988: 166).

Thus, rights are fundamentally defined in terms of individual well-being. This approach to rights is an interest-based theory, which is distinguishable from a choice theory of rights. Where the interest theory grounds rights in the interest or well-being of the right holder, the choice theory holds that a right exists when the right holder is able to exercise control over their claim on another's duty (Green 1991: 319). Freeman suggests that the difference between the two approaches is one of justification against identification of rights, where the interest justifies the right, but we may identify the right by the right holder's ability to hold another to a duty (Freeman 1995: 29).[9] At worst, however, the choice theory restricts rights to those choices already available within a particular political environment. While this interpretation may be reasonable for the identification of rights, ignoring the justification risks removing the aspirational character, replacing what *should* happen with what *can* happen, and thus undermining a key aspect of the social change function of rights. As such the interest theory forms the focus of this work, in which the social foundation, rather than the legal manifestation, of rights is discussed. Social forms and the context of choice demonstrate that some aspects of life that we deem to be important are culturally dependent. Thus, significant aspects of an individual's well-being or interest, in so far as they are defined, influenced or mediated through the local context of choice, are variable across cultures. As previously noted, 'a person's well-being depends to a large extent on success in socially defined and determined pursuits and activities' (Raz: 1988: 309). This relationship between well-being and social context, and thus between the interest theory and culture, defines the 'cultural theory of rights' and has implications for both individual and collective rights.

The first result of the relationship between the individual and community is the impact that cultural considerations have on how individual rights are understood. One effect of individual rights is to uphold for all an aspect of society that reflects the content of the right. Thus rights contribute to 'collective goods' or communally held assets (such as respect, tolerance and so forth) that define the character of society (ibid., p. 199). The point here is not that all individual rights exist for the preservation of a liberal culture, but that the rights that we consider fundamental cannot be seen separately from or as being in competition with the collective or shared aspects of society (ibid., p. 254). Through reinforcing social forms and context of choice, individual rights both protect the well-being of the individual and foster a society in which that aspect of well-being is held to be important. However, the reverse is also true. As well-being is itself to an extent determined by social forms, any attempt to transpose rights from one cultural context to another must be certain that the individual interest is in fact being addressed. The imposition of a right without reference to social forms risks undermining an aspect of life that defines well-being.

The second result of considering rights and culture is collective rights. Collective rights arise when interests that are valuable to the individual have a collective aspect, but are not reducible to individual interests. What, then, are those aspects of life that are important to us collectively and cannot be described individually? Green (1991: 321) narrows collective goods to *shared goods*, defined as those where their 'public aspect ... partly constitutes what is valuable about them'. Thus, if certain goods or assets are collectively held and valuable as a result of being shared, then the interest that an individual has in such goods cannot be held separately from the collective. If the interest in such a shared asset is sufficient to hold others under a duty, then a collective right will result. A useful example here is provided by language. Clearly, in a shared enterprise, the value 'lies in the process of creating and recreating language rather than any end product that might be said to be useful to individuals as individuals' (Reaume 1994). The interest, therefore, is held by individuals, but in a shared good, and the protection of that shared good serves members of the language-speaking group. Moreover, duties entailed in language rights cannot be justified on the basis of the utility of language to an individual; the value of language is necessarily collective in nature. Language rights must, therefore, be protected as collective rights. Goods such as language are worthy of protection, however, because of the part they play in the well-being of the individual. To put it another way, the context of choice of the individual is determined by cultural assets, such as language, that are shared goods. These assets are designated as rights because of the importance that they have in forming an individual's notions of well-being and self-respect.

Much of the foregoing is summarized by what Gould describes as a 'truism' of social philosophy: 'we [are required to] characterise the human not only atomistically but socially as well, where characteristics are not only interpreted but constructed through the concrete interactions of particular ... individuals' (Gould 2001: 77). This aspect of human life, expressed through concepts such as the social form and realized in feelings of identity, is explicitly acknowledged in the above description of human rights. The interconnectivity of individual interests with collective aspects of society is at the heart of the relationship between rights and culture. As has been seen, individual well-being is defined within the social forms that exist within a cultural community, and rights are in turn defined by individual interest or well-being. This relationship not only gives rise to collective rights to cultural assets, but is also reflected in the nature of individual rights. The cultural theory of rights, therefore, demonstrates that development or other interventions that are predicated on a rights-based approach must consider those shared cultural assets that play an important role in the well-being and self-respect of individuals.

Rights-based policy through the cultural theory lens

Rights-based approaches have been operationalized by a range of inter-governmental, governmental and non-governmental organizations, and across a range of fields.[10] The policies that these organizations embrace demonstrate the institutional understanding of the role of rights within their work. However, while the meaning of a rights-based approach is variable not only between but also within different fields, common features can be observed. One extensive survey suggests that, for those organizations that have fully embraced the rights-based approach: '[t]he human rights principles underlying [policy and programming] are: accountability, equity, non-discrimination and participation. Situations are analysed through a human rights analysis framework, which ... poses questions about power relations within society: political, economic, social and cultural' (Nguyen 2002: 6).[11]

When viewed from the perspective of the cultural theory of rights, the emphasis on participation comes closest to acknowledging the need to ground rights in the local context and to consider local social forms. The only direct reference to culture is made in the context of power relations (more on which below), positioning culture in opposition to the achievement of rights. However, a more detailed understanding can be gained by considering specific policies. Oxfam is unusual in making a direct reference to identity in their rights-based policy. 'The right to an identity' is a core programme aim: 'Through educating and campaigning, Oxfam will help to change the policies and practices of those institutions that fail to respect the identity and value of people who are excluded because of their ethnic, cultural or other identity' (Oxfam 2001: 15). Oxfam's focus here is on institutional non-discrimination and, while this policy does not rule out group rights, no mention is made of the role of identity in shaping well-being (although it is possible that this may be inferred). However, through the 'right to be heard', Oxfam provides for participation that supports the local definition of problems: 'Marginalized people will achieve their civil and political rights; will have an effective voice in influencing decisions affecting their lives; and will gain the moral support and skills they need to exercise these rights' (ibid., p. 13).

ActionAid elaborate further on this point, with a perspective on participation that ensures meaningful local input to programming:

> Participation in decision making that will affect you is a right, but is also a practical necessity if the right policies are to work. Effective participation requires creating opportunities and capabilities for people who are poor to analyse their own situation and possible solutions, take decisions in their own way, and build trusting relationships with those who support them. (ActionAid 1999: 3)

Thus, within Oxfam and ActionAid, participation is taken to include a direct input into the decisions that are made as part of the development process. While not explicitly stated, room is left within such a policy for local definitions or interpretations of rights, although there is no encouragement given to such a course of action. These two organizations reflect the norm in policy descriptions of rights-based approaches, with the role of culture and identity largely restricted to non-discrimination; no reflection on the synergy between culture, community and rights; and no guidance as to how or if these considerations should be incorporated into the processes of local decision-making.

One aspect of rights-based approaches that appears uncontested in policy is the efficacy of rights analysis for exposing power relationships. This is frequently seen as a major and natural role for rights; as Moser and Norton point out, 'a rights perspective provides a robust framework for examining some key aspects of the vertical power relations and institutions that shape people's livelihood capabilities' (Moser and Norton 2001: 16). As such, power analysis forms a central pillar of the rights-based policy framework proposed by Moser and Norton. At the analytical level,[12] the role of rights in their framework is to 'elaborate the ways in which poor people's claims are processed into outcomes by multiple structures of authority and control that operate at different levels ... [The analytical level requires] a better understanding of the way power impacts on the production and reproduction of poverty and insecurity' (ibid., p. 17).

The role of power in the processing of claims is therefore central to the analysis and should be considered in terms of perpetuating impoverishment. However, for this approach to be successful, it is pointed out that social factors must be taken into account: 'rigorous analysis [is required] of the associated social and political processes that determine the likelihood of poor people's claims being reflected in the definition, interpretation or implementation of rights ... [The analytical level] also calls for the identification of social characteristics (gender, citizenship, social status, ethnicity etc.) that empower, or disempower, people in different arenas of negotiation' (ibid.).

Here, Moser and Norton explicitly acknowledge the existence of local perceptions of rights. Indeed, an important feature of their approach is the recognition of different layers of authority: 'the legal realm covers not only "rights" but also norms – defined as explicit or implicit societal rules governing behaviour' (ibid., p. 22). However, the role of this analysis is to define those aspects of social characteristics that 'empower or disempower' in the claiming of rights. This view of social context is reinforced by example: 'international human rights law and national statutory codes theoretically may give women protection against domestic violence, while ... societal norms deny and values effectively denies them this right' (ibid.).

Social context is thus presented as a largely negative force, without a constructive role within the rights framework, and power is essentially viewed from the perspective of enabling or obstructing claims for rights. While unquestionably valid and an important contribution of rights to development practice, this focus is frequently presented and to the exclusion of the role of power relations in defining the local context of choice – and therefore the issues of well-being and individual interest that underpin rights. It is proposed that these considerations should also be seen as a contribution that flows directly from the use of rights.

Implications of a cultural theory of rights

The understanding of rights developed in the first part of this chapter is absent from the policies examined above. Three core recommendations are therefore proposed as a framework for ensuring that the role of culture in individual well-being is integrated into rights-based approaches.

1. *Different manifestations of rights* The relationship between rights and the character of society reflects the important place of rights in social, political and legal discourse. To discuss rights is to discuss issues that determine the nature of the community within which we live. A right can therefore be a threatening concept if it is new, unusual or inappropriate to a society. This is as much true in liberal societies that embrace rights as it would be if the language of rights were introduced as a new concept. Northern liberal governments enter reservations to and derogate from rights treaties as a matter of course, while the 'margin of appreciation' doctrine allows the European Court of Human Rights to defer to local (national) understandings of rights. While such processes may be subject to cynical manipulation, they also serve an important function by accounting for the local context of choice or social forms as understood at the level of political rhetoric. Differences between Europe and America on the relationship between the death penalty and the right to life provide a pertinent example. Rights are therefore framed locally as, on the one hand, the individual interests that rights protect are subject to local social forms, while, on the other hand, the character of societies (which rights reinforce) differ across communities and through time. The implication is therefore that those using rights as a basis for an intervention cannot assume that rights resonate with the local social forms and therefore that the manifestation of a right, while based on the same interest, may change. Moreover, the use of the language of rights may be perceived as a challenge or threat to a community if transferred, unchanged, from one context to another.

2. *Effecting change from within* The analysis of social forms also offers a constructive approach for implementing rights-based interventions. An understanding of the importance of social forms to individual freedom demonstrates, to restate Raz (1988: 291), that 'improving the well-being of a person can normally only be done through his goals. If they are bad for him the way to help him is to get him to change them, and not to frustrate their realization.' The identification of social forms, important communal practices, collective metaphors and so forth can be used to facilitate change from within, rather than attempting to force change from without. Dialogue on rights referenced to existing social forms (perhaps via interests) offers an opportunity to make rights language meaningful. Where confrontation may shrink or reinforce the local context of choice, a discussion of the interests that ground rights that is referenced to social forms is likely to connect with the goals of individuals, thereby expanding their context of choice rather than challenging it directly.[13]

3. *Rights and power* Claims for collective rights most clearly draw attention to those aspects of society that are important in defining well-being for individuals within that community. However, seen through the lens of power, collective rights sustain hegemonic, illiberal cultures and serve to suppress individual choice. The assessment of power relations as part of a rights-based analysis can provide significant insight into the structures of society and expose institutionalized abuse and privilege. While rights dovetail into power analysis by demonstrating which rights are denied and those responsible, the focus of this work is to highlight that rights *also* have a complementary function: rights should direct attention towards the culturally framed interests of individuals, as well as towards mechanisms of denial. A rights analysis with an exclusive focus on power may bypass the role that power holders play in social practices and in influencing the context of choice, thus missing both their role in the well-being of the community and possibility that power holders may themselves be the most effective agents of change.

Rights-based approaches in practice

The following two examples demonstrate how the above recommendations have been implemented in practice. Rather than being intended as representative of rights-based practice, they have been selected specifically to illustrate the implications of the cultural theory of rights.

Health and human rights Female genital mutilation (FGM)[14] presents particular problems for practitioners as it is a highly ingrained social phenomenon in many communities, and may also be a sensitive or even taboo subject for discussion. While the practice is culturally important, it can also be particularly physically and mentally harmful, and as such contravenes numerous human rights statutes: the Convention on the Elimination of All Forms of Discrimination Against Women (CEDAW) calls for the ending of FGM, while the Convention on the Rights of the Child (CRC) requires children's rights to be upheld, including protection from any practice that is harmful. Moreover, the Vienna Programme of Action requires 'the eradication of conflicts ... between rights of women and ... customary practices', a diplomatic reference to FGM. The Beijing Programme of Action, arising from the Fourth UN Conference on Women, considers FGM to be a form of sexual discrimination.

The significance of FGM to communities, however, can be considerable. According to Program for Appropriate Technology in Health (PATH), an NGO with expertise in behaviour change communication and experience in working with FGM:

girls receive elaborate social recognition and support at the time of FGM, not only for coming of age, but also for facing the physical pain ... Young girls anticipate and enjoy the attention, new clothes, exotic food, gifts and peer companionship that are part of the rite of passage ... Mothers also look forward to this event because it represents the culmination of multiple achievements. It illustrates that a mother has reared her daughter well ... For fathers ... FGM is a chance to show off their wealth, and to negotiate with prospective in-laws for a bride-price. For grandparents, it is a time ... to hand down ancestral teachings. (Mohamed et al. 2002: 73)

While FGM remains near universal in many areas,[15] some individuals and communities are starting to question the practice, not least due to the expense of the ceremonies and the tension created by competition between families (ibid., pp. 73–4). Capitalizing on this, PATH have developed an intervention strategy that follows two guiding principles. The first aspect of the approach is to support facilitative dialogue. However, initiating dialogue can be problematic:

When initiating a new program, the resistance to 'interference from outsiders', whether Westerners or non-local citizens, can rapidly spread. It is important to avoid a 'blame campaign' that vilifies those who practice FGM. An important step is to identify existing community-based groups that are interested in the subject, through which dialogue on FGM can be internally driven. (ibid., p. 71)

The second principle is a focus on promoting cultural strengths: 'By understanding the role that FGM plays in culture, and maintaining the healthy aspects of that role through other practices, the community's fear that change will lead to social disintegration will be minimised ... It is important to understand the various socio-cultural dimensions and pressures that can affect the ability of individuals to change' (ibid.).

Working with local organizations, PATH have followed these principles to develop an 'alternative rites of passage' approach to address FGM. Locally designed, the programme includes 'all the aspects of the traditional coming-of-age ceremony – seclusion, information sharing, and celebration – but no cutting of the genitalia. The alternative ceremony was called Ntanira Na Mugambo – "circumcision by words"' (ibid., p. 74). By introducing this alternative while also supporting the establishment of a non-circumcision community alongside the traditional community, a significant reduction in FGM has been experienced, with 200 families from one district adopting the alternative rite within a year.[16]

CARE, working in Kenya, Ethiopia and the Sudan, have explored the direct role that rights can play in combating FGM. Having found that health education had resulted in less severe forms of genital cutting, rather than its cessation, CARE were keen to use rights in order to integrate 'social well-being' into ongoing reproductive health activities.[17] However, staff were uncomfortable with introducing rights concepts at community level, particularly when dealing with such a sensitive topic: 'To what extent should we educate *community members* on rights issues (as defined in international treaties and conventions), violations of rights, and community responsibilities to uphold certain rights? Would such an approach be too top-down and too Western-dominated?' (Igras et al., 2002: 3; emphasis in original).

To combat this concern, CARE initiated a study into community-level understandings of rights and the social norms that uphold them. In the counties included in the study,[18] the project revealed that: local languages had words for rights; basic needs such as food, shelter, health and respect were commonly understood as rights; religion and culture (understood to mean social norms) define rights; well-defined concepts of those responsible for upholding rights exist; and FGM was not considered by the communities to be a rights issue (ibid., p. 5–6).[19] Having gained an insight into rights issues as defined by the local communities, a number of implications for programming were established. Primarily, staff concluded that approaches to FGM would have to vary depending on the local situation. While general agreement was found between international standards and local interpretations of rights to a good life, it was concluded that 'It would be prudent to look at rights programming from both the international and local perspectives, letting each serve a "check and balance" function for the other' (ibid., p. 6). Moreover, 'In order to develop approaches that ring true with communities with which we work, we must understand how communities think about rights and responsibilities and what community institutions promote rights equally among its membership' (ibid).

The importance of those with responsibility for shaping and upholding rights led the project to engage with influential members of society: 'In Ethiopia project staff invited religious leaders to come together to develop a consensus on the position of religion and [FGM]. In Kenya, project staff approached elders and local religious leaders on the issue of protecting those who were publicly stating they were against the practice of [FGM]' (ibid., p. 10).

Finally, it was noted that in Ethiopia, where the communities involved were extremely isolated, the role of rights was indirect, and 'the project never spoke directly to communities about rights that were violated with the practice of [FGM]' (ibid., p. 7).

SUMMARY OF RELATIONSHIP TO THEORY By assessing local interpretations of rights, the CARE approach offers a methodology for implementing rights-based interventions. Understanding the local social forms and understandings of 'rights' reveals how appropriate rights may be in a given situation. By engaging with the mechanisms that support or define social forms, the work of reform may be achieved from within rather than without; 'power' structures can thus be engaged in a constructive mode as an important social factor. The PATH approach similarly facilitates change by understanding the cultural context. Having established that FGM is a manifestation of important social forms, and a goal for many in the community, the 'alternative rights of passage' approach maintains many of the features of FGM that are important cultural markers. Thus the approach is able to offer an alternative goal, based on the existing social forms. It is notable that for CARE in Ethiopia and PATH, direct reference to rights violations is avoided, thus avoiding a 'blame campaign' and reducing the potential for resistance to outsiders with the associated closing of group ranks. When such a crucial aspect of identity is the target of the intervention, tackling it via prescriptive, judgemental rights language risks closing down opportunities for change.

Development and human rights ActionAid's long-standing presence in Somaliland[20] operates on the basis of supporting solutions to locally defined problems. ActionAid Somaliland (AAS) initially operated a conventional top-down management structure, with operations flowing from a director based in London, via an office in Mogadishu into the districts and communities. However, after AAS suspended operations in 1991 following heavy fighting in the region, work resumed in the Sanaag region in 1992, with operations now determined by those communities that AAS had maintained links with. AAS activities later expanded into neighbouring Togdheer. The conflict had resulted in the collapse of the institutions of central government, but, as the numerous inter-clan peace conferences demonstrated, governance structures remained strong in the country. A core aspect of AAS's work now lies in developing further institutional capacities around essential resources in order to support the needs of the population (Le Mare 2003).

While the state is usually perceived to be the provider of the needs that rights represent, AAS notes: 'local people have created robust institutional arrangements to provide water or manage fisheries ... [i]n AAS we have consistently demonstrated the ability of local people to create working institutional arrangements' (AAS 2002: 3). This observation drives AAS's approach. Having developed expertise in the areas of governance, institutions and experiential learning, the issues surrounding problem-solving are well understood by AAS:

A major problem is the question, 'What is the problem?' If we accept that we perceive reality [individually], and assign meaning to the observations and experience, then we arrive at problem constructs which are relevant to the individual ... Yet, human beings cannot survive as individuals, [they] need to develop cooperation and interdependence ... The problem then becomes 'How can we pool together the unique and different perceptions of individuals, so that a group of people arrive at a mutually acceptable definition of a problem?' Unless this collective understanding of a problem is reached, the solution will not address the needs of the group. (ibid., p. 8)

Collectively defining problems and identifying their solutions is the function of institutions, which AAS support at the village level, aiding with the process of forming 'small scale constitutions' for the management of local resources (Le Mare 2003). Underlying this approach is the belief that direct intervention denies the right of the beneficiary to gain experiences from his or her own worldview. Instead, AAS supports 'learning by doing': 'All humans have the experience of problem solving. This creates knowledge, which can be applied to tasks of defining problems and taking action to solve them. This builds new knowledge, which can be used in another cycle of knowledge-action-experience' (AAS 2002: 6).

Thus, AAS operate by helping local people to achieve sustainable collective action through user-groups or community-based organizations (CBOs). A major function in this approach is to operate as a conduit between donors and local organizations. The trust of communities is developed by establishing a relationship based on a 'contract', in which AAS offers funding for community defined operations, if the community chooses to take it (Le Mare 2003). The condition attached to the contract is that full participation of all stakeholders occurs in the establishment and resolution of problems. Beyond this, the approach is not prescriptive. Thus, the poor must be represented in the decision-making process, and men and women are present as different stakeholders. However, 'AAS believes that sociological evolution has assigned different roles to men and women. These roles have cultural, traditional, political, spatial and temporal contexts' (AAS 2002: 7).

The approach acknowledges that equity and justice must be applied to gender issues, but that equity and justice are themselves contextual, informed by the 'community viewpoints of both men and women' (ibid., p. 4). To establish these views, AAS help communities with their own gender analysis studies. Along with this, the people of Sanaag and Togdheer have completed a number of community reviews, which were themselves designed and facilitated by local CBOs. Furthermore, the CBOs also identified local experts to perform studies on water and pastoralism, and a review of institutions, while the CBOs themselves have carried out needs assessment studies, establishing the priorities of local communities. All of these locally defined perspectives are combined to form the strategic plan for the two regions, for which AAS suggests appropriate governance models and secures funding (ibid., p. 9).[21]

SUMMARY OF RELATIONSHIP TO THEORY. For ActionAid in Somaliland discussions of 'rights' must take place in the context of problem definition and solving, which, when performed by all stakeholders in a communal and participatory context, is the establishment of a consensus on the local understanding of justice and the rights of groups and individuals.[22] The approach is summed up with respect to gender, an issue that is conventionally framed in terms of power relations:

> Do members of that society have a problem with the way men's and women's roles have evolved? If 'Yes' then it is for them to define the problem, state whether they desire change and state the transformation they desire. We (outsiders or non-members of the society) can state our opinion on how the status-quo might advance a situation of poverty for a section of society as part of discussion but do we have a right to force change? (Le Mare 2003)

As Le Mare's final comment suggests, the approach is not one of communities operating in isolation from Western or non-local ideas, innovations or perceptions, but that it is for the community to respond to those ideas. Devolving power away from AAS and into the institutions ensures that priorities are not tempered by Western perceptions of what is important in life. As the cultural theory points out, rights aim to mediate interests on behalf of well-being, but well-being is itself influenced by cultural context.

Conclusion

Having focused on the importance of community and culture to the well-being of individuals, it is important to reiterate that this work does not seek to attack the value of individual rights, nor does it imply that legal rights and power analysis are not valuable tools in achieving the objectives of organizations that use a rights-based approach. It is not contested that the employment of rights from this perspective has had a considerable effect in improving the lives of many people. However, it is a central aim of this work to demonstrate that there is more to rights than an adversarial approach of claim-making against power holders. A shift of focus towards the interrelationship between culture, individual well-being and rights exposes a second mode of rights-based practice that retains the achievement of rights as an overarching goal but offers an alternative process based on constructive engagement with communities. While legal rights are called for in the struggle for citizenship by many, the examples in this chapter suggest that a more nuanced understanding of rights is necessary when engaging with issues that are closely tied to images of identity, or when recourse to the state is impossible. More broadly, understanding the role that culture plays in individual well-being should prevent an assumption that legal rights alone offer an appropriate course of action when the aim of an intervention is to help individuals and communities improve their own circumstances on their own terms. The interest theory is central to ensuring that rights-based approaches are relevant for such communities, defining rights in terms of aspirations for individual well-being: if this is accepted, then the challenge for rights-based practitioners is to take up the fight for those interests and to recognize the important role played by shared cultural assets.

As the review of policy demonstrates, current interpretations of rights-based approaches, while variable, generally exclude specific references to the relationship between rights and culture. On this reading, to include consideration of the cultural context implies an understanding of 'good programming practice', rather than an understanding of the nature of rights. As an increasing number of organizations embrace the rhetoric of rights, it is important to understand what it is that the language of rights represents. Returning to theory demonstrates that an approach based on rights is one that is rooted in individual interests, and that one such interest is those aspects of life that are shared in community with others. The cultural theory of rights presented here encapsulates this understanding and reveals implications for rights practice, proposed as important additions to the existing framework of rights-based approaches:

1. Different manifestations of rights. Local social forms and differences in context of choice dictate that the same actions do not have the same meanings in different places or at different times. Thus, it cannot be assumed that a particular conception of rights will resonate with the local social forms: the interests that rights represent may therefore give rise to alternative manifestations of a right. In the FGM example, local understandings of rights concepts were assessed in order to understand why cultural practices are sustained, the appropriateness of the legal rights framework, and to reduce the danger of a rights-based intervention becoming a top-down strategy that directly challenges the community. In Somaliland, the facilitative approach adopted by ActionAid naturally leads to the local

definition of rights (without being isolated from external interpretations), using an intervention designed to ensure that all stakeholders were able to define their own interests.

2. Effecting change from within. The identification of social forms, important communal practices, collective metaphors and so forth can be used to facilitate change from within, rather than attempting to force change and frustrate the goals of many in the community. Dialogue on rights referenced to existing social forms offers an opportunity to make rights language meaningful and thus expand the context of choice from within which individuals define their own goals and well-being. The 'alternative rites of passage' approach used by PATH in combating FGM explicitly acknowledges the value of cultural practices to members of the community. By maintaining all aspects of the process apart from genital cutting, an important cultural commodity is retained. In Somaliland, the provision of and support for institutions allows communication of ideas within and between communities, and opens a space for social forms and the context of choice to be renegotiated rather than displaced.

3. Rights and power. While power analysis frequently demonstrates the mechanisms of rights denial, group rights to shared goods draw attention to those aspects of society that are important in defining well-being for individuals within that community. A rights analysis with an exclusively negative focus on power may bypass the role that power holders play in social practices and in influencing the context of choice, thus missing both their role in the well-being of the community and the possibility that power holders may themselves be the most effective agents of change. A constructive use of power analysis is illustrated by the positive engagement with local 'power' structures by CARE to provide a mechanism for change that is in sympathy with social practices. For ActionAid, rather than using power analysis based on liberal rights, the institutional processes adopted allow for local assessment of the value of community structures and practices.

These conclusions all go beyond the use of rights as a straightforward legal mechanism for making claims and correcting power imbalances. They may not, therefore, be relevant in communities that directly frame their struggle in these terms. However, it is important to recognize that the issues raised above should not merely be considered as instrumental in achieving the aims of a rights-based approach, but rather reflect a core aspect of rights. The theory of rights developed in this work holds individual interests to be the underlying foundation for rights and, as a result, the implications regarding culture and community must necessarily be embedded in a rights-based approach.

Notes

1 Stavenhagen suggests three definitions of 'culture': as capital, as creativity, or as a total way of life. In this work, the third view is assumed in references to culture, meaning 'the sum total of the material and spiritual activities and products of a given social group ... a coherent and self-contained system of values, and symbols as well as a set of practices that a specific group reproduces over time and provides individuals with the signposts and meanings for behaviour' (Stavenhagen 1998: 5).

2 Van Dyke summarizes that liberals 'are protective and solicitous of the individual ... in various international documents such as the covenants on human rights, they have secured the spelling out of rights for individuals and are making the promotion of these rights a major issue' (Van Dyke 1979: 21).

3 This quote refers to work that examines the problem of bringing rights to the struggle of the Mapuche people in Chile. It should be noted that practitioners working with rights-based approaches have considered the impact of culture and identity (indeed, the case studies in this chapter identify two examples; see also Molyneux and Lazar 2003: 88–93); the function of this chapter, however, is to demonstrate that such a consideration should flow directly from the use of rights, rather than incidentally or in addition to it.

4 Which is not to say that a common culture is *never* instrumental in group formation.

5 Raz and Kymlicka are by no means the only philosophers to approach this issue, which is central to the communitarian school, nor are they by any means the first. See, for example, Van Dyke's earlier work on the liberal approach to group rights (Van Dyke 1977), or, earlier still, Hegel's critique of liberalism and the interdependency of the individual and community (Kymlicka 2002: 209).

6 Ethnic or indigenous groups may or may not form minorities; it is the group aspect that is important here.

7 Comprehensive goals being those of particular importance (Raz 1988: 308).

8 See, for example, Kymlicka (1989: 53–75, 208). Self-determination is the most obvious exception, but has also been one of the most inconsistently interpreted rights (Hannum 1992: 175–84).

9 As both Freeman and Green point out, this view does not make the interest and choice theories mutually exclusive.

10 For example, United Nations agencies such as UNDP and UNICEF, the UK Department for International Development, and NGOs such as ActionAid, Oxfam, Save the Children and International Alert all have policies that are 'rights-based', and operate across such fields as development, humanitarianism, health and conflict resolution.

11 Similar principles are found in the IDS study 'The Rise of Rights' (2003).

12 The framework operates at three levels: normative, analytical and operational.

13 It is notable that this conclusion is similar to An Na'im's 'cross-cultural' approach to relativism (An-Na'im 1992: 37).

14 Also, female genital cutting (FGC) or female genital circumcision (also FGC).

15 In some communities in Ethiopia, Kenya and the Sudan, CARE report near universal use of FGM (Igras et al. 2002).

16 The scheme has now expanded to other districts, with variations to the rite depending on local traditions (Mohamed et al. 2002: 76).

17 Beyond health, FGM has social consequences. By becoming eligible for marriage, girls' educational and income-generating opportunities are curtailed, either due to marriage or ongoing health problems resulting from FGM. Moreover, families that decide not to follow the practice face ostracism and may lose their social safety nets that the local community provide (Igras et al. 2002: 16).

18 Areas within Ethiopia and Kenya.

19 Some considered circumcision to be a right.

20 Since 1980, when the regions that ActionAid now work in were in the Republic of Somalia. Following civil war in the south of the country, the north-west region (Somaliland) declared itself independent, assuming the colonial name for the area. See: <http://www.actionaid.org/worldwideactivities/africa/somaliland/somaliland.shtml>

21 The studies identified water and pastoralism as areas of particular concern, along with education and healthcare.

22 ActionAid continue to monitor operations to ensure that their principles are being adhered to. If they are not, the contract is broken, and AAS support will be withdrawn (Le Mare 2003).

References

ActionAid (1999) *Fighting Poverty Together: ActionAid's Strategy 1999–2003* (London: ActionAid).

ActionAid Somaliland (2002) 'Country Strategy Paper', ActionAid internal document.

An-Na'im, A. A. (1992) 'Toward a Cross-Cultural Approach to Defining International Human Rights Standards', in A. A. An-Na'im (ed.), *Human Rights in Cross-Cultural Perspectives: A Quest for Consensus* (Philadelphia: University of Pennsylvania Press).

Bowen, J. R. (1996) 'The Myth of Global Ethnic Conflict', *Journal of Democracy*, 7 (4): 3–14.

Buchanan, A. E. (1989) 'Assessing the Communitarian Critique of Liberalism', *Ethics*, 99 (4): 852–82.

CARE (2002) *Defining Characteristics of a Rights-Based Approach, Promoting Rights and Responsibilities*, February (Atlanta, GA: CARE).

Cohen, R. (1999) 'The Making of Ethnicity: A Modest Defence of Primordialism', in E. Mortimer (ed.), *People, Nation and State: The Meaning of Ethnicity and Nationalism* (London: I.B. Tauris).

Comaroff, J. and J. Comaroff (1992) *Ethnography and the Historical Imagination* (Boulder, CO: Westview Press).

Fisher, E. and A. Acre (2003) 'Institutionalising Rights into Local Claim Making Processes', *Ontrac*, 23: 8.

Fishman, J. (1972) *The Sociology of Language* (Rowley, MA: Newbury House).

Freeman, M. (1995) 'Are There Any Collective Human Rights?', in D. Beetham (ed.), *Politics and Human Rights* (Oxford: Blackwell).

Gould, C. G. (2001) 'Two Concepts of Universality and the Problem of Cultural Relativism', in C. G. Gould and P. Pasquino (eds), *Cultural Identity and the Nation-State* (Oxford: Rowman and Littlefield).

Green, L. (1991) 'Two Views of Collective Rights', *Canadian Journal of Law and Jurisprudence*, IV (2): 315–27.

Hannum, H. (1992) 'Self-Determination as a Human Right', in R. P. Claude and B. H. Weston (eds), *Human Rights in the World Community* (Philadelphia: University of Pennsylvania Press).

Horowitz, D. L. (1985) *Ethnic Groups in Conflict* (Berkeley, CA: University of California Press).

IDS (2003) 'The Rise of Rights', *IDS Policy Briefing*, 17. <http://www.un.or.th/ohchr/Issues/RBA/rba.htm>

Igras, S., J. Muteshi, A. WoldeMariam and S. Ali (2002) 'Integrating Rights-Based Approaches into Community Based Health Projects: Experiences from the Prevention of Female Genital Cutting Project in East Africa' (CARE). <http://www.careusa.org/careswork/whatwedo/health/hpub.asp>

Kymlicka, W. (1989) 'Liberalism, Individualism and Minority Rights', in A. C. Hutchinson and L. J. M. Green (eds), *Law and the Community* (Toronto: Carswell).

— (1995) *Multicultural Citizenship* (Oxford: Clarendon Press).

— (2002) *Contemporary Political Philosophy* (Oxford: Oxford University Press).

Le Mare, R. (2003) ActionAid Somaliland. Response to Questions (on file with the author).

Mohamed, A., K. Ringheim, S. Bloodworth and K. Gryboski (2002) 'Girls at Risk: Community Approaches to End Female Genital Mutilation and Treating Women Injured by the Practice', in *Reproductive Health Rights – Reaching the Hardly Reached*, PATH: 73. <http://www.path.org/materials.php>

Mohan, G. and J. Holland (2001) 'Human Rights and Development in Africa: Moral Intrusion or Empowering Opportunity?' *Review of African Political Economy*, 8.

Molyneux, M. and S. Lazar (2003) *Doing the Rights Thing* (London: ITGD Publishing).

Moser, C. and A. Norton (2001) *To Claim Our Rights: Livelihood Security, Human Rights and Sustainable Development* (Overseas Development Institute). <http://www.odi.org.uk/pppg/activities/concepts_analysis/rights inaction/Publications/ToClaimOurRights.html>

Nguyen, F. (2002) *Emerging Features of a Rights-Based Development Policy of UN, Development Cooperation and NGO Agencies*, Discussion Paper, OHCHR

Asia-Pacific Human Rights Roundtable no. 1. <http://www.un.or.th/ohchr/ Issues/RBA/rba.htm>

Oxfam (2001) *Towards Global Equity: Strategic Plan 2001–2004* (Oxfam). <http://www.oxfam.org/eng/about_strat.htm>

Ranger, T. (1999) 'The Nature of Ethnicity: Lessons From Africa', in E. Mortimer (ed.), *People, Nation and State: The Meaning of Ethnicity and Nationalism* (London: I.B. Tauris).

Raz, J. (1988) *The Morality of Freedom* (Oxford: Clarendon Press).

Reaume, D. (1994) 'The Group Right to Linguistic Security: Whose Right, What Duties?', in J. Baker (ed.), *Group Rights* (Toronto: University of Toronto Press).

Sano, H.-O. (2000) 'Development and Human Rights: The Necessary, but Partial, Integration of Human Rights and Development', *Human Rights Quarterly* 22 (3): 734–53.

Smith, A. D. (1980) *The Ethnic Revival* (Cambridge: Cambridge University Press).

Stavenhagen, R. (1998) 'Cultural Rights: A Social Science Perspective', in H. Niec (ed.), *Cultural Rights and Wrongs* (Paris: UNESCO Publishing).

Van Dyke, V. (1977) 'The Individual, the State and Ethnic Communities in Political Theory', *World Politics*, 29 (3): 343–69.

— (1979) 'Collective Entities of Moral Rights: Problems in Liberal Democratic Thought', *The Journal of Politics*, 44 (1).

Linking rights and culture

Conclusion

OLIVIA BALL

This Conclusion returns to the questions raised in the Introduction to see what insights may be gleaned from the intervening chapters. The Introduction outlines critiques of rights-based approaches (RBAs) found in the literature and the following is an attempt to evaluate and, where possible, respond to those critiques.

Is there evidence for the claimed complementarity between human rights and development, humanitarianism and conflict resolution in the search for more holistic, longer-term solutions?

There is a close fit between the principles or values (or 'p'olitics) of human rights and more recent understandings of sustainable development. Both aspire to ideals of participation, equality, non-discrimination, accountability, transparency and justice. This 'code of behaviour' can inform the process of *how* development as well as humanitarian relief and conflict resolution are conducted, while human rights norms[1] can inform their *goals* (Jonsson).[2] Process and outcomes receive equal attention (Jones; Galant and Parlevliet).

A rights-based approach helps uncover the root causes of underdevelopment, conflict and even 'natural' disasters such as famine. The approach also asks *who* is performing this analysis. To achieve sustainable development, ActionAid's partners in India work 'through close interaction with people suffering [rights] denials', drawing upon Freirian methods of conscientization, whereby people 'reflect on their own social reality, reasons for poverty and powerlessness so that they can take social action against it' (Akerkar).

A rights-based approach emphasizes civil and political rights, some of which mirror the development ideal of empowerment.[3] Antunes and Romano see human rights-based development and empowerment as complementary approaches. For Akerkar, empowerment means 'enabling the poor to gain and keep control over the development process'; not just control over the work of non-governmental organizations (NGOs), but over broader economic and political factors that influence development. Action-Aid combines an empowerment agenda with a more traditional 'service delivery approach' (which is rightly retained, writes Mander, for cases of 'extreme and chronic' suffering). A rights-based approach reminds us that service delivery is, however, a means to an end (Jones); people are the *raison d'être* of aid, development and conflict resolution (Mander).

Poverty impedes enjoyment of civil, cultural, economic, political and social rights. When poverty/impoverishment is understood as a human rights violation, a rights-based approach is necessarily pro-poor. ActionAid India 'takes sides unambiguously with the poor' (Akerkar); a stance Mander calls solidarity. A rights-based approach to development focuses attention on 'exclusion, discrimination, disparities and injustice' (Jonsson). It protects people who are poor by refusing to accept poverty, inequality and the violation of civil and political rights as evils necessary to the pursuit of national prosperity (Jonsson). In taking sides with those whose rights are most denied (Mander), RBAs are also pro-women, pro-children and pro-indigenous, favouring sexual, racial and religious minorities and people with disabilities.

Despite the difficulty of finding an acceptable adjudicator or process to decide competing rights claims, Jarman advocates a rights-based approach to conflict resolution, although not necessarily a legal approach. For long-term results, a 'sustained programme of mediation' is preferred. It has of late become possible to use human rights as a basis for dialogue in Northern Ireland, wherein all parties' claims and allegations are set against a common standard. Achieving mutual recognition of human rights may not automatically resolve a conflict, especially where rights asserted by one group impede those of another, but rights can provide a foundation for negotiation, a language for respectful debate. Dialogue in isolation is not enough: conflict resolution will benefit from a 'broad political culture in which rights, respect and responsibilities sit in some form of balance' (Jarman).

Galant and Parlevliet take us beyond the too-simplistic 'justice versus peace' debate, demonstrating how process is critical when intervening in favour of both human rights and peace. They find that the negotiable parameters of human rights imperatives allow room for just resolution of conflict with respect for cultural diversity. Thus there seems ample complementarity between the methods and goals of RBAs and the aims and effective practice of development, humanitarianism and conflict resolution. Long-term solutions are more likely where a 'rights culture' is fostered, the rights violations at the root of poverty, crisis and conflict are identified, and the most marginalized people are empowered to claim their rights.

Is it possible to say in what circumstances coordination, notably with states, leads to negative results or positive outcomes?

International aid and cooperation to achieve development is not charity, but a human right.[4] CARE International has recognized this in its work to 'fundraise' on behalf of the fledgling Afghan government. NGOs risk diminishing states' responsibilities when they deliver substitute services, while a partnership or funding relationship with a government and inter-governmental organization (IGO) may compromise their independence and advocacy role. CARE deftly avoids both these pitfalls by advocating for greater resources for the Karzai administration, while simultaneously holding it publicly to account for its use of those resources to further development and human rights (O'Brien).

O'Brien highlights the grave dangers of perceived cosiness with government in a volatile context such as Afghanistan, where aid workers, both foreign and local, are attacked and killed by anti-government forces. The use of military personnel to perform development work can likewise endanger NGOs' perceived independence and staff. The blurring of roles is sometimes deliberate in the contest for 'hearts and minds' when armed forces pursue military as well as political and public relations goals.

Other contributors describe working with (rather than against) governments, assisting them to understand and fulfil their responsibilities. Such partnerships need to be transparent, however, and balanced by advocacy, lobbying and critique (Gready and Ensor). In Rwanda, CARE attempts to promote respect for rights and call attention to violations (Jones); an example, perhaps, of 'coordination infused with unequal power' (Gready and Ensor), when CARE risks prosecution or expulsion for perceived 'divisiveness'. Oxfam finds it cannot always maintain the balance: 'Some governments are not committed to protecting and promoting rights; even in cases where they express commitment, they may lack the necessary resources. And at times, Oxfam refrains from pressuring governments about specific violations, for fear of risking legitimacy or of creating future risks to staff and programmes' (Brouwer et al.).

A recurring refrain in the present volume is a call for greater coordination and collaboration between NGOs to streamline their efforts and maximize their impact. NGOs should look both 'horizontally' and 'vertically' to form 'larger coalition alliances' with like-minded partners (Akerkar), strengthening 'the links between local, state and national civil society organizations ... in order to increase the pressure on the State and to attain social control over its actions, exchange knowledge and experiences and strengthen all the actors in this struggle[5] ... [C]ivil society actors must act in concert with jointly constructed political platforms' (Antunes and Romano). Jones concurs, emphasizing long-term, mutually reinforcing coordination among rights-based NGOs.

Founded in 1995, Oxfam International is an expression of this collaborative impulse, bringing under one umbrella twelve 'like-minded independent non-government organizations, who wanted to work together internationally to achieve greater impact in reducing poverty by their collective efforts'.[6] Brouwer et al. write of the benefits to Oxfam of internal coherence, consistency and a 'common language' as well as flexibility, adaptability and innovation within the confederation. While there are differences within the organization that they would prefer were 'narrowed', diversity can be an advantage, allowing different parts to rely on and learn from others' strengths and experience. The same may be said of IGOs. Jonsson sees opportunities for cooperation among the various wings of the United Nations: rights-based approaches are 'new to all UN agencies and could therefore become an effective catalyst in the efforts to move towards a real UN team-approach, including joint programming'.

Coordination between state and non-state actors serves a variety of useful functions, increasing the capacity of rights holders and duty bearers, and assisting the latter to understand and fulfil their responsibilities. It relies on good faith and carries risks. Retaining independence and the perception thereof (transparency) may protect NGOs' advocacy role and the safety of staff. For partnerships to be successful, participating actors (and others) should be open to debate and to challenging power relations, responsibilities and roles within the development arena. Coordination within and between civil society actors is less problematic and very much encouraged to enhance efficiency and effectiveness.

Do NGOs and IGOs have the capacity to operationalize rights-based interventions (especially when it involves working outside traditional areas of knowledge and competence)?

A development organization that has embraced an RBA fights for civil and political rights as well as economic, social and cultural rights. It seeks structural change and just power relations rather than, or in addition to, technical fixes and service delivery. Where funds and personnel are already stretched, these additional demands – spanning training, organizational change, analysis, programming and evaluation – can spell overreach.

A theme in this volume is the fundamental importance of a rights-focused analysis to a rights-based approach.[7] Analysis is the essential first step to putting theory into practice. Analysis and evaluation must be repeated throughout the praxis cycle. Taking a rights-based approach to these familiar functions may require specialist staff and training, human rights education for all participants and dedicated funding (Okille). Oxfam is one NGO that admits shortcomings in this area: 'the Oxfams have not gone far enough in helping all staff to understand human rights instruments and principles' (Brouwer et al.). Organizational and institutional change, like development itself, is complex and slow.

Jarman writes of the human rights education and training necessary to reform the police in Northern Ireland. Writing of legal and justice reform, Tomas identifies numerous gaps in knowledge and failures to evaluate and learn from experience. He points to the need for further research in this area if government and NGO aid to the legal sector is to be egalitarian and pro-poor without undermining informal justice systems and cultural differences.

Operationalizing RBAs is taking most IGOs and NGOs beyond familiar territory and proven capacity. New tasks include rights-based analysis, understanding and promoting civil and political rights, lobbying and advocacy as well as additional research and evaluation. Capacity building will require a basket of measures: human rights education, professional development for existing staff in rights-based tools and techniques, perhaps new staff or access to external specialists, new funds and/or budgetary sacrifices elsewhere and, moreover, the cultivation of institutional 'memory' – a repository of learning and experience that remembers and records past lessons and feeds the results of evaluations back into the system for continuous learning and continuity over time. The capacity of many will fall short of this ideal, but it is a standard to which the practitioner-contributors to this book aspire with some success.

In what ways do human rights politicize NGO work, and is such work too political or not political enough?

Aid and development are inherently political, because they use and allocate resources and power. Whether this is a good or a bad thing depends on what values inform that process. The debate around politicization of aid is mired in the muddy use of terms. Big-P Politics is partisan, promoting particular (self-serving) actors and non-consensual interests and values. It is from such agendas and allegiances that peace and development work ought to be free. Small-p politics is quite another thing (O'Brien). A rights-based approach to development is thoroughly 'p'olitical, infused with 'certain core, higher, consensual or universal' values (Gready and Ensor), namely, the values of human rights: equality, justice, non-discrimination, participation, diversity and, ultimately, peace.[8]

O'Brien highlights how being too close to government or positioning an organization in opposition to government (or other power-broker) can both be difficult and dangerous for development, humanitarian and conflict resolution agencies. Arguing that 'impartiality', 'independence' and 'neutrality' are themselves 'p'olitical values, he examines how an NGO's history, philosophies and fundraising mechanisms will influence its relationship with 'P'olitical players. Stoddard (cited in O'Brien) contrasts 'Dunantist' NGOs, concerned with independence from state funding and influence, with 'Wilsonian' NGOs, which 'see themselves as ambassadors for American public values' and may risk being seen as instruments of American public policy.[9] A rights-based approach is different again, 'taking sides' unselfconsciously as a matter of principle rather than 'P'olitics. It will denounce rights violations regardless of who commits them and defend the impoverished and rights-abused, no matter who they are.

Mander examines how 'the identification of needs itself is a political process'. Ensor follows with a discussion of how it is also a cultural process. They and other contributors draw the same conclusion: that it must be the 'beneficiaries' of development endeavours who frame their interests and identify their rights. For external/Northern actors, supporting and funding rights-based interventions, rather than leading them, is in itself a 'p'olitical stance.

Duffield (cited in Gready and Ensor) doubts development is political (enough) to 'alter outcomes'. Development, if it is to succeed, must acquire political savvy and breadth of vision. It has got to go after the big fish. Grassroots projects are undermined at every turn by towering 'P'olitical forces. Children's rights, for example, 'are affected by government policies and budget decisions, by World Bank loans and IMF policy prescriptions, by World Trade Organization rules, and by the programmes of donors, UN agencies and NGOs. However, few mainstream development agencies and government departments pay much attention' (Theis and O'Kane).

An RBA means Northern actors must take action domestically and globally to 'enhance the capacity' of their Southern partners to succeed in their struggles for justice (Manji, cited in Mander). This may mean public awareness raising and human rights education and more overtly 'p'olitical activities such as 'naming and shaming' state and non-state actors; lobbying Northern governments, international financial institutions and IGOs; critiquing foreign policy, trade pacts and aid budgets; mounting consumer boycotts; fighting legal battles; participating in global people's movements and so on. Oxfam exemplifies a Northern NGO working to link the local and the global, and stressing the need for supporters to lobby their home government for policies that further social justice (Brouwer et al.).

Big-picture, small-p, pro-poor political action in defiance of power, profit and 'P'olitics is a necessary part of rights-based development, whether one works with or against the state. The sensitivities and risks involved may compel some NGOs to re-examine their interpretation of impartiality, neutrality and independence.

Are human rights a new form of imperialism, used to provide an increasingly intrusive attack on sovereignty, democracy and political debate/processes?

Allegations that human rights are a form of (Western) cultural imperialism are not repeated by practitioners in this volume. Ensor makes a convincing case, however, for a rights-based approach that understands that human needs, interests, dignity and rights are defined within a cultural frame of reference and may therefore be defined differently by people of different cultures: 'the manifestation of a right, whilst based on the same interest, may change'. Although development may seek to expand freedom, our received culture sets boundaries on our range of choices. Rather than advocating cultural relativism or the imposition of universal values, he favours inter-cultural dialogue, with international and local perspectives each serving 'a "check and balance" function for the other' (Igras, Muteshi, WoldeMariam and Ali, cited in Ensor). Similarly, Jones describes an RBA that builds on existing 'values and norms in Rwandan culture/society and encourag[es] open discussion where there are tensions'. For Jones, the universal aspect of human rights remains important as it lends legitimacy. Galant and Parlevliet find that 'specific political, historical and cultural conditions [can] be taken into account', while 'fundamental rights standards remain the same across the board'. Participation is again the key, with communities involved in establishing the content of their rights.

Jones observes a parallel issue in microcosm, in a scenario that will be familiar to many international NGOs attempting organizational change. He perceives resistance among local members of staff to the initially 'high-level' introduction of rights-based approaches at CARE Rwanda, although they may not express it openly. He exposes a tension between top-down versus bottom-up approaches to organizational change. There is an obvious contradiction in attempting to impose a participatory model of development. CARE has tried to solve this difficulty by identifying the more receptive employees and giving them training and positions of leadership in the hope that they will have more influence than foreign staff. Despite cultural reluctance to criticize superiors, these leaders have, in turn, arraigned CARE for lapses in its rights-based practice, which has to be a healthy sign. By contrast, one has a sense in the Brazilian example of a 'home-grown' rights movement, not driven from above/outside by ActionAid International or other external actors.

Rather than undermining democracy, a far stronger impression one gains from this volume is of rights-based approaches supporting and promoting democracy, both as a means to an end and an end in itself. ActionAid India emphasizes citizenship and freedom, works to 'strengthen

284

democratic processes' and has succeeded, claims Akerkar, in expanding 'democratic spaces'. Since 'neither rights nor justice can be given to a passive and inert group of people ... [s]ustainable justice requires their central and active agency in all processes connected with identifying, accessing and securing their rights. Rights approaches therefore are in their very nature profoundly democratic' (Mander). People must 'influence and coerce' the state, continues Mander, to act in defence of human rights 'by directly participating in governance'.

Antunes and Romano describe their work similarly as an attempt to assert 'social control' over the levers of governance in order that the state might be responsive to human rights claims. They grapple with the challenge of making government accountable to the people, especially poor and marginalized people. Their public policy proposals – their development objectives – emerge through public consultation. They encounter the obvious difficulty with international human rights norms: how to enforce them in national and local contexts. 'It is crucial that participatory spaces at [local, state and federal level] are institutionalized and their decision-making power defined; so that they become independent of the political power of the day.'

What they seek, essentially, is to establish and institutionalize a workable, effective, durable model of radical democracy. ActionAid India declares 'participatory and deliberative democracy' to be a human right (Akerkar). Popular sovereignty expressed through representative democracy is an established right in international law.[10] The human rights principle of participation, however, means the right to genuine democracy is much deeper and broader. Without a genuinely democratic basis, other human rights are hollow, and perhaps elusive.

Mander laments that 'participatory methods have been often reduced to technical instruments rather than [being] genuinely democratizing'. Tomas, an advocate of legal reform, observes that 'formal recognition of a particular right is not enough. Rights also need to be seized from below.' There is little known, he claims, about how development can effectively support this process. An ongoing challenge for RBAs is to realize their participatory ideal and, ultimately, reinvent democracy.

RBAs lend themselves to a 'both-and' solution to the universalism versus cultural relativism debate. It similarly embraces both bottom-up and top-down approaches, but first and foremost it emphasizes participation. Far from attacking democracy, diminishing (popular) sovereignty or stifling political debate, rights-based actors must strive in everything to support these processes.

Does the rights-based approach seek a radical transformation of the prevailing economic and political order, a 'mere seizure of power within the existing order', to provide alternatives (to neo-liberalism, empire), or is it hopelessly compromised by complicity and cooption?

Although contributors do not address this question explicitly, it is none the less made clear that real structural change is necessary. Ensor warns against an exclusive focus on individual rights, which neo-liberalism tends to reinforce. The authors agree, as we have seen, that an RBA is democratic and pro-poor: its antithesis is the 'free' market. 'Under the ideology of the free market, the market "decides" vital social matters' that the people are entitled to decide. 'Not surprisingly, the free market *always* decides that some people will get (stay) rich and others will get (stay) poor' (Lummis 2002: 5). Mander shows how 'social insurance and social assistance' are neither just nor effective in the face of neo-liberalism: people still 'fall through the cracks in market-led economic development'. Rights-based approaches oppose this. Mander defends state-regulated markets and argues for 'strong redistributive measures' such as land reform, poor communities' access to and control of forest and water resources, 'food and work as legal entitlements, budgetary reallocations to benefit poor people, legal and judicial reforms for the poor, and their access to mainstream financial resources. None of this can be left in markets, and all of this requires vibrant, strong, interventionist states with high legitimacy, authority but also genuine accountability.' Mander is refreshingly bold in his transforming vision, seeking to counter neo-liberalism with redistributive justice ensured by an interventionist state.

Rieff says NGOs aim too high; they will never bring peace, end human rights abuses, or 'stamp out government corruption' (cited in O'Brien). If not NGOs, who does Reiff suppose is the likely or proper agent to wring such changes? More than being 'compromised by complicity and co-option', the development sector is hampered by inertia, poor coordination and timidity. There are times when its aim is not high enough. Its 'challenges to power often appear local and fragmentary ... rather than systemic, with structural factors often beyond [their] control' (Gready and Ensor). It is possibly too early to say whether rights-based development will succeed in transforming development and society. Observes O'Brien:

> the world rarely works in simple, linear, cause-and-effect patterns. Rather, organizations change like organisms, over time and when a multitude of forces come together ... [A]gencies that adopt new humanitarianism are already transforming themselves and will continue to do so. In aiming to take responsibility for the consequences of their work, and in holding

others responsible also, they are having a real and meaningful impact on the contexts in which they work. Certainly they can do more ...

The 'prevailing economic and political order' reproduces poverty and disparities of power and is inimical to rights. An RBA seeks the seizure of power and decision-making through accountability, participation and democracy, appropriating and reappropriating these key terms and their meaning. Real change is necessary if the goals of development are to be realized. If it can reinvent democracy and thereby development, RBA will generate alternatives to the prevailing order, and some alternatives will without doubt be radically transformative.

To what extent is 'force' – in forms ranging from aid conditionality to war – a characteristic of the rights-based approach? Is this use of 'force' legitimate?

The RBA emphasis on process as well as outcomes renders force suspect (to say the least) as a method of promoting rights and development, let alone peace. Evidence suggests that force, whatever its purpose, violates rights and breeds violence. In Jarman's experience, a rights-based approach compares favourably with force as a means of resolving conflict in Northern Ireland. Moreover, he regards human rights as a remedy for the violent assertion of group interests. A culture of rights is evident when, for example, police see their role as protecting human rights rather than being impeded by them.

Some contributors warn against heavy-handedness in certain situations of rights abuse. Nepalese child activists have found it is best to avoid being 'overly negative or confrontational' (Theis and O'Kane). Rights offenders, especially non-state actors breaching rights within their own community – such as practitioners and parents in societies that engage in female genital mutilation (Ensor) – may close ranks and react defensively to a rights critique perceived as a threat to culture and identity. A respectful, holistic, with-rather-than-against approach is likely to bear more fruit in such circumstances. Respect for culture and community is not some ploy in the rights arsenal, however, but an embodiment of the human rights values of equality and diversity and an expression of respect for cultural rights.[11]

'The use of a moral argument seeks to put war beyond debate' (Rieff, paraphrased by Gready and Ensor) and to demonize opponents, both political opponents and opponents of war. That modern Western nations feel obliged to find such justifications for waging war reflects, perhaps, an increasing rejection of the use of military force. Observes Rieff: cooption has been 'the historic destiny of most, if not all, large moral ideas'. Cooption is an ever-present danger where power seeks to mask itself with sheep's clothing, appropriating the language and manners of what is acceptable to society. Ought NGOs therefore to abandon debased language and theory, regardless of their merits? And be accused of being fickle or fashionable, vulnerable to Duffield's claim that an RBA is mere periodic makeover (2001: 223)? Surely, states' cynical use of human rights language to defend indefensible aggression is no reason to abandon a defence of human rights. Rather, it is a call to contest the misuse and appropriation of progressive ideals to entrench the status quo.

Whether human rights ought ever to form part of a well-intentioned justification for war, and whether rights-based NGOs can thereby support war, is another matter again. The logical extension of NGOs taking sides in favour of human rights is not necessarily to support war, although some have done so. Any just-war theory requires, among other things, the exhaustion of all other avenues short of force. Should aid conditionality have similar prerequisites? Should populations be punished, with either the dropping of bombs or the withholding of aid, for the actions of their government? Can anyone ever rightly call for violent deliverance on behalf of another? Given the emphasis of RBAs on participation, how should a plea 'from below' for some form of coercive action to address rights violations[12] be answered? How, in practice, can an external actor reliably identify the voice of 'the people' in circumstances of oppression? Is unilateral military action ever justified? What of the role of the United Nations, the rule of international law and the increasing part NGOs play in such arenas? Such questions, though relevant to the policy and practice of development, humanitarian and conflict resolution actors in the increasingly 'P'oliticized contexts in which they work, are beyond the scope of the present volume.

The legitimacy of force and the legitimate role of aid and development agencies in any use of force are complex issues not fully explored here. Human rights theory, at least, would suggest that decisions regarding the use of coercion and force ought to be made by participatory means, and ought to respect, in method and purpose, human rights and associated principles.

Is the adoption of rights-based approaches more than rhetoric and repackaging? If so, what are the obligations and value added?

How does rights-based development differ from what's gone before? After all, 'principles such as participation and solidarity with the poor' are neither new to development nor unique to RBAs (Jones). Mander summarizes critiques of more traditional development models, illustrating why an RBA not only adds value, but is essential to redeem the development project. A 'techno-managerial' approach sees poverty as a problem that 'can be overcome simply with better managed schemes and technology'. Without a rights-based approach, service-delivery NGOs are vulnerable to (at least) two charges: neglecting 'issues of power and structural injustice' and 'enabling the state to abdicate' its human rights responsibilities. In this way, a 'basic needs' (without rights) approach can reinforce 'the existing oppressive order'. No, 'it is impossible', writes Mander, 'to address basic needs sustainably without enforcing basic rights'.

Worse than needs-driven development is supply-driven aid, which takes more account of donors' inconvenient surpluses,[13] or what 'boomerang' assistance might benefit the donor's economy or political standing,[14] than recipients' needs or entitlements. In contrast, RBAs add value to development efforts by supporting people to determine their own rights and make their own claims on duty bearers, while supporting duty bearers to hear and respond to those claims. O'Brien describes how the Afghan government 'radically' reoriented its relationship with its donors in favour of 'a responsibility model of giving'.

Rights advocates refuse to accept human needs as 'a private issue of individual survival' (Antunes and Romano). Someone who merely has un-met needs may inspire compassion or indifference, but only the altruistic and the charitable will respond. Recasting that same person as a rights holder acknowledges their agency and dignity. The ideals of participation, equality, accountability and transparency – embraced by many humanitarian and development actors as best practice – from a rights-based perspective become mandatory instead of optional (Jones). This is a tangibly different way of working.

Whereas 'concepts such as poverty, vulnerability, deprivation and inequality do not necessarily impute causality', rights identify those responsible and their duties to rectify the situation. With a rights-based approach, people are not so much poor as impoverished, marginalized and socially excluded; poor 'is not what they are, but what they have been made' (Mander). Rights entail responsibilities; they construct relationships: and this is a new, political face to development and humanitarianism. A person with rights grievances corresponds to a person or actor who is violating or failing to fulfil their rights; the rights paradigm seeks to identify who is responsible, and pursues strategies of support and pressure so that the relevant actors take responsibility morally and legally, to respect, protect and promote rights.

For several authors (e.g. Jonsson; Ensor), an advantage of RBAs is multiple avenues of approach. The struggle for justice may be conducted by social and political as well as legal means. It also recognizes multiple actors and their multiple roles (as rights holders and, potentially, duty bearers), necessitating new kinds of relationships in a globalized world. Further, the human rights doctrine of indivisibility dictates that human well-being must be regarded holistically. Development and humanitarian workers must take seriously the interdependence of rights by working for civil and political rights as well as the more traditional concerns of health, education and livelihood. An RBA entails a 'continuous fight for citizenship' (Antunes and Romano). These conceptual developments are, in themselves, added value.

Antunes and Romano describe the RBA movement in Brazil as attempting to expand accepted human rights into new realms, including a right to 'collective ownership of land' and 'access to natural resources independent of property'. A number of other contributors write of 'new' rights they and their constituents identify and claim, as natural rights idealism seeks forms of recognition and enforcement: the right to dignity (Mander; Jones), to humanitarian assistance (Sphere Project) and 'entitlement rights' (Akerkar); Oxfam defends the 'right to an identity' and the 'right to be heard' (Brouwer et al.); CARE recognizes the right to 'solidarity with communities' and the promotion of social justice (Jones); Mander argues for a right to good governance.[15] Creative uses of legal norms and non-adversarial approaches to rights (Ensor; Theis and O'Kane) do not mean the legal basis of rights is abandoned. On the contrary, in such creativity lies the origin of legal rights.

All this is not a matter of repackaging the same old approach to development. Although there are inevitably times when RBA is merely 'institutional rhetoric' (Brouwer et al.), and there is nothing to prevent an organization from adopting the trimmings without any substance, O'Brien sees 'rights-based thinking' as having a deeper impact, having 'transformed the identity of self-proclaimed rights-based NGOs'. Transforming identity, attitude and intention – no small feat in itself – is a necessary part of transforming practice. Understanding theory and adopting rights language has helped bring rights to life in the daily conduct of development, humanitarian and conflict resolution work.

If social contracts are creating new circuits of rights and responsibilities, and reinterpreting rights indivisibility, how are these rights being made real?

Rights have always been violated and protected by non-state agents. In Jarman's case study, Northern Irish Catholics complain of human rights abuses by both state and non-state actors, including police, security forces, paramilitary groups and civilians. Traditional social contract theory puts the onus on states to rein in non-state abuses. A new interpretation of the social contract assigns *duties* to non-state actors as well. Writes Tomas: 'human rights fill a void that is seen at the root of development failure: a platform to demand accountability', to demand that rights be 'made real'. Thus we find numerous accountability mechanisms emerging in the development sector such as the Sphere Project (Gready and Ensor).

Many of the means of securing enforcement described in this volume rely on political and social, rather than or alongside legal, processes. CARE, for example, combines innovative tools of accountability with the right of children to have a voice in matters concerning them (Jones). For many of the actors involved – IGOs, NGOs and their constituencies – this is a way of more consistently transporting rights discourse and reality into everyday lives. This is expressed by Galant and Parlevliet's multi-layered understanding of rights as rules and as structures/institutions, relationships and processes. Thus rights are made real through human rights education and training in contexts ranging from the workplace to the family (Okille); through reformulated interactions between NGOs/IGOs, their donors and constituencies (Jones); through lobbying for policy and political change at local, national and international levels (Brouwer et al.; Antunes and Romano); through attitudinal and behavioural change (Brouwer et al.; Theis and O'Kane); through positive examples of participation and rights in action (Theis and O'Kane); and through indigenous means of adjudication and enforcement (Tomas; Ensor).

A legal approach, for its part, can help make rights real in a number of ways. Rights have legal force where needs do not. Universal standards provide a 'common language', expressing

> in authoritative and internationally accepted terminology the essential elements for achieving human development and global justice. The unequal power relations that constrain human development can be confronted more forcefully when international principles and instruments of human rights can be brought to bear on national legislation and, in turn, citizens can draw on both levels to demand their rights. (Brouwer et al.)

International human rights law is meant to be translated into more readily enforceable domestic law. Tomas and Mander each show how law reform will be a central component of some human rights struggles. Not because law is a panacea, but precisely because there are cases where 'law may act against justice' (Mander) and must be made at least compatible with human rights. There are material benefits to a legal approach to human rights protection, beyond what satisfaction may be gained in court. Jarman welcomes progress towards not just compatibility but the full protection of human rights in Northern Irish domestic law: the more the police see upholding the law and upholding human rights as one and the same thing, the more they are likely to respect and protect human rights and the less they are likely to abuse them.

Enforcement and accountability remain, none the less, a sticking point for the human rights movement and other rights-based endeavours. In the enlarged rights framework outlined above, NGOs or IGOs may see themselves as duty bearers but what happens if they fail to deliver? What powers do beneficiaries really have to seek redress? Globalization and the relative dominance of non-state entities, including for example multi-national corporations, present new challenges for enforcement regimes that were already struggling to keep up. A 'holistic interpretation' of indivisibility may offer new ways to approach enforcement of rights from a variety of directions, including attention to 'multiple levels from the local to the global', top-down and bottom-up approaches to enforcement, public and private spheres, the legal, political, economic, social and the everyday (Gready and Ensor). These all provide both opportunities and new challenges. Practitioners have begun to experiment with relevant models to further enforcement, but there is still a long way to go to render this ambitious rights agenda real.

Is the balance sheet in favour of rights-based development still relatively empty?

The outcome of the second human rights revolution is far from apparent or understood. The present volume represents the first major attempt to draw together field experiences of rights-based approaches in development and to analyse their potential and achievements. Evaluation is difficult; crediting particular methods with observed results, where they occur, is confounded by the fact that 'outcomes are contingent on factors beyond agency control'. Rights-based approaches of their nature aim for more than 'technical or quantifiable outcomes': they seek 'political transformation' (Gready and Ensor). O'Brien and Jones discuss the complex nature of organizational change as well as social, economic and political change. Success in human rights terms – that 'frightening burden and inspiring possibility' (O'Brien) – necessitates substantial change.

The present volume provides numerous examples of right-based successes. Brouwer et al. cite concrete achievements of Oxfam's RBA, such as improved market access for Ethiopian coffee farmers. The new face of policing in Northern Ireland is not perfect, asserts Jarman, but there has been 'some recognizable impact ... on the ground' of the human rights-based approach to peace-building. Okille's evaluation of human rights education in Uganda among teachers, doctors, lawyers, accountants, NGO workers and journalists shows measurable changes in attitudes and behaviour in both their professional and private lives. Said one participant: 'Rights and governance should start with the family.' Training graduates seemed to interpret RBAs holistically and were keen to share their insights with others.

Galant and Parlevliet's account of squatters violently evicting other squatters – an example of complex indivisibility involving not only non-state perpetrators of human rights abuses, but perpetrators who are themselves victims of human rights violations – shows clearly how human rights abuses can lead to further abuses and, conversely, how addressing abuses can have a knock-on effect in preventing further conflict and abuse with sustainable results.

Outcomes, whether social, political or legal, are only part of the story, however. The RBA emphasis on process suggests new ways of assessing the effectiveness of development, humanitarian relief and conflict resolution. To focus not only on what is achieved, but also on how it is achieved, methods of evaluating qualities such as participation, transparency and accountability are needed.[16] Simply stimulating debate on these issues may be itself a measure of success.

From the practical experience of applying rights-based approaches so far, what lessons can be learnt and what challenges remain?

Although RBAs may take development, humanitarian and conflict resolution actors into new domains and may demand of them new levels of accountability, we are reminded that the state retains primacy in rights discourse. Mander seeks a strong, 'activist', even 'caring' state that goes 'well beyond' the provision of services to act to protect and fulfil human rights. NGOs must pressure and support the state to understand and assume these responsibilities and the state should, in turn, 'acknowledge, create, nurture, provide resources for, and actively support, all efforts by people and their organizations for the solution of their own problems'. Donor governments, for their part, may advocate RBAs but must also recognize the duties they bear to their international constituencies. Neither the law nor the state on its own, however, can realize the aims of the rights-based approach: a range of means, different actors and reformulated relationships are required.

Choosing whether to work 'with or against' a government is perhaps not as difficult as attempting both at once. It is a challenge for NGOs to take on (what rights discourse views as) state responsibilities, for example, while also pressing governments to resume those tasks. Rather than balance advocacy and partnership, agencies often favour one or the other. Antunes and Romano note that, 'having a right established in law is only one of the steps necessary to fulfil that right ... The biggest problem in the fight for existing or new rights is how to consolidate [rights-based] policies as government practices and obligations, in order not to depend on politically favourable governments.' Brouwer et al., too, cite 'working with governments who lack commitment' as a challenge. Jones suggests exploiting 'windows of opportunity' when they arise in difficult political environments, whether they be the existence of pro-rights legislation, 'democratization and decentralisation policies', opportunities for consultation and education, international pressure for good governance and so forth.

A foremost lesson from the field is the first step in a rights-based approach: 'diagnosing' or analysing the problem, the actors involved and power dynamics in human rights terms. In addition to analytical and policy skills and political judgement, ActionAid Brazil's tactical use of the media to educate, embarrass and influence public opinion highlights the usefulness of adroit media liaison for the modern IGO and NGO (Antunes and Romano). Human rights education is not mere communications strategy, however, but an important long-term objective of any human rights-based approach (e.g. Jarman; Okille; Brouwer et al.; Jones; Antunes and Romano).

The demands of RBAs span all the components of development from conceptualizing problems to evaluation. Jones recommends a move away from the short-term focus of project-based funding and evaluating immediate impact; brief planning, budgeting and reporting cycles cannot accommodate the structural change RBAs demand. The hardest lesson and greatest challenge for agencies, if they are to embrace rights, may be how to change themselves. An RBA will change an organization's own structure and budgetary priorities:[17] the analysis and advocacy that is the heart of RBA requires 'specific human and financial resources' (O'Brien). The 'paradigm shift' to a rights-based approach 'cannot take place overnight ... [I]nternal, organizational change ... is extremely difficult because it shines the spotlight on our own shortcomings' (Jones). For CARE International, rights-based approaches were adopted as part of 'an internal push to become a more principled organization' (Jones). Introducing new rights-based concepts and practices, Oxfam has found it sensible to build on what already makes sense to staff (Brouwer et al.). Human rights education in Uganda led the manager of one NGO to adopt a rights-based approach to management (Okille), making rights real in the office, every day. Internal coherence, consistency, transparency and integrity will be important for any human rights-based organization to embody.

Another strong theme is the democratic imperative, which empowers beneficiaries to participate actively in development, humanitarian and conflict resolution processes. Achieving real democracy, writ large and small, remains a major challenge. Intervening actors must 'walk the talk', striving for congruence of message and practice, both in their external relations and in the way they treat their staff. Employees, volunteers and partner organizations are more likely to use participatory practices, for example, if they have experienced and accepted the method themselves, and this can present a challenge. While 'top-down' and 'bottom-up' approaches may stand in tension, new interpretations of indivisibility suggest both can have merit and be used in tandem, as Jones describes working successfully in Rwanda.

The more democratic and participatory their practices, the more NGOs will be able to deflect accusations of being unrepresentative. Improved accountability will also strengthen their standing in this regard. Brouwer et al. write of the need for Oxfam to 'raise the bar' on its own accountability. As we have seen, developing and implementing effective accountability mechanisms of various kinds presents an ongoing challenge.

O'Brien faces the hard fact that a genuine RBA may give some donors cold feet, meaning an RBA may have serious financial consequences for aid NGOs. Some may shy away from human rights rather than risk organizational extinction. He shows how CARE took this risk and how it paid off, both for the organization and its achievements in Afghanistan. O'Brien stops short of the next logical step in his discussion of the costs and risks of a rights-based approach. He suggests a consistent and transparent RBA as a solution to the 'P'oliticization of aid and as a way of protecting the lives of aid workers, but this same approach, if effective, could conceivably place aid workers at risk from the powerful and influential actors who perpetrate rights abuses. Such actors may feel threatened by rights-based NGOs that 'step on toes' in pursuit of a just cause and may retaliate.[18] Protecting their workers from various threats remains a grave challenge. Taking a fresh look at how they interpret and implement neutrality, impartiality and independence may play a part in this.[19]

A rights-based approach certainly adds complexity to an NGO's brief (or provides a clearer view of the complexity of the task). Those complexities include, potentially, balancing collaboration with independence, global and local perspectives and action, the public and private realms, service delivery and advocacy, justice and peace, and emergency responses and long-term goals. Antunes and Romano describe the challenge of shifting a public-charity model of hunger relief towards a rights-based approach to food security. Social welfare programmes the world over would face similar challenges. They argue that an emergency response to child malnutrition is necessary, but so is structural change.

Galant and Parlevliet pose a topical dilemma in relation to social and economic rights: will addressing the just demands of rights abusers encourage abuse? The resolution of conflict in a squatter settlement outside Cape Town is an unlikely echo of political leaders who refuse to 'negotiate with terrorists' for fear of the precedent it might set for the effectiveness of violence (assuming, for present purposes at least, that some terrorists are also victims of rights violations). And yet Galtung would encourage exactly such negotiation with 'terrorists' if we are to overcome this impasse.[20]

A number of important matters remain for other practitioners to illuminate. Too rarely do conflict resolution, humanitarian, development and human rights discourses speak to environmental concerns. Armed conflict and poverty (and over-consumption) have an immense impact on the environment.[21] Meanwhile, environmental degradation takes a disproportionate toll on the poor and must be part of development planning and post-conflict reconstruction. Other issues that remain unexamined here include how a rights-based development or conflict resolution NGO might deal with the thorny issue of self-determination, a rights claim they will encounter in the field. Certain issues already alluded to – such as whether force can be used to advance rights and development, how government can be made accountable to the people and how rights can systematically be made enforceable and real – are only partially answered here and need further consideration as matters of daily practical relevance.

It would appear that at least the right questions are being asked, and debate is ongoing. The practitioner contributors to this volume provide ample evidence that real change is occurring both within their organizations and in their work, indicating that the conversation between rights and development is yielding results and likely to continue.

Notes

1 The general terms used in human rights treaties can be both an asset and a source of frustration. For those seeking clarification, international norms and standards are increasingly being fleshed out by various authoritative sources including the general comments of human rights treaty bodies, guidelines of specialized agencies of the UN – such as UNICEF, UNESCO, WHO, the ILO and FAO – pronouncements of international human rights conferences, judicial interpretations of, say, the right to life, in national and regional jurisdictions and various other documents such as the Limburg Principles and Maastricht Guidelines.

2 Citations in this chapter refer to contributions to the present volume, unless otherwise indicated.

3 For ActionAid India, transparency in development is an aspect of empowerment of the poor. Aid is transparent when the people are in control of the development process (Akerkar).

4 International Covenant on Economic, Social and Cultural Rights (ICE-SCR), Article 2(1). See also UN Committee on Economic, Social and Cultural Rights (1990) CESCR General Comment 3: The nature of States parties' obligations (Art. 2, para. 1), UN Doc E/1991/23, Office of the High Commissioner for Human Rights, Geneva <www.unhchr.ch/tbs/doc.nsf>, para. 13.

5 Boundaries between roles appear permeable at Mutirão. With a strategy emphasizing coordination and collaboration between NGOs and community-based organizations and mass mobilization and participation of the public to exert pressure on the state, Antunes and Romano cite examples of how development workers and volunteers share in data gathering, analysis, policy development and service delivery.

6 'History of Oxfam International', Oxfam International website <www.oxfam.org/eng/about_who.htm>

7 Elements of right-based analyses described in this book include identifying:

- 'the problem(s)' and what rights are involved, as defined by those affected
- rights holders and duty bearers, including multiple roles
- knock-on effect of violations that lead to other violations and/or impede ability to fulfil duties
- interplay of civil and political rights and economic, social and cultural rights to uncover root causes of unmet basic needs
- impact of gender, age, disability, race, religion, sexual orientation, caste and class, etc.
- political processes for claiming rights
- power-brokers in formal and informal power structures, including politicians, bureaucrats, judges, economists, media, intelligentsia (Baxi, cited in Mander) and local patrons and 'bosses' (Antunes and Romano)
- internal political forces within government that affect policy outcomes
- human rights implications of government spending, i.e budget analysis (Mander)
- other political forces, i.e. power relations, human and material resources, vested interests in change versus the status quo
- existing/indigenous accountability structures
- relevant international and domestic law and available mechanisms for enforcement
- risks (to staff, future funding, rights holders, etc.)

Instruments and techniques have been developed to assist in analysis, including Jones's causal-responsibility analysis tool (adapted from UNICEF). It is critical to ask who is performing the analysis, and to strive for genuine participation of affected groups.

8 The Universal Declaration of Human Rights (UDHR) views human rights as 'the foundation of ... peace in the world'. Understanding and disseminating

this truth has never been more urgent, as human rights and freedoms are besieged the world over in the name of peace and security.

9 Even these distinctions are increasingly blurred. In 2004 the Taliban issued a statement claiming responsibility for the murder of five MSF staff members in Afghanistan: 'Organizations like Médecins Sans Frontières work for American interests and are therefore targets for us' (Weissman 2004).

10 UDHR Article 21(3), also the International Covenant on Civil and Political Rights, Article 25.

11 Human rights relating to cultural diversity and integrity include: the right to cultural participation; the right to enjoy the arts; conservation, development and diffusion of culture; protection of cultural heritage; freedom for creative activity; protection of persons belonging to ethnic, religious or linguistic minorities; freedom of assembly and association; the right to education; freedom of thought, conscience and religion; freedom of opinion and expression; and the principle of non-discrimination. Defending its system of universal norms of which these rights form part, the UN website asserts that, 'universal human rights are a modern achievement, new to all cultures. Human rights are neither representative of, nor oriented towards, one culture to the exclusion of others' (Ayton-Shenker 1995).

12 For example, trade and sports sanctions against apartheid South Africa.

13 In an early example of such self-serving pragmatism, the United States disposed of food surpluses it had accumulated during the First World War as famine relief to Russia in 1921. This almost forgotten response to an immense crisis was certainly philanthropic, but also served US economic and 'P'olitical interests, Herbert Hoover hoping that a grateful populace might overthrow its Bolshevik 'oppressors' (Patenaude 2002).

14 The tendency of Australian official aid to be spent on Australian wages, goods and services gave rise to the epithet, 'boomerang aid'. Of course, Australia is not the only donor nation to 'P'oliticize its aid in this way. The World Bank has estimated that 'tied' aid (paid to for-profit businesses) is 20–25 per cent more expensive than 'untied' aid (AID/WATCH 2005: 1) and has been condemned by the international community. The UK untied its programme in 1997 (O'Connor 2003).

15 Mander reminds us that the good governance agenda is no more politically neutral than development: 'governance is "good" only to the extent that it benefits the social groups who are impoverished, oppressed and socially vulnerable and excluded'. Is the mainstream enthusiasm for good governance another instance of both appropriation – the establishment stealing buzz words (participation, transparency, accountability, etc.) from the human rights movement – and avoidance – state and non-state powers feigning reform while deftly dodging the real issues?

16 The anti-corruption NGO Transparency International offers a 'Corruption Fighters' Tool Kit', including '46 exciting tools from around the world', which highlights 'the potential of civil society to create mechanisms for monitoring public institutions and to demand and promote accountable and responsive public administration' (Transparency International 2004).

17 Theis and O'Kane advocate 'mainstreaming' rights as one way to

realign a rights-based organization, and call for broader mainstreaming of rights concerns throughout governance institutions. A potential pitfall of this approach, however, is withdrawal of funding from, in their case, children's organizations once child rights and interests are considered to be mainstream. 'Mainstreaming' is sometimes a buzz word used in the hope of making a problem (like rights claims) go away.

18 Jones writes of the risks associated with rights work in Rwanda. This is a threat with which traditional human rights defenders around the world are well familiar. In 2000 the UN Commission on Human Rights established the post of Special Representative of the Secretary-General on Human Rights Defenders to support implementation of the 1998 Declaration on Human Rights Defenders (see <www.ohchr.org/english/issues/defenders>).

19 Most aid workers would claim to be neutral, says O'Brien, but neutrality amid 'P'olitics has varied meanings. The Red Cross's old-school neutrality prevents it from engaging in any 'controversies of a political, racial, religious or ideological nature' (<www.icrc.org>). 'New humanitarians' have a new take on neutrality, exemplified by the outspoken MSF. These NGOs refuse any or significant government funding in order to retain an independent voice with which they might impartially 'name and shame' as justice demands. Some states have expelled MSF or refused it entry to avenge or avoid national or international exposure. The threat of limited access to people in need is a dilemma of neutrality and a risk associated with a rights-based approach. Perhaps the presence of a 'silent-neutral' NGO such as the Red Cross can justify the 'vocal-neutral' approach of a rights-based NGO, and vice versa.

20 Innovative peace scholar Johan Galtung contrasts his 'peace approach' with the prevalent 'security approach' in which the Other is constructed as 'evil ... somebody with whom one would never negotiate since there is no grievance and no basis for any solution' (Galtung 2004a). He recommends secret negotiations with 'terrorists' about 'stopping violence in return for withdrawal, and about reconciliation' (Galtung 2004b).

21 Armed conflict is, increasingly, 'an assault on the planet. From the massive defoliation of Viet Nam to the threat of nuclear fallout, we declare war not only on our enemies, but on our fragile ecology' (Mackay 2004: 215, cited in Tieman and Ball 2004: 20). People living in poverty may harm their environment because of their limited freedom and lack of alternatives, e.g. felling forests for fuel, clearing and tilling marginal land, over-fishing and hunting threatened species. Meanwhile, unsustainable development such as giant dam projects and so-called Green Revolution agriculture pollute land and water and destroy countless species and their habitats.

References

AID/WATCH (2005) 'Australian Aid: The Boomerang Effect' (Erskineville NSW: AID/WATCH), February. <www.aidwatch.org.au>

Ayton-Shenker, D. (1995) 'The Challenge of Human Rights and Cultural Diversity', United Nations Background Note, UN Department of Public Information. <www.un.org/rights/dpi1627e.htm>

Duffield, M. (2001) *Global Governance and the New Wars: The Merging of Development and Security* (London: Zed Books).

Freire, P. (2000) *Pedagogy of the Oppressed*, trans. M. Bergman Ramos (New York: Continuum).

Galtung, J. (2004a) 'The Security Approach and the Peace Approach: Some Cultural Factors Conditioning the Choice', World Culture Open, UN NYC, Building Peace Through Harmonious Diversity Panel: Global Governance, Peacemaking and Social Harmony, 10 September. <www.transcend.org/t_database/articles.php?ida=491>

— (2004b) 'What Would Peace between Washington and Al Queda/Iraq Look Like? Some Points for Presidential Candidates to Consider', *Transcend*, 11 September. <www.transcend.org/t_database/articles.php?ida=490>

Lummis, C. D. (2002) 'Foreword', in R. Swift, *The No-nonsense Guide to Democracy* (Oxford: New Internationalist Publications).

Mackay, H. (2004) *Right & Wrong: How to Decide for Yourself* (Sydney: Hodder).

O'Connor, T. (2003) 'Report: Australian Aid Budget Fails Commitment to Developing Countries' (Erskineville NSW: AID/WATCH), 16 May. <www.aidwatch.org.au>

Patenaude, B. M. (2002) *The Big Show in Bololand: The American Relief Expedition to Soviet Russia in the Famine of 1921* (Palo Alto, CA: Stanford University Press).

Tieman, G. and O. Ball (2004) *Blood on the Planet: The Who, What, Where and When of Armed Conflict in the World Today*, report for the Justice and International Mission Unit of the Synod of Victoria and Tasmania, Uniting Church in Australia, Melbourne.

Transparency International (2004) 'Corruption Fighters' Tool Kit Special Edition 2004: Teaching Integrity to Youth: Examples from 11 Countries' (Berlin: Transparency International). <www.transparency.org>

Weissman, F. (2004) 'Military Humanitarianism: A Deadly Confusion' (Paris: Médecins Sans Frontières). <www.msf.org>

Contributors

Supriya Akerkar has an undergraduate degree in law and a master's degree in Development Studies from the Institute of Social Studies, The Hague, Netherlands. She has worked with the mass organization of *adivasis* in the state of Maharashtra, India, for a number of years, and has done policy research work focusing on the rights of *adivasis* and other marginalized groups over common property resources such as forests. She has written several publications on these issues. She was a part of the ActionAid team that responded to the Kutch Earthquake and the communal violence in Ahmedabad in Gujarat, and is currently working as the Regional Manager of ActionAid's Bhubaneshwar office.

Marta Antunes is an economist (Technical University of Lisbon) with a master's degree in Development, Agriculture and Society, specializing in International Studies, at the Federal Rural University of Rio de Janeiro. She is working as Technical Adviser of the Governance Programme in ActionAid Brasil and her main activities include local development projects, fundraising and research assistance in national and international research projects such as *Linking Rights, Participation and Power – Brazilian Country Study* (IDS and Just Associates) and *Critical Watch* (ActionAid Brasil/DFID/IDS). Her research interests are empowerment, rights, participation, poverty, gender and rural issues.

Olivia Ball is originally a psychologist and community development worker experienced in working with refugees in her hometown of Melbourne. Retraining in development studies, she managed development projects in the South Pacific. She graduated with distinction with an MA in Human Rights from the University of London, joining the teaching staff the following year. She has undertaken human rights research and campaign work in academia and the NGO sector in Britain and Australia. She is now an Adjunct Research Fellow with the Centre for Human Rights Education at Curtin University in Perth, and her publications include *Blood on the Planet: Armed Conflict Around the World* (Uniting Church in Australia, Melbourne 2004), *Every Morning, Just like Coffee: Torture in Cameroon* (Medical Foundation for the Care of Victims of Torture, London 2002), *Toloa Rainforest Reserve: A Guidebook for Visitors* (Vava'u Press, Suva 2001) and articles for *New Internationalist*.

Marjolein I. Brouwer has worked for Novib/Oxfam Netherlands for over eight years, advising the organization on human rights issues. In that capacity she was also involved in advising on the relevant sections relating to rights-based approaches within the Oxfam International Strategic Plan. Before joining Novib, she worked for various UN agencies for nearly nine years: in Zambia, with the UNHCR, and in Switzerland, with the Centre for Human Rights (now the Office of the High Commissioner for Human Rights). In Geneva, her specific field of research was on the right to development and economic, social and cultural rights. Marjolein started her professional career with the Dutch section of Amnesty International. She holds master's degrees in Criminology (1982) and Law (1984).

Jonathan Ensor holds an MA in Human Rights from the University of London. Having spent two years researching the theory and application of rights-based approaches, he now works as Research Officer at the Immigration Advisory Service in London. He also holds a PhD from the University of York, where he previously worked and published as a lecturer in engineering.

Ghalib Galant has been working in the area of conflict management for the past 12 years. As a practitioner he has been involved in managing conflict in various communities and organizations, and, for the last seven years, as a Labour Commissioner in South Africa, in the workplace. A Senior Associate with the Centre for Conflict Resolution, he has worked closely with the Human Rights and Conflict Management Programme in designing and delivering capacity-building programmes in human rights and conflict management and providing technical assistance to both civil society actors and national human rights institutions in South Africa and in Africa. He has also led several investigative missions in Southern Africa on behalf of the International Federation for Human Rights Leagues (FIDH). Galant is a former Director of the Social Law Project at the University of the Western Cape, a labour service organization that focuses on training government, trade unions and employers in labour law as well as providing research and facilitation in the areas of policy formulation and institution-building. Holding a BA and an LLB (both from the University of Cape Town), he has written and presented papers often on topics in labour law, managing diversity, human rights and conflict management. Currently he heads SynergyWorks, a small consultancy focusing on training, facilitation and institution-building.

Heather Grady is the Global Lead on Rights and Institutional Accountability for Oxfam Great Britain. Before that she was Oxfam's Regional Director for East Asia, based in Thailand, managing a programme covering nine countries including Indonesia, Cambodia, Vietnam, China and Burma. Prior to becoming Regional Director in 2000, she was the Country Representative of Oxfam Great Britain in Vietnam, where she resided from 1993 until 2000. Previously Heather worked with Save the Children in Palestine and Sudan, and over the years has worked in China, Taiwan and Egypt for academic and development institutions. Heather has a BA from Smith College (with a concentration in

Government and Chinese language) and a master's in Public Administration from Harvard University. She has authored several articles, and co-authored one of the first books on PRA methodology.

Paul Gready is a Senior Lecturer in Human Rights at the Institute of Commonwealth Studies, University of London. He has worked for and undertaken consultancies for a number of human rights organizations, mostly in the UK and South Africa, including Amnesty International and the Centre for the Study of Violence and Reconciliation, Johannesburg. His academic publications include *Writing as Resistance: Life Stories of Imprisonment, Exile and Homecoming from Apartheid South Africa* (Lexington Books, 2003) and the edited volumes *Political Transition: Politics and Cultures* (Pluto Press, 2003) and *Fighting for Human Rights* (Routledge, 2004). He has published articles recently in *Conflict, Development and Security*, *Health and Human Rights*, the *International Journal of Human Rights*, and the *South African Journal on Human Rights* and *Third World Quarterly*, on issues ranging from transitional justice to globalization.

Neil Jarman is the Director of the Institute for Conflict Research, an independent not for profit organization based in Belfast. He has worked for many years on issues of public order, police reform, human rights and violence during the political transition in Northern Ireland. More recent work has been focused on racist and homophobic violence and the changing social and demographic make-up of the region.

Andrew S. Jones has worked for ten years for CARE, initially in Ecuador and subsequently at CARE USA headquarters, in CARE's Nairobi office, and most recently with CARE Rwanda. His current position is Assistant Country Director, in charge of programmes. Prior to moving to Rwanda, he served from 1998 to 2002 as CARE's inaugural global human rights and rights-based programming adviser, based initially in Atlanta and subsequently in Nairobi. In this position, he spearheaded CARE's efforts to integrate rights-based approaches, providing training and technical advice and support to CARE country offices worldwide and initiating a newsletter and peer learning network for the ongoing exchange of information and dialogue. He holds a master's degree in Public and International Affairs from Princeton's Woodrow Wilson School and a law degree (Juris Doctorate) from the University of Virginia.

Urban Jonsson has a PhD in Food Science and Technology from the University of Gothenburg, Sweden, and has conducted post-doctoral studies in economics, nutrition and the philosophy of science. He has 24 years of work experience with UNICEF, most recently as Regional Director, Eastern and Southern Africa. Jonsson is currently working as Senior Adviser to the Executive Director (UNICEF) on Human Rights-Based Programming.

303

Harsh Mander is a social worker and writer. He worked in the Indian Administrative Service in the predominantly tribal states of Madhya Pradesh and Chhatisgarh for almost two decades, mainly as the head of the district governments of tribal districts. He is associated with social causes and movements, such as communal harmony, tribal, *dalit* and disability rights, the right to information, custodial justice, homeless people and bonded labour. He writes and speaks regularly on issues of social justice. His books include *Unheard Voices: Stories of Forgotten Lives* (Penguin, India), *Cry, My Beloved Country: Reflections on the Gujarat Carnage 2002 and its Aftermath*, and *The Ripped Chest: Public Policy and Poor in India*. He was awarded the Rajiv Gandhi National Sadbhavana Award for peace work, and the M.A. Thomas National Human Rights Award 2002. He worked as Country Director of ActionAid India for four and a half years (September 1999–March 2004). He is at present convenor of Aman Biradari, a people's campaign for communal harmony and justice, founding member of Anhad, Director of the Centre for Equity Studies, Delhi, Visiting Professor, Jamia Millia University, Delhi, and he writes a column for *Hindustan Times*.

Paul O'Brien was the Advocacy Coordinator for CARE International in Afghanistan from November 2001 to August 2004. He now works for the government of Afghanistan as an adviser on their Poverty Reduction Strategy, amongst other things. After graduating from Harvard Law School in 1993, Mr O'Brien co-founded the Legal Resources Foundation in Kenya, practised law with Cravath Swaine and Moore in New York, and was President of the Echoing Green Foundation. From 1998 to November 2001 he was CARE's Africa Policy Adviser. His publications include *The Benefits–Harms Package* (1999), *A Training Manual for Human Rights and Rights Based Approaches* (2001), and 'Politicized Humanitarianism' in the *Harvard Human Rights Journal* (Spring 2004).

Claire O'Kane has recently joined Save the Children UK's Head Office as their Global Care and Protection Adviser. From March 2003 to September 2004 she was the Child Rights Adviser with Save the Children UK's Afghanistan programme. Claire is the author of Save the Children's (South and Central Asia) regional flagship publication *Children and Young People as Citizens: Partners for Social Change* (2003). This was produced while she was the regional Children Citizenship and Governance Coordinator for Save the Children Alliance in South and Central Asia (2001–2003). Claire is a qualified social worker with a decade of fieldwork, research and advocacy experience in the field of child rights, participation and protection in South and Central Asia and the UK.

Pamela Ashanut Okille trained as a lawyer and holds an LL.M. She has over five years' experience in managing and implementing development programmes in human rights, gender, civil society, democratization and good governance.

Her employers have included Ugandan civil society organizations, a regional ecumenical organization operating in the Great Lakes and Horn of Africa, and an international development agency. Currently she is working as an independent consultant. Her clients include CARE International (East Africa Regional Management Unit, Rwanda, and Uganda), Christian Aid (South Sudan Programme), DANIDA, International Foundation for Election Systems (IFES), and the British Council.

Michelle Parlevliet has been working on human rights, transitional justice, peacebuilding and conflict management for nearly ten years. She was the Manager of the Human Rights and Conflict Management Programme at the Centre for Conflict Resolution (CCR) for over five years from its inception in 1999. In this context she designed and delivered capacity-building programmes in human rights and conflict management, provided technical assistance and facilitation, and conducted research. She has worked with a wide range of actors throughout Africa, and in Denmark, Norway and Northern Ireland; she also acts as a lead facilitator for a capacity-building project of the United Nations System Staff College on Early Warning and Preventive Measures. Prior to joining the Centre, she worked as a researcher for the South African Truth and Reconciliation Commission. Holding a MA in Political Science (University of Amsterdam, *cum laude*) and a MA in International Peace Studies (University of Notre Dame, US), she has published widely on various topics, including the relationship between human rights and conflict management. Much of her work since 2004 has focused on national human rights institutions, conflict resolution and peacebuilding; and on human rights in conflict interventions and peacebuilding processes. From March 2005, she is acting as an independent consultant, providing training and facilitation and undertaking research.

Jorge O. Romano is an anthropologist specializing in social anthropology, with a PhD in Development, Agriculture and Society from the Federal Rural University of Rio de Janeiro. He is presently the Country Director of ActionAid Brasil. Previously, he was Executive Secretary of the non-profit association Redcapa, a network of institutions for capacity building and teaching agriculture and rural development policies in Latin America and the Caribbean. Since 1985 he has been working as an adviser for multilateral and international non-governmental institutions (FAO, IICA, IDRC, OXFAM, NOVIB, EZE, Ford Foundation, Greenpeace, IIED), Brazilian non-governmental institutions and social movements (IBASE, AS-PTA, National Council of Rubber Collectors, DNTR-CUT) and Brazilian governmental agencies (CAPES, CNPq, FINEP, INEP), among others. He has also been working as a Professor of the Post-Graduation Program in Development, Agriculture and Society at the Federal Rural University of Rio de Janeiro, since 1984. He has published very widely.

Joachim Theis has worked for almost 20 years in international development in Africa, the Middle East and Asia. He has been involved in Participatory Poverty Assessments and Poverty Reduction Strategies, research on child labour, and in promoting rights-based approaches and children's participation in Asia and the Pacific. He has written about rights-based approaches, participatory research methods, monitoring and evaluation methodologies, and child and youth participation. He currently works in UNICEF's Regional Office for East Asia and the Pacific on youth programming. He holds a PhD in social anthropology and an MA in Development Studies, Social Anthropology and Middle Eastern Studies.

Amparo Tomas has been working on the development of rights-based approaches for UNDP since 2000, as Justice and Human Rights Officer in UNDP Philippines (2000–2002) and as Task Facilitator for the regional UNDP Access to Justice Initiative in Asia and the Pacific since 2003. In the course of her work, she has assisted development actors in designing and implementing programmes attempting to apply a rights-based perspective; developed training manuals, guidelines and other tools for development practitioners; conducted training for UNDP, OHCHR, UN Country Teams and UNDP government counterparts; compiled lessons learned on the application of a human rights approach; and contributed to overall UNDP policy on the issue. Amparo Tomas is a political scientist with a master's degree in International Studies from the Diplomatic School of Madrid. Prior to her experience in UNDP, she worked with NGOs and government organizations in Spain and Thailand.

Valerie Gnide Traore has been at Oxfam America for the past three years, during which she led the organizational learning process on the rights-based approach. Among other things, she developed training modules and oversaw the development of case studies around the approach. She was also a country specialist for Amnesty International USA covering Senegal, Sierra Leone and Côte d'Ivoire. Valerie is currently based in the Oxfam America West Africa regional office as the Regional Information and Communication Officer. She is a graduate of the University of Indianapolis.

Dereje Wordofa is currently working for Oxfam GB as Head of the Regional Policy Team, based in Oxford. Prior to this, he was Programme Representative for Oxfam GB in Uganda (1999–2002), and worked for Save the Children in Ethiopia for ten years. He has worked on participatory approaches and has been leading on political and civil rights. He holds an MSc in Social Policy Planning in Developing Countries from the London School of Economics.

Index